This is a social history of political polarization as it evolved in one city over three and a half decades before the Spanish Civil War. As such it is a book about the long-term origins of the war as seen "from below." More broadly it is an analysis of the evolution of political culture during the transition from elite to mass politics.

The book focuses on the interplay between the three main forces that competed for political control: the conservative monarchist/Catholics, the democratic republicans and the revolutionary trade movement. It then demonstrates how the failure of the democratic option, as embodied in the Second Republic of the 1930s, polarized the country towards revolution and counter-revolution.

This is different from other Civil War studies, since it tries to understand the relationship between organized political forces and the "masses" they sought to reach. In doing so it reveals a rich canvas of participants and activities, from trade unions and strikes to female consumer riots, and community-based protests to republican parties and secular rituals. In the process the book engages in recent theoretical debates about gender and politics, class formation, the public sphere and the formation of political culture.

From mobilization to civil war

From mobilization to civil war

The politics of polarization in the Spanish city of
Gijón, 1900–1937

~

PAMELA BETH RADCLIFF

CAMBRIDGE
UNIVERSITY PRESS

Published by the Press Syndicate of the University of Cambridge
The Pitt Building, Trumpington Street, Cambridge CB2 1RP
40 West 20th Street, New York, NY 10011-4211, USA
10 Stamford Road, Oakleigh, Melbourne 3166, Australia

First Published 1996

Printed in Great Britain at the University Press, Cambridge

A catalogue record for this book is available from the British Library

Library of Congress cataloguing in publication data
Radcliff, Pamela Beth
From mobilization to civil war: the politics of polarization in the Spanish city of Gijón,
1900–1937/Pamela Beth Radcliff.
p. cm.
Includes bibliographical references.
ISBN 0 521 56213 9 (hc)
1. Gijón (Spain) – Politics and government. 2. Polarization (Social sciences)
3. Spain – History – Civil War, 1936–1939 – Causes – Case studies. I. Title.
DP402.G46R33 1996

946′ 19 – dc20   95-51799 CIP

ISBN 0 521 56213 9 hardback

To my daughter, Olivia

Contents

~

List of maps	*Page* xi
List of tables	xii
Acknowledgments	xiii
Glossary of terms and abbreviations	xvi
Introduction	1
1 A turning point: the city in 1900	16
PART I Patterns of life in working-class Gijón	59
2 The structural context: economy, demography and urban space, 1900–1936	62
3 Culture and community in working-class Gijón	87
PART II Institutional forces of opposition: republicans and anarchosyndicalists	115
4 The republican parties and municipal politics, 1900–1930	118
5 The republicans in power: municipal politics, 1931–1936	142
6 The trade union movement, 1900–1936	167
PART III Defining an oppositional culture: the struggle over the public sphere	195
7 Republican culture: a nation of citizens	199
8 Labor movement culture: the brotherhood of workers	226
PART IV The urban battlefield: conflict and collective action, 1901–1936	249
9 Conflict and collective action, 1901–1930	253

10 Conflict and collective action during the Republic,
    1931–1936   280

Conclusion   305

Appendix 1: Wage and price movement   315
Appendix 2: Occupations by status category   322
Appendix 3: Supplementary tables   326
Select bibliography   327
Index   347

Maps

~

1 Spain   *page* xviii
2 Gijón to the 1840s   22
3 Expansion in the 1850s and 1860s   24
4 The *Plano de Ensanche* of 1867 (Arenal)   25
5 Parcelization and working-class settlements   26
6 Twentieth-century working-class settlements   79
7 Industrial Asturias   294

Tables

∼

1	Unions in Gijón, 1899	*page* 48
2	Population of Gijón, 1887–1930	73
3	Years of residence in Gijón	74
4	Population of the township of Gijón, 1887–1930	76
5	Birthplace and residence of marriage partners in Gijón	77
6	Residence of middle-class families in Gijón	80
7	Population growth in La Calzada and El Llano	82
8	Occupational pattern in the "mixed" neighborhoods of Gijón, 1920	84
9	Literacy and residence	85
10	Union organization, 1910	175
11	Union organization, 1931–1934: Confederación Nacional de Trabajo (CNT)	190
12	Union organization of clerical and low-level professional workers (December 1936)	191

Acknowledgments

~

While it is impossible to begin to thank all of the people who have helped me over the ten years since I began work on this project, I am grateful for the opportunity to thank a few of them for the advice, support and criticism they offered during the various stages from dissertation to book.

Foremost on the list is my thesis advisor, Edward Malefakis, who tried to teach me how to be both rigorous and poetic, to check the accuracy of every figure while bringing out the human interest in buried details. From the first draft of my master's degree essay, on which every line was marked up with nearly illegible comments, he tirelessly and meticulously forced me to think about what I wanted to say and how best to say it. I have also benefitted from the ongoing support of Temma Kaplan, who has always encouraged me to push my work further and incorporate new ways of thinking about social history. In particular, many of the insights about gender and collective action that are incorporated here I owe to her.

My years at Columbia were also enriched by the presence of Robert Moeller, whose seminar on labor history first drew me into the field, Michael Hanagan, who was an invaluable resource on quantitative methodological questions, and Robert Paxton, who helped clarify the arguments of the dissertation after reading an earlier draft. I am also indebted to the graduate students' dissertation reading group, which digested the earliest versions of these chapters and provided a much needed community support group during the isolating process of writing a dissertation.

In the several trips I made to Spain, numerous people assisted me in the daunting task of locating materials and getting access to them. Members of the faculty at the University of Oviedo were most helpful, notably the chair of the history department, David Ruiz, who shared his knowledge of Asturian labor history, economics professor Germán Ojeda, historian Jorge Uria, and professor of geography, Ramón Alvargonzález, who was very generous with his time and in introducing me to the problems of urban geography. In Gijón, I am grateful for the assistance of Patricio Aduriz, a local historian who ran the Hemeroteca Provincial and who shared his expertise on the Ateneo Casino Obrero, and I would like to thank his successor at the Hemeroteca, José Manuel Gutiérrez, who helped expedite a follow-up research trip to Gijón. I am also indebted to Padre Patac, the librarian who managed the collection of Asturian materials in the Jesuit college, and who seemed to have memorized the location of every document in the library. Both Aduriz and Patac went out of their way to insure that I had access to everything I needed. I also want to mention Ramón Alvarez Palomo, an anarchist who lived in Gijón in the 1930s and generously shared his experiences with me, and Manuel Suárez Cortina and Angeles Barrio Alonso, who helped me locate anarchist materials. Finally, I am grateful to the numerous public officials, in archives, libraries and record offices, who were willing to go out of their way to help me to negotiate the bureaucratic preconditions for accessing materials.

I would also like to thank several people who read various chapters of the book manuscript and offered insightful comments as well as encouragement, including David Ringrose, Cynthia Truant, José Alvarez Junco, Adrian Shubert, David Luft, Leonard Smith, Bill Deverell and David Gutiérrez. In addition, I want to thank Bonne Wagner for her beautiful maps and Henry Sanabria for assisting with the final preparation of the manuscript. I am also grateful to Jennifer Zeitlin for helping me with the statistical analysis and making sure I knew what to do with it.

This manuscript would not have been possible without the financial support provided by several grants. The pre-dissertation grant awarded by the Latin American and Iberian Institute at Columbia University was invaluable in getting me started. The body of the research was carried out under the auspices of a Fulbright fellowship, and I would like to thank the Commission, as well as Patricia Zahniser, who managed the program in Madrid and did everything she could to make our lives easier. The completion of the dissertation was made possible by a grant from the Whiting Foundation. Further research was conducted with the help of a grant from the Center for German and European Studies at the University of California, and the release time provided by the UCSD Affirmative Action Faculty Career Development Award gave me time to write revisions. Finally, Richard Attiyeh, Vice-Chancellor for Research at UCSD, generously provided me with subvention funds for publication.

I am grateful to my editor at Cambridge University Press, William Davies, who gave my manuscript special consideration, and to my copy-editor, Virginia Catmur, whose meticulous and thoughtful reading of the manuscript improved its final version considerably.

My greatest debt is to my family and friends, who have encouraged me through this long process and helped keep it all in perspective. My mother, Gladys Radcliff, and my grandmother, Marguerite Vanden Heuvel, instilled a love of learning from early on, and my husband, Bill Perry, saw me through the final stages. Rita Perry and Ann Del Priore gave me those needed precious hours to finish the conclusion after my daughter was born. Finally, I want to thank my daughter Olivia, whose entry into this world provided me with the inspiration to finish this chapter in my life.

Glossary of terms and abbreviations

~

ACH	Asociación de Cultura e Higiene
aldea	rural residential district
Alianza Obrera	alliance between anarchosyndicalist, socialist and communist trade unions and parties, signed in March 1934, for the purpose of co-ordinating revolutionary action
AMO	Asociación Musical Obrera (workers' musical association)
AP	Acción Popular (Catholic party)
AP	Agremiación Patronal (employers' organization)
AR	Alianza Republicana
armadores	ship owners/outfitters
ateneo	athenaeum/cultural society
barrio	neighborhood
bienio	two-year period
cacique	political boss
carnet	membership card
casa del pueblo	trade union headquarters/worker center
CEDA	Confederación Española de Derechas Autónomas (right-wing confederation)
cenetista	member of CNT
cigarrera	cigarette maker
ciudadela	inexpensive housing units constructed in interior patios
CNT	Confederación Nacional de Trabajo (anarcho-syndicalist trade union organization)

comadres	godmothers
consumo	consumption tax
CRT	Confederación Regional de Trabajo (anarcho-syndicalist trade union organization)
ensanche	style of urban development
FAI	Federación Anarquista Ibérica
faísta	member of FAI
gaita	Asturian musical instrument
IR	Izquierda Republicana (left republican party)
IRS	Instituto de Reformas Sociales
LI	Liga de Inquilinos (tenants' association)
paseo	a communal stroll
PCE	Partido Comunista Español
PF	Partido Federal
pidalista	follower of Conservative politician Alejandro Pidal y Mon
Pósito	Pósito de Pescadores (fishermen's association)
POUM	Partido Obrero de Unificación Marxista (Trotskyist party)
PRLD	Partido Republicano Liberal Demócrata (reformist)
PSOE	Partido Socialista Obrero de España (workers' socialist party)
romería	saint's day festival
Rula	fish auction house
SDIP	Sindicato de Defensa de Intereses Públicos
tertulia	debating society
treintista	supporter of the September 1, 1931 manifesto issued by thirty *cenetistas*, arguing for a more moderate CNT
turno	the controlled alternation of political power between the Liberal and Conservative parties during the Restoration regime
ugetista	member of UGT
UGT	Unión General de Trabajadores (socialist trade union organization)
UR	Unión Republicana (left republican party)
velada	celebration
verbena	festival on the eve of a saint's day

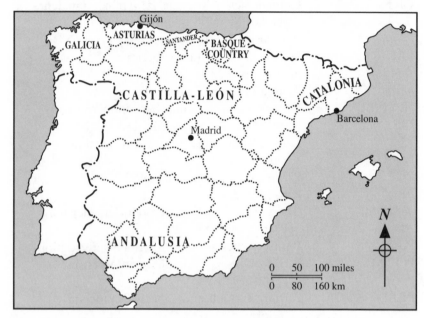

Map 1 Spain

Introduction

~

This book analyzes the polarization of political culture in a Spanish city, the northern industrial port of Gijón. Through an analysis of the mass mobilization of Spanish society and the failed efforts to incorporate the masses into a stable political system, the book aims both to elucidate the long-term origins of the Spanish Civil War and to shed new light on the transition to mass politics that confronted European countries in the nineteenth and early twentieth centuries. In the process, the book explores new ways of understanding the formation of political identity in the emerging age of mass politics.

The challenge of popular mobilization generated varying degrees of political crisis across Europe, but Spain experienced a particularly acute form that led to unchecked polarization and civil war, the so-called "two Spains" in mortal combat.[1] The turning point for Spain was the disastrous war with the United States in 1898 that opened the first fissures in the monarchist regime after two decades of political stability. From 1898 until the Civil War, the country experienced an intensifying effort to achieve political legitimation that pitted the

---

[1] The use of the term the "two Spains" originated with late-nineteenth-century reformers, who saw the country as divided between a modernizing, secular and democratic sector, and a backward, ultramontane and monarchist sector. For the best exploration of this trope, see Edward Malefakis, "The Civil War in Historical and Theoretical Perspective," *El País*, March 2, 1986. Some historians have argued that the image of fragmentation, of multiple divisions, better describes the country's political anatomy: see Santos Juliá Díaz, *Madrid: 1931–1934: de la fiesta popular a la lucha de clases* (Madrid: Siglo Veintiuno, 1984), and Manuel Tuñón de Lara, "La Guerra Civil Española, medio siglo después," in *La Guerra Civil Española: 50 años después*, ed. Manuel Tuñón de Lara (Barcelona: Editorial Labor, 1985). In any event, all historians would agree on the existence of deep political, social and cultural fissures.

1

forces of the old elitist regime against emergent challengers who sought to organize the masses against them. Thus, a declining monarchist/Catholic establishment tried to defend its domination against both a republican democratic and a revolutionary class-based alternative. The struggle culminated during the Second Republic of the 1930s, when the republican attempt to incorporate the masses into a liberal democratic regime failed and the country became polarized into revolutionary and counter-revolutionary forces. Instead of a coherent political program that could unite the country, its culture of polarization led to civil war. The book chronicles this evolution as it unfolded in one tumultuous city.

A local study offers the opportunity to understand these changes from the perspective of ordinary men and women. Moreover, in the context of early-twentieth-century Spanish politics, the local study is the best vehicle for grasping the dynamics of polarization and the origins of civil war. Even throughout the Republic of the 1930s, the political center of gravity remained at the local level, while national political parties, trade union federations and associations had done little to solidify a national political culture or national public sphere. One could argue that the Second Republic itself was in part a failed attempt to create a unified national political culture that could channel the diverse forms of mobilization into an integrated nation. As a result, Spanish political culture during this period needs to be pieced together from local experience rather than inferred from national institutions.

From this perspective, the city of Gijón provides an excellent case study in the politics of polarization. Gijón was one of a dozen "red cities" in Spain, with a strong conservative establishment and a revolutionary labor movement that evolved into the most powerful political force in the city by the Civil War.[2] From the turn of the century, when the city first consolidated its industrial and commercial transformation, its residents quickly gained a reputation for contentious and sustained political mobilization. Gijón clinched its reputation in October 1934 when revolutionary forces mounted the barricades as part of a regional revolt against an increasingly conservative Republic. However, in

---

[2] The "red city" has been a favorite subject for labor historians attempting to understand the mechanisms of successful mobilization. See, for example, Helmut Gruber, *Red Vienna: Experiment in Working-Class Culture, 1919–1934* (Oxford: Oxford University Press, 1991); Juliá Díaz, *Madrid: 1931–1934*; John Merriman, *The Red City: Limoges and the French Nineteenth Century* (Oxford: Oxford University Press, 1985), and Temma Kaplan, *Red City, Blue Period: Social Movements in Picasso's Barcelona* (Berkeley: University of California Press, 1992).

addition to the forces of revolution and counter-revolution, the city also maintained a solid republican democratic movement that helped mobilize the popular classes and competed with the labor movement for their loyalty. The eventual eclipse of the republican project in this three-way political struggle thus provides a microcosmic version of the national crisis that ended in polarization and civil war.

While the story of polarization is a familiar one, what this study brings is a new understanding of urban political culture that opens up a more complex arena of struggle and introduces a wider spectrum of participants.[3] Instead of being confined to the realm of formal institutional struggle, political culture takes shape in the broader realm of public values, collective action and symbolic expression.[4] Thus, the battleground extends from government institutions to a contested public sphere, and was peopled, in this case, by a diverse popular community that ranged from republican politicians to poor housewives. In this view, politics consisted of collective contests over power relations that took place in a number of different arenas, from the workplace and the city hall, to the cultural center, the neighborhood and the streets of the city. In other words, it penetrated the day-to-day structure of power as it was lived and breathed by ordinary men and women.[5] Their experience of this structure helped constitute the political culture that organized their collective lives and which could then link up to a national political culture beyond their immediate world.

To understand how political culture takes shape in this contentious environment, I have employed the concept of hegemonic struggle.[6]

---

[3] Although that of the origins of the Civil War is the most investigated question in the history of modern Spain, the debate is generally carried on within a narrow theoretical framework that focuses on traditional political and economic history. The call for Spanish historiography to be more theoretical and more comparative was the central theme of a series of papers presented at a round-table debate on "Spanish Historiography: The State of the Art," at Tufts University on May 19, 1994.

[4] Along these lines, see Lynn Hunt's influential definition of political culture in the introduction to *Politics, Culture and Class in the French Revolution* (Berkeley: University of California Press, 1984).

[5] On pushing the boundaries of the "political," see the essays in *Culture, Power and History*, ed. Nicholas Dirks, Geoff Eley and Sherry Ortner (Princeton: Princeton University Press, 1994). In the introduction to the latter volume, the editors acknowledge the "radically deinstitutionalized understanding of the political process, in which questions of conformity and opposition . . . are all displaced from the conventional institutional arena for studying them (that is, the state and public organizations in the narrow sense) onto a variety of settings previously regarded as 'nonpolitical,' including the workplace, the street, the deviant or criminal subculture, the recreational domain, and, above all, the family and the home" (p. 4).

[6] In utilizing the concept of hegemony, I have been influenced by the theoretical work of the "cultural studies" group at the University of Birmingham, who have used Gramsci's

The concept conveys the sense of competing systems of power and legitimacy, vying for control in a complex matrix of domination, consent and resistance. As John Clarke and Stuart Hall define it, hegemony is the "total social authority" that can "win and shape consent so that the granting of legitimacy of the dominant classes appears not only spontaneous but natural and normal."[7] Since hegemony is always incomplete, it implies a constant "war of position" or at least negotiation, which leaves room both for resistance and for organized counter-hegemonic attacks, such as those launched by the republicans and the labor movement in Spain.[8] While hegemony is always in flux, it oscillates between periods of stability and crisis that provide more or less space for opposition.[9] In the Spanish case, the 1898 defeat opened up a crisis of hegemony in the old regime that encouraged the formation of counter-hegemonic projects. The following decades witnessed the struggle between three competing hegemonic projects, none of which succeeded in maintaining or winning the "total social authority" needed to legitimate it.

The rivalry over social authority is crucial because it implies that hegemony requires more than simple domination of the state. Consent has to be won in the more open space of civil society or the public sphere, an intermediate realm in which private citizens come together and organize themselves as public participants in the body politic. In fact, as Geoff Eley has argued, it is precisely in the public sphere that the true limits of hegemony are tested.[10] As theorized by Habermas, the classic public sphere developed as an independent

framework to organize their problematic on the relationship between culture and society. For an intellectual genealogy of "cultural studies," see the essay by Stuart Hall, "Cultural Studies and the Centre: Some Problematics and Problems," in *Culture, Media, Language: Working Papers in Cultural Studies, 1972–1979*, ed. Stuart Hall et al. (London: Hutchinson, 1980). For a more critical outside view, see David Harris, *From Class Struggle to the Politics of Pleasure: The Effects of Gramscianism on Cultural Studies* (London: Routledge, 1992).

[7] "Subcultures, Cultures and Class," in *Resistance through Ritual: Youth Subcultures in Post-War Britain*, ed. Stuart Hall and Tony Jefferson (London: Hutchinson, 1976), 38.

[8] In Geoff Eley and Keith Nield's words: hegemony "is not a fixed and immutable *condition*, more or less permanent until totally displaced by determined revolutionary action, but is an institutionally negotiable *process* in which the social and political forces of contest, breakdown and transformation are constantly in play": "Why Does Social History Ignore Politics?," *Social History*, 5 (May 1980), 269.

[9] Richard Johnson emphasizes this flexibility in the concept of hegemony: "Barrington Moore, Perry Anderson and English Social Development," in *Culture, Media, Language*, 63–64.

[10] "Nations, Publics and Political Culture," in *Habermas and the Public Sphere*, ed. Craig Calhoun (Cambridge, MA: MIT Press, 1992), 322–323. Conversely, without a developed civil society, there is no need for complex mechanisms of winning consent.

arena of "rational – critical" debate in which free-thinking citizens banded together to combat the arbitrary authority of the state.[11] However, critics have exposed his idealized version of a public sphere as ungrounded in class and gender hierarchies, and have instead posited an arena of contested discourse in which different "publics" struggle to assert their competing visions of the world.[12]

These publics are formed not only in elite debating clubs and literary societies, but in the broader networks of urban sociability, from voluntary associations to cafés, taverns and neighborhoods. Within this more inclusive understanding of the public, other actors become visible, in particular working-class men and women who constructed their own networks outside the links of elite sociability. These networks, or "clusters of communication,"[13] form the building blocks of local public spheres, which in turn constitute the foundation for a national sphere of public discourse. At both the local and national levels, the public sphere can then be mobilized towards competing hegemonic projects. Thus, both the republicans and the labor movement sought to "structure attention" in the public sphere by winning popular acceptance of their own set of institutions, symbols, rituals and collective values and by undermining those of the hegemonic Catholic culture.[14]

This understanding of a contested and variegated public sphere brings into question broader assumptions about the mechanisms of mass mobilization and the identity of political actors and groups. In particular, it has important implications for the relationship between gender and politics. One of the major limitations of Habermas' conception of the public sphere is that it accepts the "natural" division between the public and the private, thus assuming the irrelevance of the family in political life.[15] Since, within this division of the world,

---

[11] Jurgen Habermas, *The Structural Transformation of the Public Sphere: An Inquiry into a Category of Bourgeois Society* (1962; reprint, Cambridge, MA: MIT Press, 1989), 93–95, 100–117.
[12] See, for example, the articles in *Habermas*, especially those by Calhoun, Eley, Fraser and Ryan.
[13] Craig Calhoun uses "clusters of communication" to conceptualize the variegated nature of the public sphere: "Introduction: Habermas and the Public Sphere," in *Habermas*, 37.
[14] "Some structuring of attention, imposed by dominant ideology, hegemonic powers, or social movements, must always exist": Craig Calhoun, "Introduction," 37.
[15] See Nancy Fraser, "Rethinking the Public Sphere: A Contribution to the Critique of Actually Existing Democracy," in *Habermas*, 131–132. For an extended critique of the public/private division within liberal theory, see Carole Pateman, "Feminist Critiques of the Public/Private Dichotomy," in *The Disorder of Women: Democracy, Feminism and Political Theory* (Stanford: Stanford University Press, 1989).

women were identified with the family, and many did not participate in paid employment or in formal political institutions, the classic understanding of the public sphere, like conventional histories of politics, failed to leave conceptual room for women as political actors in the modern period.

In fact, women entered the public sphere, but through their own (classed) networks. Instead of being excluded from public debate, they maintained discourses on issues that directly concerned them.[16] Thus, most working-class women belonged to a world of female sociability constructed around their caretaking role in the family. While their concerns often arose out of their responsibilities in the private sphere, however, these concerns pushed them into an informal female associational life that could also form the basis for political activism. In particular, working-class women continued to engage in a politics of consumer protest, which depended on their collective identity as shoppers and their ability to mobilize in the public spaces they shared. Within the more inclusive framework of a public sphere comprised of "clusters of communication" and a variety of publics, we can begin to locate women as political actors and to recognize their participation in the formation of "modern" political culture. From this perspective, the book attempts to integrate gender into the grand narrative of the emergence of mass politics.

The gendering of this narrative exposes other limitations with conventional models of political mobilization. In the traditional Marxist paradigm of mobilization, economic class formed the basis for politicization, and political identity was reduced to structural determinants. Although labor historians have continued to refine notions of class and class consciousness, there has been no agreement on a new definition of class that is more inclusive without being hopelessly vague or losing touch altogether with economic relationships.[17] Some

---

[16] As Nancy Fraser argues, "the view that women were excluded from the public sphere turns out to be ideological; it rests on a class and gender-based notion of publicity, one which accepts at face value the bourgeois public's claim to be *the* public": "Rethinking," 116. For a case study of American women's alternative routes to public life, see Mary Ryan, *Women in Public: Between Banners and Ballots, 1825–1880* (Baltimore: Johns Hopkins University Press, 1990).

[17] Labor historians since E. P. Thompson have been refining notions of class beyond the original strictly economistic definition, with increasingly sophisticated and contingent versions of class formation. For a cogent discussion of the state of the question, see Ronald Aminzade's introduction to *Ballots and Barricades: Class Formation and Republican Politics in France, 1830–1871* (Princeton: Princeton University Press, 1993). However, as they have done so, the term has become increasingly vague. As William Reddy put it, class has become no more than a fuzzy dividing line between empowerment and

have followed the "linguistic turn" in social history and redefined class in terms of discursive practice, cutting its links to a "real" material base.[18] Others have tried to free class from its reductionist origins while positing a contingent relationship between consciousness and material relations, or "superstructure" and "base."[19] In fact, the framing of political outcomes in terms of hegemonic struggle has been one way of theorizing this contingency.

While this study adopts the hegemonic framework of contingent mobilization, it does not equate hegemonic struggle with class struggle. That is, I view class as one axis around which mass mobilization and politicization in the industrialized world occurs, but not as its exclusive source. Thus, "class" is one possible political construction of certain economic relationships, and the formation of class consciousness arises out of the appeal of specific organizations that claim solidarity on the basis of individuals' relationship to the means of

impotence, and as Ira Katznelson wrote, "class has soaked up so much meaning that it has become bulky to use." Reddy concludes that class cannot be salvaged, while Katznelson argues that it can be: William Reddy, *Money and Liberty in Modern Europe: A Critique of Historical Understanding* (Cambridge: Cambridge University Press, 1987), 30; Ira Katznelson, "Working-Class Formation: Constructing Cases and Comparisons," in *Working Class Formation: Nineteenth-Century Patterns in Western Europe and the United States*, ed. Ira Katznelson and Aristide Zolberg (Princeton: Princeton University Press, 1986), 14.

[18] Two classic examples, in terms of the evolution of their own work, are Joan Scott and Gareth Stedman Jones. See Scott's *Gender and the Politics of History* (New York: Columbia University Press, 1988), and Stedman Jones' "Rethinking Chartism," in *Languages of Class: Studies in English Working Class History, 1832–1982* (Cambridge: Cambridge University Press, 1984). See also Patrick Joyce, *Visions of the People. Industrial England and the Question of Class, c. 1848–1914* (Cambridge: Cambridge University Press, 1991), and his introduction to *The Historical Meanings of Work* (Cambridge: Cambridge University Press, 1987). For a stimulating discussion of the implications of the "linguistic turn," from both approving and critical perspectives, see the essays in *Rethinking Labor History* ed. Lenard R. Berlanstein (Urbana: University of Illinois Press, 1993). For a thoughtful critique that focuses on Stedman Jones' work, see David Mayfield and Susan Thorne, "Social History and its Discontents: Gareth Stedman Jones and the Politics of Language," *Social History*, 17:2 (May 1992).

[19] From a labor history perspective, one of the most systematic attempts to theorize this relationship is Ira Katznelson's introduction to *Working Class Formation*. See also the essays by Christopher Johnson, Ronald Aminzade and Michael Hanagan in *Rethinking Labor History*. Some applied examples are: Louise Tilly, *Politics and Class in Milan* (Oxford: Oxford University Press, 1992); Donald Bell, *Sesto San Giovanni: Workers, Culture and Politics in an Italian Town, 1880–1922* (New Brunswick: Rutgers University Press, 1986); Michael Hanagan, *The Logic of Solidarity: Artisans and Industrial Workers in Three French Towns, 1871–1914* (Urbana: University of Illinois Press, 1980); Tyler Stovall, *The Rise of the Paris Red Belt* (Berkeley: University of California Press, 1990); and Elinor Accampo, *Industrialization, Family Life and Class Relations: St.Chamond, 1815–1914* (Berkeley: University of California Press, 1989). From a different perspective, the "cultural studies" group at the University of Birmingham has also focused on articulating a non-reductionist relationship between productive relations and social formation.

production. In addition to class, other axes of solidarity in the urban setting revolved around neighborhoods, gendered sociability patterns, and the "networks of debt" established between shopkeepers and their poor clients. These axes were linked by social and economic ties, but not necessarily by strict class identity. To communicate this flexible relationship, I posit a more general dividing line between "popular" and "elite," rich and poor, the few and the many, without implying a mechanistic economic and social barrier.

These axes of solidarity created a crisscross of networks that could coalesce into what I have called popular and elite communities. Thus, "community," defined as the "extent to which people are knit together as social actors,"[20] speaks to the ties and networks established between individuals without specifying a particular trajectory of collective consciousness. Those ties could be short term or evolve into a more enduring tradition of the collective defense of perceived interests. Urban communities could be built around tightly knit occupational groups and families, or well-established neighborhoods with common concerns. At another level, these communities could link up with each other into a city-wide popular community that could challenge the power of conservative elites. What drew the elements of this opposition together was what we might call a "radical – populist" sense of the "little man's/little woman's" right to a decent life, as against the exploitation of landlords, employers, speculators and the government. In more global terms, they demanded that the rhythms of the urban industrial city be geared to the needs of its ordinary residents instead of its owners.[21] On the level of day-to-day life, this was what hegemonic struggle boiled down to for the urban popular classes.

This understanding of urban popular mobilization is not employed to replace class as a monolithic causal factor but to share a more com-

---

[20] Craig J. Calhoun, "The Radicalism of Tradition: Community Strength or Venerable Disguise and Borrowed Language," *American Journal of Sociology*, 88:5 (1983), 897. See also Craig Calhoun, "Community: Toward a Variable Conceptualization for Comparative Research," *Social History*, 5:1 (1980) and David Garrioch, *Neighbourhood and Community in Paris, 1740–1790* (Cambridge: Cambridge University Press, 1986).

[21] In articulating a popular urban agenda, I have been influenced by Manuel Castells' work on urban social movements. Castells argues for an independent category of urban-oriented collective action, which is rooted in the power structures of urban life, and which he distinguishes from class-based labor struggle. Thus, he sees the city as a "social product" that generates its own field of contestation. See *The City and the Grassroots: A Cross-Cultural Theory of Urban Social Movements* (Berkeley: University of California Press, 1983) for an empirical and theoretical exploration of the relationship between urban social movements and urban change.

plex arena of politicization. Even co-existence, however, clashes with many accounts of the emergence of "modern" mass politics, in which there is an implicit time line that moves from community-based pre-industrial conflict to "modern" interest group or class politics.[22] In this account of the "modernization" of politics, class follows community both chronologically and ontologically. Instead of disappearing with the emergence of class-based political identity, I would argue that other sources of mobilization have simply been ignored by labor historians privileging class consciousness. Once again, it is often women's politics, frequently organized around community issues, that have gotten lost in the transition.[23]

Once we acknowledge the complex milieu of mass mobilization at the grass-roots level, we can examine the formal institutional actors that attempted to assert their leadership over this mass constituency and to mobilize it behind a specific hegemonic project. These were the republican movement, divided into a number of political parties, and the labor movement, split between the Socialist federation (UGT) and the anarchosyndicalist federation (CNT). Both claimed to be the voice of popular opposition, and both expended a great deal of energy wooing the lower classes, but each articulated a different vision of popular empowerment. The republicans represented the attempt to integrate the masses into a reformed liberal democratic regime, and one of the major tasks of the book is to understand the failure of this attempt in Spain, which culminated during the tragic Second Republic. On the other hand, the labor movement promised to establish a revolutionary workers' regime, organized around either a Marxist or anarchosyndicalist model. In some form or another, these two versions of mass politics challenged elite regimes all across Europe in the late nineteenth and early twentieth centuries.

The republicans' ideological agenda was rooted in Enlightenment

---

[22] The idea of a time line of forms of protest, in which there is an evolution of methods, groups and repertoires, is associated with Charles Tilly. See, for example, "Charivaris, Repertoires, and Urban Politics," in *French Cities in the Nineteenth Century*, ed. John Merriman (New York: Holmes and Meier, 1981) and "European Violence and Collective Action Since 1700," *Social Research*, 53:1 (1986).

[23] Efforts have been made to integrate poor women into a version of class relations that doesn't marginalize them, but their inclusion remains problematic. For example, Katznelson's introduction to *Working Class Formation* does not seriously consider the issue. For a discussion of the continued marginalization of gender in the master narrative of labor history, see Ava Baron, "Gender and Labor History: Learning from the Past, Looking to the Future," in *Work Engendered: Toward a New History of American Labor*, ed. Ava Baron (Ithaca: Cornell University Press, 1991) and Joan Scott, "On Language, Gender and Working Class History," in *Gender and the Politics of History*.

ideas of popular sovereignty, private property and equal citizenship. Beyond basic liberal and democratic precepts, the republicans were committed to the "modernization" of society, which included everything from industrialization to mass education and secularization. In pursuing this course, they hoped to wrest Spain from the clutches of the old-regime aristocratic and clerical elite that refused to give up the reigns of power. During the First Republic (1873–1874), they had seized the opportunity to direct national politics, but after its rapid demise, republicanism retreated to local strongholds like Gijón until the establishment of the Second Republic (1931–1939).

The republicans' position in Spain's political spectrum can best be understood in comparison with their French counterparts. In both countries, republicanism attempted to negotiate the transition to mass democratic politics without losing control to revolutionary or counter-revolutionary forces. But the French republicans succeeded where the Spanish did not. First, they hammered out an ideological synthesis to consolidate the movement and successfully attracted large numbers of lower-class Frenchmen into their movement.[24] As part of this synthesis, French republicans drew on a powerful cultural idiom, the revolutionary tradition inherited from 1789 and reinforced in 1830, 1848 and 1870. Then, after the establishment of the Third Republic, they continued to pursue the goal of mass integration through education, cultural rituals and political outreach.[25] The Spanish republicans attempted to follow this path, but could not overcome the numerous obstacles. Their failure, as a result of both internal and external problems, was a crucial part of the road to civil war.[26]

The other major institutional voice of opposition was the labor

[24] On the building of a cross-class republican coalition in the early and mid-nineteenth century see Raymond Huard, *Le Mouvement Républicain en Bas-Languedoc: 1848–1881* (Paris: Presses de la Fondation nationale des sciences politiques, 1982); Sanford Elwitt, *The Making of the Third Republic* (Baton Rouge: Louisiana State University Press, 1975); and Aminzade, *Ballots and Barricades.*

[25] The degree of success achieved is a matter of debate, but the contrast to the Spanish case is clear. On the debate, see Roger Magraw, *A History of the French Working Class* (Oxford: Blackwell, 1992), vol. II, part 5. For an account that emphasizes successful integration, see Sanford Elwitt, *The Third Republic Defended: Bourgeois Reform in France* (Baton Rouge: Louisiana State University Press, 1986).

[26] Despite their importance, they are one of the most understudied political forces in modern Spanish history. Conservative historians under the Franco regime ignored them, and leftist historians have focused on anarchism and socialism. For a discussion of this problem see Nigel Townson's introduction to a new anthology intended to begin the recovery of the history of republicanism: *El republicanismo en España, 1830–1977*, ed. Nigel Townson (Madrid: Alianza Editorial, 1994).

10

movement, in particular the anarchosyndicalist federation, which was the strongest sector of the labor movement in Spain until the Second Republic, and the most powerful in Gijón through the Civil War.[27] Anarchosyndicalism evolved out of the nineteenth-century anarchist movement that flourished during the 1860s and 70s, but was displaced in most European countries by Marxist socialism towards the end of the century.[28] Twentieth-century anarchosyndicalism retained the anarchist commitment to direct action, its rejection of electoral politics, and its revolutionary fervor, but combined these with a greater dedication to trade union organization. Through this new interest in institutional mass mobilization, anarchosyndicalism made another effort to capture the labor movement for anarchism.

Its greatest success was achieved in Spain, where the national federation formed in 1910 (CNT) grew into the largest labor organization in the country by the end of the First World War.[29] This success gave Spain's labor movement a unique configuration, which has generated a number of general theories to explain what anarchism represented.[30] However, the praxis of the CNT tends to escape the confines of such

[27] The other major branch of the labor movement was the UGT, affiliated with the Marxist Socialist party. In addition, there was a small "yellow" or Catholic union movement. The national anarchosyndicalist federation, the CNT, was founded in 1910 with 30,000 members, but ballooned to several hundred thousand in 1919 (up to 800,000, but the figures are disputed) before it collapsed during the Dictatorship: Antonio Bar, *La CNT en los años rojos: del sindicalismo revolucionario al anarcosindicalismo, 1910–1926* (Madrid: Akal Editor, 1981), 492. The Socialist party (PSOE) was founded in 1879, and the UGT in 1882, but both grew slowly until the Republic. In 1919, the UGT had only 200,000 members: Raymond Carr, *Modern Spain, 1875–1980* (Oxford: Oxford University Press, 1980), 88. After 1931, the UGT expanded to over one million members, its rapid growth tied largely to the Socialists' prominent position in the new government. In contrast, the CNT never fully recovered its 1919 numerical peak: its national congresses in June 1931 and July 1936 represented between 500,000 and 550,000 members: Murray Bookchin, *The Spanish Anarchists: The Heroic Years, 1868–1936* (New York: Harper and Row, 1977), 234 and 290.

[28] The rivalry between Bakunin and Marx in the First International set up the competition between two versions of the revolutionary organization of the poor. In terms of its impact on Spain, the classic works are Max Nettlau, *La Première Internationale en Espagne, 1868–1888* (Dordrecht: D. Reidel, 1969) and Josep Termes Ardévol, *Anarquismo y sindicalismo en España: la Primera Internacional, 1864–1881* (Barcelona: Crítica, 1972).

[29] It also played a role in the major French federation, the CGT, but the impact of revolutionary syndicalist ideas on the French labor movement is disputed. Peter Stearns' classic book, *Revolutionary Syndicalism and French Labor* (New Brunswick: Rutgers University Press, 1974) argues that the syndicalists represented a small minority, no more than 10% of the small number of unionized workers, and that their radical rhetoric was out of touch with most workers. See Roger Magraw for a counter-argument: *French Working Class*, vol. II, 103–117.

[30] Explanations for the "survival" of anarchism in Spain after it declined as a mass organization in most other countries include economic "backwardness," national character, religiosity, and weak state formation. For a fuller discussion of the debates, see Chapter 6.

11

theories. Because of its decentralized and loose national structure, its strength and identity lay in local federations that were shaped as much by the political culture of the place as by any fixed platform imposed from above. The result was a heterogeneous and flexible anarchosyndicalist movement whose role in Spanish politics is difficult to pin down.

Nevertheless, in broad terms, the CNT thrived on the widespread suspicion of the possibility of change through governmental channels. In other words, it reflected the crisis of political legitimacy that plagued first the Restoration Monarchy (1875–1930) and then the Second Republic. Thus, the CNT symbolized the political skepticism that the republicans had to overcome in order to consolidate popular support for the Republic. While in practice the distinction between anarchists and republicans was not always so clear, their approaches represented two alternative routes to popular empowerment.

Within this general framework of the crisis of political legitimacy, local political cultures developed their own versions of conflict and resolution. In some cities and towns, Socialists predominated over anarchosyndicalists and republicans, while in others, like Gijón, the Socialists barely existed, and in still other (mostly rural) locales the monarchist/clerical elite remained virtually unchallenged through the entire period. While this local variation confirms the importance of local studies, it also means that no single case can be a paradigmatic version of the larger conflict. Thus, this study of Gijón cannot be made to stand for the whole, just as the whole is empty without its parts.

What, then, is the significance of an analysis of the political culture of Gijón? While Gijón was not paradigmatic, it does represent an important segment of Spain's political geography: the highly mobilized industrial city. It was in cities like Gijón that mass mobilization began in the late nineteenth and early twentieth centuries. It was there, also, that the discourses of numerous local public spheres carved out a space in the stagnant Restoration political system. This ferment then nurtured the development of the counter-hegemonic challenges that eventually burst to the surface of national politics in the 1930s. In other words, Gijón was part of the urban industrial sector that opened up Spain's hegemonic crisis and forced the challenge of mass politics on a conservative, rural-based elite.[31] Thus, while Gijón's local

---

[31] Rural agrarian Spain still represented the majority of the population in 1930: about 25% of the population lived in cities over 30,000, and about 26% worked in the secondary sector, versus 46% in the primary: Adrian Shubert, *A Social History of Modern Spain*

political culture had its own unique shape, it formed part of a larger pattern of grass-roots mobilization that set the political agenda in early-twentieth-century Spain.

In order to reconstruct the origins and evolution of Gijón's political culture, the book is organized into a series of thematic layers that breaks down the process of polarization into discrete factors. Thus, following an introductory chapter on the city in 1900, it is divided into four main parts, each of which covers the entire chronological period. Part I explores the social and economic milieu that favored the coalescence of an oppositional popular community among the lower classes. The second part presents the two major institutional players, the republicans and the anarchosyndicalists, and examines their attempts to win popular support through formal institutional change. The third part carries this analysis into the public sphere, where the struggle for hegemony was waged through collective rituals, public symbols and educational and entertainment centers. And finally, the fourth part follows the battle into the streets and workplace, where it was waged through various forms of direct confrontation and conflict. The goal is to construct a multi-layered picture of the hegemonic battle that ended in polarization and civil war.

Within this broad outline, Chapter 1 introduces the city in the aftermath of the hegemonic break of 1898, when the forces of opposition were just taking shape, but before any major chinks had opened in the conservative political system of the Restoration. The city government was comfortably controlled by the Conservative party, and the realm of public culture was the domain of its ally, the Catholic Church. Before the turn of the century, there was no trade union movement to speak of, few strikes or other popular protests, and only one poor neighborhood with significant community ties. This chapter provides a point of departure for the rest of the book.

Chapter 2 looks at the economic and urban developments that provided a framework for the patterns of popular and working-class life in the city. On a general level, they brought thousands of poor residents to the city, created new neighborhoods for them to live in, and dramatized the economic distinctions between the "haves" and "have-nots." Although these structural factors do not explain popular

(London: Unwin Hyman, 1990), 46, and Ramón Tamames, *La República y la era de Franco* (Madrid: Alianza Editorial, 1983), 66.

mobilization, they did establish a backdrop of socio-economic segregation that potentially could provide the building blocks of popular solidarity.

Chapter 3 examines how poor residents translated the reality of economic and residential segregation into the segregated sociability that characterized popular culture in the city. Although divided by gender and neighborhood, there were enough elements of common culture that set them apart from the wealthier residents in the "other" Gijón. As Catholic reformer Arboleya put it in poetic terms: "each of the two Gijóns seem like completely distinct populations: the first is a Gijón populated by workers, darkened by smoke, and encircled in the piercing noise of trucks and machines; the second is the Gijón of the elegant, of happiness, of light, of pleasant pastimes."[32] Out of the distinction between these two Gijóns came the rough parameters of a shifting popular realm potentially drawn together by shared grievances and social ties and networks.

Chapters 4 and 5 examine the republicans' efforts to shape and direct an oppositional municipal politics based on this popular constituency. Chapter 4 concentrates on the pre-republican years, as the local republican movement tried to carve out an oppositional space through control of the city council. Its failure to do this in all but symbolic terms left a legacy of weakness that hindered the legitimization of the Republic when it was finally established in 1931. Chapter 5 looks at city politics under the Republic, and argues that even with the change of regime the local republicans could not implement a program of social and economic reform to satisfy their popular constituency. The upshot is that republicanism failed, for a variety of reasons, to demonstrate the possibility of significant social reform through the democratic process.

Chapter 6 analyzes the emergence and consolidation of the anarchosyndicalist-dominated labor movement as a major political alternative. Despite its formal apolitical stance, the CNT played an important political role, both in tacitly supporting the republicans in joint oppositional efforts, and in articulating a more direct route to popular empowerment when governmental channels failed. Through an effective strategy of co-operation and antagonism, pragmatism and

---

[32] Maximiliano Arboleya Martínez was a prominent figure in the provincial and national social Catholic reform movement, which tried to convince the Church hierarchy of the need to take into account workers' material needs. The quote is from *Gijón veraniego* (Gijón: La Industria, 1914).

revolutionary zeal, the local CNT was perfectly positioned to take over popular leadership in case the republicans could not deliver.

Chapters 7 and 8 examine first the republican and then the labor movement's efforts to establish their popular leadership in the public sphere. Through the "invention" of new traditions, symbols and rituals, and the pursuit of mass education and indoctrination, they each sought to cut loose the popular classes from Catholic public culture and define an oppositional public sphere that would provide a powerful common identity for a new Spain: for republicans, the "nation of citizens" and for the labor movement, the "brotherhood of workers." Both chapters argue, however, that neither republican nor labor movement culture was strong enough to stand alone, which left the Republic without a clear sense of cultural identity that could unify the forces of change around it.

Finally, Chapters 9 and 10 place all of the actors on the urban battlefield, where the process of polarization took its most visible form in a growing tradition of direct conflict and collective action that juxtaposed popular and elite forces. The boundaries between the two sides fluctuated, and different players moved in and out of the spotlight, but the basic dynamic only strengthened and solidified over time. What emerged was an activist populist voice that pursued change through the channel of direct mass mobilization. Chapter 9 looks at the inception and establishment of this dynamic of conflict before the Republic, and Chapter 10 takes it through the peacetime Republic and its culmination in armed rebellion in October 1934 and finally civil war in July 1936. The recourse to armed rebellion by both sides signaled the death of the democratic alternative and the triumph of force over consent in the hegemonic struggle. The struggle would only be resolved after a bitter civil war, which finally gave the victorious Franco regime the power it needed to forcibly impose unity and authority on a polarized society.

1

A turning point: the city in 1900

~

At the onset of the twentieth century, Gijón's fortunes seemed to be directly opposed to those of the rest of the country. As Spain sagged under the weight of military defeat and economic crisis, Gijón was poised for industrial take-off. The war with the United States that brought an inglorious end to Spain's coveted imperial identity had a quite different effect in Gijón. A wave of repatriated capital from Asturians in the colonies[1] created an unparalleled growth spurt that put the province and its major industrial city on the map.

> Asturias is in fashion. All the newspapers speak of an Asturian economic renaissance that will lead to a national renaissance . . . Individual initiative in work has increased greatly in Asturias, and in it we see the remedy for the great damage caused by general inaction and weakness.[2]

In this heady atmosphere, many people believed not only that Asturias would take its place as the newest industrial region, after Catalonia and the Basque country, but that it would assist in sparking a national recovery. Thus, while the nation plunged into pessimistic analysis of its decline, Asturias radiated success.

---

[1] In the *Heraldo de Asturias,* October 10, 1897, Juan F. Llana commented on the importance of Asturian interests in Cuba: "Asturias is the province of Spain that has the most investment in Cuba . . . there are 200,000 Asturians in Cuba. Commerce, banking, industry, and agriculture are all in their hands. Asturians are almost always the civil authorities, the elected representatives, the city councilmen . . . Asturians, Galicians, Catalans and Basques are the premiere capitalists of the island": quoted in Luis G. San Miguel, *De la sociedad aristocrática a la sociedad industrial en la España del siglo XIX* (Madrid: Edicusa, 1973), 146.

[2] Salvador Canals, *Asturias: información sobre su presente estado moral y material* (Madrid: M. Romero, 1900), 1.

Despite the apparent uniqueness of the regional and local trajectory of development, the *fin de siècle* marked a similar turning point for both city and nation. In stark terms, it signaled a hegemonic break, the beginning of a long-term crisis of authority that would only be resolved on the battlefield of the Civil War, several decades later.[3] At the national level, the humiliating collapse of the remnants of empire dealt a serious blow to the legitimacy of the monarchy and brought into question the capacity of the traditional elites to lead Spain into the twentieth century. While the crisis of confidence had no immediate political consequences, it opened a space in which opposition groups could begin to articulate counter-hegemonic challenges to the regime.

Although the crisis was national in scope, it was at the local level that the challenges took concrete shape. In particular, it was in cities and urban centers like Gijón, which were undergoing social and economic transformations, that opposition political cultures began to take root, both in the realm of formal electoral politics and in the broader public sphere. The dynamism of these cities and towns, scattered throughout Spain, but concentrated in peripheral regions like Catalonia, the Basque country and Asturias, clashed with a stagnant political system designed to resist change. As a result, the hegemonic confrontation that would eventually encompass the entire country began on local battlefields like these, where the uncontested political culture of the early Restoration gave way to a culture of contention and then polarization. Because this kind of mobilization did not break the surface of national politics until the Second Republic of the 1930s, it is in these local political cultures that we can best track the early evolution of Spain's hegemonic crisis.

Within this framework, Gijón's *fin de siècle* political culture is an ideal place to start such a long-term analysis. Although the city had been undergoing tremendous economic and social changes in recent decades, its political system was firmly in the hands of traditional elites, while a public sphere of independent political discourse and debate was just beginning to emerge. Thus, 1900 marks the beginning of the story of breakdown and polarization that would culminate thirty-six years later in civil war. This chapter sets the stage for this local

---

[3] On the crisis of 1898 as a hegemonic break, see Carlos Serrano, "¿1900?," in *1900 en España*, ed. Carlos Serrano and Serge Salaün (Madrid: Espasa Calpe, 1991), 16–17, and Manuel Tuñón de Lara, "La Guerra Civil Española, medio siglo después," in *La Guerra Civil Española: 50 años después*, ed. M. Tuñón de Lara (Barcelona: Editorial Labor, 1985), 12.

story of polarization with an analysis of Gijón's economic, social, political and cultural contours at the point of hegemonic break.

Economic dynamism

In less than a century, Gijón had made the transition from a large fishing village of 5,000 inhabitants to a mid-sized industrial city of 47,544.[4] Since the war against Napoleon had devastated the city, the majority of this demographic expansion occurred in the last half of the century, most dramatically between 1887 and 1900, when the population grew by 35%. These figures make perfect sense within the context of the city's economic evolution. Gijón had always been a small commercial center, given its location and the fact that Asturias was bordered on the south by a mountain range, but poor roads kept it isolated and prevented large-scale transport.[5] The turning point came with the construction of the Carretera Carbonera (1842), or "Coal Highway," and the Ferrocarril Langreo (1854), a railroad connecting the Nalón mining valley to the port city. A second rail line to Asturias' other major mining basin, opened in 1885, completed the transport network. With the infrastructure in place, the latter part of the century unfolded as Gijón's golden age of expansion and industrialization.

The linchpin of expansion was Gijón's role as a commercial port for the export of coal and iron ore from the interior of the province. In 1840, barely a few hundred tons of coal passed through the port; by 1872, that number was 143,000 tons and rising.[6] The city added piecemeal to its overworked port facilities, but committed itself in 1892 to build a large, modern port on the outskirts. The project of "El Musel" took twenty years to complete, but it endowed Gijón with the premiere port in the region and one of the major ports in Spain.

[4] To put this figure in its national context, in 1900 the largest Spanish cities were Madrid and Barcelona, each with over 500,000 inhabitants. Gijón was about the same size as a handful of major northern port cities like San Sebastián, La Coruña and Santander. It was also the fourth largest of seventy-eight cities over 20,000 that were not provincial capitals. Nine of these cities were located in the province of Asturias, making it one of the most urbanized in the country. The Asturian capital of Oviedo had 48,000 residents, and the next largest city in Asturias was Avilés, with 25,682 residents: Delegación Regional, Oviedo. Instituto Geográfico y Estadístico, Censo de la Población, 1900, 1910.
[5] The first project for a road to connect Asturias with Castilla was proposed in the 1760s, but owing to a combination of local rivalries and the fiscal poverty of the state, it was not completed until the 1830s: Javier Varela, Jovellanos (Madrid: Alianza Editorial, 1988), 79–81.
[6] Avance, August 14, 1932.

Both directly and indirectly, Gijón's commercial expansion triggered growth in the industrial sector. Before 1850, Gijón's meager
industrial offerings are clearly expressed in the observations of a contemporary traveler:

> There are three private chapels in the town; one stearic candle factory,
> another factory of lime, a tannery, three canneries and a glass factory;
> seventeen boarding houses, thirty-eight stores, a café, a hostel; and
> there are about 1,000 men employed in carpentry, locksmithery and
> other industries and 2,000 women cigarette makers.[7]

By the end of the century, this picture had changed dramatically. Even
before the post-1898 boom, a surprised Catalan visitor could marvel,
"I repeat that I had no idea Gijón was so industrial and, even more,
that she made such perfect products."[8] The commercial traffic sparked
the creation of two major industries: metallurgy and shipbuilding.
Thus, between 1865 and 1874, the number of steam-powered ships
in Gijón's fleet had risen from four to thirty-four, most of them built
in local shipyards.[9] The first large metallurgical factory was opened in
1879 by a French capitalist, who chose Gijón because of its convenient
location near the ore and coal deposits of the mining basin.[10] After
Moreda y Gijón consolidated and updated its equipment in 1895, it
became the third largest iron and steel plant in Asturias. In classic
"take-off" effect, metallurgy created spin-off industries, like machine
building, smelting, and petroleum refining.

In addition to her "perfect products," Gijón had the good fortune
to possess a pristine beach and mild summer weather. The city turned
these advantages into a booming tourist trade as soon as the transport
network could bring people as well as coal, in this case to escape the
heat of the central *meseta*. Gijón's tourist reputation was secured
when, in 1858, Queen Isabella and her family summered there. In
addition to bringing the city prestige and revenue, tourism also stimulated commercial growth, especially in the areas of construction and
public services, entertainment and luxury goods. The city's two faces,

---

[7] Juan Hunquera Huergo, quoted in Joaquín A. Bonet, *Biografía de la villa y puerto de
Gijón*, vol. I (Gijón: La Industria, 1968), 238.
[8] From an article written in the local paper by the prominent anarchist, Federico Urales,
"Sobre cosas y casos en Gijón," *El Noroeste*, May 8, 1898.
[9] Ramón María Alvargonzález Rodríguez, *Gijón: industrialización y crecimiento urbano*
(Asturias: Ayalga Ediciones, 1977), 26–27.
[10] Angeles Barrio Alonso, *El anarquismo en Gijón: industrialización y movimiento obrero,
1850–1910* (Gijón: Silverio Cañada, 1982), 36.

of summer resort and industrial powerhouse, came together in a brilliantly successful exposition of Gijón's products and industry, organized for visitors in the summer of 1899.[11]

All of this commercial and industrial infrastructure set the stage for the turn-of-the-century boom. The years between 1898 and 1901 witnessed the most rapid economic growth in Asturias until the "miracle" of the 1960s. The combination of "the benefits of the export of iron ore with the repatriation of colonial capital produced a sharp rise in investment" and sparked a boom that "reached its true significance in the two northern industrial regions: Asturias and the Basque country."[12] It affected nearly all sectors, but was concentrated in banking, mining and metals, shipping and the service sector. Dozens of new enterprises opened their doors and existing companies expanded through incorporation and diversification.

Equally important, perhaps, was the palpable sense of wealth that permeated the province:

> In small as well as big ways one can observe in Asturias an abundance of money. The well-stocked warehouses demonstrate it; the many active markets, the lack of street begging in the important towns; the increase in urban property; the legion of traveling salesmen that traverse the province; the rarity of mercantile bankruptcy, and above all, the financial success of recently launched businesses.[13]

In this passage are summed up all of the optimism, the sense of unlimited possibilities, the dynamism that characterized the Asturian and Gijonese economy in 1900. When the city leaders looked forward, they envisioned a continuation of this growth; what they did not realize was that they had reached the pinnacle and were about to start the descent.

The contours of the city: the two faces of Gijón

In the meantime, Gijón's economic expansion had begun to change the character of the town itself. Everything from its physical appear-

---

[11] The national journal *Blanco y Negro* dedicated a page to the Exposition in their August 19, 1899 issue.

[12] T. Jiménez Araya, "Formación de capital y fluctuaciones económicas. Materiales para el estudio de un indicador: creación de sociedades mercantiles en España entre 1886 y 1970," *Hacienda Pública Española*, 27 (1974), quoted in Juan Antonio Vázquez García, "El ciclo económico en Asturias, 1886–1973: un análisis comparativo," *BIDEA*, 105–106 (1982), 466.

[13] Canals, *Asturias*, 13.

ance to its moral fiber seemed to be in flux, to the delight of modernists and to the horror of others who warned of decadence and the ugliness of the industrial landscape. As in most industrializing towns, the city was inundated with immigrant workers who arrived along with the factories.[14] The settling of these thousands of new residents created many of the contours of the twentieth-century city. But, unlike most industrial cities, Gijón also had to accommodate thousands of temporary residents of a very different class – its tourists. This combination helped to reinforce the sense of Gijón's split personality, on the one hand of playground of the leisure class and on the other of industrial powerhouse. In other words, it created an exaggerated version of the characteristic segregation of the early-twentieth-century industrial city. By 1900, the two faces of the city were already sketched in, leaving the twentieth century to fill in the details.

The ancient city, dating from pre-Roman times and re-built in the fifteenth century, remained enclosed in the head-shaped promontory of land later called Cimadavilla, or the "upper town." The phenomenon of horizontal as opposed to vertical segregation began in the later eighteenth century as the town's early commercial activity attracted more artisans and sailors, who populated the area just outside the bottleneck entrance to Cima. Named La Rueda, or the wheel, its streets still carry names like "furnace," "warehouse" and "market" that once reflected its character and inhabitants.[15] (See Map 2.) Nevertheless, the old city of Cima retained the socially mixed character of the early modern city, well into the early nineteenth century. Today, the juxtaposition of the old palace of the Conde de Revillagigedo and rows of tiny stone houses bear witness to the past composition of the neighborhood.[16]

By the mid-nineteenth century, however, this configuration began to change. The installation of the tobacco factory in Cima in 1842, coupled with the aging and decay of the old city center's buildings, triggered the exodus of the wealthy and the proletarianization of the

---

[14] The growth of the worker population is difficult to calculate, since statistics are often contradictory and leave out certain categories of workers, notably female. Angeles Barrio reviews the various estimates and concludes that there were about 11,000 male industrial workers and 4,000 female workers in 1900. The only comparison that exists is the estimated 2,000–3,000 workers in the 1857 census: Barrio, *Anarquismo en Gijón*, 65–67.

[15] Aladino Fernández García *et al.*, *Geografía de Asturias: geografía humanal: geografía urbana: Langreo, Mieres y Gijón* (Asturias: Ayalga Ediciones, 1982), 177.

[16] As Javier Varela writes of the mid-eighteenth century: "There resided noble rentiers, who controlled the city government, the artisans who fulfilled their basic needs, the 'gente del mar,' dedicated to fishing, and a dozen merchants": *Jovellanos*, 15.

21

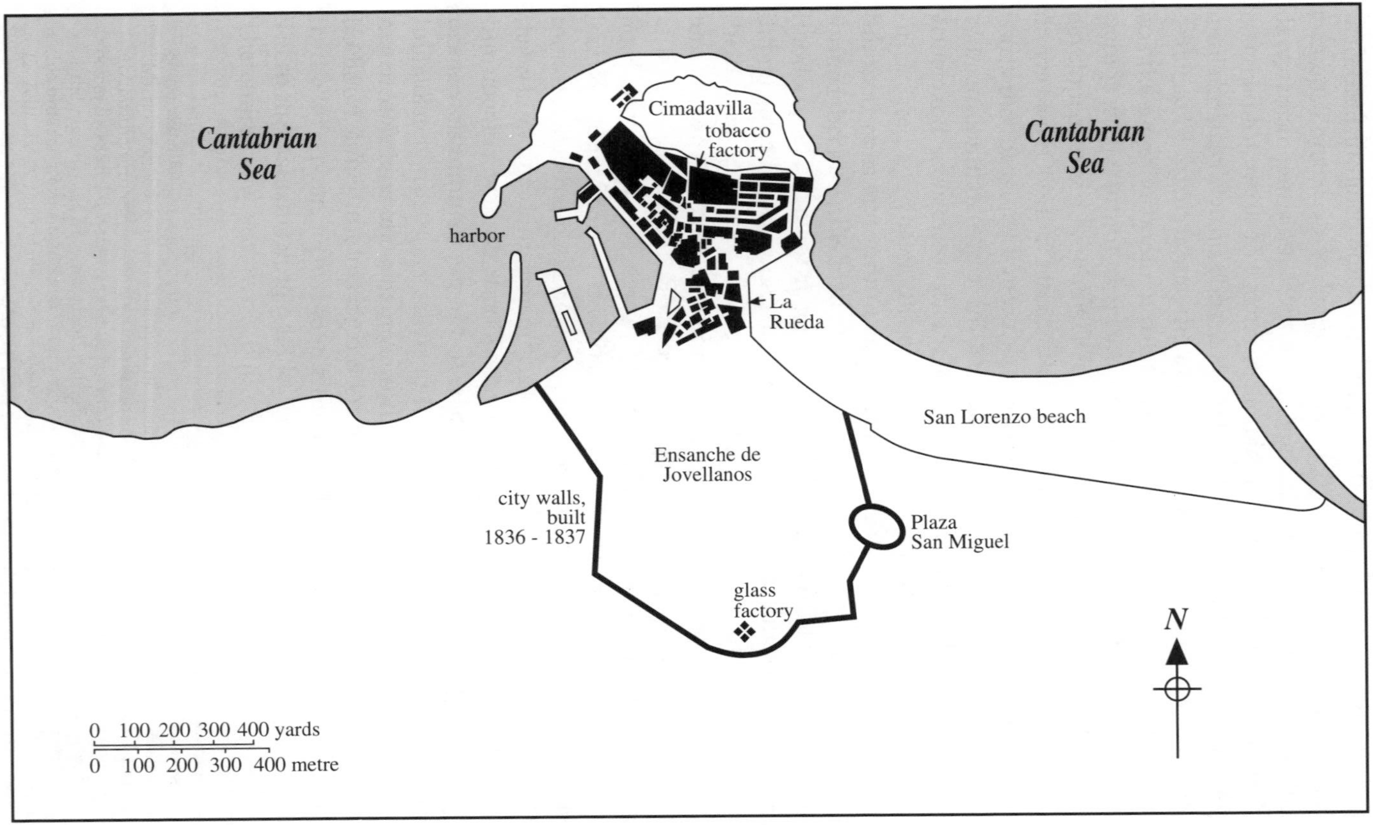

Map 2 Gijón to the 1840s

Cantabrian Sea

Cantabrian Sea

harbor

Cimadavilla
tobacco factory

La Rueda

San Lorenzo beach

city walls, built
1836 - 1837

Ensanche de
Jovellanos

Plaza
San Miguel

glass factory

N

0 100 200 300 400 yards
0 100 200 300 400 metre

neighborhood.[17] As workers moved into Gijón, they gravitated to Cima and its inexpensive housing. By the 1870s, it had been transformed into the city's first working-class *barrio*. The local government put its official stamp on this transformation when, in 1865, it moved its administrative apparatus to a new city hall outside Cimadavilla.[18]

With the old city center abandoned to the popular classes, the wealthy residents moved into a new commercial and residential center constructed on the outskirts. Instead of modernizing the old quarter, with its narrow, twisted streets, Gijón, like many other Spanish cities, built an alternative downtown that was to express the personality of a modern, prosperous city. This area, the *ensanche*, consisted of wide, straight streets, perfect for impressive façades and busy commerce. (See Map 3.) This blueprint for urban development, first implemented in Barcelona in the 1860s, became the standard model of urban planning in late-nineteenth and early-twentieth-century Spain.[19]

As the orderly grid of the *ensanche* expanded to the east (see Map 4), the city also spread in a much more haphazard fashion to the south and the west (see Map 5). Stimulated by the railroad station and the port to the west and the "Coal Highway" to the south, the majority of the city's factories were built in these areas. Since many of them were located far from the city center, private entrepreneurs took the initiative of constructing cheap housing to attract and accommodate the new worker population. Thus, the two faces of the city took shape, working-class Gijón to the west and south, and elite Gijón to the east. However, unlike the eastern *ensanche*, the new factory suburbs followed no plan. As elsewhere in Spain, the municipal government paid little attention to construction outside the *ensanche*, which was left entirely in the hands of private businessmen.[20]

Gijón's first new factory suburb was Natahoyo, a narrow strip of land bounded by the sea on one side and the railway station on the

[17] Alvargonzález, *Gijón*, 108.

[18] This process of decay and proletarianization of the old city center repeated itself in a number of Spanish cities during this same period. See Brigitte Magnien, "Cultura urbana," in *1900 en España*, 110–111.

[19] The plan presented by the Barcelona architect Ildefonso Cerdá in 1860 was used as a model for most cities (Magnien, "Cultura urbana," 112). Interestingly, Gijón's first plan had been drawn up in the late eighteenth century by the far-sighted Jovellanos, even though it was not implemented until the 1860s. Gaspar Melchor de Jovellanos was Gijón's most illustrious son, who, in addition to being one of the premiere figures of the Spanish Enlightenment, took a great interest in the economic development of his native city and province.

[20] Magnien, "Cultura urbana," 113.

23

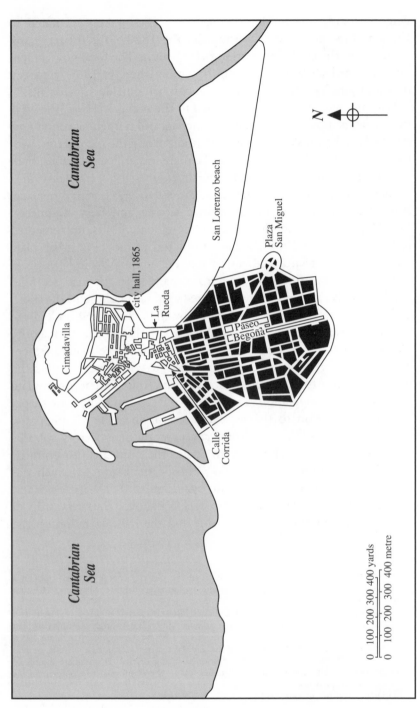

Map 3 Expansion in the 1850s and 1860s

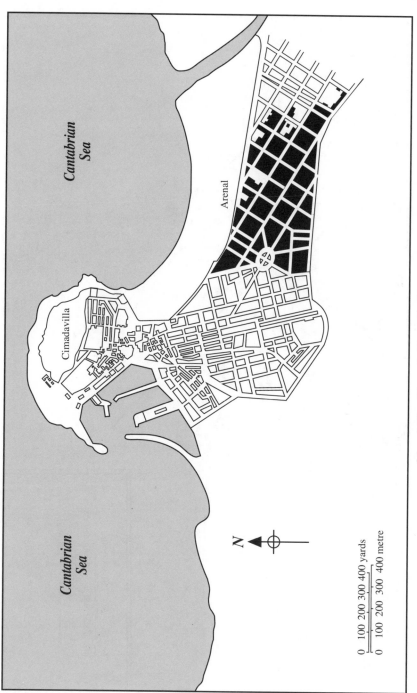

Cantabrian
Sea

Cantabrian
Sea

Cimadavilla

Arenal

N

0 100 200 300 400 yards
0 100 200 300 400 metre

Map 4 The *Plano de Ensanche* of 1867 (Arenal)

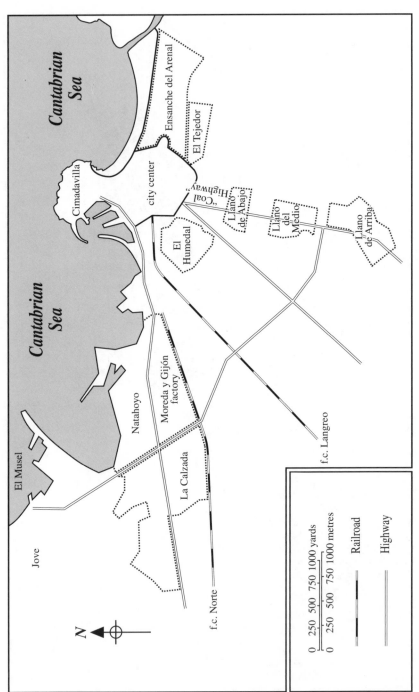

Map 5 Parcelization and working-class settlements

other. The first factory – a ceramic manufacturing plant – went up here in 1876, but it was the construction of Moreda y Gijón in 1879 that established a critical industrial mass. When the limits of this strip were exhausted, industrial and residential development moved further west from Natahoyo into a new barrio, La Calzada, which formed the center of twentieth-century expansion to the west.[21] The first factory (textiles) was erected there in 1899, but the completion of El Musel in 1912 provided the best reason for industries to settle there. In addition to this westward movement, clusters of cheap housing sprang up at isolated intervals in the swampy south end of the city, in areas that would become the neighborhoods of Humedal, Tejedor and El Llano. El Llano, situated on the "Coal Highway," was at this point too far from the industrial center in Natahoyo to attract many residents, but by the 1930s it would become one of the most important working-class neighborhoods in the city.[22] Thus, in 1900, the only areas that could be called full-fledged working-class neighborhoods were Natahoyo and Cimadavilla, the just-born and the centuries old.

Within this basic pattern of expansion, the two faces of the city solidified. In addition to bourgeois residents, the *ensanche* attracted most of the new banks, cafés and luxury stores that accompanied Gijón's growth. By the turn of the century, high-society life revolved around the fashionable Calle Corrida, which remained the symbol of leisure-class Gijón through the 1930s.[23] To enhance this image, the business community and the city government poured their energies into giving the new downtown area all the accoutrements of a modern city, including the triumphal inauguration of electric street lights on the Calle Corrida just before the turn of the century. This was the Gijón that tourists raved over, about which it could be said: "Gijón is an enchanting, educated, happy, clean and healthy place; I don't believe there is a better place to spend the summer and avoid the heat."[24]

The contrast with the industrial city spreading to the west could not have been greater. Visually, the haphazard and unco-ordinated

[21] According to the 1888 census, La Calzada contained 561 residents. By 1930, over 3,200 people lived there: Delegación Regional, Oviedo. Instituto Geográfico y Estadístico, *Nomenclator de España: Provincia de Oviedo*, 1888 and 1930.

[22] In 1888, there were 288 people living in El Llano, compared to about 5,500 in 1930 (because of re-districting, it is difficult to calculate an exact number): *Nomenclator*, 1888 and 1930, and Archivo Municipal de Gijón, *Censos de la Población*, 1900 and 1930.

[23] L. Villar Sangenis, *Noticiero – Guía de Gijón* (Gijón: Imprenta Lino, 1911), 25–26.

[24] *Blanco y Negro*, August 19, 1899.

settlements were completely at odds with the geometric order of the downtown grid. Further, the ignored suburbs suffered from a lack of basic amenities and public services. Since these areas operated as private fiefdoms subject to no public regulations, owners had no financial incentives to improve the quality of life. City officials did not have much more control over downtown development, but there the tourist industry and the potential profits motivated greater attention to comfort, convenience and aesthetics.[25] As the first anarchist newspaper grumbled in 1901, the Calle Corrida was always under improvement: from the clock to the statue of Jovellanos (1891) to the paving of the street (1901), while in the outer reaches of the city the streets were virtually impassable on rainy days.[26] Since the new worker areas were outside the city limits, there was no running water, no electricity, sewers, telephones or even transport into Gijón until the streetcars began operating in the 1890s. In 1904 residents of Natahoyo lacked even a mailbox for posting letters.[27] More generally, as late as 1911, almost 90% of the public services provided by the city were located in the center districts.[28]

While the two faces of the city could not have looked more different, a common thread united them: the primacy of business interests in shaping Gijón's urban environment. This identity clearly set Gijón off from what had long been Asturias' premiere city and its capital, Oviedo, just 30 km inland. Besides being a provincial capital, Oviedo was the seat of a bishopric and the home of a major university. With these institutions, the capital retained its reputation as the intellectual and cultural center of the province; instead of businessmen, its most important citizens were professors, bureaucrats and clergymen.

These distinct personalities gave rise to a series of familiar stereotypes about the rival cities.[29] The Gijonese were both admired and

---

[25] On the history of urban planning in Gijón see Moisés Llordén Miñambres, *La producción de suelo urbano en Gijón 1860–1975* (Oviedo: Gráficas Summa, 1978). As he points out, the only serious attempt at public urban planning before the 1970s occurred during the Civil War, under the Popular Front government. On the national level, Brigitte Magnien notes that in 1900 there were virtually no effective laws imposing minimum services on local governments, which meant that all improvements had to come from local initiative: "Cultura urbana," 115.

[26] *Defensa del Obrero*, November 19, 1901.

[27] *El Noroeste*, April 2, 1904.

[28] The exact figure was 88.8% in 1911; by 1951 that number had dropped to 51.72%: Alvargonzález, *Gijón*, 239 and 241.

[29] The commercial versus intellectual orientation of the two cities dated back to the eighteenth century, when Gijón was a town of 2,500 people. For example, when Jovellanos fought to open an institution of higher learning in Gijón, he proposed an institute focused on "practical sciences," to balance the University of Oviedo, which was dedicated to "intellectual sciences." The Real Instituto Asturiano de Náutica y Minerología was in

reviled as hard driving and ambitious, while the Oviedans were viewed as more cautious and contemplative, less sharp but more metaphysical. One of the clearest descriptions of the Gijonese stereotype came from Federico Urales, a Catalan of metaphysical bent who chronicled his visit to Gijón in the local newspaper:

> If I could put into the brain of this simple people the acquired civiliz-
> ation of certain intellectual centers, without altering the lovely color of
> their cheeks, nor the healthy and passionate sentiments of their hearts,
> I would have achieved the greatest triumph. But elsewhere, where there
> are ideas, there is no passion, because people lack the physical power
> to feel them; and here, where there are passions, there are no ideas
> because of the lack of education to sustain them.[30]

While it would be difficult to document the absence of ideas in turn-of-the-century Gijón, the kind of thriving public sphere of politi-cal and intellectual debate that Urales was used to in Barcelona was certainly lacking. Gijón's entrepreneurs and officials had turned the city into a bustling, cosmopolitan commercial center, but its political culture was still that of a sleepy village. Thus, by 1900, Gijón had undergone a dramatic economic, social and spatial transformation while its intellectual and political culture remained mired in the stifling conventions of the nineteenth-century Restoration:

> In spite of the surprising development that Gijón has undergone in the
> last few years, her character and appearance, that is to say, her basic
> structure, has not changed greatly. The same established families, the
> same surnames of the past, the same privileges of the old Gijón. This
> fact is perfectly explicable, given that the dramatic rise in population is
> concentrated in the working class, who have been moving to the town
> by the thousands, attracted by the factories, industries and maritime
> activities that offer jobs for thousands of workers.

This passage, located in a contemporary coffee-table history of Astur-ias, articulates perfectly the elites' uncritical acknowledgement of what had been up to that point the certainties of Restoration politics.[31]

Restoration politics before 1900

The fact that these historians could so easily dismiss the politically disruptive potential of thousands of workers, despite the existence of

---

fact established in 1893, the beginning of a tradition of technical education that would extend into the twentieth century: Varela, *Jovellanos*, 87–89.

[30] "Sobre cosas y casos en Gijón."

[31] Fermín Canella y Secades and Octavio Bellmunt y Traves, *Asturias* (Oviedo, 1895), 271.

universal male suffrage, captures the essence of Restoration politics. On paper, the Restoration system incorporated mass political participation, but in practice it operated within a tightly closed political circle. Although this contradiction existed in virtually all late-nineteenth-century representative regimes, it was particularly pronounced in Spain. Thus, the remarkable stability achieved was less a sign of general contentment than an indication of the elite compromise that had been struck between absolutists and liberals.

After a chaotic republican interval in the mid-1870s, the monarchy was restored in 1876, guided by one of Spain's most influential statesmen, Antonio Cánovas del Castillo. One of Cánovas' main concerns was to establish a parliamentary system that could negotiate transitions without the interference of the army. To incorporate as broad a spectrum of monarchist political opinion as possible, Cánovas grouped the conservative and center-right elements into his Conservative party while his opponent Práxedes Sagasta attracted the moderate left-center with his Liberal party. Cánovas planned to allow each party to have its turn in forming governments, but was more concerned with stability than with democratic process. Thus, the designated schedule for rotation was based not on a set interval or on the whim of the voters, but on the "exhaustion of the situation." This condition, once agreed upon by the political players, would lead the king to appoint a ministry from the opposition party. Because the two party leaders and the king made this decision, a new ministry was put in the peculiar position of "making" a new majority in the Cortes through the holding of elections whose results everyone knew beforehand. While apparently awkward, the mechanism of what became known as the *turno* institutionalized the peaceful transfer of authority for the first time in Spanish parliamentary history.

However, these manipulated elections created a powerful role for local political bosses, called *caciques*, who were charged with securing the required majority for the government's candidate. This system of *caciquismo*, which used the local influence of individuals who could dispense favors in return for political support, became one of the primary characteristics and major pillars of the Restoration regime.[32] *Caciquismo* ruled Asturian politics as well, but its exact form differed from the general Spanish model. Rather than a periodically shifting

---

[32] The best general study on *caciquismo* is José Varela Ortega, *Los amigos políticos: partidos, elecciones y caciquismo en la Restauración, 1875–1900* (Madrid: Alianza Editorial, 1977).

balance of power, the Conservatives dominated regional politics. At the apex of the Conservative political machine was Alejandro Pidal y Mon, the region's most famous and powerful *cacique*. Although not Asturian by birth, Pidal reserved a parliamentary seat there for his entire political life, spanning some thirty years.[33] During the year he ruled from Madrid, while in the summers he held court in his home in wealthy Somió (a suburb of Gijón); there he "established his central headquarters, where all his subjects came to receive orders on controlling the various townships and electoral districts in the province. In this way, Pidal ruled his fief of Asturias."[34]

Another pillar of the regime was the Catholic Church, which often worked in tandem with the *caciques* to influence and manipulate the population. The "King and Church" bond had been formed during the Reconquest and solidified during the Napoleonic occupation and the First Republic. The result was a regime in which Church and State were perhaps more closely intertwined than in any other late-nineteenth-century parliamentary system. In this alliance, the Church contributed all of its moral and political support to upholding the regime.[35] In return, the civil authorities allowed the Church great latitude in controlling both public culture and private life.

The political influence of the Church and the *caciques* permeated the country, but it was strongest in rural districts where the priest and the landowner held sway over an uneducated populace. In 1900, Spain was still largely a rural country, with over 65% of the population engaged in agriculture. Even in Asturias, one of the more industrialized regions, 69% worked in agriculture, with only 14% in industry and 16% in the tertiary sector.[36] Those employed in these latter sectors were almost entirely concentrated in Gijón, Oviedo and the mining towns of the central basin. The size and concentration of the industrial population allowed rural Asturias to dominate the regional political

---

[33] Pidal was financially linked to Asturias through interests in the metal and mining industries. He began as an ultramontane politician at war with the Restoration state, but in the early 1880s he changed course and decided to collaborate. It is from this period that his real political power dates. In 1884, Cánovas named him Minister of Development, and he remained on the provincial and national political scene until close to his death in 1913: David Ruiz, *Asturias contemporánea, 1808–1936* (Madrid: Siglo Veintiuno, 1975), 35.

[34] Antonio Oliveros, *Asturias en el resurgimiento español* (Madrid: Juan Bravo, 1935; reprint, Gijón: Silverio Cañada, 1982), 46. Oliveros was editor of the reformist newspaper, *El Noroeste*, after 1917.

[35] As Manuel Tuñón de Lara put it, the Church was the fundamental organ of the reproduction of ideas that upheld the regime: "La Guerra Civil," 11.

[36] Ruiz, *Asturias contemporánea*, 189.

establishment even as urban centers like Gijón came to dominate the provincial economy. The way electoral districts were drawn, for example, allowed the rural areas of Llanera and Carreño to swamp Gijón's urban vote in any national or provincial elections.

In local elections, voting districts were similarly balanced: urban neighborhoods were paired with one of the *aldeas* (rural suburbs). Throughout the period, these *aldeas* rarely failed to return a unanimous bloc of votes for the conservative candidate, although their impact lessened as the percentage of urban residents in the township increased.[37] The only formal political opposition was provided by a variety of republican parties, a few of whose candidates managed to get elected to the city council without ever threatening the monarchist majority. Usually, republicans ran in two or three safe districts, which monarchists did not even bother to contest. Thus, for example, in 1899, the city council consisted of three republicans and twenty-seven monarchists.[38]

This kind of predictable election generated considerable apathy on the part of the population. As the British vice-consul reported in 1892, "the people in general had no faith in the purity of the elections, and showed such indifference as to support the idea that they lacked an interest in politics as it existed in other European countries."[39] In the 1899 parliamentary elections, for example, the Conservative candidate and his republican opponent ran a close race in the city, with the former gaining 465 and the latter 370 votes. However, 60% of the 2,100 electors did not even vote. When the votes of Llanera and Carreño were added, the final tally for the parliamentary district gave the Conservative Rendueles over 5,000 votes and the republican de Labra only 862.[40] This landslide victory was achieved through a combination of skewed districting, apathy and the manipulation of rural voters.

The electoral machinery operated in the context of a wide range of strategies and tools that the conservative establishment maintained to control political expression. The government granted ample powers to suppress dissent, whether articulated in speeches, newspaper articles

---

[37] In 1900, Gijón's rural districts contained 2,205 electors, compared to 2,247 in the urban districts. The majority of the electors in the rural districts were farmers, with sprinklings of workers and artisans. By 1930, the number of rural voters had doubled, to 4,572, but city districts accounted for 12,090 electors: Delegación Regional, Oviedo. Instituto Geográfico y Estadístico. *Censo electoral de la provincia de Oviedo*, 1900 and 1930.

[38] *El Noroeste*, May 19, 1899.

[39] Varela Ortega, *Los amigos políticos*, 394.

[40] *El Noroeste*, April 17, 1899.

or demonstrations. Laws made it easy to censor criticism, and judges co-operated in enforcing them. Public order was maintained by units of local police as well as a strong contingent of the Guardia Civil, or Civil Guard. The Guards were part of a national police force, first organized to patrol rural areas, but which had also become extremely effective in intimidating disturbers of the urban status quo, whether they were beggars, strikers or city councilmen.[41]

For example, on February 11, 1900, the local republican parties planned to celebrate the anniversary of the establishment of the Republic, in a symbolic but powerful display of dissent.[42] The republicans applied for a permit to hold a public demonstration, during which they intended to dedicate a plaque to one of the fathers of local republicanism, Tomás Zarracina, in a ceremony in front of his house. They also purchased 300 loaves of bread to distribute to the poor, thus linking the Republic to the fate of the downtrodden masses. To participate in this momentous event, the organizers invited representatives from Oviedo and Mieres, scheduled to arrive on a morning train.

On February 10th, however, the government suddenly revoked permission to hold public rallies, in anticipation of nationwide celebrations of the anniversary. A circular distributed to the Civil Governors of the provinces gave orders "to be prepared to dissolve by force" any public demonstration that might form.[43] In Gijón, dozens of extra Civil Guards were shipped in as reinforcements. When the regional delegates arrived at the train station, they were escorted by cordons of Guards to the republican headquarters. Crowds assembled outside and attempted to march to Zarracina's house, but mounted officers dispersed groups by charging into them. Republican leaders finally ordered people to go home, and the few who could fit into party headquarters held a subdued rally and supervised the distribution of the bread. The ironic finale to this event was that two days later the mayor approved a small public ceremony to uncover the plaque, but this concession only reinforced the powerlessness of the opposition. Instead of invoking the power and compassion of the Republic, the event had conveyed its humiliation and defeat.

More broadly, the event captures the image of republicanism during

---

[41] On the origins and evolution of the Guardia Civil, see Diego López Garrido, *La Guardia Civil y los orígenes del Estado centralista* (Barcelona: Editorial Ariel, 1982).
[42] The following account was found in *El Noroeste*, February 10, 12 and 13, 1900.
[43] Circular núm. 107 del Ministro Gobernación a los Gobernadores de las Provincias, AHN, Serie Gobernación, Legajo 5A, núm. 8.

these years. The failure of the Republic had demoralized and confused the movement, leaving it unable to create a viable new strategy. Instead, it fractured into a variety of splinter groups which fought bitterly among themselves, agreeing only on the pure form of the regime.[44] The republicans' collective political message thus became little more than an incantation, which was most effective in commemorative celebrations like the event described above. In fact, the republicans may have attracted more respect as persecuted martyrs than as opposition leaders.

The image of republican leaders fleeing horses' hooves epitomizes the political culture of Gijón and most of Spain in 1900. The symbiosis of a weak and divided formal opposition and a manipulative and repressive establishment provided the elements of Restoration stability. Thus, even during a period of rapid social change, the old families ran the city through a combination of "carrot and stick" diplomacy, granting favors and punishing the ungrateful in a style more reminiscent of *noblesse oblige* than of democratic accountability. While the two faces of Gijón were taking shape, they had not yet opened a political dialog. Nevertheless, there were cracks in the apparently seamless hegemony of the old families. Although they did not show up in the election results, voices of opposition existed. In the nineteenth century, none of these voices was powerful enough to launch an attack on the Restoration, but in the twentieth century their combined impact shook the fortress to its foundations.

Nineteenth-century oppositional traditions: the emerging public sphere

To see the budding oppositional voices, it is necessary to look beyond the formal political arena to the broader discourse of the public sphere, where the true limits of hegemony are tested. In the stagnant world of Restoration electoral politics, Gijón, like other new urban centers, was starting to develop an infrastructure of urban culture and sociability in which independent public debate could take place. This infrastructure, which included all the formal and informal institutions of

---

[44] After the demise of the Republic, four main splinter groups formed: Salmerón's Centralists, Ruiz Zorilla's Progressives, Castelar's Possibilists and Pi y Margall's Federalists. For a brief overview of these tendencies, see Carlos Dardé Morales, "Los republicanos," in *Historia General de España y América*, vol. XVI–2 (Madrid: Ediciones Rialpe, 1981), 130–140.

urban sociability, from the press to theaters, cafés, and voluntary associations, to marketplaces and neighborhoods, helped constitute the city's emerging public sphere.

The actors in this broadly defined public sphere were many, but it is possible to identify several different oppositional currents that opened up avenues for expressing discontent in the barren political climate before 1900. While these currents were too weak to have much immediate impact, they began to muddy the clarity of the dominant hegemonic framework and formed the basis for what would become articulated oppositional paradigms in the twentieth century. In other words, the emerging public sphere provided an incubator in which the seeds of future counter-hegemonic challenges could be nourished.

In particular, we can identify the formation of three different blueprints for uniting and empowering the Gijón of Cimadavilla and Natahoyo. One blueprint was offered by the republican intellectuals who sought to mold future democratic citizens through their cultural and educational associations. Another blueprint was articulated by anarchosyndicalists, who envisioned an alternative network of economic associations that would launch a radical challenge to the system. And finally, a third, more informal blueprint was provided by working-class women, who practiced a politics of radical direct action built on neighborhood networks that was aimed at reforming discrete parts of the system. The three blueprints overlapped in certain areas and conflicted in others, but together they created the available language of change and opposition in twentieth-century Gijón. Within the parameters of this language of protest, different groups fought to define an oppositional culture that would represent the popular face of Gijón. Moreover, they set patterns for mobilization that would define the twentieth-century repertoire of collective action.[45] Between them, they provided what would become the standard weapons: of alternative education, of the strike and of the consumer protest.

The reformers: the pursuit of intellectual and cultural regeneration
While the republican electoral opposition of the late nineteenth century made little impact, in Gijón and other cities groups and

---

[45] This useful term is associated with Charles Tilly, whose work emphasizes how these repertoires become part of the lexicon of mobilization, even as they adapt to new situations. See Charles Tilly, "Britain Creates the Social Movement," in *Social Conflict and the*

individuals associated with republicanism pursued a more successful strategy of cultural subversion in the public sphere.[46] This strategy emerged from the broader republican mission, which transcended the electoral goal of installing a new regime to encompass a world view dedicated to the "modernization" of Spanish society, which, in this view, was stagnating under the anachronistic survival of the old regime.[47] Central to this broader mission was the construction of the intellectual and symbolic foundations for what the republicans perceived to be a modern society, that is, a secular and democratic one. In other words, they endeavored to destroy the "webs of significance" that entangled Spaniards in a monarchist and clerical society, that made them "subjects" instead of "citizens."[48] If the republicans could create a nation of people who thought like citizens, not subjects, they could undermine the hegemony of the traditional elites, erode the stability of the Restoration and usher the country into the twentieth century.

The essence of this transformation was education, to which, like liberal democrats elsewhere, they ascribed almost mystical powers. Education, in the broadest sense of the word, performed the double function of preparing people for their role in the new society and of helping to construct its foundations. Their ideas on pedagogical content were simple. If one gave individuals an education that stressed independent thinking, freedom from religious indoctrination and intellectual exploration, they would naturally reject the hierarchy and blind faith that tied them to the old regime and embrace the liberal democratic values of republican culture.

Political Order in Modern Britain, ed. James Cronin and Jonathan Schneer (New Brunswick: Rutgers University Press, 1982).

[46] The distinction between the formal political weakness and the cultural impact of the republicans is explored in more depth in Pamela Radcliff, "Republican Politics and Culture in Turn of the Century Gijón," in *Republicanismo en España*, ed. Nigel Townson (Madrid: Alianza Editorial, 1994). By "cultural subversion," I mean the capacity to shape and influence value-systems, traditions and symbolic practices, as opposed to the capacity to shape government policy and institutions.

[47] On the dimensions of the republican project, see José Alvarez Junco, *El emperador del paralelo: Lerroux y la demagogia populista* (Madrid: Alianza Editorial, 1990): "More than a simple current of opinion or a political party, republicanism was a concept of the universe, a conjunction of beliefs, guided by reason, about the fortunes and destiny of humanity": p. 185. For a good portrait of late-nineteenth-century republican culture, see also Angel Duarte i Montserrat, *El republicanisme català a la fi del segle XIX* (Vic: Eumo Editorial, 1987).

[48] "Believing . . . that man is an animal suspended in webs of significance he himself has spun, I take culture to be those webs": Clifford Geertz, *The Interpretation of Cultures: Selected Essays* (New York: Basic Books, 1973), 5.

Achieving this transformation was an especially daunting task in the Spanish context. In the first place, the republicans had to create a new educational agenda, but more importantly they had to reach the millions of Spaniards who were simply left out of the existing state educational system. In contrast to France, the Spanish government had never made a serious effort to implement universal public education.[49] While this fact posed an enormous challenge for educational reformers, it also provided a great opportunity to socialize the alienated masses. A few alternative institutions existed already, particularly Giner de los Ríos' Institución Libre de Enseñanza,[50] but the movement of alternative education gained momentum in the crisis atmosphere after 1898.[51]

One of the most important centers of this educational reform movement was Asturias, where the consequences of industrialization intensified the general problem of alienated masses. From the Asturian republicans' perspective, the most crucial problem facing Spain was the integration of the new worker population, which was both politically and economically marginalized.[52] Thus, the general task of creating a nation of citizens merged with the "social question."[53] In this revised problematic, education was also the key to reconciling the tensions between capital and labor.

While theoretically women constituted half of the marginalized masses, in reality the reformers paid more attention to the gulf between classes than to that dividing the sexes. One of the few republi-

---

[49] Although a law of 1857 had imposed obligatory schooling for children between age six and nine, by 1900 the state would have had to build 10,000 more primary schools to accommodate every child. As a result, 71.6% of the population was illiterate in 1887, and 63.8% in 1900. See Jean-Louis Guereña, "Las instituciones culturales: políticas educativas," in *1900 en España*.

[50] Giner de los Ríos founded the Instituto after the fall of the First Republic, when he and other professors were fired from university appointments. The school was based on the philosophy that education was not designed to mold students into accepting dogmatic belief structures, but to free their minds to follow their own consciences.

[51] The crisis of 1898 generated a broad cultural and political critique known as "regenerationism." The republicans were part of this movement, but it covered a more diverse political spectrum and only lasted a few years as a so-called movement. On regenerationism, or the "generation of 1898," as it is called, see E. Inman Fox, *La crisis intelectual del '98* (Madrid: Edicusa, 1976) and Manuel Tuñón de Lara, *La quiebra del '98* (Madrid: Sarpe, 1986).

[52] According to Angeles Barrio, there were over 35,000 male industrial workers in Asturias in 1901, including miners, factory employees and artisans. About a third of these lived in Gijón, and another third were miners: *Anarquismo en Gijón*, 65–67.

[53] In this context, it is interesting that one of the major educational reformers, Aniceto Sela, had financial interests in the Asturian mining industry: Francisco Erice Sebares, *La burguesía industrial asturiana, 1885–1920* (Madrid: Silverio Cañada, 1980), 276.

can propagandists to raise the gender issue was Belén Sárraga, who caused quite a stir when she gave a talk in Gijón in 1899.[54] She pointed out that the religious divide between men and women was a consequence of the separate lives they led: "while the man is in the club defending democratic ideas, the woman, at the confessional, sells out the husband and forms a conspiracy against him."[55] While most male republicans no doubt agreed with her basic analysis, they only belatedly realized its implications when faced with the need to republicanize newly enfranchised women under the Second Republic. In the meantime, Sárraga remained an anomaly in a male republican world. When Melquíades Alvarez, Asturias' republican rising star, was asked to speak at a rally with Sárraga, he bluntly refused: "women should not be involved in these activities."[56]

In practice then, the movement for educational and cultural reform targeted and reached largely men, specifically from the lower classes. The focus on working-class men rather than women of any class stemmed partly from implicit assumptions about gender and citizenship but more directly from the threat posed by organizations competing for the ear of working-class men. As revolutionary ideologies took root in Asturias towards the end of the century, part of the reformers' concern was to dissuade workers from being seduced by calls to class struggle:

> There is nothing more baneful for everyone, than the constitution of political groups based on opposition and social antipathy. The formation of these groups, that usually call themselves workers' parties, with egotistical and demoralizing programs, is due partly to the ignorance in which vital classes like the working class still live, and partly to a stupid pride and mistaken education which is supposed to deal with that ignorance.[57]

The dangers of this combination of antipathy and ignorance are dramatically argued in a short story by one of the Asturian reformers, Leopoldo Alas, called "El Jornalero" (The Laborer). The hero is a poor intellectual who works in the library researching an article about

---

[54] Sárraga was one of the few prominent women in the early-twentieth-century republican movement. On her role, see María Dolores Ramos, "Belén Sárraga y la pervivencia de la idea federal en Málaga, 1889–1933," *Jábega*, 53 (1986).

[55] *El Noroeste*, September 12, 1899.

[56] *Aurora Social*, October 7, 1899.

[57] From an article by one of the reformers, González Posada, "La educación del obrero," *BILE* (1889), 306.

social disturbances in some town long ago. One day he is accosted by a group of anarchists who want to kill him and set the library on fire. The scholar tries to convince the anarchists that "science is impartial, history is neutral. These books ... are innocent ... they don't say either 'yes' or 'no'; here there are all opinions," but they are too ignorant to realize they are only hurting themselves.[58] The reformers, then, were like the hero of the story, standing at the door of civilization and faced with the challenge of letting in the masses without allowing them to burn down the edifice.

The most important concrete expression of the republican educational agenda in Asturias was the University Extension, promoted by a group of professors at the University of Oviedo.[59] As Aniceto Sela explained: "our universities, perhaps more than any others, need to open our doors, go down to the people, educate them, collaborate in the great project of national education in a way that gives more immediate results than does our primary mission of cultivating the pure sciences."[60] The extension program first appeared at the University of Zaragoza in 1893, after which it spread to other cities, but it reached its apogee in Asturias.[61] The University of Oviedo inaugurated its program in 1898, followed by a branch in Gijón the next year. The Extension was the first free adult education system in the country, linked to the existing university system but financed largely out of the founders' pockets. It sponsored lectures, excursions and mini-courses designed to appeal to manual laborers, but all with the same underlying message of self-help, class harmony and anti-clericalism.

The activities of the high-profile University Extension helped to reinforce the goals of an older and more humble organization in

---

[58] Leopoldo Alas, "El Jornalero," in *El Señor y lo demás cuentos* (Madrid: Talleres Calpe, 1919), 170.

[59] Without a university of its own, Gijón was influenced by the intellectual initiatives of the University of Oviedo. The reformers included the noted novelist, Leopoldo Alas ("Clarín"), as well as prominent academics, the most important of whom were A. Alvarez Buylla, Rafael Altamira and Aniceto Sela, all of whom achieved national prominence. For more on these men, see Leontina Alonso Iglesias and Asunción García Prendes, "La Extensión Universitaria de Oviedo, 1898–1910" (Tesina, University of Oviedo, 1974), 8–11.

[60] Quoted in Jean Louis Guereña, "La Projection sociale de l'Université à la fin du XIXe siècle: L'Extension Universitaire en Espagne," *Higher Education and Society. Historical Perspectives*, 1 (1985), 212.

[61] On the Extensión Universitaria, in addition to Guereña, see Maryse Villapadierna, "Les 'clases populares' organisées par l'Extension universitaire d'Oviedo (début du XXe siècle)," in Jean-René Aymes *et al.*, *L'Enseignement primaire en Espagne et en Amérique Latine du XVIIIe siècle à nos jours. Politiques éducatives et réalités scolaires* (Tours: Publications de l'Université de Tours, 1986).

Gijón, the Ateneo Casino Obrero. The Ateneo was founded in 1881, through the combined efforts of republican businessman Eladio Carreño and a group of artisans whose *tertulia* formed the basis of the organization.[62] At the official founding, the membership consisted of 560 men, most of them engaged in artisanal trades like carpentry, engraving and masonry. Progressive businessmen like Carreño lent financial and organizational support, but the institution was operated by and for men of the humble classes. While the earliest *ateneos* in Spain served the middle and upper classes, Gijón's was one of the first of a new generation, dedicated to raising the cultural level of the working classes.[63] Although it did not have the intellectual weight of the University Extension, the goals of the Ateneo fit squarely into the broad reformist agenda – to establish primary and adult education and to provide honest and civilized distraction for its working-class members.[64] "Civilized" meant sober and non-violent, an alternative to both the tavern and extremist politics. As with the University Extension program, the founders were confident that an exposure to books, music and healthy debate would point workers towards the path of good citizenship. At the founding ceremony for the Ateneo, the keynote speaker expressed this hope in a speech entitled: "Give me the ability to teach and I will transform the world":

> Your mission, gentlemen, is much easier here than in other areas. The Gijonese worker is sober, honorable and hard-working. He professes political doctrines, he has ideals, but he doesn't pursue them outside of the legal framework. Because he is not easily deceived, he doesn't believe that the riot can achieve anything serious or fundamental.[65]

Although the Ateneo failed to keep the Gijonese worker on this reformist path, it was crucial in promoting the idea of social progress through education. Between the Ateneo and the later University Extension program, by 1900 this concept was fully integrated into

---

[62] The *tertulia*, or debating society, was a popular institution in Spain after the 1830s, and helped to define Spain as, in Raymond Carr's words, a "discussing society": *Spain: 1808– 1939* (Oxford: Oxford University Press, 1975), 207.

[63] An *ateneo* (athenaeum) is a "scientific and literary association dedicated to raising the intellectual level of its associates through discussions, lectures and courses." The first athenaeums appeared in Paris in the late eighteenth century, with the first Spanish one established in Madrid in 1820. The first worker *ateneo* was the Ateneo Catalán de la Clase Obrera de Barcelona, founded in 1861: Pere Solà, *Els ateneus obrers i la cultura popular a Catalunya, 1900–1939* (Barcelona: Ediciones la Magrana, 1978), 39–40.

[64] Juan Teófilo Gallego Catalán, *La educación popular en Gijón* (Gijón, 1907), 57.

[65] Journalist Evaristo Escalera, quoted in Patricio Aduriz, "Centenario del gijonés Ateneo Casino Obrero," *El Comercio,* July 19, 1981.

the local political discourse. As a result, the secular cultural center evolved as one of the basic oppositional weapons of the twentieth century.

Despite the continued influence of these institutions, the republicans' cultural and educational impact was probably greatest during the last decades of the nineteenth century. Before the 1890s, workers interested in political dialogue and self-improvement had nowhere to go other than the republican organizations. In contrast to more established cities like Madrid and Barcelona, Gijón had no anarchist or socialist tradition leading back to the First International,[66] and no history of trade unionism other than the guilds that had been abolished in the eighteenth century.[67] Thus, the path of politicization for workers led inevitably through republicanism, whether or not it stopped there.[68]

Of the republican parties, the Federalists played by far the most important part in this process of education. In an 1884 survey of Ateneo Obrero members, all the respondents "declared themselves to be republican, and, in general, Federalists."[69] Likewise, an anarchist writing about the early 1890s declared: "the workers of Gijón were all Federals."[70] As elsewhere in Spain, the Federalist party carved out a special niche among the humble classes for its unique appeals to

[66] For the early history of trade unionism in Barcelona, see Manuel Izard, *Industrialización y obrerismo. Las Tres Clases de Vapor (1869–1913)* (Barcelona: Ediciones Ariel, 1973). For the early anarchist and socialist movements see Josep Termes Ardévol, *Anarquismo y sindicalismo en España: la Primera Internacional, 1864–1881* (Barcelona: Crítica, 1972); Santiago Castillo, *Historia del socialismo español*, vol. I : *1870–1909* (Barcelona: Conjunto Editorialista, 1989), and George Esenwein, *Anarchist Ideology and the Working Class Movement in Spain, 1868–1898* (Berkeley: University of California Press, 1989).

[67] A wonderful source from this period is the survey of Ateneo Obrero members commissioned by the Instituto de Reformas Sociales and published in 1885: Fernando García Arenal, *Datos para el estudio de la cuestión social* (1885; reprint, Gijón: Silverio Cañada, 1980). He reported that: "at the present time, there are neither guilds nor any free association that has replaced these former trade and professional organizations," pp. 6–7.

[68] As Pere Gabriel argues, however, even where socialism or anarchism appeared early, republicans played an important role in working-class politicization: "El marginament del republicanisme i l'obrerisme," *L'Avenc*, 85 (1985). Two good local studies of this relationship at the turn of the century are Angel Duarte i Montserrat, *El republicanisme català* and Ramir Reig Armero, *Obrers i ciutadans. Blasquisme i moviment obrer: Valencia, 1898–1910* (Valencia: Institució Alfons el Magnánim, 1982).
For a similar argument about French republicanism and workers, see Ronald Aminzade, *Ballots and Barricades: Class Formation and Republican Politics in France, 1830–1871* (Princeton: Princeton University Press, 1993).

[69] García Arenal. *Datos*, 80.

[70] Rogelio Fernández, *Suplemento Revista Blanca*, May 28, 1901. "To attribute the working-class movement in this city to either Socialists or anarchists demonstrates a lack of knowledge about what Gijón was like in that era ... the workers of Gijón were federalists."

Proudhonian notions of social and economic justice.[71] In contrast, the other republican parties offered a more liberal view of economic inequality that stressed individual effort over social responsibility. Because the Federalists played such an important role in educating and politicizing workers in the last decades of the nineteenth century, they can be credited with training many of the men who went on to lead twentieth-century anarchist and socialist organizations.[72] Two personal histories, of a socialist and an anarchist militant, exemplify this point. José Valdés' political involvement began in 1887 when, "like everyone who was progressive in those days," he joined the Federalist party. Youths who disliked the drunken socializing of the taverns could go to the Casino Federal and listen to an impressive variety of speakers, including Eladio Carreño, the founder of republicanism (and the Ateneo) in Gijón. In debates there, he said, you could listen to the most advanced ideas that attracted all lovers of liberty. The only exposure he got to more radical ideas was through negative newspaper stories of labor movements in Paris or Germany. In 1890, José, like many Asturians, went to Cuba to find work. There, he encountered anarchism. His final conversion resulted from a trip to the United States, where the extremes of wealth and poverty convinced him that the Republic was not the paradise it claimed to be. In 1901, when he wrote this story, Valdés had returned to Gijón and was serving as the president of the woodcarvers' union.[73]

Juan Leal first joined the Federalist party in 1896, "like all workers who were political at the time." He lived in Natahoyo, the most radical of all the neighborhoods, and, he said, the source of all progressive ideas. The generation of these ideas mostly took place in the workshop

---

[71] This social and economic dimension of Federalism was a crucial part of its intellectual foundations. For a selection of founder Pi y Margall's writings that emphasizes this dimension see Francisco Pi y Margall, *Pensamiento social* (Madrid: Editorial Ciencia Nueva, 1968). For a more general history of the origins of the movement, see Charles Hennessey, *The Federal Republic in Spain: Pi y Margall and the Federal Republican Movement 1868–1874* (Oxford: Oxford University Press, 1962) and Antoni Jutglar, *Pi y Margall y el republicanismo federal* (Madrid: Taurus, 1975).

[72] Two of the most well-documented political journeys were those of Socialist Manuel Vigil and anarchist Eleuterio Quintanilla, both key figures in the origins of the labor movement in Gijón. Vigil's politicization began with the Federalist *El Grito del Pueblo*, and his first political post was that of librarian for the republican center at age eighteen. See his "Recuerdos de un octogenario," a memoir written in 1955 and published in *Estudios de Historia Social*, 18–19 (1981), 322–323. Anarchist leader Eleuterio Quintanilla's politicization began with his Federalist employer giving him reading materials and inviting him to meetings. See Ramón Alvarez Palomo's biography, *Eleuterio Quintanilla* (Mexico: Editores Mexicanos Unidos, 1973).

[73] *Defensa del Obrero*, October 17, 1901.

42

of Joaquín, the shoemaker, where everyone would gather and discuss all the issues of the day. One of the regulars at Joaquín's was Víctor Huergo, soon to become an important figure in the Socialist party. Huergo eventually converted Juan himself.[74]

Despite such stories, the trajectory from republicanism to radical working-class organizations should not be oversimplified. In classic Marxist historiography, it was assumed that "bourgeois" republicanism passed the torch of working-class politicization to the "authentic" labor movement at some designated historical moment, usually the foundation of the First International. However, republicanism and its reformist vision did not simply fade away once the radical working-class organizations appeared. In an oppositional culture in which political boundaries often blurred, republicans and anarchists both competed for the loyalty and support of working-class Gijón. In the process, the republicans did much to shape the city's oppositional culture, which absorbed their principles of anti-clericalism, of the power of education, and of the importance of the cultural battlefield. In the end, however, the republicans failed to assert their hegemony and lost control of the oppositional forces. Their vision of social harmony never came to terms with the city's growing polarization, and as a result, could not build the bridges that would have provided the foundation for their project. In the context of polarization, the radical opposition articulated this gulf in a political language that resonated more with the popular classes of Gijón.

Radical working-class politics: the first trade unions

The labor movement that articulated this radical alternative evolved within the parameters of local and national conditions, as well as according to the general set of European patterns.[75] Thus, the process of unionization in Gijón was part of the European wave of class-based associationism in the later nineteenth and early twentieth centuries. However, unlike the labor movement in Germany or England, union organization remained for the time being a local phenomenon in Spain. The striking unevenness of Spain's regional development and the general lack of political integration made it difficult for a coherent

---

[74] *Aurora Social,* April 7, 1900.
[75] The lack of a single model of development has been amply demonstrated. See especially the introduction to *Working Class Formation: Nineteenth Century Patterns in Western Europe and the United States,* ed. Ira Katznelson and Aristide Zolberg (Princeton: Princeton University Press, 1986).

national movement to emerge. Thus, like Barcelona, Madrid and Bilbao, Gijón developed a movement with an identity all its own.

The most striking characteristic of the early trade union movement in Gijón was the struggle between anarchist and Socialist hegemony.[76] Outside of Spain, by the end of the nineteenth century anarchism had either been defeated by Marxism or reformist trade unionism, or had withdrawn from the labor movement to pursue individual acts of terror.[77] Even in Italy, the other major country where it took root in the 1860s, the labor movement had converted to Marxism by the 1880s.[78] Spain, then, remained one of the few countries where anarchism still competed to define the shape of the labor movement. Within Spain, the city of Gijón was a major battleground. Barcelona had long established its anarchist loyalties,[79] as had the *latifundista* areas of Andalusia,[80] while Bilbao and the mining towns of central Asturias had adopted a socialist orientation.[81] By 1900, therefore, Gijón constituted one of the most important contested territories.

The story began in 1891, when a dockworker named Francisco Cadavieco founded a local branch (Agrupación) of the Socialist party (PSOE), thereby constituting the first formal working-class organization in the city. By the following year, the 300 new members inaugurated their first Workers' Center (Centro Obrero) and announced their

[76] While anarchism and socialism fought to define a workerist alternative, republicanism remained a third force in this fluid period of definition. As Ramir Reig put it, in reference to Valencia: "the complex relations among the three groups, from collaboration to conflict, in terms of leadership and of the mutual influence and indeterminate orientation of the rank and file, is one of the most revealing aspects of the labor movement": *Obrers i ciutadans*, 26.

[77] As José Alvarez Junco notes, anarchism's strength in Spain only became distinctive in Europe in the twentieth century, and more particularly with the formation of the CNT in 1910: "El anarquismo en la España contemporánea," *Anales de Historia contemporánea*, 5 (1986), 190–191.

[78] On the rise and decline of Italian anarchism, see Nunzio Pernicone, *Italian Anarchism, 1864–1892* (Princeton: Princeton University Press, 1993).

[79] This traditional characterization has been disputed by Pere Gabriel, who argues that Socialists had more influence than acknowledged in the early years of the century: "Sindicalismo y sindicatos socialistas en Cataluña. La UGT, 1888–1938," *Historia Social*, 8 (1990).

[80] On nineteenth-century anarchism in Andalusia, see Temma Kaplan, *Anarchists of Andalusia, 1868–1903* (Princeton: Princeton University Press, 1977) and Jacques Maurice, *El anarquismo andaluz: campesinos y sindicalistas, 1868–1936* (Barcelona: Editorial Crítica, 1990).

[81] On the origins of the Socialist movement in the Basque country, see Juan Pablo Fusi, *Política obrera en el país vasco, 1880–1923* (Madrid: Turner, 1975). On the mining region of Asturias, see Adrian Shubert, *The Road to Revolution in Spain: The Coal Miners of Asturias, 1860–1934* (Urbana: University of Illinois Press, 1987) and David Ruiz, *El movimiento obrero en Asturias: de la industrialización a la II República* (Oviedo: Amigos de Asturias, 1968).

existence by organizing a few strikes. As elsewhere in Europe, the older, once-guilded trades, like carpentry, masonry and cabinet-making, formed the nucleus of this movement.[82] Nevertheless, it is difficult to gauge the continuity these artisans felt with older forms of associationism. As the Ateneo survey revealed, the guilds were no more than a distant memory, with the important exception of the guild of fishermen and dock workers, which had survived until recent years.[83] Given Cadavieco's trade, it may be that the dockworkers transmitted the memory if not the reality of an organizational tradition based on work identity.

After only a few years of activity, however, repression broke the back of the organization. In the years following an anarchist uprising in Jerez de la Frontera in 1892, the government cracked down on all dissident organizations, and the local unions shared the fate of most of their comrades around the country. By 1894, only the Socialist nucleus and a handful of dockworkers remained.[84]

The early socialist presence in Gijón is well documented, but the anarchists' origins are harder to trace. The Ateneo survey of 1884 asserted that no one declared himself an anarchist, "even though . . . all of them have a more or less clear idea of the existence and aspirations of those that are situated on the extreme left of the advanced parties."[85] This evidence is not unequivocal proof, but if a nucleus of anarchists existed in the early 1880s, these education-minded artisans would have been obvious candidates. By the early 1890s, some sources report anarchist activity, but others insist on their insignificance until the end of the decade.[86]

The likely scenario is that a few anarchists appeared in the early nineties but contributed little to the process of unionization. Manuel Vigil remembered the anarchists as pure troublemakers, in particular a man named Martín, who disrupted one May 1st celebration with

[82] The literature tying artisans to the origins of trade unionism is vast, beginning with E. P. Thompson, *The Making of the English Working Class* (New York: Pantheon Books, 1963). See, for example, Ronald Aminzade, *Class, Politics and Early Industrial Capitalism: A Study of Mid-Nineteenth Century Toulouse* (Albany: State University of New York Press, 1981) and Joan W. Scott, *The Glassworkers of Carmaux* (Cambridge, MA: Harvard University Press, 1974).

[83] García Arenal, *Datos*, 6–7.

[84] Socialist Manuel Vigil narrated the early history of the labor movement in a series of articles in *El Socialista*, March 23 and 29, 1901.

[85] García Arenal, *Datos*, 80.

[86] Historian Angeles Barrio argues that they appeared later (*Anarquismo en Gijón*, 102), while Manuel Vigil, in his series of articles for *El Socialista*, March 23 and 29, 1901, blames anarchists for the collapse of the early unionization drive.

his "Catalan accent, his presumption and his absurd manner," not to mention the glass of *anís* and water he gulped down during his oration. According to Vigil, local authorities expelled Martín from Gijón soon after, but not until he had converted the metalworkers at Moreda y Gijón to anarchism, leaving them bereft of organization.[87]

While Vigil's story is an openly hostile source, his description of Martín rings true in the context of Spanish anarchism in the 1890s. In a spiralling cycle of repression and violence, the anarchist-inspired trade unions of the 1870s and early 1880s collapsed, and anarchists abandoned strategies of mass organization in favor of underground militant activity and spectacular acts of terrorism, like the bomb that exploded at the Corpus Christi parade in Barcelona in 1896.[88] After that bombing, the government passed a blanket anti-terrorist law that allowed the authorities to indiscriminately round up and jail anarchists. The atmosphere of persecution permeated Gijón's first anarchist newspaper. In one article, "¡Alerta!," the author claimed that police had been collecting information on anarchists in preparation for a repeat of the mass arrests that had occurred in Catalonia.[89] In this climate, union building could hardly have been a high priority.

Nevertheless, around the turn of the century the anarchist movement entered a new phase. The cycle of violence inflamed by individual acts of terror had nearly snuffed out the movement, and the time seemed ripe to return to mass organizing.[90] Under the guise of anarchosyndicalism, the anarchists plunged once again into the battle for the hearts and minds of the workers. Like the Socialists, anarchosyndical-

---

[87] *El Socialista*, March 23 and 29, 1901.

[88] On anarchism during this decade, see Rafael Núñez Florencio, *El terrorismo anarquista, 1888–1909* (Madrid: Siglo Veintiuno, 1983) and Esenwein, *Anarchist Ideology.* Joan Casanovas marks the conversion to terrorism by the trade union anarchists of Catalonia with the dissolution of the Federación de Trabajadores de la Región Española in 1888: "Pere Esteve: un anarquista català a cavall de dos mons i de dues generacions," *L'Avenç*, 162 (1992), 20.

[89] *Fraternidad*, July 14, 1900.

[90] The pattern in Spain followed an international trend, although not all anarchists gave up the pursuit of "propaganda by the deed." At the international anarchist conference in Paris in 1900, the majority accepted the weapon of the general strike as the best means to advance the revolution. Thus, it returned to the idea of economic, work-based organizations as the units of struggle. In this new form, anarchism influenced the formation of the CGT in France and the IWW in the United States. On anarchosyndicalism, see George Woodcock, "Syndicalism Defined," in *The Anarchist Reader* (Glasgow: Fontana, 1980). On the IWW see Salvatore Salerno, *Red November, Black November* (New York: State University of New York Press, 1989). On France see Peter Stearns, *Revolutionary Syndicalism and French Labor* (Rutgers: Rutgers University Press, 1974).

ists argued that workers associated by trade were best equipped to wage economic warfare against the employers. But unlike the Socialists, they relied completely on this economic warfare to advance them towards the revolution. Whereas the Socialists created a division of power and responsibility between their political arm (the party) and their economic arm, the anarchosyndicalists invested all decision-making in the syndicates and refused to participate in electoral politics. In practice, Socialist and anarchist unions often fought for similar short-term goals, but the underlying assumptions infused these activities with a very different tone.

Thus, by the time of Gijón's second and more successful union drive in 1899–1900, the Socialists faced a kind of challenge from the anarchists which was different from that of the early part of the decade. Instead of playing the role of spoiler and provocateur, the anarchist movement now presented a serious alternative strategy of organization. As a result, the labor movement turned into a battleground in which neither side could claim victory. Not until the end of the following decade did the anarchists emerge victorious from this bruising battle for control over the potentially powerful labor movement.

None of this could have been predicted in 1898 when the Socialists' patient groundwork at last seemed to be paying off. The smoldering ashes of unionization suddenly exploded into a conflagration, when some thirty to thirty-nine "societies of resistance" were constituted between the years of 1898 and 1900.[91] Contemporary observers were as amazed by the rapidity of the process as we are in retrospect. On May 7, 1899, *El Noroeste* reported that "recently, they have begun to organize with such precipitation that a day doesn't go by without the celebration of one or more meetings of workers from different trades." By November of 1899, the Socialist newspaper *Aurora Social* boasted that over a dozen trades had unionized (see Table 1).

In the subsequent months other trades followed suit: the tinsmiths and cabinet-makers in December, street cleaners, cartwrights and hairdressers in January 1900, graphic artists and tailors in February, and in March, the *chocolateros*, wheelwrights and gas factory workers.[92] At

[91] Barrio, *Anarquismo en Gijón*, 103, says thirty; Manuel Vigil, in *El Socialista*, April 12, 1901, says thirty-nine.
[92] *Fraternidad*, February 3, February 17, March 11, 1900. *Aurora Social*, December 3 and 23, 1899, January 27, February 17 and 24, March 10, 1900.

Table 1 *Unions in Gijón, 1899*

Profession	Members
Masons	501
Dockworkers	478
Fishermen	400
Glassmakers	231
Carpenters	230
Painters	112
Metalworkers	100
Woodcarvers	99
Locksmiths	88
Potters	83
Bakers	66
Tobacco (men)	35
Flour dealers	26
"Mixed"	95
Shoemakers	68
Total	2,612

the height of the organizing drive, there were some 5,500 unionized workers, about half of the male worker population.[93]

As is clear from the list of new unions, the backbone of the labor movement still comprised the classic male artisanal worker. Although there were plenty of women workers in Gijón – seamstresses, cigarette makers and weavers – few of them jumped on the bandwagon initiated by the male workers. Even when some female trades unionized in later decades, the trade union movement remained a male-dominated organizational form that did not always connect with female concerns and priorities. Thus, the two most high-profile oppositional frameworks of the twentieth century, the trade union and the cultural center, appealed largely to men.

In 1900, however, this limitation did not seem to be a problem for the labor movement. A series of successful strikes had inspired the unions to reach for the brass ring of the eight-hour day. Incredibly, by March 1900, the entire construction industry as well as the dock-

[93] According to Vigil: *El Socialista*, April 19, 1901.

workers, some 2,500 individuals, had won this coveted prize.[94] Moreover, it had been achieved with remarkably little resistance from the
city's employers. The lightning attack of the new movement caught
the owners off guard, making them appear impotent in the face of
the formidable power of collective labor. The drama of this moment
was not lost on activists outside of Gijón, either. Overnight, Gijón
joined the ranks of cities like Barcelona that militants looked to in
awe and envy. From Paris, Errico Malatesta could plausibly boast that
the "Gijonese worker is in the vanguard in Spain."[95]

Why did the union movement scale such heights in so short a time?
Clearly the impetus behind the successful union drive was the economic conjuncture. Money was flowing into Asturias, business was
expanding, labor was in demand, and yet salaries lagged behind those
of other major industrial centers. Employers gave in easily in part
because they were unprepared for the assault, but also because they
had an economic cushion to work with. Within a couple of years, all
this changed. The boom fizzled out, employers frightened by the
power of the labor movement began to co-ordinate their own defense
and the turf war within the ranks began to corrode the solid front of
labor that had brought such dramatic results.

The Socialists first mentioned the interference of anarchists in late
1899,[96] and by the spring of the next year their influence was
strong enough to defeat a vote for the local federation to join the
Unión General de Trabajadores, the Socialist trade union federation
(UGT). By that point, anarchists and Socialists held separate rallies,
in which they attacked each other and lobbied for mass support.
The Socialists accused the anarchists of being provocateurs and
assassins, while anarchists responded by painting the Socialists as
mere political opportunists, charlatans palming hands to get votes
and personal power. In defense against their reputation as criminals,
the anarchists insisted they were scapegoated for the terrorism of a
few individuals.[97] The anarchists' protestations of respectability provide tangible evidence of the evolution from "propaganda by the
deed" to mass organizing. With this convergence, the main substan-

---

[94] *Fraternidad*, March 11, 1900.
[95] Quoted in Pachín de Melás, "Convulsiones sociales en Gijón," *La Prensa*, November
25, 1934.
[96] *La Aurora Social*, October 21, 1899. The article observed that the "lighthouse of anarchism" had moved from Oviedo to Gijón, blinding the sailors in its false light.
[97] *Fraternidad*, July 1, 1900. *Aurora Social*, June 9 and 23, 1900.

tive point of disagreement between Socialists and anarchists was the issue of political participation, but each movement also maintained a more ineffable difference in tone: moderation versus intransigence.

As the union movement struggled amidst factional disputes that began literally to tear it apart, its opponents took advantage of the respite to recoup their own forces. By the spring of 1900, the radical press warned that the bosses were forming their own association:

> It is rumored that various bourgeois of this town are trying to form a type of association with the "noble" goal of breaking the organization of the unionized workers, in order to thus rob them of all the improvements in the conditions of work that they have achieved.[98]

By July, the rumored Agremiación Patronal (AP) had materialized. In the same year, businessmen announced the formation of a Chamber of Commerce and a Unión Mercantil e Industrial to defend the interests of big business in Gijón. After this point in time, workers faced a united front in their workplace struggles, and easy victories like the eight-hour day campaign became a thing of the past. By 1900, then, a process of polarization in the workplace was well under way.

The development of a powerful and intransigent capitalist front helped to legitimate the more intransigent radicalism of the anarchists. Likewise, the anarchist rejection of electoral politics made sense to many people who observed the seemingly impregnable Restoration system. In addition, the well-established republican movement already provided a blueprint for pursuing change within the system. In this context, the Socialist movement's combination of moderate trade unionism and electoral politics could not find its niche in Gijón's oppositional culture. As a result, anarchism came to dominate not only the labor movement but also the language of radical opposition in the city. Thus, by the early twentieth century, the two poles of radical and reformist opposition were positioned to compete for the loyalty of Gijón's popular classes.

Women and the tradition of consumer protests
While the establishment of these opposing traditions certainly marked a watershed in the local history of popular protest movements, it reveals a distinctly masculine version of politics. As noted earlier, both

---

[98] *Aurora Social*, May 12, 1900.

of these movements comprised mainly working-class men, so their existence tells us little about the political role of women of the lower classes. In fact, it is common to assume that since most women did not join the ranks of unions or political parties they were largely apolitical. Likewise, since women were identified with the private sphere of home and family, their absence from the nineteenth-century public sphere has often been taken for granted. Thus, women, especially from the working classes, are often written out of the narrative of modern politics.

Through questioning narrow definitions of modern politics and the public sphere, however, we can locate working-class women's sphere of political activity. This activity emerged out of the daily networks of female sociability, which were the marketplace and the neighborhood instead of the trade union, the *ateneo* or the *tertulia*. In other words, working-class women constituted their own "cluster of communication" in the public sphere in the places where they congregated and debated their issues of collective concern.[99] For women involved in the daily provisioning of their families, one of their main common concerns was guaranteeing the consumption of goods and services necessary for basic survival and comfort. As a result, their political action often took the form of the consumer protest, well known to historians of early modern Europe, but often overlooked as a "modern" form of politics. In fact, this form of protest survived in the twentieth century as a predominantly female form of politics. Moreover, through the consumer protest, working-class women provided an alternative blueprint for political opposition, a blueprint that lacked the formal structure of the cultural center or the trade union but which retained significant power to mobilize community action.

Women's presence in food riots has been accepted as paradigmatic since E. P. Thompson's article on the eighteenth-century moral economy.[100] As Thompson and others have argued, the riot, especially the consumer riot, was one of the fundamental political weapons of the poor before the establishment of trade unions and working-class parties. Instead of an act of random violence, the food riot was a

---

[99] Craig Calhoun argues that "clusters of communication" can form around different issues, categories, or geographical units, like neighborhoods: "Introduction: Habermas and the Public Sphere," in *Habermas and the Public Sphere*, ed. Craig Calhoun (Cambridge, MA: MIT Press, 1992), 38.

[100] E. P. Thompson, "The Moral Economy of the English Crowd in the 18th Century," *Past and Present*, 50 (1971).

sophisticated dialogue between the people and the government over the formation of public policy.[101] The problem is that this market tradition has been treated implicitly as a stage in the modernization of protest, in which there is an appropriate evolution of collective action, in its forms, its motives and its participants.[102] In this scheme, eighteenth-century bread riots by consumer mobs give way to workers' strikes and political demonstrations; the politicized worker replaces the consumer, who increasingly targets power at its central source, the national government. Once a time line is in place, historians view certain types of protest as meaningful only in specific contexts.[103]

In fact, women continued to take to the streets over consumption issues, long after the formation of trade union movements. Because of the social division of labor in industrial societies, women remained the most sensitive to marketplace issues and continued to mobilize around them.[104] And because of their continued marginalization in conventional political systems, they still embraced forms of direct confrontation that bypassed legal mechanisms of redress.[105] While the incidence of the traditional food riot declined along with subsistence crises, it was replaced by battles over prices, rents, services and short-

---

[101] On eighteenth-century consumer riots see, in addition to Thompson, Louise Tilly, "The Food Riot as a Form of Political Conflict in France," *Journal of Interdisciplinary History*, 2 (1971), and John Bohstedt, "Gender, Household and Community Politics: Women in English Riots, 1790–1810," *Past and Present*, 120 (1988). Bohstedt insists that women's participation in riots has been overestimated, but his statistical findings demonstrate a strong presence in, particularly, food riots. See also Thompson's discussion of women and food riots in his reconsideration of the moral economy article, where he specifically addresses Bohstedt: "The Moral Economy Revisited," in *Customs in Common* (London: Merlin Press, 1991), 305–336.

[102] The term "modernization of protest" comes from Charles Tilly, "The Modernization of Protest in France, 1845–1855," in *The Dimensions of Quantitative Research in History*, ed. W. O. Aydelotte *et al.* (Princeton: Princeton University Press, 1972). However, the concept has been implicit in many labor history studies since Eric Hobsbawm, *Primitive Rebels: Studies in Archaic Forms of Social Movement in the 19th and 20th Centuries* (New York: Norton, 1959).

[103] Thus, in most articles about food riots in the twentieth century, the authors must explain why these atavistic protests have reappeared. For example, see Anthony James Coles, "The Moral Economy of the Crowd: Some Twentieth Century Food Riots," *Journal of British Studies*, 18 (1978); William Friedburger, "War, Prosperity and Hunger: The New York Food Riots of 1917," *Labor History*, 25 (1984); and María Luz Arriero, "Los motines de subsistencias en España, 1895–1905," *Estudios de Historia Social*, 30 (1984).

[104] Much of the theoretical basis for this distinction was laid in Temma Kaplan's oft-quoted article, "Female Consciousness and Collective Action: The Case of Barcelona, 1910–1918," *Signs*, 7 (1982). See also Pamela Radcliff, "Elite Women Workers and Collective Action: The Cigarette Makers of Gijón, 1890–1930," *Journal of Social History*, 27:1 (September 1993).

[105] Paul Hanson emphasizes this point in his article, "The *vie chère* Riots of 1911: Traditional Protests in Modern Garb," *Journal of Social History*, 21 (Spring 1988), 464.

ages of other essential goods. Women did not always dominate these struggles, but they often did. Moreover, when women organized protests, it was more often than not around these kinds of broadly defined consumption issues. As a result, these protests constituted the most coherent expression of working-class women's political identity.

The coherence emerged not from the links of formal organizations or ideological manifestos, but from the strikingly similar way that these public protests unfolded, in both content and form. The participant was the irate consumer, angry at the government or a businessman for not providing the expected goods or services that popular notions of justice demanded. Organization was spontaneous, often unfolding at the immediate location of the problem. Targets and goals were usually specific, and the participants were often prepared to hold the line until these goals were met. Moreover, within the limited scope of the attack, they were willing to employ coercion and violence to achieve their aims. The drama of members of the "weaker sex" engaged in violent public confrontation was often enough to bring the authorities to their knees.

A few examples should make these parameters clearer. In one instance, a dispute arose between a property owner and the women of Tremañes, one of Gijón's peripheral districts, just beyond La Calzada. The owner closed off a road that had always provided access to the river for women carrying their loads of washing. Seventy residents sent a petition to the mayor, but while these negotiations bogged down, the women took matters into their own hands. They took down the new wall, stone by stone, did their washing and went home. The owner rebuilt the wall and the women repeated the process. Finally, the mayor warned the owner that it would be messy and unpopular to stop the women by force, and he reluctantly conceded.[106]

In a different kind of situation, outraged women pursued the same kind of direct confrontation. The protest began when twenty-one women and two men from La Calzada blocked one of the highways into the city to prevent the entry of high-priced milk into Gijón. They were arrested and taken downtown to the jail, but this proved to be only the opening act. A large group of mostly female residents from La Calzada followed them into town and demonstrated outside the jail, asking for their release. Others went to the city hall and still others

---

[106] *El Noroeste*, January 19, 1900.

succeeded in blocking traffic on the street where the courthouse was located. These women dispersed peacefully, but at the end of the work day, female workers from the textile factory in La Calzada also marched to the jail to express their protests. They would not go home until the mayor assured them that the prisoners would be released the next day.[107] Significantly, the unit of mobilization in both these cases was the neighborhood, in particular two of the peripheral *barrios* that were just establishing their identity during this period. As these areas developed, often without vital services, neglected and forgotten by downtown Gijón, residents shared a whole range of consumption issues that provided a new focus for the traditional consumer protest. Women continued to form links based on their role as providers of goods and services for their families, but the shape of the industrial city created a new form of solidarity rooted in the problems of neighborhood consumption. As a result, the traditional links that women formed became the fundamental building blocks for the neighborhood community of the twentieth century. Thus, instead of a pre-industrial hangover, this blueprint for collective action was crucial to the formation of what would become one of the most powerful centers of oppositional culture, the working-class neighborhood.

The most dramatic consumer protests, however, crossed neighborhood lines to envelop the entire city. The most famous such event in local history occurred in May of 1898, when thousands of women took to the streets to express their hatred of an unpopular food tax, the *consumo*.[108] It began in the oldest working-class neighborhood, Cimadavilla, when a customs official confiscated two fish from a woman fishmonger who had not paid the new tax on seafood. Immediately, the other sellers in the fishmarket closed their stalls and marched behind their banner to the city hall, just outside the neighborhood. When the mayor did not appear to talk to them, they took to the streets again, walking back to the cigarette factory in Cima. There they convinced the 1,800 cigarette makers to join in solidarity. The entire crowd of over 2,000 women and children returned to the

---

[107] *El Noroeste*, January 13, 1900.

[108] This riot formed part of a pattern of such events that occurred all over the country around the turn of the century, the results of spiraling prices for agricultural goods that began in 1898. At a time of rising prices, the always unpopular *consumo* absorbed much of the rage. It was first instituted in 1845, lifted in 1868, then reimposed in 1874. On this broader wave of riots, see María Luz Arriero, "Los motines," and Carlos Serrano, *Le Tour du Peuple* (Madrid: Casa de Velázquez, 1987). The narrative of the local riot relies on *El Noroeste*, May 3 and 4, 1898.

city hall, but after more silence from city officials, the crowd marched by other factories, calling on all of their women workers to walk out.[109]

The demonstration had been peaceful up to then, but in the afternoon, with still no response from the authorities, it turned violent. From the original issue of the fish, the cry broadened to include the other necessities made expensive through the hated tax. When the focus turned to the price of bread, the women went to Tomás Zarracina's flour factory, threw rocks and broke all of the windows. A clerk tried in vain to get a commission of the demonstrators to express their demands "reasonably." Instead, they entered and tore open sacks of grain. Afterwards they headed towards Zarracina's house, pelting it, too, with stones. The next stop was the office of *consumo* administration, where documents were brought out and burned in the street. Other symbols of tax collection received similar treatment. Finally, local officials called out the soldiers to "calm them down," but their shots into the air only increased the excitement. When darkness fell, the women went home voluntarily, probably to cook dinner and rest.

The next day the rioting began again, with a violence never before seen in Gijón, according to the newspapers. First the women shut down the office where farmers registered their produce. Then they sacked several bakeries (one owned by another noted republican) and Zarracina's chocolate factory. They took the sacks of cocoa, coffee and cinnamon to the streets and sold them for a fraction of their market price to any passer-by. Although the chocolate factory was the first target unrelated to the *consumo* issue, it formed part of a clear pattern. From the rioters' point of view, food, whether basic or luxury items, should be made available to everyone at affordable prices.

By this time, the city and regional government had finally coordinated a response, and the Civil Governor, speaking from the balcony of the city hall, promised the crowd that the *consumos* would be dropped.[110] There were further shouts that the mayor should be sacked, and a committee of women presented a petition to the mayor demanding his resignation. With such a loss of confidence in his

---

[109] Arriero, "Los motines," reports that the predominance of women, especially in the early stages, was a common feature of all the riots: p. 213.

[110] While this may sound surprising, María Luz Arriero ("Los motines") reports that it was not uncommon for local authorities to suspend the *consumos* as a result of popular pressure, but they usually attempted to reimpose them as soon as possible (p. 223). However, after this wave of riots (in May of 1898 alone there were eighty-three), the government in 1904 lifted the *consumos* on the most basic foodstuffs, like wheat, flour and salt. By 1911, they had been replaced by other taxes (p. 200).

leadership, the mayor agreed to step down. The announcement of his resignation drew cheers from the crowd, which finally went home peacefully.

The *consumo* riot nicely demonstrates the kinds of links formed between poor women, whether they were wage earners or not. Although the immediate instigators of the protest were sellers not buyers, its escalation depended to a large degree on all of the women's common concerns as household managers. But equally interesting, the protest demonstrates where this blueprint diverged from the other forms of oppositional culture in the city. The republicans considered themselves the voice of the people, but in this case their business interests contradicted those of the female protesters. The juxtaposition of the republican ceremony to honor Zarracina with the women's looting of his warehouses makes this point clearly. Moreover, at a moment when the male trade union movement was just forming, it showed little interest in supporting the protest. In fact, a delegation of workers went to the newspaper to express disgust with its riotous disorganization.[111]

The republicans were critical of the disregard for private property, and the workers were disdainful of the lack of an ideological and organizational structure. Thus, this type of protest did not fit neatly on the reformist/radical spectrum defined by the parties and trade unions. On the one hand, it favored the use of radical direct action that ignored the legal process. On the other hand, the goals were usually reformist in nature, directed towards changing a particular manifestation of the system. Given the divergent agendas, it is easy to see why working-class women were not easily absorbed into the mainstream opposition.

So how, then, did this tradition of collective action figure into the larger oppositional culture taking shape in Gijón? On the most basic level the consumer protest, in all of its new forms, remained part of the repertoire of collective action up to the Civil War. Thus, it joined the strike, the election and the cultural event as one available political weapon. And while the consumer protest was not linked to a formal institutional base, it did help to solidify the new working-class neighborhoods, which would become important informal units of association. More subtly, it articulated a set of issues that could appeal to

---

[111] Again, María Luz Arriero affirms this response on a national level. The Socialist party officially disapproved, and the worker press called the participants "people without ideas" and "archaic rioters" ("Los motines," 214).

a broad spectrum of Gijón's lower classes, particularly the women, and provide a basis for community mobilization that extended beyond the workplace. Eventually, both republicans and anarchists absorbed the lesson that their appeals for support ran deeper and wider when they could incorporate these concerns into their political agendas. In fact, the impact of the opposition was greatest when it was able to harness the weapons of all three blueprints into a concerted attack on the Gijón of the old families.

In 1900, however, the elements for this attack were not in place. The political fortress of the Restoration held firm, despite the changing economic and social contours of the city. Thus, the increasingly complex city still officially spoke with a single voice. The two faces of Gijón were emerging in the divisions between the downtown and the new peripheral *barrios*, but the process had not yet solidified into contrasting identities. Furthermore, there was only the hint that these contrasting identities would become increasingly antagonistic to one another, that they would polarize rather than come to some sort of accommodation. As a result, it was also unclear what role the existing oppositional traditions would play in the evolving saga of the city's political evolution. In the nineteenth century they remained fragmented and dispersed, incapable of sustaining an assault on the establishment or defining a clear alternative. Through them, we can see the opening of cracks in the system, but there was no way to predict its unraveling or the path that process would take. For this reason, the turn of the century is a critical point, in the history of Gijón as well as in Spain at large. The old regime could either renovate by incorporating new elements into itself or it could encourage the process of polarization by hunkering down – politically, socially, culturally – in the bunker. Since all attempts at renovation failed, the story of this book is about polarization, and about how Gijón and the rest of the country arrived at July 1936.

PART I

Patterns of life in working-class Gijón

~

From the late nineteenth century to the Civil War, Gijón's political climate was transformed, from a model of Restoration order to a hotbed of radicalism. Much of this transformation depended on the politicization and participation of the large working-class population, many of them recently arrived on the scene in 1900. The forces of opposition, both republicans and anarchists, targeted this population as the most marginalized and discontented, and thus the most likely to join the struggle against the old regime. Their numbers were such that without them, no popular oppositional movement could have rooted itself in the city. Thus, at a basic constituency level, the working-class population was at the fulcrum of Gijón's political evolution in the twentieth century. Before attempting to interpret that evolution, it makes sense to begin with an analysis of the collective life experience of this new political and social force. The following two chapters will explore the patterns of life in working-class Gijón, and their relationship to the political evolution of the city.

The presumption of links between "patterns of life" and political behavior does not imply a deterministic connection. Instead, the economic, social and cultural conditions of daily life provide a context in which political choices get made. The context then encourages or discourages certain types of responses, from solidarity to fragmentation, from integration to polarization, from conservatism to radicalization. But this context is only one factor in the equation. Equally important is the existing political dynamic, and the ways in which it dialectically reinforces or undermines lessons drawn from the patterns of daily life. The point is that these patterns constitute some of the building blocks of political consciousness, without furnishing a definitive blueprint for construction.

Chapters 2 and 3 will make the case that, in early-twentieth-century Gijón, there existed ample building blocks for an oppositional politics. That is, the economic, social and cultural conditions of daily life among the working-class population provided a fertile environment for both alienation from the existing system and mobilization against it. Both factors are essential to political radicalization, since alienation alone may lead to indifference and apathy, but without it the capacity to mobilize has no focus. The keys to alienation were insecurity and segregation, two central characteristics of the spatial and economic development of the city. The economic context brought great disparities of wealth and poverty, as well as the volatile combination of good wages and high unemployment. The spatial context created a physical barrier between rich and poor that further emphasized the disparities, as did the division between an elite culture based in the wealthy downtown area and a popular culture based in the poorer peripheral neighborhoods.

The factors encouraging mobilization were equally compelling. Out of the alienation of segregation, the poorer residential areas evolved towards neighborhood communities, with networks of sociability that provided the basis for solidarity. The rootedness of these communities was further reinforced by Gijón's demographic pattern, which combined slow growth with intra-provincial immigration. Despite the dramatic changes of industrialization, the city was characterized more by residential stability than uprootedness. While living, working and playing together, Gijón's poorer residents welded the bonds that formed the basis for collective action.

With built-in grievances and the capacity to mobilize, it is predictable that Gijón's working-class population was courted by all the opposition groups in the city. Likewise, it is not surprising that residents in the working-class neighborhoods responded to the various calls to arms that were issued. Nevertheless, the patterns of life in working-class Gijón could not have predicted with certainty the final outcome of polarization and Civil War. The building blocks could have been put together in different ways, with this scenario one of several that might have arisen from the same conditions. Within the range of possible scenarios, however, polarization – the breakdown of communication between the two Gijóns – was a plausible outcome. Given the political dynamic that unfolded, with an immobile traditional elite, a largely ineffec-

60

tual reformist elite and a vibrant radical labor movement, it is easy to see how the segregated sociability of Gijón's working-class community translated into polarization and the armed barricades of 1934 and 1936.

2

The structural context: economy, demography and urban space, 1900–1936

~

Structural phenomena can no longer be relied on to predict political formations, as the debate over "exceptionalisms" has demonstrated the variety of possible responses to the development of capitalism and industrialization.[1] Nevertheless, the lack of deterministic links does not mean that no links exist. The specifics of structural evolution in each city, region or country provide a material context that the political discourse must take into account. At some level, this discourse has to formulate a response to that environment, not the only response, but one possible response. This is not to say that economic development is the base, while all else is flimsy superstructure; it is simply a recognition that the material structure of life is one of the factors that shapes the lived experience of people. Moreover, its impact differs among groups of people, depending on gender, occupation, residence and so on. In the broadest sense, then, the structural context is part of the fabric out of which people's lives are constructed, and out of which they construct their lives.

Although the unit of analysis here is the city, Gijón's economic structure must be placed against the background of the larger Spanish picture. Historians still disagree on many of the fundamental character-

[1] See E. P. Thompson, "The Peculiarities of the English," in *The Poverty of Theory and Other Essays* (New York: Monthly Review Press, 1978); David Blackbourn and Geoff Eley, *The Peculiarities of German History: Bourgeois Society and Politics in the Nineteenth Century* (Oxford: Oxford University Press, 1984); Aristide Zolberg, "How Many Exceptionalisms?," in *Working Class Formation: Nineteenth-Century Patterns in Western Europe and the United States*, ed. Ira Katznelson and A. Zolberg (Princeton: Princeton University Press, 1986); and Adrian Shubert, *A Social History of Modern Spain* (London: Unwin Hyman, 1990).

istics of economic development in the nineteenth and early twentieth centuries, but all agree that the country's industrial transformation was slower and more uneven than in the majority of the western European countries.[2] It began the process with the early industrializers, but fell further behind over the course of the nineteenth century. By 1910, for example, the level of industrialization per capita was about the same as in Russia, lower not only than in Britain or Germany, but also than in Italy and Hungary.[3]

However, this statistic glosses over the dramatic regional differences in the impact of industrialization within Spain. In fact, it is the unevenness of transformation more than any aggregate level of "backwardness" that best characterized the shape of the Spanish economy. The majority of the country's industry was located in the provinces of Catalonia, the heart of Spain's textile industry, and the Basque country, the center of mining and metallurgy. In a distant third place was Asturias, which also used its mineral resources as a springboard to industrialization. One of the cities that used this springboard was Gijón, which thus became the major industrial city in one of the three important industrial regions in an otherwise largely agricultural economy.

In this kind of highly segmented economy, the local economic unit is particularly important in defining structural context. Thus, Gijón followed a unique pattern of growth and development that left its mark on the city's residents. To piece together this pattern and to highlight its salient characteristics and their impact, this chapter will analyze the cycles of economic growth, the changing demographic configuration of the population and the spatial organization of the city, which, in combination, constituted the specific structural context of the city.

The three major elements of this context were economic insecurity, demographic stability, and spatial segregation. After the expansion of the late nineteenth century, the following decades were plagued by cycles of famine and relative plenty. The result was not unrelieved

---

[2] Disagreement centers on the causes of this slowness, as well as on its extent – "failure," "stagnation," or "slow growth." For a summary of the historiography, see Gabriel Tortella's preface to Leandro Prados de la Escosura, *De imperio a nación: crecimiento y atraso económico en España, 1780–1930* (Madrid: Alianza Editorial, 1988). A revisionist position, emphasizing steady, if not rapid growth, can be found in Adrian Shubert, *A Social History of Modern Spain*, Chapter 1, and David Ringrose, *Patterns, Events and Preconceptions: Revisiting the Structure of Spanish History, 1700–1900* (Cambridge: Cambridge University Press, 1996).
[3] Prados de la Escosura, *De imperio*, 168.

poverty but unpredictability and insecurity. Partly as a result of this stop-and-start economy, Gijón did not continue to attract immigrants at the expected rate. After the turn of the century then, the population became more rooted instead of uprooted, more intimate than anonymous. Nevertheless, intimacy was also shaped by the physical contours of the city, which continued the pattern of spatial segregation set in the nineteenth century. The placement of factories in the peripheral districts of the city created a ring of industrial neighborhoods that came to epitomize the social and economic divisions in the city.

This configuration of structural patterns did not engender political conflict, but it did provide a favorable environment for it. The economy produced grievances without leaving people completely impoverished and bereft of resources. Residential segregation and demographic stability created a fertile environment for associational life and neighborhood solidarity. Given the right circumstances, the combination of grievances and solidarity was a good base out of which to build an oppositional movement, and segregation could be used to fuel political polarization. Whether or not this kind of political culture developed would depend on a variety of factors, but the structural conditions encouraged rather than hindered mobilization.[4]

Economic structure and development: growth and instability

The economic development that culminated with the turn-of-the-century boom turned Asturias from an agricultural to an industrializing province, and paved the way for Gijón to become its premiere industrial city. By 1930, the province contained 130,000 salaried workers, including almost 30,000 miners. In 1900, Asturias employed only 14% of its labor in industry; by 1930 the figure was 41%, well

---

[4] The underlying assumptions about the kind of structural factors that encourage mobilization come from traditions as distinct as those epitomized by Charles Tilly and E. P. Thompson, both of whom emphasized that mobilization was more likely rooted in social cohesion than in disintegration, extreme poverty or disequilibrium. For a summary of both types of theories, see Jack Goldstone's introduction to *Revolutions: Theoretical, Comparative and Historical Studies*, ed. Jack Goldstone (San Diego: Harcourt, Brace, Jovanovich, 1986). On social cohesion, see E. P. Thompson, *The Making of the English Working Class* (New York: Pantheon Books, 1964) and Charles Tilly and Edward Shorter, *From Mobilization to Revolution* (Reading: Addison-Wesley, 1978). On disequilibrium, see Neil J. Smelser, *Theory of Collective Action* (New York: Free Press, 1963) and Clark Kerr and Abraham Siegel, "The Interindustry Propensity to Strike – An International Comparison," in *Industrial Conflict*, ed. Arthur Kornhauser *et al.* (New York: McGraw-Hill, 1954).

over the national average.[5] Gijón, with its major port, its 185 factories and 15,000 workers, was the most concentrated source of this industrial strength.[6]

Moreover, Gijón was the only full-scale, diversified industrial city in the province. Single-industry mining towns dotted the central basin, the western and eastern interior produced mostly agricultural products, the coastal towns specialized in fishing and some commerce, and Oviedo remained the bureaucratic and intellectual capital. With its combined strengths in commerce, large-scale and small-scale production, capital and consumer goods, Gijón was comparable in shape, if not in scale, to a city like Barcelona. Like Barcelona, the city did not depend on a few large factories, but retained a varied collection of enterprises, including numerous workshops with fewer than ten employees.[7]

The combination of this diversity and the lack of precise data make an exact breakdown of Gijón's economic structure impossible to reconstruct. Nevertheless, we can draw some broad outlines, particularly because the basic industrial shape of the city did not change after the turn of the century.[8] The city's largest and most concentrated industry continued to be metallurgy and steel production, a sector of the economy that employed several thousand workers.[9] Moreda y

[5] In the *Censo de la Población* for 1900, the national average was 15%; in 1930, it was 31%.

[6] *Guía oficial para 1930 por la Feria de Muestras Asturianas* (Gijón: La Fé, 1930). Evidence of this concentration can be gleaned from tax assessment figures. The provincial government assessed municipalities' industrial wealth and assigned a lump sum for each city to pay. The cities listed below cover the spectrum of the province: Mieres was a mining town, Avilés was one of the smaller ports, and Oviedo was the provincial capital. By 1920, Gijón was assessed at 50% more than its closest competitor (1912 figures in parentheses): 398,590 pts. (351,272 pts.); Oviedo, 254,528 pts. (260,055 pts.); Avilés, 81,894 pts. (82,674 pts.); Mieres, 30,796 pts. (27,271 pts.); data from the *Boletín Oficial de la Provincia de Oviedo*, 1912 and 1920.

[7] The proliferation of small workshops was still a characteristic of Gijón's economy in 1962: Luis García Peláez and José Benito A.Buylla, "Localización geográfica de las industrias de Gijón," *BIDEA*, 45 (1962), 92. On Barcelona's industrial structure, see Pere Gabriel, "La població obrera catalana, una població industrial?," *Estudios de Historia Social*, 32–33 (enero – junio 1985).

[8] Ramón Alvargonzález notes that there were only a handful of new enterprises created between 1903 and the Civil War, as businessmen concentrated on consolidating their nineteenth-century investments: *Gijón: industrialización y crecimiento urbano* (Asturias: Ayalga Ediciones, 1977), 35.

[9] It was this industry that distinguished the province as a whole, if we look at the distribution of factory production within Asturias, and in comparison to Catalonia and Spain as a whole. Food processing represented 40% of Spain's total factory production, 16% of Catalonia's, and 41% of Asturias'; textiles represented 26%, 56%, and 0.5% respectively, and metals 8%, 7%, and 38%. (Unfortunately, the Basque country is not included in these

Gijón, one of the three largest steel-making factories in the province, employed around 1,000 workers in the 1930s.[10] The five largest iron-working plants were also located in Gijón, including Laviada y Co., with 600 employees in 1920, Astilleros Riera with 315, also in 1920, and Constructora Gijonesa, with 120 in 1914. We can estimate, then, about 2,500 metalworkers employed in factories with over 100 workers, 1,600 of those in two plants. At least several hundred more labored in smaller workshops.[11]

The other sector that employed a comparable number of workers was construction, but the shape of the industry was very different. Several hundred skilled craftsmen were employed in woodworking and furniture-making shops, which were generally small to medium-sized; for example, in 1914, Hijos de Aquilino Lantero employed 125 men and the Compañía Gijonesa de Maderas had 90. The rest of the approximately 3,000 men in the industry worked on building sites, employed by a variety of contractors. Because of the nature of the work, seasonal unemployment and lack of job security were very high in this volatile business. In addition, because much of the work required only unskilled labor, the construction industry constituted a catch-all sector for the city's least trained men.

Aside from metalworking and construction, there were a number of other important industries. One of the first factories in the city had been for glass-making (1844), and by the 1930s three major plants employed 750 glassmakers. There was also a large ceramics factory, the Fábrica de Loza, with 350 workers in 1900. The textile industry, which dated from 1898, employed about 600 women and 110 men between three factories. The other concentration of female workers was the tobacco factory, with over 1,000 women and a handful of men at the end of the 1920s. In addition to these major employers, there were numerous smaller concerns that made everything from chocolate to light bulbs.

---

statistics.) See Jordi Nadal, "La Industria fabril española en 1900: una aproximación," in *La economía española en el siglo XX*, ed. Jordi Nadal *et al.* (Madrid: Ariel, 1987.)

[10] The largest factory was Duro-Felguera, which employed 4,000 men, virtually the entire active population of the town of La Felguera.

[11] The Instituto de Reformas Sociales listed the five largest iron-working plants, which each produced from 900 to 1,400 tons a year, and acknowledged the existence of a number of smaller workshops, producing between 200 and 400 tons a year, on which they could not obtain statistics: *Informes de los inspectores de trabajo sobre la influencia de la guerra Europea en las industrias españolas, 1917–1918*, vol. II (Madrid: Sucesora de M. Minuesa de los Ríos, 1919), 20.

In keeping with its dual identity as a commercial and industrial center, Gijón's port activities continued to occupy a central role in the local economy. The smaller port in Cimadavilla housed the largest fishing fleet in the province, which hauled in more than four times as much fish as its closest competitor.[12] The fishing trade as a whole, including fishermen, sailors, sellers, machinists, etc., provided employment for over 2,200 people. The transatlantic port of El Musel had become, by 1930, the largest "coal" port in the country, and the most important passenger port in the north of Spain. Between 1910 and 1930, the amount of coal leaving Gijón rose from 433,000 tons to 1,936,289 tons, which constituted over half of the coal shipped out of the province.[13] In addition to cargo, between 4,000 and 8,000 passengers a year entered and left the province through Gijón.[14] In order to maintain this busy port, there was a permanent crew of 400 workers employed by the Junta de Obras, the corporation that managed operations and repaired the infrastructure.

Through this brief sketch of Gijón's economic structure, one can get a sense of the city's wealth, its productivity and its stature. But there is a darker side to this story of economic power. After the dizzying growth following the Cuban war, the local and provincial economies faltered and never regained this momentum or even sustained a secure level of growth. Instead, Asturias experienced a roller-coaster ride of stagnation and expansion that finally ground to a halt with the depression of the 1930s. This combination of wealth and volatility created a curious mixture of high hopes and dashed expectations, of bustling activity and empty factories, of high salaries and unemployment. The most coherent legacy of this mixture was insecurity, especially for those at the bottom of the ladder who could not cushion themselves against the uncertain future.

The grand explanation for this pattern is difficult to pinpoint, since it is linked to the larger debate about the problems of Spanish industrialization. Historians have argued for the primacy of a variety of factors, from the poor quality of the natural resources, to the poverty of the internal market, to the lack of competitiveness on the international

---

[12] Ramón Argüelles, *Regionalismo económico asturiano* (Gijón: La Fé, 1934), 40. In 1933, Gijón brought in 9 million pts. worth of fish, versus 2.7 million for Luanco, and 2.3 million for San Esteban de Pravia.

[13] *Avance*, August 14, 1932. The amount of coal mined in Asturias in 1930 was 4,700,000 tons; 3,500,000 tons of that was sent out by sea.

[14] Bernardo del Llano, *Noticiero – Guía de Gijón* (Gijón, 1925), 21–22.

market. If we look at the single case of Asturian coal, the major problem seems to be competitiveness. Spain was actually a net importer of coal, which was cheaper to bring in from England than to transport from Asturias. Some have placed the blame on the quality of Asturian coal, but others have emphasized the tendency of the Asturian bourgeoisie (as in other regions) to rely on protectionism and government contracts instead of modernizing to compete on the international market.[15] Whatever the precise causes, the consequences were clear. The economic expansion of the mining industry and of the other linked businesses in the province was fraught with tension, frustration and insecurity.

The roller-coaster began its descent in 1902–1903, as the investment boom receded, and did not resume climbing until the onset of the First World War. The conjunctural reasons for the slowdown are not entirely clear, but the delay in completing "El Musel" and the shortsightedness of the native bourgeoisie in discouraging outside investment have been cited.[16] Over-extended companies folded or retrenched, and investment fell off dramatically. In one four-month period in Gijón, for example, thirty-eight businesses declared bankruptcy.[17] The war turned the economy around temporarily by increasing the competitiveness of Asturian coal. With the shortage induced by the disruptions and demands of the war, the skyrocketing price of coal dramatically increased demand, even for the more expensive Asturian product.[18] For several years, the mines and metallurgical plants ran at full tilt, utilizing the newly completed port of El Musel (1912) to increase the volume of exports. Although the boom bypassed some industries, especially those that depended on expensive imports, workers in struggling industries like textiles or construction could usually find other work.[19]

The prosperity that derived from economic crisis abroad could not last long after the crisis subsided. By 1921, the effect of renewed pro-

---

[15] On this question, see Adrian Shubert, *The Road to Revolution in Spain: The Coal Miners of Asturias, 1860–1934* (Urbana: University of Illinois Press, 1987), 25–31; Juan A.Vázquez García, *La cuestión hullera en Asturias, 1918–1935* (Oviedo: Instituto de Estudios Asturianos, 1985); and Prados de la Escosura, *De imperio*, Chapter 4.

[16] Alvargonzález, *Gijón*, 35. See also Juan Antonio Vázquez, "El ciclo económico en Asturias, 1886–1973," *BIDEA*, 105–106 (1982).

[17] *Boletín Oficial de la Provincia de Oviedo*, 1905.

[18] For example, the price of steel jumped from 22 pts./kilo in 1914 to 70 pts./kilo in 1918: IRS, *Informes de los inspectores*, 152.

[19] Information on the uneven impact of the war is contained in the IRS report, *Informes de los inspectores*, 126–155.

duction in Britain began to be felt, and the Asturian economy fell into another slump.[20] By the end of the 1920s, the province was just showing signs of recovery when the deeper crisis of the 1930s set in.[21] Not until well after the Civil War did Asturias regain its economic momentum. In the meantime, the republican years were fraught with tensions over who should be blamed for squandering the economic potential that had seemed so solid in 1900 and 1915.

The economic instability expressed in this cyclical pattern becomes more palpable if we look at its impact on the city's lower classes. While there is not enough data to draw firm conclusions on the standard of living, the general pattern that emerges fits the overall economic picture of wealth mixed with insecurity. Thus, wages remained fairly high, keeping pace with inflation, but so did the danger of losing one's job. Although unions were able to secure wage increases, they could not protect workers against lay-offs. And because of the periodic slumps, unemployment could happen to anyone; it was a fear and a reality that affected every worker and his/her family. In this way, economic insecurity became part of the fabric of working-class culture in the city.

It started in 1903, when stories about unemployment and emigration began to replace glowing descriptions of economic conquest. "Now, in Oviedo, in Gijón and everywhere, the work crisis is creating gloomy scenes in the theater of the miserable proletarian home . . . "[22] No absolute unemployment figures exist, but the Socialist newspaper *Aurora Social* reported in 1904 that 3,000 men had left Gijón to find temporary employment, while hundreds more remained jobless at home.[23] The Cocina Económica, a privately funded soup kitchen, printed pleas for more donations, as demand had overwhelmed their resources, "given the overabundance of needy workers, and thus the great need of a goodly part of the working class."[24]

The complaints tapered off once the world war broke out, but by 1921 they returned. "Workers are leaving. Every day expeditions of men leave for other points, either within or outside the province, in

[20] As Adrian Shubert points out, the Asturian mine owners did not use their windfall profits to invest in the modernization that would have allowed them to remain competitive after the war: *Road to Revolution*, 54.
[21] Juan Antonio Vázquez, "El ciclo económico en Asturias, 1886–1973," 451. Vázquez notes that Barcelona never slumped as far as Asturias, and had reached pre-war levels of production by the late 1920s.
[22] *Aurora Social*, January 1, 1904.
[23] *Aurora Social*, May 15, 1904.
[24] *El Noroeste*, April 23, 1904.

search of work. This parade of men has taken on the character of a virtual exodus."[25] As usual, exact statistics are not forthcoming. Moreda y Gijón, the city's biggest factory, laid off 350 of its 1,000 employees between 1919 and 1921. Broader estimates ran the gamut from the anarchist federation's 4,000 to the government's claim of 900. The first number seems high, but *El Noroeste* called the government's figure ridiculously low.[26] Whatever the true figure was, it was great enough to fuel the kind of pessimism expressed by this writer in 1927:

> Contrary to what has been occurring during previous winters, it is notable that this winter there has been more activity in the construction industry. Clearly this activity does not begin to correspond with what Gijón needs, given the number of unemployed workers, but at least we can say that we have avoided the nearly complete paralysis of the past few years.[27]

By the 1930s, as Asturias' slump folded into the world-wide depression, the figure of 4,000 unemployed had become a low estimate. One reporter's terse description of Gijón in 1934 as a "cemetery of industries" sums up both the economic situation and the prevailing mood.[28]

In contrast to the drama of unemployment, the movement of prices and wages over the period seems remarkably stable. From what can be pieced together from the fragmentary data, those with the good fortune to stay employed fared pretty well. (See Appendix 1 on methods and data.) As in other ways, the beginning of the century seems to have been a crucial turning point. In 1885, the first inquiry into living standards concluded that only a master artisan could afford to feed his family a basic diet, even one heavy in bread and potatoes.[29] But between 1898 and 1900, Asturian wages, which had lagged behind those of other industrial regions, doubled. While prices rose steadily, it is unlikely that they also doubled.[30] After the recession set

---

[25] *El Noroeste*, "The Exodus," January 5, 1921.
[26] *El Noroeste*, January 10, 1923 for the anarchist figures, and May 26, 1926 for the government estimate.
[27] *El Noroeste*, February 12, 1927.
[28] *Avance*, March 9, 1934.
[29] Fernando García Arenal, *Datos para el estudio de la cuestión social: información hecha en el Ateneo-Casino Obrero de Gijón* (1885; reprint, Gijón: Silverio Cañada, 1980), 36–41. See Appendix 1 for details on his calculations.
[30] Comparing Arenal's 1885 prices to those of Tuñón de Lara's from 1900, cited in Angeles Barrio Alonso, *El anarquismo en Gijón: industrialización y movimiento obrero, 1850–1910* (Gijón: Silverio Cañada, 1982), p. 84, bread rose from 0.32 to 0.40 pts. a kilo, while potatoes stayed constant at 0.15 pts. a kilo. (Because of a series of bad harvests, bread

in in 1903, wages did not rise again until 1914,[31] but price movement was also sluggish.[32] Clearly workers were worse off than they were in 1900, but the psychological impact of the decline may have been worse than the material impact. The cycle of boom followed by bust created a set of high expectations that were doomed to be disappointed by the crisis-ridden Asturian economy.

The war brought with it both wage increases and rampant inflation, but again there does not seem to be a dramatic divergence. According to wage figures for the province, the average worker, skilled or unskilled, earned 225% more in 1920 than in 1914. Women, who began at a much lower level, averaged 242% of what they received in 1914.[33] On the other hand, national price indexes show increases of just over 200% for the same period: meat at 215, vegetables and fruits at 204, and other edible items, from potatoes to olive oil, averaged 223. Provincial indexes reveal variations from as low as 130 for rice to as high as 300 for eggs or 400 for fish.[34] Viewed on this broad level, there does not seem to be a dramatic overall decline in standard of living. Undoubtedly, the war caused economic hardship, but more through temporary shortages of essential goods, long lines and short-term fluctuations than through long-term impoverishment.

By the early 1920s, prices and wages had both stabilized in a way that maintained worker living standards over the next fifteen years. Both indexes rose slowly, with wages at times even surpassing price increases.[35] The general picture, then, does not point to a dramatically deteriorating standard of living, either over the period as a whole or in the years leading up to the Civil War. Nor does it indicate an

prices were unusually high between 1898 and 1903.) It is difficult to say how comparable these figures are, given that Tuñón de Lara's are national averages, but they are all that exist.

[31] Serial wage statistics for provinces appeared in 1914, with the publication of the *Anuario Estadístico de España*, 1915.

[32] The only figures come from a republican rally in 1909, where one speaker estimated a 76% price rise between 1855 and 1909. Another speaker calculated a subsistence daily family diet that would cost 3.62 pts., which represents a 30% rise over García Arenal's 1885 figures. Since the percentages of food groups listed by each are different, the comparison can only be used as an estimate: *El Noroeste*, May 21 and 23, 1909. Compiling national estimates, Jordi Maluquer de Motes concludes that wages climbed slightly more than prices during the 1900–1914 period: "De la crisis colonial a la guerra europea: veinte años de economía española," in *La economía española*, 90–94.

[33] *Anuario Estadístico de España*, 1920.

[34] Ministerio de Trabajo, Dirección General de Estadística, "Precios al por mayor y números índices, 1913–1941," *Boletín de Estadística* (Madrid, 1941) and *Anuario Estadístico de España*, 1920.

[35] Again, I am relying on less than adequate data to reach this conclusion, since the price schedules represent the average taken from all cities in Spain, while wages only apply to the city of Oviedo. I have simply assumed that the general trends are accurate.

endemic level of privation, as was found, for example, among farm laborers on the *latifundias* in Andalusia. Thus, the struggle for survival was not as relentless or unyielding as in these desperately poor regions. What seems more characteristic of an industrial city like Gijón was the unevenness and unpredictability of survival. There were good wages when work was to be had, but lay-offs always loomed in the background; wages generally kept pace with prices, but sudden price hikes or shortages could disrupt a tight family budget.

More subtly, there is evidence that the insecurity affected occupational mobility as well. Data from marriage records in the 1930s confirms the lack of generational social mobility out of manual labor.[36] However, there appears to be downward mobility even within the category of manual labor, since significant numbers of skilled workers had sons who ended up in the unskilled category.[37] Another indication of greater permeability on the downward side was the fate of small businessmen. Over two-thirds of businessmen's sons were employed as either manual laborers or white-collar employees.[38] While the sample size is too small to draw firm conclusions, it does reinforce the image of a contradictory and complex economic environment, defined by the tension between high expectations and their frequent frustration.

Demographic stability

In contrast to this picture of tension and instability, the city's demographic structure was characterized by relative stability. As a result of the uneven expansion of the economy, Gijón's population grew more slowly than might be expected for the largest industrial city in the province. Instead of being transformed by hordes of immigrants, Gijón managed to retain an intimacy that belied its image as a major city. Most of the immigrants who did move to the city came from the surrounding *aldeas* or the rural regions of the province. Thus, even the

---

[36] From the *Registro Civil de matrimonios* of Gijón, 1933–1936. In 1933, marriage record forms began to record the occupations of the husband and wife, as well as those of their parents. Of the 400 marriages recorded between 1933 and 1936, 300 included information on father/son occupations.

[37] Of the seventy-one fathers-of-the-groom who were skilled workers, thirty of the sons engaged in skilled labor, six entered white-collar work, and thirty-five, or 49%, became unskilled laborers.

[38] Of thirty-four businessmen, twenty-four (70%) were either clerks or laborers. Some of the clerks were undoubtedly working in their fathers' businesses, but others were probably second sons or victims of failed enterprises.

Table 2 *Population of Gijón, 1887–1930*

	Population (township)	Rate of growth	Yearly rate
1887	35,170	–	
1900	47,544	35.00%	2.69%
1910	55,248	16.20%	1.62%
1920	57,573	4.21%	0.42%
1930	78,239	35.90%	3.59%

new arrivals could probably plug in fairly easily to existing networks of families and friends who had come from the same *pueblo*.[39] In Gijón, then, the process of industrialization did not seem to be accompanied by the uprootedness and fluidity that is often associated with it.

The most dramatic changes occurred in the period before 1900 and after 1920, when fairly rapid expansion brought two waves of workers into the city. Between 1900 and 1920, however, the rate of population growth dropped dramatically, creating a stable period in which new immigrants could be incorporated into the life of the city (see Table 2).[40] With the spurt of growth in the 1920s, the population of the township (including the city and its rural *aldeas*) grew by about 60% between 1900 and 1930, certainly not a negligible figure, but not in the league of the fastest-growing northern city, Bilbao, which more than doubled its population between 1887 and 1900, and then doubled it again between 1900 and 1930.[41]

As a result of this growth, Gijón had become a mid-sized city, the fifteenth largest in the country in 1930. Perhaps more significantly, it was the second largest city with over 20,000 inhabitants that was not

[39] On the non-dislocating impact of short-distance migration, see William Sewell, *Structure and Mobility: The Men and Women of Marseille, 1820–1870* (Cambridge: Cambridge University Press, 1985), and Leslie Moch, *Paths to the City: Regional Migration in 19th Century France* (Beverly Hills: Sage Publications, 1983), 22–24.

[40] All of the following demographic information is taken from the *Censo de la Población de España*, except where otherwise noted.

[41] Gijón's growth was similar to the other medium-sized port cities on the Atlantic coast, with the exception of Bilbao. It also matched the growth of the Asturian capital of Oviedo. Figures for these cities for 1900 (1930 in parentheses) are: La Coruña, 43,971 (74,132); San Sebastián, 37,800 (78,430); Santander, 54,694 (85,117); Bilbao, 83,306 (161,987); Oviedo, 48,103 (75,463). (In 1887, Bilbao had only 32,734 inhabitants.) In contrast to these other cities, the mining towns of Asturias grew much more rapidly, most of them ballooning from villages to small cities in only a few years: Mieres, 1887: 568; 1900: 2,813; 1930: 6,501; Felguera, 1887: 59; 1900: 3,721; 1930: 4,581.

Table 3 *Years of residence in Gijón (adults over fifteen years of age)*

	1900	1910	1920	1930
Over 20 yrs. (or always)	57.0%	57%	67.0%	69.0%
Over 10 yrs.	70.0%	74%	79.0%	81.0%
1–5 yrs.	19.6%	15%	14.6%	12.5%

a provincial capital. This ranking highlights the fact that Gijón's growth was purely a factor of economic opportunity and not swelling numbers of government bureaucrats. With this consideration in mind, Gijón can be seen as one of the dozen prominent cities in the country: important, but not in the highest class reserved for Madrid, Barcelona, Bilbao and a few other cities.[42]

Nevertheless, because of its generally slow to moderate growth during the first two decades, Gijón's population looks surprisingly stable for a major city. Throughout the entire period, a full two-thirds of the inhabitants had been born in Gijón and lived there all of their lives.[43] Moreover, many of the immigrants who arrived before or around the turn of the century appear to have stayed put. Thus, the percentage of the population that had lived in the city for at least ten years continued to rise, despite the influx of newcomers in the 1920s (see Table 3).[44] In 1930, then, 80% of the population, whether we count only adults or include children, had lived in Gijón for at least ten years. By the time a new wave of immigrants arrived in the 1920s, the community would have been established enough to absorb them without destabilizing its collective identity.

Even the new arrivals did not come from very far away. All but a handful of Gijón's residents were born within the province of Asturias (917 out of 1,000), a fact that added to the intimacy of the population

---

[42] Madrid had 950,000 residents in 1930; Barcelona had 1 million.

[43] The information is taken from samples of the local population census for the years 1900, 1910, 1920 and 1930: born in Gijón: 1900, 66.5%; 1910, 66.6%; 1920, 66.1%; 1930, 66.4%; lived always: 1900, 63.6%; 1910, 62.3%; 1920, 65.7%; 1930, 67.6%. There is a slight confusion between these two categories, since some people were born in the city, but left for a few years, or lived in Gijón all their lives, despite being born elsewhere. However, the overall figures are so close that I will use the "born in Gijón" figures to refer to people who had always lived in the city.

[44] As would be expected, for the whole population the numbers are slightly higher, but the increase over the years is less dramatic: over twenty years: 1900, 68%; 1910, 68%; 1920, 73%; 1930, 74%; over ten years: 1900, 75.6%; 1910, 78%; 1920, 80%; 1930, 82%; one to five years: 1900, 17%; 1910, 13.8%; 1920, 13.9%; 1930, 12%.

structure.[45] Thus, the newcomers shared with older residents a sense of Asturian culture and identity, a linkage which must have made integration easier. In contrast, in the city of Barcelona in 1930, only 688 out of 1,000 residents came from within the province, in Bilbao the number was 620, and in Madrid it was only 574. The reason for this difference is that the economic growth in Asturias was never great enough to absorb its own excess population, let alone reach beyond its borders. For example, during the decade of the 1920s, when Gijón's population grew by 35%, the population of the province as a whole declined, presumably to emigration.[46] Clearly, the vast majority of Gijón's new residents came from the shrinking small towns and villages of Asturias.[47]

On the local level, we can see this dynamic within the township of Gijón, which included the urbanized center, the unincorporated suburbs and the rural *aldeas* that surrounded the city.[48] In 1887, the number of people living in the rural and urban parts of the township was about the same, but by 1930, the distribution had changed dramatically (see Table 4).[49] Thus, while the city and its working-class suburbs had more than doubled, the *aldeas* had grown by less than a third. It seems plausible to infer that, in addition to being Asturian, many of the new urban residents were also natives of the township itself. The circle of immigration appears even more intimate from this perspective.

This impression is reinforced if we look at the register of marriages recorded in the township over the period.[50] The register reveals both

---

[45] Interestingly, the mining towns showed a much more diverse immigration structure, depending, it seemed, on the individual mining company. The percentages of non-Asturian born workers ranged from a low of 8% to a high of 50%: Shubert, *The Road to Revolution*, 39.

[46] In crude terms, the provincial population was growing, but if we take into account the natural population increase, Oviedo lost 4.62% of its population, presumably to emigration. In contrast, the province of Catalonia grew by 13.73%, above and beyond its natural growth rate.

[47] Most of the towns in Asturias with under 10,000 inhabitants showed increasingly negative growth rates. On the crisis in the countryside, see Shubert, *The Road to Revolution*, Chapter 1.

[48] These figures are calculated from both the *Nomenclator de la Provincia de Oviedo* and the local *Censo de la Población*.

[49] The separate figures on the unincorporated suburbs cannot be compared, since many of the original areas had been incorporated into the city limits. However, since none of the *aldeas* were incorporated, the overall urban/rural figures are comparable.

[50] Before 1933, the registers only recorded residence and birthplace of the couple. After this, they record birthplace information on both parents and grandparents, as well as occupations. I took a sample of about 25% from each year: 107 from 1900 and 105 from 1915.

Table 4 *Population of the township of Gijón, 1887–1930*

Population	Residents	Percentage of total
1887		
Rural *aldeas*	15,101	42.9%
Gijón (city)	17,978	51.0%
Unincorporated industrial suburbs	2,091	6.1%
1930		
Rural *aldeas*	19,306	24.6%
Gijón (city)	52,653	67.0%
Unincorporated areas	6,313	8.0%

strong intra-township links as well as evidence of the changing rural/ urban center of gravity within its borders (see Table 5). The internal linkages are strongest in 1900, when three-fourths of all the couples had local origins. By 1933, the insularity had declined somewhat, but the majority of marriages were still contracted between people born in the township of Gijón. The appearance of insularity magnifies if we look at the generational linkages of the native couples who married in the 1930s. Of those natives, 71% of the brides and 84% of the grooms had at least one parent born in the township of Gijón. Of this same group, 63% of the brides and 53% of the grooms had at least one set of native grandparents. At least for the inhabitants who chose to marry in the city, then, the links to the township at large often went back one or two generations. Within this pattern, we can see the evidence of rural/urban migration. Whereas in 1900 the largest number of marriages were contracted between rurally based couples, by 1933 the situation had been reversed: a full 40% of the couples were natives of the city itself. Of these 40%, nearly half had at least one parent who was also born in the city. In contrast, the previous generation of grandparents were nearly all born in the *aldeas*.[51]

---

[51] The rural/urban transition also comes through in generational changes in occupations recorded in the marriage records. In the 1933–1936 sample (25%) of 300 marriages, seventy fathers-of-the-groom and sixty fathers-of-the-bride listed their occupation as farmers. Of the first group, only sixteen of their sons remained farmers; fifty-four, or 77%, of them went into industrial jobs, many of them as unskilled laborers. Of the fathers-of-the-bride, only seventeen of their daughters married farmers, while forty-three married men in industrial jobs.

Table 5 *Birthplace and residence of marriage partners in Gijón*

	1900	1915	1933–1936
Born in *aldea*/reside in *aldea*	35.0%	20%	13%
Born in *aldea*/reside in city	17.7%	14%	11%
Born in city/reside in city	23.8%	27%	40%
Other	23.5%	39%	36%

While not conclusive, the demographic data suggests that pre-Civil War Gijón, despite its aspirations to cosmopolitan status, remained a very provincial city. The majority of the city's inhabitants shared similar backgrounds, either as natives of the city, transplants from the nearby *aldeas*, or immigrants from the surrounding provincial countryside. The evolution of Gijón's demographic structure in the post-Civil War period serves as a contrast; in 1950, only 53% of the city's residents were natives, and by 1975, that number had dropped to 42%. In mushrooming peripheral districts like La Calzada and Pumarín, it was as low as 30%.[52] In other words, despite all of the physical changes that Gijón had undergone by 1936, from industrialization to demographic expansion to the cafés and theaters of city life, it had not lost the intimacy characteristic of a smaller and less dynamic town. While this demographic intimacy does not in itself explain Gijón's political evolution, we can see in it the potential building blocks of collective action. Given the right circumstances, the residents of Gijón could turn the bonds created by familiarity into a form of political solidarity that would cross occupational and workplace boundaries. In fact, it would be this kind of diffuse solidarity that gave Gijón's oppositional culture much of its power.

Human geography: the segregation of urban space

To further explore the structural antecedents of this solidarity, it is necessary to ask not only where people came from, but where in the city they settled. If patterns of sociability develop partly out of the interactions of daily life, then it is important to get a sense of the

---

[52] Aladino Fernández García *et al.*, *Geografía de Asturias*, vol. II: *Geografía humanal: Geografía urbana: Langreo, Mieres y Gijón* (Asturias: Ayalga Ediciones, 1982), 163. In addition, the non-Asturian-born population had risen to 23% by 1975.

internal social geography of the city (see Map 6). Impressionistic sources give us the unequivocal sense of a city divided into rich and poor, downtown and periphery, working-class and elite neighborhoods. While there was no formal policy dictating this segregation, "due to very difficult obstacles that are nearly impossible to solve, in reality one has to notice it," as one housing commission report put it.[53] In a more poetic rendition of the phenomenon, a priest from Oviedo penned this description: "Each of the two Gijóns seem like completely distinct populations: the first is a Gijón populated by workers, darkened by smoke, encircled in the piercing noise of trucks and machines; the second is the Gijón of the elegant, of light, of pleasant pastimes."[54]

This neat juxtaposition of two cities does not hold up under the scrutiny of census data on occupation and residence, however. In fact, there seems to be more of a continuum that runs from the clearly working-class districts, to the mixed areas, to the elite downtown. Some people of all occupational categories are scattered throughout the city, and even the downtown neighborhood had a substantial working-class population. Thus, there seems to be a discrepancy between the structural map and the rhetoric of the divided city.

In reality, we are faced not so much with a discrepancy as with a problem of interpretation. Even though a substantial grey area eluded the category of elite or working-class district, it was the extremes that came to define how the residents saw their own city. Observers like the priest were not lying when they described the two cities of dark and light. They simply fastened on the dramatic gap between the two ends of the continuum and ignored the muddy terrain in the middle. As a result, the contrast between the two extremes, between the downtown area and certain working-class neighborhoods (notably Cima, Natahoyo, El Llano and La Calzada), came both to epitomize and to reinforce the social and economic polarization of the city. Moreover, these working-class *barrios* became the physical representation of all working-class Gijón, no matter where the individual working-class families lived. In other words, the geographical concept of the two Gijóns was a combi-

---

[53] Junta local para el fomento y mejora de casas baratas, *Memoria del ejercicio de 1916* (Gijón: La Fé, 1917), 20. The junta was established in 1916, charged with evaluating the housing situation and proposing solutions to the scarcity of low-income housing.

[54] Maximiliano Arboleya, in *Gijón veraniego* (Gijón: La Industria, 1914).

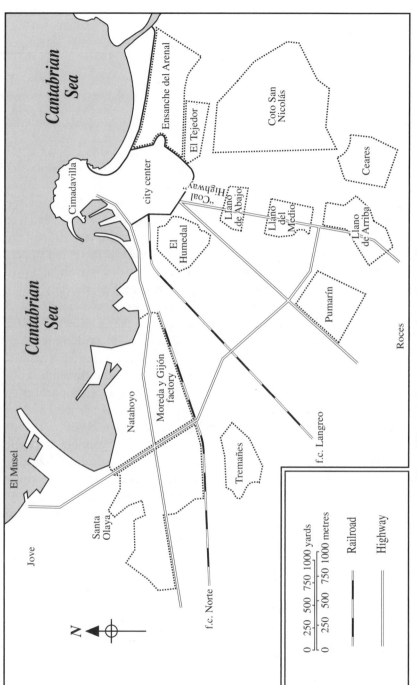

Map 6 Twentieth-century working-class settlements

Table 6 *Residence of middle-class families in Gijón*

	1900	1910	1920	1930
Downtown	24%	25%	28%	26%
Mixed areas	10%	13%	15%	14%
Working-class *barrios*	7%	7%	7%	8%

nation of residential patterns and a dominant interpretive framework that emphasized polarization and segregation.

The structural basis for this interpretation can be found in the contrast between the four prominent working-class *barrios* and the downtown district.[55] The downtown area, from the city hall to the *ensanche*, contained by far the largest percentage of lower- to upper-middle-class families in the city (see Table 6).[56] Moreover, these downtown residents constituted a substantial majority of the city's elite population; in 1900, 72% of all middle- and upper-class families lived in the center. This number began to drop over the years as the center filled up and as some wealthy residents moved to the garden suburb of Somió, but the concentration of elite families in the center remained steady.[57] This image of the center is enhanced by the distribution of the city's live-in servant population. In almost direct proportion to the percentages of middle-class families living in the center, 81% of the city's servants resided there in 1900, and 65% in 1930.

In addition to the middle- and upper-middle-class families and their servants, the center contained the greatest concentration of that category which most aspired to middle-class stature: the white-collar employees – in 1900, 75% of these families lived in the center.[58] As with the middle- and upper-class families, this percentage began to

[55] I created the categories of "downtown," "working-class" and "mixed" from a combination of electoral districts, popular identity and occupational breakdown. Unless otherwise noted, the figures were calculated from the raw data of the local population census. See Appendix 2 for a list of occupations and the status categories they were assigned to: upper-middle, lower-middle, white-collar, skilled, semi-skilled, unskilled.

[56] Figures based on the occupation of male adults. Unfortunately, it is difficult to distinguish between upper- and lower-middle-class households, so these classifications have generally been grouped together. People who list their occupation as businessman or industrialist could be owners of the corner grocery store or a factory that employs 200 workers. See Appendix 2 on occupational categories.

[57] The percentage slowly declined, from 59% in 1910, to 53% in 1920, and 48.3% in 1930.

[58] Most of those defined as "white-collar" were *empleados* and *dependientes*, office workers and store clerks. See Appendix 2.

80

drop as the center filled up, and white-collar families moved into the mixed districts, but there were still more of them in the center than anywhere else.[59] If we add the percentage of middle and upper classes, white-collar workers and students (normally a sign of family wealth) living in the center, these groups constituted 44% of the population of that district in 1900, and 55% in 1930. This combination gave the center a distinct identity: a strong nucleus of wealthy families and a healthy cushion of non-manual laborers who identified either up the social ladder or horizontally across it rather than down.

This critical mass of non-manual labor did not imply the absence of manual laborers. Their proportion of the downtown population declined over the years, from 40% to 36% in 1930, but their presence was still substantial. Nevertheless, this population seemed to contribute little to the character of the district. They were often hidden in attic apartments, or in structures called *ciudadelas*, which were jammed into the interior spaces between blocks of buildings. Only the grand façades of elegant apartments could be seen from the street, while the *ciudadelas* had to be entered through a narrow walkway between the buildings. Thus, the poor could live in the center without having their presence acknowledged.[60] In addition, the overall percentage of Gijón's working-class families who lived in the center dropped substantially, from 30% to 20%, indicating that the center of gravity of working-class life moved increasingly away from the downtown district.

The new center of gravity settled in the expanding *barrios* of Natahoyo, Cima, La Calzada and El Llano, as factories and cheap housing attracted poorer residents.[61] The image of internal migration towards the outskirts is supported by the rates of population growth in these areas, which far outstripped that of the city as a whole. The most

---

[59] The percentages of white-collar and middle-class families in each neighborhood tended to follow a similar trajectory, which seems to indicate that white-collar families strove towards a middle-class identity for themselves. The fact that few white-collar families moved into working-class neighborhoods seems to confirm this. The percentage of all white-collar families who lived in the center dropped from 75% to 44% in 1930, as the percentage in mixed areas rose from 21% to 40%.

[60] Most of the *ciudadelas*, one-story rectangular blocks, were built in the 1870s and 80s; by 1891, there were 63 of them, divided into 178 units and housing 1,078 people. By the 1920s, that number had doubled, partly through overcrowding and partly through the construction of second stories on some of the buildings: Moisés Llordén Miñambres, *La producción de suelo urbano en Gijón, 1860–1975* (Oviedo: Gráficas Summa, 1978), 52–53, and Francisco Quirós Linares, "Patios, corrales y ciudadelas," *Ería*, 3 (1982).

[61] These neighborhoods housed 30% of the working-class population in 1900 and 44% in 1930.

Table 7 *Population growth in La Calzada and El Llano (estimates)*

	La Calzada	El Llano
1887	–	288
1900	700	994
1910	1,500	1,822
1920	2,500	3,144
1930	3,280	7,910 (inflated by re-districting)

dramatic expansion was in La Calzada and El Llano, which were virtually empty in the nineteenth century (see Table 7).[62] Cima's and Natahoyo's growth were controlled by their physical boundaries. Thus, Natahoyo peaked at a population of about 2,000 by the 1910s, while Cimadavilla squeezed in another 1,000 residents to put its population at 4,000 by 1930. And there was no doubt about the character of these neighborhoods. The presence of most of the city's factories helped provide a visual distinction between the Gijón "darkened by smoke" and the downtown area, while the census verifies who lived there. About three-quarters of the residents of these areas belonged to working-class families (82% in 1900 and 70% in 1930).[63]

Further evidence of economic segregation is provided by the neighborhood mortality statistics compiled by a local doctor in 1915, which offer a stark picture of residential contrasts. Whereas the mortality rate for residents on the Calle Corrida was 15.50/1,000, in Cimadavilla it was 32.02 and in El Llano it reached 43.68/1,000.[64]

The reasons for these high rates are not hard to find, although the specifics differed in each neighborhood. Cima, as the oldest popular neighborhood, had some of the worst housing in the city. Many of the buildings were eighteenth-century stone structures, cold, damp and airless. In addition, the inhabitants literally lived on top of one

[62] Neighborhood population figures had to be calculated from the censuses and the *Nomenclator General de España para la provincia de Oviedo*. There were some discrepancies between the two sources in the case of La Calzada: the *Nomenclator* declared 1,744 residents in 1920, while my calculations from the census yielded 2,500. Likewise, in 1930, it claimed 3,286, while I counted 3,547. For El Llano, the problem was different. Re-districting before the 1930 census made it impossible to come up with a comparative figure. The 1930 figure may be inflated by as much as 2,500.
[63] These percentages could be as much as 9% higher because of the category of "without employment." Because it is difficult to interpret, this 9% have not been included in any of the classifications.
[64] Junta local para el fomento y mejora de casas baratas, *Memoria*, 53.

another, since the houses bordered on narrow, maze-like streets and dead-end alleys. Overcrowding added to the density, as 1,000 more people crammed into the neighborhood between 1900 and 1930. El Llano, on the other hand, had plenty of space, but it was built on a poorly drained swamp. Between stagnant pools of water that spread disease, and periodic floods that wiped out homes, the area was the most unhealthy of the city. On top of these problems, its open spaces were used as dumping grounds for trash and refuse.[65] Natahoyo's and La Calzada's structural problems were less acute, but they shared the basic urbanization problems of El Llano. For example, Natahoyo was not granted a sewer system until June of 1925, after floods caused "thick fecal matter" to float through the streets.[66] Despite the subtle differences between the neighborhoods, these urban health problems came to constitute one of the defining features of working-class Gijón.

While the basic elements of this poor industrial belt remained constant, there were also some important changes in its composition. Whereas in 1900 this area was largely populated by unskilled workers, by 1930 other social groups had moved in. A few of these were middle-class and white-collar residents, which caused the overall percentage of workers to decline.[67] But more dramatic was the addition of a significant number of skilled workers. In 1900, 71% of the workers in these four *barrios* were unskilled, and only 13% skilled, but by 1920 the gap between the two categories had been reduced to 58% and 25%.[68] At the same time, the percentage of skilled workers living in the center declined.

In other words, there was almost a direct transfer of skilled workers from the center to the working-class *barrios* between 1900 and 1930.[69] Thus, the physical and social distance between skilled workers and middle classes increased over time, just as the distance within the population of manual laborers decreased. The fact that white-collar

[65] Complaints about garbage dumps were numerous: see *El Noroeste*, January 2, 1900, May 31, 1917 and July 26, 1931.

[66] *El Noroeste*, April 17 and June 25, 1925.

[67] Between 1900 and 1920 the overall percentage of manual laborers fell from 82% to 74%, as the percentage of middle- and upper-middle-class and white-collar workers rose from 6% to 14%. This non-worker presence was still much smaller than in the other city districts.

[68] The majority of those with artisan trades were defined as skilled, while the unskilled identified themselves as "workers": *jornaleros, obreros*, etc. Most of those in the semi-skilled category were seamen who lived in Cimadavilla. See Appendix 2.

[69] In 1900, 51% of skilled workers lived in the center, and 9% of them lived in working-class districts. In 1930, 38% of them lived in the center, while 28% lived in working-class areas.

Table 8 *Occupational pattern in the "mixed" neighborhoods of Gijón, 1920*

	Center	Mixed	Working-class
Middle classes	28%	15%	7%
White-collar	20%	25%	7%
Manual laborers	30%	57%	75%

workers did not accompany the skilled workers in their migration to the outskirts must have solidified the social distinctions between manual and non-manual labor, and between these *barrios* and the rest of the city. At the same time, these new skilled residents probably contributed much to changing the character of these *barrios*, from desolate outposts for the very poorest to neighborhoods with articulated identities.

Between the two extremes of the southwestern *barrios* and the downtown, there were a number of mixed neighborhoods whose occupational pattern tended to fall somewhere in between. The most established of these areas was the late-nineteenth-century expansion east of the *ensanche*, called Arenal, but they also included the expansion to the southeast in what would be called the Coto San Nicolás and El Tejedor, and the area directly south of downtown, named El Humedal (see Map 6).[70] Each of these neighborhoods looked more like the southwestern *barrios* in their substantial population of manual laborers, but contained larger percentages of middle-class and white-collar families (see Table 8). The significant minority of white-collar workers who lived in the mixed areas seems to epitomize perfectly the liminal identity of these districts that rarely appear in the sources as coherent entities. While contemporaries spoke as if the Calle Corrida or El Llano had their own personalities, El Humedal and the others remained shadowy agglomerations never endowed with clear social, and later, political, identities.

This liminal identity is neatly expressed in the correlation between

[70] Population estimates from the censuses give the following figures for El Tejedor/Coto San Nicolás: 1900, 2,058; 1920, 3,816; 1930, 3,500. The figures for 1930 are skewed because of re-districting, which transferred as many as 2,500 residents from El Tejedor to El Llano. The figures for El Humedal are: 1900, 3,164; 1920, 3,900; 1930, 6,563.

Table 9 *Literacy and residence (percentage of residents over seven years of age who could not read or write)*

	Center	Mixed	Working-class
1900	13.0%	30.0%	37.0%
1910	10.0%	19.2%	26.8%
1920	5.7%	14.0%	19.5%
1930	2.4%	4.4%	7.0%

literacy and residence shown in Table 9. While illiteracy levels declined across the board, at every stage there was a continuum in which the mixed districts lay somewhere in between the two extremes. As a result of this ambiguous status, these areas never developed a clear collective identity within the political geography of the city. People spoke of the city as divided into two, epitomized by the contrast between the beach and the factories, or the wide streets of the *ensanche* and the chaotic clumps of El Llano. It is difficult to know how the residents of El Humedal or El Tejedor saw themselves within this juxtaposition, but it is possible that they were pushed into identifying with either of the two extremes. The urbanization problems that they shared with the working-class neighborhoods may have been one link that drew these areas together. In any case, the residential structure of the city left a complicated mark on its social geography. The census data provides clear evidence that economic segregation was a prominent feature of the urban landscape. But the reasons why residents emphasized the totalizing nature of this segregation lie beyond the scope of the numbers.

Thus, the existence of segregation, like the other components of Gijón's structural development, provided a context for people's lives without determining how it would filter into their social and political identity. The industrial expansion of the city gave it a new shape, with mushrooming factory suburbs ringed around the commercial and tourist center of the city, and with a distinct residential composition for each area. And yet, because of the unevenness of the economic growth and development, these changes took place fairly slowly. The result was a surprisingly stable population that appeared increasingly rooted in the city. But the uneven growth also created insecurity as well as stability. On the one hand, industrialization had brought wealth and jobs, on the other hand it could not consistently sustain them. The resulting mixture could have pointed in a variety of political directions, but the fact that residents were able to form a broadly based oppositional community out of this context is not surprising. We are still left with the burden of explaining how this occurred, but at least we can see the building blocks that the residents had at their disposal. What they did with those blocks is another story.

3

Culture and community in working-class Gijón

~

Within the demographic and structural context provided by an industrializing city, Gijón's working classes interpreted and shaped the contours of their everyday existence. These contours delineated the culture of working-class life in the city.[1] This culture was characterized by a segregated sociability: a series of networks and linkages rooted in the social and residential gap between rich and poor residents of the city. These networks then formed the building blocks for a working-class community that could potentially unite the city's poorer residents. The community was not monolithic or static, as it was often divided by gender and by neighborhood. Nevertheless, when viewed from the outside, it was clear that the members of this community shared more than they differed in their way of life. On some basic level, the culture of working-class life gave the poorer residents of the city a common ground that set them apart from their wealthier

---

[1] The concept of working-class culture derives from several theoretical sources. First, it is based on the broad epistemological definition of culture used by scholars like Clifford Geertz and Raymond Williams. In Williams' words, "culture is ordinary: that is the first fact. Every human society has its own shape, its own purposes, its own meanings": from "Defining a Democratic Culture," in *Resources of Hope: Culture, Democracy and Socialism* (New York: Verso, 1989), 4. Second, it is based on the ideas about hegemony, power and culture developed at the Centre for Contemporary Cultural Studies at the University of Birmingham. Following Gramsci, scholars like Stuart Hall and Richard Johnson have set out to understand the relationship between the dominant culture and the subordinate culture of the working class. Thus, the "shared meaning" that defines a cultural milieu is problematized by class and power relations. See Richard Johnson's "Three Problematics: Elements of a Theory of Working Class Culture," in *Working Class Culture: Studies in History and Theory*, ed. John Clarke, Chas Chitcher and Richard Johnson (London: Hutchinson, 1979) and Stuart Hall, "Notes on Deconstructing the 'Popular,'" in *People's History and Socialist Theory*, ed. Raphael Samuel (London: Routledge and Kegan Paul, 1981).

counterparts. As a local teacher wrote in 1906, "Where can they meet each other in order to develop friendships and mutual respect? Not in school, nor in the street, in the workshop, the factory, in sum, nowhere."[2]

The common ground was both spatial and social, based, on the one hand, in residential segregation and, on the other, in activities that derived from one's social position in the city. Arguably, residential segregation had a greater impact on sociability in working-class neighborhoods, because wealthier residents had the mobility to establish long-distance ties. Thus, working-class networks were rooted more firmly in the neighborhoods in which they lived.[3] The centrality of the neighborhood in defining working-class sociability was doubly important for working-class women, since many of them held no employment outside the home, and most of their duties were located close to their homes. Within or beyond the neighborhood, one's social position was primary in determining who one congregated with, where and for what purpose. In both its social and spatial senses, this segregation encouraged networks that helped create a sense of shared culture and community among Gijón's working-class residents.

The role of such community networks in the larger hegemonic struggle was complex. In the broadest sense, the evolution of a dense network of informal ties provided the building blocks of a variegated civil society that could articulate more than elite interests. In other words, the associational links of working-class culture made it easier to formulate a collective popular voice that could participate in the city's developing public sphere. Thus, the city's vibrant working-class culture established its own "clusters of communication" that could be organized and mobilized into an oppositional public sphere, given the right conditions and an effective strategy of mobilization.[4] In fact, both anarchists and republicans would attempt to mobilize the city's working-class culture and channel it into their own version of a counter-hegemonic assault from the public sphere.

---

[2] Teófilo Gallego, *La educación popular en Gijón* (Gijón, 1907), 18–19.

[3] On neighborhoods and working-class life, see: Tyler Stovall, *The Rise of the Paris Red Belt* (Berkeley: University of California Press, 1990); Daniel Jalla, "Le Quartier comme territoire et comme représentation: les 'barrières' ouvrières de Turin au début du XX siècle," *Mouvement Social*, 118 (1982); and Jerry White, *The Rothschild Buildings: Life in an East End Tenement Block, 1887–1920* (London: Routledge and Kegan Paul, 1980).

[4] Craig Calhoun uses "clusters of communication" to suggest subdivisions within a non-monolithic public sphere: "Introduction: Habermas and the Public Sphere," in *Habermas and the Public Sphere*, ed. Craig Calhoun (Cambridge, MA: MIT Press, 1992), 38.

Clearly, a segregated working-class culture does not lead inevitably to a counter-hegemonic assault or a politics of polarization, but it could.[5] The networks of community life were resources that could be mobilized behind political goals and community grievances could provide an agenda for a politics of polarization.[6] The formal oppositional forces of the city understood this potential and targeted the working-class community as their main constituency. Their success in building a mass following thus depended on their ability to understand and interpret its demands. In fact, these formal political forces never completely absorbed the community, leaving a space for an informal politics shaped largely, as argued in Chapter 1, by gendered concerns. As a result, the working-class community played a central role in the evolving political culture of the city; both as the target of formal organizations and as the instigator of its own agenda.

It is important to emphasize the distinction between worker culture and the formal political organizations often associated with the working class. In traditional labor historiography, they were too often conflated, but recent scholars have emphasized the need to distinguish worker or working-class culture from the culture of the labor movement or political parties that sought to represent the working class.[7] Worker culture is constructed out of the patterns of everyday life in a capitalist society, while labor movement culture represents a specific oppositional response to these patterns on the part of a segment of

---

[5] There is a lively debate about whether a segregated working-class community hinders radical politicization and leads more to integration than opposition, or whether it has a more subversive impact. For examples of those who stress its conservative impact, see Standish Meacham, *A Life Apart: The English Working Class, 1890–1914* (London: Thames and Hudson, 1977); Peter Stearns, "Efforts at Continuity in Working Class Culture," *Journal of Modern History*, 52:4 (1980); Gareth Stedman Jones, "Class Expression vs. Social Control," *History Workshop*, 4 (Autumn 1977); and Gunther Roth, *The Social Democrats in Imperial Germany: a Study in Working Class Isolation and National Integration* (Totowa: Barnes and Noble, 1963).

I would argue that there is nothing inherently integrative about a segregated working-class community, and that the key to what direction it takes lies in the political context.

[6] Craig Calhoun defines community as the "extent to which people are knit together as social actors." He also poses the notion of community networks as resources: "The Radicalism of Tradition: Community Strength or Venerable Disguise and Borrowed Language," *American Journal of Sociology*, 88:5 (1983), 901.

[7] See, for example, Vernon Lidtke, *The Alternative Culture: Socialist Labor in Imperial Germany* (New York: Oxford University Press, 1985); Michael Seidman, *Workers Against Work: Labor in Paris and Barcelona during the Popular Front* (Berkeley: University of California Press, 1991); John Clarke, Chas Chitcher and Richard Johnson, eds., *Working Class Culture: Studies in History and Theory* (London: Hutchinson, 1979); Helmut Gruber, *Red Vienna: Experiments in Working Class Culture, 1919–1934* (Oxford: Oxford University Press, 1991); and Lynn Abrams, *Workers' Culture in Imperial Germany: Leisure and Recreation in the Rhineland and Westphalia* (London: Routledge, 1992).

the working-class population. There is often considerable overlap, in this case between republican, labor movement and worker culture, but keeping them analytically separate forces us to explain where they overlap and diverge and why, particularly in the case of gender politics. Understanding the relationship between all three interactive cultures can help illuminate the strengths and weaknesses of oppositional politics in Gijón as well as the dynamic of polarization in the city.

As part of this process, this chapter will explore the contours of working-class culture in Gijón as it took shape in the early twentieth century. More specifically, it will analyze the linkages and networks that emerged out of the city's social and residential segregation, and how they provided the building blocks for an increasingly solid working-class community in the city.

Social segregation: class, gender and sociability

Wherever working-class residents of the city lived, some of the networks they established and the common activities they engaged in correlated with their place in the social and economic hierarchy of the city. Within the bounds of these social networks, there were crisscrossing gender linkages, which bound working-class women together in ways that did not include men, and visa versa. These divisions were partly balanced by residential and family networks, which created common ground for both sexes, but they did not totally erase the gender gap in working-class culture.

The consequences of this gap would be extraordinarily important to the political culture of the city. The formal political organizations made their appeals to the working-class community largely through male social networks, which made it more difficult to draw women into them. Unincorporated into the formal political arena or the male-defined public sphere, working-class women pursued their own collective agendas using their gendered social networks, as in the example of the consumer riot in 1898. At certain moments, this gender gap divided and weakened the working-class community, while at other times it broadened its activities. In either case, the gendered social networks helped shape the city's political culture.

The segregated patterns of adult life began in childhood, as boys and girls, poor and wealthy children received separate and unequal educations. The poor overflowed the (single-sex) public city schools, while wealthier families sent their children to private schools, most operated by the Catholic Church. As the distance between classes was established during these years, so were ties of friendship within social groups: "It is the local school, next to houses, streets and shops, where generations of working-class children have been 'schooled,' and where ties of friendship, peer-group and marriage are forged and unmade."[8] These networks did not, however, always include both boys and girls. Many girls from poorer families attended school infrequently, and were kept at home to help their mothers with the housework.[9] Thus, while boys formed bonds of friendship among their classmates, many girls entered their mothers' social network. Another important consequence of this distinction was that illiteracy among working-class women remained significantly higher than that among men, thus making it more difficult for them to share the world of print culture.[10]

Between childhood and marriage, working-class girls and boys had more opportunities to interact and few that brought them into contact with wealthier adolescents. Teenage boys from wealthier families were more likely to continue schooling beyond the required age of twelve,[11] while working-class boys entered the workforce immediately. When they did so, the majority of them could expect to remain in the same class as their fathers. From both marriage and census records, it is evident that intra-family mobility in the working classes was quite low.[12] Thus, from late adolescence, working-class boys entered the work milieu of their fathers. This milieu provided them with a social identity, symbolized by the standard blue overalls and black beret, and

---

[8] Stuart Hall and Tony Jefferson, "Introduction" to *Resistance through Ritual: Youth Subculture in Post-War Britain* (London: Hutchinson, 1976), 43–44.

[9] In the country at large, it was not until the 1930s that the number of girls equaled the number of boys in primary school; at that point, however, 50% of both boys and girls still did not attend primary school, largely because of the lack of public schools: Adrian Shubert, *A Social History of Modern Spain* (London: Unwin Hyman, 1990), 37.

[10] In the working-class neighborhoods, levels of illiteracy among males and females over the age of seven were: 1900: men, 31%; women, 42%; 1910: men, 19.8%; women, 33.8%; 1920: men, 13.6%; women, 25.3%; 1930: men, 7%; women, 11.7%. Notice that not only was the rate of illiteracy higher among women, but it fell more slowly than that of men.

[11] Evidence for this can be garnered from the census sample. In 1900, there were fifty students over fifteen, all male, and forty-two of them lived in the wealthy city center.

[12] From the census sample, looking at households with father and son employed, we find the following percentages of father – son pairs in working-class neighborhoods who shared the same professional category (skilled, semi-skilled, or unskilled):1900, 60%; 1910, 55.6%; 1920, 54.7%; 1930, 47.4%; and the following percentages of father – son pairs with the same occupation: 1900, 60%; 1910, 53%; 1920, 47.8%; 1930, 43.3. In the 415 recorded marriages between 1933 and 1936, a full 85% of the worker fathers-of-the-groom had sons who were also workers, that is, within the broader categories of skilled, semi-skilled or unskilled.

plugged them into an associational network based on this identity. The most formal version of the network was the trade union.

Most working-class girls did not automatically enter this milieu, as the rate of female wage labor in Gijón was relatively low throughout the entire period.[13] Nevertheless, a minority of girls did, especially before they married and left home. According to the census, women were most likely to work in this period of their lives and again, if necessary, when their husbands died, but few married women stayed in the workforce.[14] Thus, a minority of mostly single women participated in the predominantly male work culture.[15]

Even this minority experienced a gendered version of the workplace milieu. In fact, they rarely worked with or alongside men. The largest category of female workers was domestic service, which created a unique work culture that did not lend itself to sociability or solidarity. Most of these women had little contact with their peers, since they lived in their employers' houses, which were located primarily in the wealthy center district.[16] The rest worked in industrial labor, most in factory or workshop settings, but even here their colleagues were largely women. The tobacco and textile factories, which employed the largest concentrations of women, about 2,300 at their peak, hired no more than a few dozen men between them. The only case of an integrated workforce was one of the metallurgical factories, which employed some 200 women as packers.[17]

The result of this segregation seems to have been a semi-independent female work culture with networks that did not always run through male channels. Evidence is sparse, but intriguing anecdotes suggest the existence of specifically female networks of both

---

[13] The rate of female wage labor in Spain was among the lowest of the European countries: in 1910, 13.5% of the Spanish workforce was female, compared to over 30% in France and England. In 1930, the number had fallen to 9.16%, because of the decline in agricultural labor: Rosa Capel Martínez, *El trabajo y la educación de la mujer* (Madrid: Ministerio de Cultura, 1984), 42 and 48. Gijón's figures are higher than the national average but still low in comparison to northern Europe: in 1930, according to the census sample, 18% of adult females were employed.

[14] For female employment rates, see Table 3.1 in Appendix 3.

[15] A major exception to this pattern was the cigarette makers, who tended to keep their artisanal identity and their jobs throughout their adult lives. See Pamela Radcliff, "Elite Women Workers and Collective Action: The Cigarette Makers of Gijón, 1890–1930," *Journal of Social History*, 27:1 (September 1993).

[16] In 1930, the census reported 2,500 domestic servants, all of them women. Of those who appeared in the census samples, the majority lived in the center district: in 1900, 135 out of 165, and in 1930, 169 out of 256.

[17] Information about women workers was gathered from editions of the *Anuario estadístico de España*, 1914–1933.

community disapproval and solidarity within the workplace setting. Two similar stories illustrate how women workers imposed a code of behavior using the familiar technique of gossip. The first involved eighteen-year-old textile worker Josefa Peinado. As a result of rumors spread about her character and her relationship with her former boy-friend, life at the factory became unbearable for her and she quit. But even then, *las malas lenguas* (the gossips) pursued her everywhere, with ironic glances and whispers. At her wits' end, she finally decided to commit suicide: she dissolved two packs of match heads into water and drank the solution.[18] The second involved another factory worker, Angelita, who had the misfortune to catch the eye of her boss. Although she was engaged to another man, other women in the fac-tory spread rumors that she was having an affair with the boss. She denied it, but her fiancé broke off relations with her, and at this point Angelita decided to run off with her employer. When police found them several days later in Madrid, the family ordered her forcible return to Gijón.[19] Whether the rumors were true or not, the stories illustrate one aspect of female community-building on the job. Gossip is a tool most commonly associated with neighborhood community control,[20] but these stories demonstrate that it could be absorbed into work culture as well. Moreover, they demonstrate the intense relation-ships that these women established in the workplace, and which have to be in place for gossip to be effective. As historian David Garrioch argues: "it was gossip . . . based on familiarity and on a degree of vigilance requiring a considerable local commitment of energy, which more than anything defined the boundaries of the community."[21]

A different kind of workplace community-building is illustrated in the famous banquet of the *comadres*, or godmothers, celebrated every year by cigarette makers in the tobacco factory and by seamstresses in a few dressmaking shops. The institution of godparenthood had originated in the middle ages as a way of extending close ties beyond

---

[18] *El Noroeste*, June 12, 1909.

[19] *El Noroeste*, April 18, 1909. Even though she was thirty years old, under Spanish law she was still subject to the will of her father.

[20] Susan Harding explains the gender specificity of gossip this way: "In a legally and ideo-logically subordinate position, and without recourse to effective institutions of their own that they can manipulate, women must defend and advance themselves with whatever everyday verbal skills, such as squabbling, finesse, and gossip, they may develop": "Women and Words in a Spanish Village," in *Toward an Anthropology for Women*, ed. Rayna Reiter (New York: Monthly Review Press, 1975), 295.

[21] David Garrioch, *Neighbourhood and Community in Paris, 1740–1790.* (Cambridge: Cam-bridge University Press, 1986), 33.

immediate blood relations. The choice of a godparent created a "formal state of friendship" that was the most sacred bond outside the immediate family.[22] By the twentieth century, the tradition had died out everywhere but in the rural Mediterranean world. In Asturias, the only ritual remnant was the banquet of the *comadres* staged by these women workers.[23] Few details of the festival exist, but it clearly signified some kind of transfer of the "formal state of friendship" to the workplace, where one's fellow workers were apparently being cast as extended family members. And because the banquet was specifically for godmothers, not godparents, it was a gendered assertion of community and friendship. Thus, the cigarette makers and seamstresses established their own gendered social networks that tied them more to other women than to male workers.

One place where young working-class men and women did meet was the street, where the daily promenade or *paseo* provided opportunities for the early stages of courtship.[24] While residents of all classes engaged in this public ritual, there were definite boundaries between the two worlds. The main street for the *paseo* was the fashionable Calle Corrida: "a privileged place in the city, where people stroll at all hours, and where the beautiful Gijonese women show off their enchantments, and the city's youth choose to spend their most savored moments."[25] While everyone was welcome, normally the elites (the *señoritas*) walked along the paved, left-hand side of the street, while the poorer women took the right, unpaved side. Beyond this spatial distinction, *señoritas* could always be identified by their lavish hats, which even the cigarette makers could not afford. As a compensation, the cigarette makers had their own promenade, called the Paseo de los Arcos, a tradition that began in the nineteenth century when there were several hundred eligible young *cigarreras* working in the factory.

---

[22] See John Bossy, "Godparenthood: The Fortunes of a Social Institution in Early Modern Christianity," in *Religion and Society in Early Modern Europe, 1500–1800*, ed. Kaspar von Greyerz (London: Allen and Unwin, 1984).

[23] "The *cigarreras* of the tobacco factory of Gijón continued to observe this festival for some time; it was a kind of corporate tea, without male participation, that tried to maintain the old traditional flavor": Joaquín Bonet, *Pequeñas historias de Gijón* (Gijón: La Industria, 1969), 40. "We know that in Gijón the festival was much more important than elsewhere, and it was observed through the first quarter of the century; later it languished": Eloy Gómez Pellón and Gema Coma González, *Fiestas de Asturias* (Oviedo: Caja de Ahorros de Asturias, 1985), 20.

[24] Kathy Peiss puts this phenomenon in the context of a new heterosocial youth culture in turn-of-the-century New York: *Cheap Amusements: Working Women and Leisure in Turn of the Century New York* (Philadelphia: Temple University Press, 1986).

[25] *El Noroeste*, February 7, 1936.

Each day after work, the women would parade down from Cimadavilla through the arches of the Plaza Mayor and past the waiting groups of admirers and suitors.[26]

In addition to these formal *paseos* in the city center, the streets of working-class neighborhoods brought together young men and women in search of entertainment and companionship. A biography of local poet Pachín de Melás explains that he met his future wife, Agapita, "in the street and in a neighborhood common to both, fundamentally working class, a neighborhood of corduroy sashes tied around the kidneys."[27] The site of Pachín's and Agapita's courtship is corroborated in a more general way by the strong correlation between social relations and residence demonstrated in the marriage records. Almost half of the couples both lived in the same neighborhood before their marriage. If the residence of the two witnesses is factored in, at least two of the four participants lived in the same neighborhood in three-fourths of the weddings, and in a third of the cases they lived on the same street.[28] Thus, patterns of courtship seemed to be embedded in residential ties, which were in turn embedded in social hierarchies. Of the marriages concluded by girls from working-class families, 83% were to men from the same class. The streets were also important to working-class socializing because they were free, in contrast to the private clubs that enclosed much elite entertainment. One good example of the indoor/outdoor barrier was the segregation of Carnival celebrations. Although all classes participated in the festivities, the rich attended private balls while the common people took to the streets with bawdy and irreverent displays considered beyond the bounds of dignified society:

> There is a marked differentiation between the parties patronized by the nobility and the *haute bourgeoisie*, refined and sumptuous dances in houses and palaces, and the festivities attended by the less favored classes, with their biting remarks and ridiculing of persons and institutions, at the same time exposing the wrongs suffered by society; these

---

[26] All of this information came from a story published in *El Noroeste*, July 19, 1921. Since the tobacco factory workforce had stopped hiring new workers, the cigarette makers had married and aged, and by the time of the article, the Paseo de los Arcos was no longer practiced.

[27] Patricio Aduriz, *Pachín de Melás* (Gijón: Imprenta La Versal, 1978), 26.

[28] *Registro Civil de Gijón*. These statistics include couples from all status levels for the years 1933–1936. Only in 1933 did the forms add information on the residence of the couple and their witnesses. Of the 400 marriages recorded between 1933 and 1936, I took a sample of about 25%, or 100 entries.

latter take the form of masked parades that march through the city singing disordered compositions that are repeated later throughout the year.[29]

Thus, Carnival resulted in the effective abandonment of the streets to the common people, adding yet another brick to the wall of segregation that separated the classes.

While working-class men and women congregated with each other in the streets during courting, when they married, their extra-familial social networks diverged again. Married men established life-long associational ties through the workplace, and they tended to spend many of their leisure hours with other men, in sociable activities centered on the discussion of current affairs. Thus, the shaping and expressing of political views was an important feature of male social life. Depending on the man's social status, he had access to taverns, barber shops, cafés and casinos, or private clubs, where the debate of contemporary issues formed the staple of conversation.[30]

For working men, the locale of choice was the tavern, followed by the barber shop. Through their steady clientele, barber shops established their niche in the social hierarchy and sometimes even a political character, as in the case of the barber shop across from the trade union headquarters which sold the anarchist *Defensa del Obrero*. From all reports, however, male social life revolved largely around the tavern.[31] Every street had its corner tavern, every tavern had its complexion, its crowd, and sometimes its political leanings. Unlike in England, Spain's taverns were unregulated, so they proliferated with industrialization in the nineteenth century. In addition to multiplying, their interiors were altered:

---

[29] Gómez Pellón and Coma González, *Fiestas de Asturias*, 21.

[30] The importance of these institutions for male sociability has long been recognized. See Eric Hobsbawm in *Laboring Men: Studies in the History of Labor* (London: Weidenfeld and Nicolson, 1964); Jon M. Kingsdale, "The Poor Man's Club: Social Functions of the Urban Working Class Saloon," *American Quarterly*, 25 (October 1973); and Roy Rozenzweig, *Eight Hours for What We Will: Workers and Leisure in an Industrial City, 1870–1920* (Cambridge: Cambridge University Press, 1983).

[31] Tavern life was the subject of numerous studies, as conservative moralists sought to demonstrate links between industrialization, alcoholism and crime. For Asturias, see Manuel Gimeno y Azcárate, *La criminalidad en Asturias, 1883–1897* (Oviedo: Escuela Tipográfica del Hospicio, 1900). For a complementary discussion in the French context, see Susanna Barrows, "After the Commune: Alcoholism, Temperance and Literature in the Early Third Republic," in *Consciousness and Class Experience in Nineteenth Century Europe*, ed. John Merriman (New York: Holmes and Meier, 1979).

with the goal that the clientele would stay for longer periods of time, thanks to the greater comfort, giving rise to the diversification of establishments, with some acquiring a specific character: this development was very important to the manner in which social relations were established in the nineteenth and the first half of the twentieth centuries.[32]

Some taverns were almost political institutions, where regular *tertulias*, often revolving around one savant, would meet.[33] On the night that Socialist León Meana was killed, for example, he had been in a bar on the Calle Ezcurdia where he and his comrades regularly discussed political issues. Their discussion lasted from 9:45 until 11:45, after which he was shot by a man lying in wait outside the door.[34] The political tenor of a bar was obviously common knowledge, with anarchist and Socialist *tertulias* strictly off limits to each other. Occasionally incidents of turf violation were reported, as when León Meana provoked a violent debate a couple of years before his death by entering a bar frequented by anarchists. His arrival was greeted with disbelief, since no one could understand why he would have ventured into hostile territory. The ensuing conflagration ended with Meana shooting one of the anarchists in the bar.[35] In yet another incident in 1932, a bar owner refused to serve a group of Socialists who walked into a bar filled with anarchist regulars. The interlopers later returned with guns and started a brawl.[36]

Conservative moralists liked to point to stories like these to prove the bestial nature of tavern life, but the significance of the violence appears more complex. It was true that many crimes of violence took place inside or near taverns,[37] but the evidence that exists suggests that many of them were not random acts but were embedded in a set of social networks. Thus, violence was common between men who knew each other, and had scores to settle. In one case, a man beat up a fellow worker after insults about his mother; in another, two men fought over a woman's honor; and in a third, a man knifed his cousin over a financial dispute. A typical story was the altercation between

---

[32] Pedro G. Quirós Corujo, *Alcohol y alcoholismo en Asturias* (Gijón: ARCANO, 1983), 559.
[33] Amaro del Rosal, "La taberna como centro de discusión política en Asturias, 1914–1920," *Los Cuadernos del Norte*, 14 (1982).
[34] *El Noroeste*, June 26, 1923.
[35] *El Noroeste*, October 28, 1921, at the trial of León Meana.
[36] *El Noroeste*, November 22, 1932.
[37] Manuel Gimeno y Azcárate's figures for the late nineteenth century indicate that nearly half of all crimes prosecuted in Asturias took place in or near taverns: *La criminalidad*, 55.

two neighbors, Arturo and Andrés, which broke out one night in a *chigre*, or dive, in Cimadavilla. When Arturo insulted Andrés' wife, Andrés taunted that he would "cagar en tu puta madre" if Arturo would step outside. They did, and Andrés ended up with a knife in his chest.[38]

In all of these cases, the violence illustrates the existence of community ties, not their disintegration. Carrying out public disputes in this context is a community act in and of itself, as David Garrioch points out: "With their set forms, gestures and language, their strong element of performance, and the publicity which accompanied them, disputes were public expressions of grievances designed to win over the onlookers, appeals to the community to bear witness and to redress the injury done."[39] From this perspective, it is not surprising that men staged many of their public disputes where they did most of their socializing, and with those whom they shared space and competed for turf. The violence was thus another expression of intimacy, a volatile intimacy that ran from rejection to solidarity, the flip side of the positive support that sustained community life.

In contrast to the work and leisure patterns of working-class men, those of their wives looked very different. Most of them, like their wealthier counterparts, were engaged in full-time house management and child care, with an average number of four children in each household.[40] But this role did not consign them to an isolated existence inside their homes. In fact, many of their daily chores and responsibilities brought them out into the streets and the courtyards of their neighborhoods, and into contact with other women on similar errands. Because modest houses lacked gas, running water, and refrigeration, women made daily trips to the public fountains and markets, and regular visits to the coal dispatchers. Likewise, laundry was done in neighborhood communal tubs by hand.

The time spent waiting in line or scrubbing dirty clothes was an opportunity to chat and exchange views. As Susan Harding points out

---

[38] Only a handful of court cases exist for the period. See AHP, Sección Audencia Provincial de Oviedo: sumarios, 1933–1935. Caja 92, #231/34.

[39] Garrioch, *Neighbourhood*, 54.

[40] The average number of children and household size does not seem to correlate clearly with social status. In 1930, for example, the mean number of children was 3.8, ranging from 3.5 in the downtown district to 4.0 in the working-class districts. The average age of the mother at the birth of the first child was also very close in all types of neighborhoods: in 1930, the mean was 24.9, ranging from 24.6 in the working-class areas to 25.2 in the downtown district.

in her study of a Spanish village, women rarely visited each other just to talk, but instead combined socializing with their common chores.[41] This pattern of socializing differed not only from that of their husbands, but also from that of wealthier wives, whose servants performed most of the public household duties. Further, it resulted in what Rayna Reiter called a "sexual geography" of spatial use.[42] While men were at the factory or the workshop during the day, the city streets were in female hands.

Even when women were at home, the design of working-class housing promoted interaction.[43] Most lower-income units faced onto a common back patio overrun by collective use. One Socialist observer, commenting on conditions in a workers' neighborhood, was especially horrified by the teeming life in the patio he visited:

> A veritable fabric of ropes criss-crossed the space, covered with clothes that had been washed by the inhabitants. Stoves here, earthen jars, boxes of garbage there; women, some washing or cleaning, others preparing lunch; an army of children, some crawling on the floor, others running, all of them barefoot, dirty, making an infernal racket, while other smaller ones, placed in boxes used as cribs, cried until they no longer could, trying to communicate that they wanted to eat. A throng of street vendors offered their specialties, pawed-over meat, horse-meat sausage, vegetables that the pigs would reject, and other merchandise of this caliber. What poverty and lack of hygiene! If there was such crowding, confusion and promiscuity in the patio, what would the rooms be like?[44]

The observer's concern about the links between immorality and density are common to reform literature.[45] Whether or not we accept his dismay, however, his observations highlight the essentially communal nature of urban working-class living in Gijón, especially among wives and children. The limitations of privacy, resources and space forced a sharing and accommodation with one's neighbors that was not part of the fabric of upper-class life.

[41] Harding, "Women and Words," 295–296.
[42] Rayna R. Reiter, "Men and Women in the South of France: Public and Private Domains," in *Towards an Anthropology of Women*, 256.
[43] Ellen Ross emphasizes this in the case of London: "Survival Networks: Women's Neighborhood Sharing in London before World War I," *History Workshop*, 15 (Spring 1983), and Kathy Peiss for turn-of-the-century New York: *Cheap Amusements*, 15.
[44] *Aurora Social*, March 3, 1900.
[45] His distaste also underlines the distinction between labor movement and working-class culture, and the ways in which the labor movement often tried to change the latter.

The combination of this lack of privacy and the general privations of working-class life encouraged women to develop what Ellen Ross called "survival networks," informal exchanges of aid and support between kin and neighbors.[46] These mutual aid networks were embedded in the social and cultural realities of working-class women's lives, reflecting both their own scarce resources and the common duties they all shared to feed, clothe and provide material comfort for their families. Most of these exchanges remain invisible in the historical record, but a few more dramatic examples were considered newsworthy. When Josefa Blanco was beaten by her husband, for example, the police report noted that three women intervened on her behalf.[47] In another incident, a young worker from Cimadavilla drowned when he fell off the dock as he was weaving along and singing early Christmas morning. When his body was finally fished out, three days later, "the whole neighborhood of Cima came down to the docks." The unpleasant task of readying the decomposed body for burial was taken up by three women of the community.[48] Support on a different scale came after one of the major disasters of the period, the "catastrophe" of El Musel, an explosion that killed eighteen port workers and injured twenty. The tragedy provoked a citywide expression of grief, but neighborhood women made their contribution by bringing the victims' wives and mothers to their houses in La Calzada and Natahoyo for emotional first aid.[49]

The networks that generated these events did not always lead to positive demonstrations of support. As with male social life, there was a disputatious flip side to this sociability. Despite the stereotype of the drunken male worker as perpetrator of violent brawls, *El Noroeste*'s daily reporting of fines and arrests included almost as many instances of women cited for public altercations. Significantly, most of these fights took place where women did much of their socializing: in the market place, and at other public gathering places. Also significantly, most of these fights occurred between women, neighbors or kin who had transgressed social rules and were being publicly challenged to make restitution. The cases of women fighting with men, husbands

---

[46] Ross, "Survival Networks." See also Judith E. Smith, "The Transformation of Family and Community Culture in Immigrant Neighborhoods, 1900–1940," in *The New England Working Class and the New Labor History*, ed. Herbert G. Gutman and Donald H. Bell (Urbana: University of Illinois Press, 1987).
[47] *El Noroeste*, July 8, 1906.
[48] *El Noroeste*, January 4, 1900.
[49] *El Noroeste*, February 26, 1913.

or not, were much rarer, perhaps to some extent because most of their public time was spent with other women. In any case, these public disputes, as with some of the bar-room brawls, were often an indication of community intimacy and interdependence rather than alienation.

Residential segregation: neighborhoods and sociability

The networks that resulted in these patterns of public disputes had a spatial as well as a social dimension: people formed relationships with those with whom they came into daily contact. For the relatively immobile working classes, the place where this contact was most likely to happen, aside from the workplace and the central markets, was the neighborhood in which they lived. Thus, a neighborhood was more than a physical arrangement of buildings and private and public space; it provided a geographical locus for community-building.

It was not, of course, a neutral locus. The division of the city into cheap residential areas dotted with factories and expensive commercial and residential sectors dictated where people could afford to live. As Robert Fishman put it, "however objective the industrial city might appear, its form rests ultimately on the values and choices of the powerful groups in the city."[50] Thus, the working-class neighborhood originated as a function of the hegemony of local elites, who wanted to banish industry and its workforce to the outskirts of the city. And yet, because of the opportunities for community-building within that context of subordination, the neighborhood could become what Gramsci called an area of "won space."[51] What is crucial about Gramsci's concept is that it implies agency: a neighborhood does not simply happen, it is constructed out of dismal rows of tenement buildings and unpaved streets. Before residents could hunker down behind the barricades in 1934, they had to forge a community within their perimeters. The evidence suggests that they achieved significant progress along this line by the 1930s.

The potential for working-class neighborhood communities lay in

[50] Robert Fishman, *Bourgeois Utopias: The Rise and Fall of Suburbia* (New York: Basic Books, 1987), 12. For more on power relations and the construction of space, see Edward W. Soja, *Postmodern Geographies: The Reassertion of Space in Critical Social Theory* (New York: Verso, 1989).
[51] Antonio Gramsci, *Selections from the Prison Notebooks* (London: Lawrence and Wishart, 1971), 43.

a number of factors, from their isolation, to the fact of daily contact, to the set of shared grievances arising from the city's neglect. Especially in the early years of the century, the new developments of Natahoyo, El Llano and La Calzada were isolated both from each other and from the city center. The three sections of El Llano stretched out for over a mile along the "Coal Highway," connected only by this major thoroughfare, which was still not fully paved by the mid-1920s.[52] The outskirts of La Calzada were almost a mile and a half from the railway station in Natahoyo, which was another half mile from the city center. Streetcars were built in 1909, but even then transport fares ate up about 7% of a worker's daily wage.[53] In addition, the streetcar service did not run between areas on the outskirts, that is, from La Calzada to the west to El Llano further south. Like the railroad system in Spain, the streetcar system funneled people in and out of the center and not along the periphery. These factors appeared to encourage workers to reside near their place of employment, although the evidence is inconclusive.[54]

The isolation of the new developments made them easy to contrast with the more favored downtown. More importantly, this contrast provoked numerous complaints about the neglect and inferior conditions of the Gijón that lay across the tracks. The spate of critical articles and letters printed in the local newspapers never let up. They complained of the scarcity of public water sources, the absence of sewers, and the poor condition of streets and sidewalks, which were often unpaved. They also cited the lack of police vigilance and street lighting, which made night travel through muddy streets even more treacherous. The complaints are summed up by a local politician who decided to take a tour of La Calzada and Natahoyo to see for himself how the workers lived. He came back with horror stories and accusations: "the streets are dirty, partially urbanized, badly lit: the city government does not realize that Gijón extends beyond the Calle Corrida and slips into the realm of labor . . . there everything is deplorable, from hygiene to decoration."[55] While residents certainly suffered from

---

[52] From a complaint in *El Noroeste*, March 10, 1925.

[53] Moisés Llordén Miñambres, *La producción de suelo urbano en Gijón, 1860–1975* (Oviedo: Gráficas Summa, 1978), 117.

[54] Unfortunately, the only information combining residence and place of employment was found on a UGT metalworkers' union list of 1913. Of the 257 members, I calculated that nearly two-thirds lived within a half a kilometer of their workplace.

[55] *El Noroeste*, September 3, 1903.

these conditions, they also created a common agenda that linked working-class residents to their neighbors.[56]

The common agenda was strengthened by the increasing residential stability of these neighborhoods. Gijón's population was generally stable, but the trend became even more marked in working-class neighborhoods. Thus, in 1900, about 30% of all city residents had lived in Gijón less than ten years. But by 1920, that number had almost halved in the working-class areas, to 16.5%. In contrast, the percentage remained about the same in the city center: 28.5%. In other words, the population of the working-class neighborhoods was the most settled in the city.[57] While these numbers cannot tell us how long people stayed in one neighborhood, the marriage statistics cited above help to fill in the gaps: the strong correlation between the street, the neighborhood, the couple and their witnesses, suggests that stability existed at this level as well as at the citywide level.

The factors that favored community-building at the neighborhood level were thus very high: from social and economic homogeneity, to residential stability, to shared grievances and physical distance from the center. In addition, there were few countervailing forces, such as competing immigrant groups or religious divisions.[58] Thus, nearly everything about life in the poorer areas pushed residents towards identifying with each other as neighbors. It is, of course, more difficult to prove that they did bond with each other and to what degree, but the existing evidence is positive. In particular, these areas witnessed a dramatic increase in neighborhood-based associations and activities, both formal and informal. From this evidence, we can infer the existence of networks of sociability and some popular level of identification with the *barrio*.

One of the major sources of neighborhood associational life in the

---

[56] Tyler Stovall makes this argument a centerpiece of his book *The Rise of the Paris Red Belt*: he argues that, in that context, class solidarity was built more out of these common concerns than out of those of the workplace (p. 4).

[57] The "mixed" neighborhoods, as usual, fell somewhere in between. The figures for those who had resided in Gijón for fewer than ten years were, for the center, 1900, 30.5%; 1920, 28.5%; for the mixed areas, 1900, 29.3%; 1920, 18.3%; and for the working-class neighborhoods, 1900, 28.4%; 1920, 16.5%.

[58] For a discussion of the forces that encourage or undermine neighborhood communities, see White, *The Rothschild Buildings*, Chapter 3, and Stovall, *Paris Red Belt*, especially pp. 156–163. Religion and immigration were more powerful issues in the American context, although in major European cities regional immigrant groups often did not integrate. In Spain, the case of Barcelona is exemplary of this phenomenon: the immigrant Andalusians were never absorbed into the Catalan working class.

poorer *barrios* was the desire to improve living conditions and to fill in the gaps in social services not provided by the city. Because of their special problems, residents of these areas were forced to be more independent from the political and social mainstream, to contrive makeshift solutions to problems and to turn to each other for support. Along these lines, one of the earliest signs of community organizing in the *barrios* was the effort to open more schools for their children, since the number of public institutions was insufficient. Thus, in 1905, residents of Llano de Arriba organized a school with primary classes during the day and adult classes at night. The project was conceived by one hundred contributors, not wealthy businessmen but workers, and several residents of the neighborhood volunteered to teach night courses.[59] At about the same time, residents of La Calzada founded a primary school, La Caridad, for children of workers and orphans, which by the 1920s enrolled almost 300 students.[60] In both cases, residents founded these schools without the assistance of any existing institutions; in other words, they were true community efforts.

After these early projects, the initiative was taken up by more formal neighborhood organizations, particularly the branches of the Ateneo and of the Asociación de Cultura e Higiene (ACH),[61] which were still opening and operating schools up to the Civil War.[62] Because the number of public schools never reached the level of demand, the need for private efforts offered a constant rallying point for neighborhood organization. The *ateneos* of both El Llano and La Calzada opened primary schools near the end of the first decade, which enrolled over 100 students by the 1930s.[63] Later,

---

[59] *El Noroeste*, January 4, 1905. The article noted that the founders had to overcome all sorts of bureaucratic obstructionism and the indifference of wealthy property owners before their project came to fruition.

[60] *El Noroeste*, January 11, 1923. The report noted that the school employed four teachers and enrolled 283 students.

[61] The Gijón central branch of the ACH was founded in 1904, for the purpose of improving social harmony and promoting the dissemination of culture among the "humble classes." Over the next two decades, half a dozen branches were formed, all but one in working-class neighborhoods, with predominantly working-class membership. The ACH was a product of republican reformers seeking to integrate workers and assert their leadership over them, but regardless of the hegemonic intent, it stimulated and organized neighborhood sentiments and energies. For more on the Ateneo and the ACH as part of the republican project, see Chapter 7.

[62] The last notice of a private neighborhood school being inaugurated was at the end of 1935, in Natahoyo. The ACH held a meeting of all parents in the *barrio* to discuss issues related to the primary school due to open in December: *El Noroeste*, November 23, 1935.

[63] *El Noroeste*, September 12, 1933.

104

the ACH branches also opened schools, like the free one in Cimada-villa attended by sixty students. Every year the school held public exams where the students displayed their skills in math, grammar, geography and drawing, in front of an admiring audience of parents and members of the ACH. The public staging of the event demon-strated that the progress of the children was as much a matter of collective pride as of individual achievement.[64]

In addition to their education projects, the branches of the ACH acted most prominently as advocates for urban improvements in the neglected neighborhoods, especially by the 1920s and 30s. When the city council erected monuments downtown but dragged its feet about sewers in Natahoyo or streetlights in La Calzada, the ACH helped organize the neighbors and promote their cases to the appropriate authorities. As one reporter noted approvingly, the ACH and its branches acted as "apprenticeships for civic participation for those who belonged, while at the same time working to overcome the crimi-nal abstention and indifference with which the city center views what happens in the peripheral barrios."[65] These activities helped to bring neighbors together and make the transition from grumbling to collec-tive action.

Through this collective action, the branches achieved numerous specific improvements that must have reinforced the positive associ-ations of working together towards a common goal. A few examples illustrate the range of achievements. Soon after its inauguration in 1915, the ACH of El Llano began offering free vaccinations for chil-dren and adults who lived in the neighborhood, and convinced the city government to install a water fountain in Llano de Arriba.[66] The ACH of La Calzada made history by inaugurating the first children's playground in Asturias, in July 1915.[67] And the ACH of Natahoyo was instrumental in getting the city to install a sewer system in the neighborhood.[68]

The actual number of residents involved in these campaigns was probably not high, but the ACH always celebrated as if the neighbor-hood had won the victory. Thus, at the dedication of the playground or the completion of the sewer system, the ACH branch would open

---

[64] The last one before the Civil War was reported in *Avance*, July 16, 1936.
[65] *El Noroeste*, October 11, 1917.
[66] *El Noroeste*, September 18, 1915.
[67] *El Noroeste*, July 30, 1915.
[68] *El Noroeste*, March 22, May 15, 1915. It was not completed, however, until 1925.

105

its doors and throw a party for the neighborhood. In June 1936, for example, one of the youngest branches, in the Barrios Nuevos in Ceares, held a ceremony for a newly installed water fountain. The ceremony was attended by city officials, representatives from all the ACH branches, and numerous members of the public, including "all the neighbors (*vecindario*) of the barrio." Afterwards, the crowd went back to ACH headquarters to celebrate and make plans for new improvements.[69] As is evident from the large attendance, even non-member residents were drawn into manifestations of neighborhood pride and solidarity.

As neighborhood identities were forged out of the need to struggle together for basic services, they were also shaped out of the need to provide local entertainment and leisure activities. In 1900, most of the festivals, cafés, theaters and casinos were located downtown, and, with the exception of street events, were affordable mainly to elite patrons. The combination of isolation from the center and poverty thus created a need for accessible entertainment that was not profitable for commercial enterprises to operate. What is interesting about the response to this need is that it was contained within and defined by neighborhood units. In other words, leisure and entertainment activities came to be a subset of neighborhood life instead of a separate category. As such, they played a central role in reinforcing neighborhood identity.

This process can be seen clearly in the manipulation of traditional rituals to fit the needs of new neighborhoods. For example, there was a popular cycle of *romerías de barrio*, or saint's day festivals, that were located in several of Gijón's rural parishes. A few of the new industrial neighborhoods not included in the original cycle decided to add on: thus, in the 1930s, El Llano created an annual *romería* during the first weekend of September. Likewise, neighborhoods began to decentralize the Carnival festivities in February by organizing their own masked balls. The first one to do this was Natahoyo, in 1913, but by the 1930s, El Llano, Calzada and Jove each staged their own, sometimes sponsored by the ACH branch in that neighborhood. By 1936, the neighborhood balls had been absorbed into Carnival tradition in Gijón, just as Carnival had been absorbed into the neighborhoods. Significantly, however, balls that

---

[69] *El Noroeste*, June 3, 1936.

were located downtown carried the name of the private clubs in which they were held; only in the working-class *barrios* did Carnival become identified with a broader neighborhood community. Thus, the new masked balls or *romerías* did more than provide entertainment for those not interested in going into the center. They became "invented traditions" that solidified identities and created histories for neighborhoods without a past.[70]

Another case of an "invented tradition" being used to bolster neighborhood identity was the increasingly elaborate neighborhood beauty pageants. These pageants functioned as preliminary rounds in the choice of Miss Gijón, but before the 1930s they passed virtually unnoticed. At this point, however, they became major events, often becoming incorporated with other facets of neighborhood associational life. Thus, the Miss Natahoyo contest of 1935 was sponsored by the ACH, which used it to promote a benefit lunch for its library.[71] Miss Llano, Miss Cima and Miss Calzada, on the other hand, were sponsored by the neighborhood soccer clubs, which staged the events during their games. Local businesses donated prizes, as in the 1936 Miss Calzada pageant, where a local seamstress made a gown for the winner.[72] Contestants were required to live in the neighborhood, as did seventeen-year-old Felisa Rodríguez, a textile worker at La Algodonera who became Miss Calzada 1936. Interestingly, as with the Carnival festivities, only the poorer neighborhoods organized the contest geographically. The other contestants for Miss Gijón were chosen in pageants held in private clubs, whose winners carried titles like Miss Sport, Miss Palerno, Miss Somió Park.[73]

In addition to these special annual events, the working-class *barrios* developed more regular outlets for leisure and entertainment. As mentioned above, a local soccer league was founded, with teams in Natahoyo, Cimadavilla, and La Calzada, among others. And, in the pattern of Carnival and the beauty contests, only teams from the working-class neighborhoods identified themselves with their neighborhood instead

---

[70] On the concept of "invented traditions," see the introduction to *The Invention of Tradition*, ed. Eric Hobsbawm and Terence Ranger (Cambridge: Cambridge University Press, 1983).
[71] *El Noroeste*, July 18, 1935.
[72] *El Noroeste*, June 16, 1936.
[73] In addition to these three, there were contests for Miss Calzada, Miss Llano, Miss Cima, Miss Natahoyo, Miss Ceares and Miss Coto San Nicolás: *El Noroeste*, August 13, 1935.

of a private sponsoring business. This fact made it doubly significant when La Calzada's soccer team made it to the finals of the Olympic playoffs in 1936.[74]

For more highbrow entertainment, neighborhood associations like the ACH began to offer a range of activities, from lectures and poetry readings to concerts and theater productions. Notices of these events first appeared just before the First World War, but by the 1930s both the events and the number of associations had multiplied dramatically. In many cases, the associations formed their own troupes of musicians, singers or actors, who would perform on what became the local circuit of neighborhood cultural stages. Within this circuit, the *ateneos* and the ACH remained the most prominent, but numerous new associations sprang up in the 1930s, with names like the Workers' Cultural and Artistic Association of Ceares, the Popular Improvement Center of El Llano, the Cultural Instruction Center of El Llano, the Neighborhood Association of Jove, the Women's Association of Natahoyo or Cimadavilla, the Libertarian Ateneo of La Calzada, and so on. Some of these had direct political affiliations and others not, but all identified themselves as neighborhood cultural institutions.

This point is an important one to make. Many of the neighborhood-based events and associations had conflicting and contrasting agendas. The libertarian *ateneos* sought to create anarchist militants, the football clubs and beauty pageants were commercial ventures sponsored by businesses, and the ACH hoped to promote social harmony between classes. And yet, whatever their organizers' intentions, these cultural products also had the effect of promoting neighborhood sociability and identity. They brought neighbors together, instilled a sense of pride in where they lived, and helped turn the poor neighborhoods into centers of social and cultural activity instead of forsaken outposts of civilization. As Stuart Hall has argued, there is no "authentic," autonomous working-class culture "which lies outside the field of force of the relations of cultural power and domination." The culture of neighborhood life, as with the culture of working-class life in general, oscillated between containment and resistance, independence and subordination.[75] Whether neighborhood sociability led to the barri-

---

[74] *Avance*, July 2, 1936. As a protest against the Nazi Olympics, an alternative Popular Olympics was planned in Barcelona for July 1936. In addition to allowing national teams to compete, it had a category for local teams. Unfortunately, the Civil War broke out shortly before the games were to be held.

[75] Hall, "Deconstructing the 'Popular,'" 232.

cades or to the pursuit of respectability depended on the nature of the political dynamic.

Whatever the outcome, it is clear that Gijón developed a vibrant neighborhood culture that peaked in the 1930s, and that it was particularly strong in the poorer sectors of the city, where a combination of factors promoted interaction and interdependence. We can see this in the way the press began to talk about these neighborhoods as if they each had a single collective voice or personality. Undoubtedly, the strongest voices belonged to the most heavily settled working-class neighborhoods of Cimadavilla, Natahoyo, La Calzada and El Llano, which, significantly, were also those that participated as neighborhoods in the revolt of October 1934. The "mixed" areas of El Humedal, El Tejedor or Coto San Nicolás appear more as geographical boundaries than as neighborhoods. And newer worker settlements, like Jove, Ceares and Tremañes, were just beginning to take shape as coherent entities in the 1930s.

A model neighborhood community: Cimadavilla

Among the most heavily settled working-class neighborhoods, there was an additional distinction between old and new, between Cimadavilla and the modern twentieth-century neighborhoods. As one article described it, "if we could personify the city, it has its heart in Cimadavilla and its brain in La Calzada . . . in Cima we have tradition, racial sentiment and folkloric character; in Calzada we have feverish activity driven by its industrial dynamism."[76] Thus, Cima exemplified the pre-industrial popular neighborhood, while La Calzada (as well as Natahoyo and El Llano) symbolized proletarian industrial Gijón. The fact that both types of popular neighborhoods survived into the 1930s is unusual in and of itself, and can be explained partly by the geographical evolution of the city, which left the artisanal neighborhood of Cima largely intact.[77]

As a result of this integrity, Cima had by far the most developed internal linkages of any neighborhood in the city, as well as the clearest public personality. As the quotation above indicates, observers loved to wax eloquent about its quaint, folkloric character and its ties to a

---

[76] In a two-page spread on La Calzada: *El Noroeste*, May 31, 1935.
[77] As Chapter 1 explained, Cima did not become transformed into the new city center. Instead, a new city center grew up at the same time that the city was industrializing, along with the ring of factory settlements. Thus, Cima was largely untouched.

pre-industrial past that was slipping away. The focus on the past, however, sometimes disguised Cima's role in the present. For the residents of newer districts, Cima was the ultimate role model of a neighborhood community. In the struggle to turn rows of buildings into neighborhoods, Cima offered a living blueprint, not simply a faded memory of community life.[78] Thus, it played a crucial role, not simply in the preservation of the past, but in the creation of vital neighborhood communities in the present. In fact, its existence can be counted as one of the factors that encouraged the process of neighborhood community-building in the newer industrial areas.

Cima's basic internal linkages were rooted in its connection to the sea, which provided work for close to half of the *barrio*'s men, and a few of its women.[79] Beyond the fact of occupational homogeneity, the fishing industry gave Cima a distinct public personality, with the daily ritual of dragging the nets up and down the hill to the docks, the smell of fish that clung to the residents, and of course the vigil awaiting the return of the boats.[80] These seemingly timeless rituals helped reinforce Cima's identity as a bastion of tradition in a rapidly changing industrial world. Other kinds of public rituals and activities further enhanced this image. Thus, it was in Cima that the only remaining confraternity celebrated its saint's day with a parade from the docks up the hill. And it was there that female fishmongers still serenaded their companions' wedding nights with a *pandorgada*, or charivari, banging pots and pans and singing bawdy songs.[81] The cigarette makers also contributed to this public culture, with their banquet of the *comadres*, the

---

[78] I'm thinking here of the contrast with David Garrioch's study of Parisian neighborhoods in the eighteenth century, in which he argues that the working-class communities of the nineteenth and twentieth centuries were heirs of these earlier popular neighborhoods, in the same way that trade unions owed a debt to the guilds. In this case, the chronological sequence does not fit: *Neighbourhood and Community*, 255–260.

[79] In 1900 in Cima seamen made up 48.3% of the sample (47% in 1930); unskilled workers 33.7% (24% in 1930); skilled workers 5.6% (7.3% in 1930); white-collar workers 5.6% (11.5% in 1930); professionals 2.2% (7.3% in 1930). Most of the women in the sample were housewives, but several were either fishmongers or cigarette makers.

[80] One writer reported how "normal" people would cross to the other side of the street when fishermen in their nankeen suits and gum boots or women with baskets of sardines walked through the center of town: José Canals, *Octubre Rojo en Asturias* (1935; reprint, Gijón: Silverio Cañada, 1984), 141–142.

[81] In one instance, a group of fishmongers performing an "improvised concert" on tin cans, mortars, ceramic pots, etc. outside the window of a newly married couple were dispersed by three guards. In another instance, the performers resisted arrest by surrounding and hitting the municipal guard who was trying to assert his authority: *El Noroeste*, May 17, 1913, and May 13, 1907.

informal parade of the Paseo de los Arcos, and their renowned receptions for royal visitors.[82]

Outsiders never quite knew what to make of Cima's world, which was, at various times, dismissed as an anachronism, praised nostalgically, or treated condescendingly as a fascinating primitive culture. In fact, the bonds of this tight-knit community proved to be quite adaptable to both "traditional" and "modern" challenges. What mattered in the end was the level of solidarity, which could be summoned under a variety of circumstances. This, then, was the lesson that Cima had to teach "modern" Gijón, particularly the new industrial settlements. By the 1930s, Cima was no longer dismissed, but respected as a poor neighborhood committed to the improvement of the Gijón "darkened by smoke," even though its methods did not always match those of the newer areas. A nice example of this flexible solidarity is a story about a new application for a traditional sign of community disapproval, the charivari.[83] When the Catholic unions refused to honor the general strike of July 1919, female strikers in Cima subjected the president of the Catholic cigarette makers' union to the humiliation of a "veritable charivari" outside her apartment window.[84] By doing so, the strikers communicated that the woman was violating not only work solidarity, but neighborhood solidarity as well. Her public humiliation at home thus transported the censure from a workplace to a community event. Or more accurately, it erased the boundaries between the two, by demonstrating that disloyalty in one realm was equated with disloyalty in the other. Whether this equation was achieved through a charivari or some other more "modern" method was inconsequential; this was the kind of solidarity the newer neighborhoods strove to imitate.

Cima demonstrated this close work and community solidarity in more formal ways as well. In the late 1920s, the families connected with the fishing industry formed a mutual aid society called the Pósito de Pescadores that had over 2,000 members of both sexes by 1931. Its functions overlapped with those of the old guilds, as well as the

---

[82] Over the years, they entertained several princesses, a queen and even King Alfonso XIII.

[83] The fact that the charivari could be adapted demonstrates, as E. P. Thompson put it, a "mode of life in which some part of the law belongs still to the community and is theirs to enforce": "Rough Music," in *Customs in Common* (London: Merlin Press, 1991), 530.

[84] *El Noroeste*, July 4, 1919.

trade unions, the ACH branches and the *ateneos*, and its identity combined elements of all of these associations. It provided mutual aid
for those in the same profession, it organized resistance against the
employers (the *armadores*, or boat outfitters), and it offered educational and cultural activities for the community.[85] In a sense, because
of its special links, Cima was able to achieve a level of integration not
possible in the other *barrios*.

In the process, the Pósito achieved some significant results. By
1933, it had opened both an elementary and a nursery school, in
an attempt to combat the perceived low rate of literacy among
fishermen. In addition, it ran an evening class on nautical skills
that, in 1932, enrolled 110 students. Further, it operated a mutual
aid society with 2,000 members, with its own pension fund and
accident insurance.[86] In 1935, the Pósito formed a choral group,
which had its inaugural performance in April, singing songs of the
sea and presenting a "seafaring scene," which captured the "ambi-
ence of the pure-blooded *barrio* of Cima, with all its characteristics
and idiosyncrasies."[87] The promotion of both the occupation and
the neighborhood was also apparent in the public lectures sponsored
by the Pósito; in one instance, local poet Pachín de Melás spoke
on "Cimadavilla in Gijón's History: Popular Culture, Ports, and
Shipwrecks," and in another, merchant marine captain Angel de la
Viña lectured on "The Fisherman in the National Economy."[88] To
pay for all of these activities, the Pósito successfully petitioned to
open its own Rula, or distribution center, for the sale of fish.[89]
Instead of paying a commission to the *armadores*, the new Rula
collected the money for the welfare of the community.[90]

The Pósito was not designed to be a society of resistance or a trade

---

[85] An article on the history of the Pósito appeared in *Avance*, August 15, 1934.
[86] *Avance*, August 28, 1932. According to a letter from lawyer Germán Cerra to the Military
Governor, he helped the Pósito organize a pension fund, as well as accident insurance
to deal with shipwrecks (October 30, 1934: AGS, J-50.)
[87] *El Noroeste*, April 16 and 17, 1935.
[88] *El Noroeste*, February 6 and December 12, 1935.
[89] Not surprisingly, the *armadores* fought tooth and nail against this project; they succeeded
in delaying its approval but could not get it scrapped. They argued that the Pósito used
violent, coercive tactics and that there was no need for two Rulas in Gijón. See letter
written by the president of the Unión de Armadores of July 5, 1931: AHN, legajo 7A,
núm.8.
[90] It began operating on a temporary basis on May 1, 1931, but received official permission
in 1933. By the end of that year, the new Rula had absorbed about a third of the local
fish distribution business, processing 2,978 kg vs. 5,795 kg for the old Rula: Ramón
Arguelles, *Regionalismo económico asturiano* (Gijón: La Fé, 1934), 40.

union, but the opposition of the *armadores* to the Rula forced it to wage an ongoing battle for survival. This struggle, while it made life difficult for the residents of Cima, also solidified its ties with the other working-class neighborhoods and the anarchist trade union federation. After all the confusion about whether Cima was traditional or modern, what mattered was that it was engaged in a struggle between the people and the elites. The only difference was that Cima based its opposition not in a trade union, but in a neighborhood community in which the networks could reach deep into the fabric of social life. In fact, all of the working-class *barrios* aspired to this kind of integration, but only Cima had all the resources to achieve it. Thus, it stood in the 1930s not as some folkloric reminder of the past, but as the most powerful example of a poor neighborhood community defending itself against the elite power structure. More than for any other area in the city, Cima was a space that had been won by its working-class residents.

While Cima represented one end of the continuum, by the 1930s similar networks of sociability permeated working-class life in the city. Men and women of the working classes had numerous opportunities to congregate and associate, and few that pushed them into the path of the city's elites. Although the specific rhythms of life may have been different for men and women, or for residents of Cima and La Calzada, the general cadence was the same. They fought for the city to clean their streets and struggled to provide education for their children; their women shopped and washed and waited in coal lines; their men drank and talked politics together in the taverns; and their families strolled down the unpaved side of the Calle Corrida. All of these small events constituted the common cultural universe of working people in Gijón. Their universe was predominantly segregated, keeping them isolated from, and uncomprehended by, the elites who belonged to casinos, attended private schools and lived and worked in downtown Gijón.

The fact that this cultural universe was both segregated and underprivileged reinforced the internal links among those who participated. A shared cultural universe that is based on the daily struggle to improve miserable conditions encourages co-operation and the combination of forces. Thus, there was an even greater tendency towards community-building within the culture of working-class life as opposed to elite culture, which could rely more on the state and individual resources to gain objectives. This tendency did not lead to a monolithic, unified working-class community, but it did create the building blocks that could potentially be joined together. The dynamic of community-building also fostered antagonism towards the elite power structure that ignored the needs of working-class Gijón. This antagonism did not equal opposition or polarization, but in the right context it could foster such a dynamic. If no bridges were built between the two faces of the city, if the grievances of the shadowed face were never addressed, and if the elites lost the ability to suppress those grievances, then segregation would become polarization, and a working-class community would congeal in opposition to downtown Gijón. The story of how this happened constitutes the remainder of the book.

PART II

Institutional forces of opposition: republicans and anarchosyndicalists

The combination of political torpor and economic and social dynamism that characterized late-nineteenth-century Gijón soon gave way to open confrontation. As the political culture of confrontation developed, the nascent oppositional traditions of the nineteenth century blossomed into full-fledged challenges to the old regime. In the realm of formal institutional politics, two main groups, the republican parties and the labor movement, led the attack on the Restoration system, each vying to define an oppositional politics that could unite the people of Gijón in battle against the establishment. Through different forms of rhetoric and organization, each sought and claimed to represent the interests of the new Gijón created by the processes of urbanization and industrialization. They both spoke a populist language of empowerment directed at the Gijón "darkened by smoke," the working classes and the new *barrios* on the margins of the city.

But the vision that each articulated was quite different. Republicans spoke about orchestrating the integration of the masses into a reformed political system that would erase the barriers between El Llano and the Calle Corrida. Anarchists and Socialists, on the other hand, spoke about polarization; their scenario called for the residents of El Llano to occupy the Calle Corrida, not make peace with it. Following the implications of these contrasting populist languages, each group worked through different institutional channels. In order for the republicans' vision of integration to be realized, they had to overhaul the governmental institutions to make them effective conduits for social and economic reform. Thus, much of the local republicans' energies were directed at the conquest and reform of the government, particularly at the municipal level. In contrast, the anarchists' vision of polarization required an alternative base of political organization: the trade union. As a result, their institutional energies were focused on constructing a powerful union federation that would provide the foundation for a new political order.

In spite of the contrasting agendas and institutional bases, the rigidity of the Restoration system in resisting change and the flexibility of their populist discourses often allowed the two groups to combine efforts, either openly or implicitly.[1] The result was a complex dynamic between co-operation and competition that could appear, at crucial moments, as a united political front with a broadly democratic vision of a new Spain. At these moments, the competing languages of polarization and integration were suspended in a powerful if unstable balance that held together as long as both republicans and trade unionists shared a sense of impotent opposition. The culmination of this united front came in April 1931, when the combined strength of republicanism and the labor movement peacefully ousted the old regime in Gijón and proclaimed a Republic, even before the official word arrived from Madrid.

At this point, however, the implicit alliance quickly began to unravel as the competing agendas reasserted themselves. Rifts opened between republicans and anarchosyndicalists over the speed and degree of fundamental reforms, but they also divided the republican camp as well. Could a republican city council in a republican state finally implement a policy of progressive reform that could unite the Gijón of El Llano with that of the Calle Corrida, or should it only fight for the masses who had been marginalized for so long? This dilemma weakened the coherence of the Republic even before the reorganized old regime forces began their counter-attack. When the right demonstrated that it would fight every reform, and the left continued to press for more rapid change, the republicans were increasingly boxed in by the dilemma. By 1936, the republican center had collapsed, as each party had to make its choice to move right or left, to join the forces of order or the workers' republic. Either way, they ceased to be the protagonists of their own regime. Those who refused to make a choice were left suspended in a political no-man's-land. When the rightist coup was thwarted in Gijón in July 1936, the

---

[1] José Alvarez Junco makes the point that the discourse of populism crossed class boundaries and allowed for broader social formations: *El emperador del paralelo: Lerroux y la demagogia populista* (Madrid: Alianza Editorial, 1990), 459.

remaining left republicans were mere junior partners to the labor movement, which set about implementing its own vision of the new order.

The following three chapters examine the evolution of the two versions of formal oppositional politics, as they unfolded in the republicans' municipal policy and the anarchosyndicalists' union-building efforts. Chapter 4 looks at the republican movement under the Restoration, while Chapter 5 focuses on the Republic. Both chapters aim to demonstrate the failure of the republicans' attempts to use municipal reform to effect political integration. Chapter 6 examines the anarchosyndicalists' success in building a powerful labor movement that could challenge republican hegemony. Particularly after 1931, the labor movement's clear rhetoric of polarization held increasing appeal in a society in which the grounds for consensus were shrinking daily.

4

The republican parties and municipal politics, 1900–1930

~

In July of 1910, the anarchist Marcelino Suárez attempted to assassinate the president of the Employers' Association, Domingo Orueta, driven to it, as he testified, by the crimes of the employers and their lackeys. Although he failed, the event provoked the most dramatic political polarization of the city since the 1901 general strike. In response to a hysterical Conservative crusade to establish law and order, crush the trade unions and replace the elected republican city council with a commission of "honorable citizens," a left alliance of the besieged groups solidified. At the heart of the coalition were the republican councilors, now in the majority, who defended the right of workers to organize, protested against the random arrests of union leaders and resisted the attempted coup by the city's financial elite. The contrast between the behavior of the old Conservative governments and the new republican-dominated city council could not have been more dramatic. The power of this left coalition seemed to augur a new era in local politics, with the republicans poised to lead the political assault on the old regime.

As the story demonstrates, the republicans had moved from the margin to the center of local politics in less than a decade. By 1909, when they captured a majority on the city council, the republican movement established itself as the most formidable opposition to the Restoration regime. Nevertheless, they had a difficult time capitalizing on this victory. From 1909 to 1923, when parliamentary politics were suspended, a series of republican city councils struggled to differentiate themselves from the Conservative era, but few concrete results backed them up. Even this limited effort was aborted in 1923, when

118

the Dictatorship replaced the elected city councils with appointed cor-
porations of the old conservative elites. Thus, instead of inaugurating
a new era, the assault of 1910 proved ephemeral. The republicans
could not turn their conquest of city hall into an effective weapon of
political change.

The republicans' failure to make a clear impact through city politics
could be partially explained by the constraints of the national political
system, and this fact kept their project alive over thirty frustrating
years. More importantly, the common enemy helped maintain a
degree of republican hegemony over the political opposition. In
reality, however, the constraints of the existing system were only part
of the problem. The internal divisions that had been a constant feature
of the movement since its inception re-emerged in yet another incarnation, as the new Reformist party competed with the "historical"
republican parties to become the primary voice of the opposition.[1]
This battle often prevented or sabotaged co-operative efforts to
implement reforms of any kind. Even without this hostility, the new
majority was deeply divided and confused about the extent of concrete
reforms it envisioned. Torn between ties to modernizing business
elites and a popular constituency, between liberal individualism and a
communitarian rhetoric, republicans could not fix on a social program
that would demonstrate their commitment to the popular classes
they were trying to attract. The limits of their social vision became
clearer after 1931, but they were also apparent in the actions of the
republican/Reformist city councils of the 1910s.

Thus, both because of the limits of the republican vision and the
constraints of the old regime, the city government did not evolve into
an effective instrument of political or social reform. The consequences
of this inefficacy were serious. On a basic level, the republican movement, broadly speaking, could not stem the tide of social and economic polarization that would make its task so difficult in 1931.

---

[1] The Reformist party was not technically republican, since it proclaimed its indifference
to the form of the regime, so long as it was open to democratization. Nevertheless, the
rigidity of the monarchist regime kept it effectively marginalized from the Restoration
system for most of the period. It also opposed the Dictatorship of Primo de Rivera, and
was an important force in the establishment of the Republic in 1931 (in Asturias). The
Reformists are thus considered part of the broadly conceived republican movement. On
the problems of defining who was a republican, see Demetrio Castro Alfín, "Los republicanos madrileños durante la primera fase de la Restauración," in *La sociedad madrileña
durante la Restauración, 1876–1931*, ed. A. Bahamonde and L. E. Otero (Madrid: Comunidad de Madrid, 1989). He also accepts a broad definition: "those who were hostile
to the system from the left" (p. 42).

Furthermore, it did not reverse the image of political impotence that hung over the movement like a shroud. Partly as a result of both of these consequences, it could not prevent the expansion of a radical labor movement that benefited from both the polarization and the impotence. With this background in place, it is much easier to understand how republican hegemony over the opposition dissipated so rapidly after April of 1931. The stage had already been set for the failed republican project of the 1930s.

City politics under conservative rule, 1901–1909

Before 1909 the story was still a simple one: all the instruments of local political power remained in the hands of the monarchist establishment, which continued to operate according to the rules of traditional elite politics.[2] The only elected body, the city council, was manipulated by the Conservative party machine, which limited the republican opposition to an impotent minority. As one local businessman commented in 1904, "Serious politics has been murdered at the hands of caciquism. There are no struggles. The radical parties, numerous but lacking in organization, are desperate, apathetic, skeptical, and remain marginalized from the electoral process."[3] In this atmosphere, there was little sense of political accountability or concern for public opinion in the actions of the city council. Gijón had not yet entered the era of mass politics.

The other institutions of local authority only magnified the lack of popular accountability, since most of them were subject directly to the central government. The municipal laws of 1877 codified an administrative apparatus that was designed to fit into "a uniform political administrative structure, subordinated and adapted to the exigencies of the centralized activities of the state."[4] Thus, the mayor was appointed by a local body of notables, the Junta Municipal, but the King had the right to veto any local decision. The mayor reported

---

[2] José Alvarez Junco argues that there is a lag between universal suffrage in 1890 and "modern" forms of mass politics which just begin to emerge around the turn of the century with politicians like Alejandro Lerroux. The actions and attitudes of Gijón's Conservative city governments before 1909 typify the old-style elite politics, unconcerned with mobilization and constituency-building: *El emperador del paralelo: Lerroux y la demogogía populista* (Madrid: Alianza Editorial, 1990).

[3] Benito Delbrouck, in *El Noroeste*, August 17, 1904.

[4] Adolfo Posada, *El régimen municipal de la ciudad moderna* (Madrid: Imprenta Clásica Española, 1916), 251.

directly to the Civil Governor, the state's representative in each province. With his ample executive powers, the Governor could overrule the actions of local mayors and city councils, as well as suspend the accords of the provincial assembly and its executive body.

The long arm of Madrid was even more visible in the presence of national military units, whose job was to maintain public order. In small towns, this presence consisted of a Civil Guard post, but in a city the size of Gijón, it included units of the regular army.[5] In normal situations, they reported to the Civil Governor, but during emergencies, military authority supplanted the civil. The guards and army units, almost always imported from other regions, often made the city seem as if it were under occupation. This thick web of institutions, linked by loyalties to Madrid and to the Restoration system, formed a comfortable cocoon in which the Conservative city government could operate with little concern for its constituency. It professed no mission to pursue serious reforms, to deal with the problems in the burgeoning industrial suburbs, or even to actively promote Gijón's economic growth. Its main task, according to an article in the right-wing paper, El Comercio, was the competent management of the always shaky municipal budget.[6] This attitude put the municipal government at odds not only with the working population, who suffered from unemployment, unsanitary neighborhoods, and unenforced labor laws, but also with many businessmen, who wanted a more activist stance on economic and commercial expansion. As one frustrated editorial put it, "Gijón does not have the kind of visionary city council that would provide leadership in this period of growth and development."[7]

Not surprisingly, the Conservative establishment could not maintain its hegemony indefinitely under these conditions. As in cities all over Spain, the pressure of social change and universal suffrage finally eroded the effectiveness of urban cacique machines. Likewise, as in other cities, it was the republicans that provided the first major challenge to the dynastic parties. Thus, from 1903, when a united

---

[5] In 1900, according to the census, the military presence in Gijón included 50 artillery men, 58 riflemen, 63 cavalry soldiers, 88 infantrymen, and several dozen military engineers and officers. In addition, there were four Civil Guard posts with a total of 40 officers. In 1910, there were 120 soldiers, 56 riflemen, and about 60 officers. The number of Civil Guards had more than doubled (96), with new posts in La Calzada, Jove and El Llano. In addition, the census shows that most of these guards came from elsewhere in Spain.

[6] El Comercio, July 11, 1907.

[7] El Noroeste, "We Need a City Government," May 8, 1903.

republican slate captured a number of city councils, republican parties began to make serious inroads in urban political establishments.[8]

In Gijón, the campaign to capture the city council also began in 1903, when republicans ran a full slate of candidates for the first time, and ended in 1909, when the Conservatives permanently lost their majority. The first breakthrough came in 1903 when the aura of republican solidarity negotiated at the national level propelled nine of the fifteen candidates to victory. For the first time, the republicans had broken out of their three "safe" districts and elected at least one representative from all seven electoral districts. Since only half of the city council went up for election each term, the new council still contained a minority of republicans, but the eighteen to twelve ratio represented a dramatic new presence for the opposition.

The tide finally turned in 1909, when national events added urgency to the ongoing campaign to defeat the Conservative forces. In Madrid, the authoritarianism of Prime Minister Antonio Maura and the "Tragic Week" in Barcelona[9] led to a series of complex alliances between liberal, republican and socialist groups which in turn spawned a variety of local coalitions in the May and December municipal elections. For the first time, parliamentary Liberals abandoned their dynastic loyalty and combined forces with some of the more conservative republicans, notably the Asturian politician Melquíades Alvarez, in a "Liberal Alliance." A few months later, the rest of the republican forces signed an agreement with the Socialist party, the Conjunción Republicana – Socialista, for the purpose "not only of defending public liberties during the present regime, but also for the more practi-

---

[8] 1903 was a significant year for the republicans in Spain. After all of the "historical" republican leaders except Salmerón had died, the different groups finally managed to unite into a single republican party in 1903, and this alliance filtered down to the local level. Thus, in the municipal elections of that year, one-sixth of all councilors elected in cities of over 60,000 inhabitants were republican. The union also produced the first dramatic Cortes victories since the First Republic. In the elections of that year, thirty-six republicans won seats, up from nineteen in 1901. The only Restoration election in which this number was surpassed was in 1910, when thirty-seven republicans were elected. Unfortunately for the republicans, the brief unity did not last: Carlos Dardé Morales, "Los republicanos," in *Historia General de España y América*, vol. XVI-2 (Madrid: Ediciones Rialpe, 1981), 150.
[9] A general strike in Barcelona unraveled into anti-clerical violence, which was met by severe government repression. The symbol of this repression was the trial and execution of freethinker Francisco Ferrer, whose ties to the uprising seemed and seem unlikely. For more on the "Tragic Week," see Joan Connelly Ullman, *The Tragic Week: A Study of Anti-Clericalism in Spain, 1875–1912* (Cambridge, MA: Harvard University Press, 1968); Joaquín Romero Maura, *La Rosa de Fuego: El obrerismo barcelonés de 1899 a 1909* (Barcelona: Grijalbo, 1975); Alvarez Junco, *El emperador*, Chapter 9.

cal and positive end of replacing this regime when the possibility arises, either peacefully or through revolution."[10]

In Gijón, the *melquiadistas*[11] enthusiastically pursued the alliance with disenchanted dynastic Liberals, who had never belonged to the local political establishment anyway. This alliance won five seats in the May election and three in December. The Republican – Socialist Conjunción, comprised of the Unión Republicana, the Federalist party and the Agrupación Socialista, fared even better. In May, the Conjunción emerged with seven seats, and in December it added six more. The final count left the Conservatives with nine out of thirty seats on the city council. After over thirty years of uncontested rule, their electoral domination had finally been broken. Nevertheless, the victory was marred by bitterness between the Liberal Alliance and the Conjunción, yet another version of the infighting that had plagued the republican camp since the First Republic.[12] As the reformist opposition took on the challenge of running the city council, it carried this disharmony with it as one of its permanent handicaps.

A new era? Reformist/republican city politics under the monarchy, 1909–1923

The defeat of the Conservatives in 1909 marked the first step in a transformation of the political establishment in the province. The once almighty Conservatives began a process of decline, accentuated by the death of their leader, Pidal, in 1914. By the end of the decade, the party had dissolved into warring factions, in a process that definitively put an end to its image of stability and invincibility. With the Liberal party in Asturias too weak to benefit from this opening, the gap left

---

[10] *El Noroeste*, November 4, 1909: from a Socialist party (PSOE) circular issued by the national committee. This was the first time the PSOE altered its traditional strategy of refusing to ally with bourgeois parties. The local Gijonese branch enthusiastically supported the change of tactics, since isolationism had gotten them nowhere in local politics. The alliance helped bring the first PSOE deputy to the Cortes, when Pablo Iglesias was elected in 1910. For a full account of the formation of the Conjunción Republicana – Socialista, see Manuel Suárez Cortina, *El reformismo en España* (Madrid: Siglo Veintiuno, 1986), 22–58, and Antonio Robes Egea, "La Conjunción Republicana – Socialista" (Ph.D. diss., Complutense University of Madrid, 1987).

[11] In May of 1909, 100 supporters of Melquíades officially constituted a political club to work for the enhancement of their leader's influence. At this point, the word *melquiadista* acquired an institutional meaning. In 1913, they formed the Reformist party: *El Noroeste*, May 13, 1909.

[12] During the electoral period, the fight was carried on in the pages of the *melquiadista El Noroeste* and the republican *El Publicador*.

by the old establishment was increasingly occupied by the new Reformist party of Melquíades Alvarez, officially formed in 1913. Its ranks were filled by "historical" republicans and Liberals who were discouraged by the inefficacy of their old parties. In addition to the weakened Conservatives and the new Reformists, the Republican – Socialist Conjunción managed to survive intact until 1918, more or less consolidating the republican left. Out of these readjustments emerged the three pillars of the post-*turno* era in Gijón: on the right, a broad monarchical coalition, reduced to defensive consolidation; in the middle, the Reformists, fast becoming the new establishment party; and on the left some version of the Republican – Socialist Conjunción.

To complicate this redrawn political spectrum, the Reformists tried to remain opposition leaders at the same time that they were taking over the political establishment. Thus, both the Reformists and the Conjunción competed for the acclamation of working-class Gijón in an ongoing battle that often confused clear categories of "left" and "right." The weakness of the Socialist presence in Gijón and the endemic crisis of "historical" republicanism further benefited the Reformists, who walked a delicate line between populist rhetoric and respectability. The result was a fierce contest to define the political opposition in the city, a contest which, ironically, remained one of the biggest obstacles to reform.

Nevertheless, there were other powerful obstacles. First, it took another decade after 1909 to break the hold of the Conservative party over Gijón's corpus of representatives in the provincial and national parliaments.[13] Furthermore, even a united republican city council would have been encased by the web of unelected institutions loyal to the regime. The role of the mayor, still an appointed position until 1917, was a case in point. Even as a member of the Conservative minority on the city council, the mayor had considerable authority over local affairs. For example, in 1915, the Conservative mayor clashed with the Reformist/republican majority on the city council

---

[13] In the provincial elections, the turning point was 1917, when Reformists won three of the four seats allotted to Gijón's electoral district in the Asturian parliament. In national elections, it was not until 1920 that the Conservatives lost their seat, held by the Conde de Revillagigedo, for the last time. In Asturias as a whole, the dynastic parties held on to a majority of the province's fourteen seats in the Cortes until the 1923 election, and even then the five Conservatives and two Liberals made up half of the delegation. For more details on elections, see Miguel Angel González Muñiz, *Los partidos políticos en Asturias* (Gijón: Centro Gráfico, 1982).

over an instance of alleged police brutality against a fisherman in Cima-davilla. Despite council resolutions and large public rallies, the law and order mayor was able to resist firing the accused officers.[14]

Even the popular election of mayors after 1917 did not change the picture dramatically. In a telling memo to Madrid in 1920, Asturias' Civil Governor admitted that he had to rely almost exclusively on the Civil Guard and other agents of the central government to carry out his orders, since many of the province's mayors were Socialist.[15] In another example of the capacity and willingness to bypass local elected authority, the Civil Governor and the provincial military commander issued a decree in 1918 to confiscate all firearms. To enforce the law, the Civil Guard were empowered to frisk suspicious-looking people on the street and to levy fines for any infractions they uncovered.[16] Thus, the most powerful executive and police functions remained in the hands of authorities imposed by, and loyal to, the government in Madrid. In holding onto these powers, even in the face of electoral defeat, the Restoration demonstrated its rigid refusal to adapt to a changing world.

The limitations that derived from operating within the Restoration regime were serious, but the republicans' own crippling disunity was perhaps their biggest handicap. Disunity was certainly nothing new, as the factions had been mud-slinging for decades. But this battle was waged from within the local seat of power, not on its margins. The bitter and often petty disputes now took place not in obscure republi-can clubs but in the broad daylight of city hall. Ironically, the higher stakes intensified rather than softened the viciousness of the exchanges, thus further undermining the entire movement.

The character as well as the locus of the feuds was changing, too. Throughout Spain, a younger generation of republican activists chal-lenged the viability of the "historical" parties to lead the movement into the future.[17] Men like Melquíades Alvarez and Alejandro Lerroux formed new organizations, more attuned to mass mobilization and party-building than the old groups, and more flexible in their

[14] The story unfolds over several months, with important installments in *El Noroeste* on January 5, February 2, 4, 20, 25, 26, March 24, 26, 28, 30, April 8, September 21, 1915.
[15] September 8, 1920: AHN, Serie, Gobernación, 58A, núm.4.
[16] Telegrams, December 20, 1918 and July 18, 1923, and press release, 1921, undated: AHN, Serie, Gobernación, Legajo 3A, núm.1 and 2 and Legajo 58A, núm.16.
[17] For a brilliant analysis of this important transition in republican politics, see Alvarez Junco, *El emperador*.

strategies for getting power.[18] At the national level, these new forces clearly contributed to a marked decline of the "historical" parties, which never reasserted hegemony over the republican movement.[19] In Gijón, the rise of Melquíades paralleled the erosion of the Union and Federalist parties, both in terms of electoral support and institutional cohesion. By the end of the decade, these parties had virtually disintegrated. Nevertheless, the republicans still had enough strength to sabotage and undermine Reformist leadership. The result was an especially noisy and well-armed version of republican divisiveness, in which each side claimed to occupy the political left and personify the true voice of the people.

The philosophical crux of the division between the two groups was Melquíades' willingness to compromise formal republican principles to pursue what he claimed were the larger goals of democratization. In fact, before he formally declared this tactical flexibility, "historical" republicans and *melquiadistas* formed a brief alliance in 1910 (the latter joined the Conjunción) that achieved the impressive victory of electing Melquíades as the first non-monarchist Cortes representative from Asturias. When he won, people danced in the streets in a premature celebration of the death of the Conservative machine. The harmony between the two camps lasted through the next year, when Melquíades distinguished himself in the Cortes as a vocal defender of republican values, calling for an end to the war in Morocco and a re-opening of the Ferrer treason case. In the local *El Porvenir*, mouthpiece of the Conjunción, an editorial praised him in effusive terms,

---

[18] This transition was aided by the deaths of all of the old leaders: Castelar and Pi y Margall at the turn of the century, Salmerón in 1908, and the post-Zorilla leader of the Progressive party, Esquerdo, in 1912. On Lerroux's activities in Catalonia during these years, see Joan B.Culla i Clarà, *El republicanisme lerrouxista a Catalunya (1901–1923)* (Barcelona: Curial, 1986). On Melquíades Alvarez, see Maximiano García Venero, *Melquíades Alvarez: historia de un liberal* (Madrid: Ediciones Tebas, 1975).
   A third new force was *blasquismo*, which emerged out of a split in the Valencian Federalist party. Led by novelist Blasco Ibáñez, the local organization shared many of the populist characteristics of Lerroux's Radical party in Catalonia but never gained national stature. See the excellent studies by Ramir Reig Armero, *Obrers i ciutadans. Blasquisme i moviment obrer: Valencia, 1898–1910* (Valencia: Institució Alfons el Magnánim, 1982) and *Blasquistas y clericales. La lucha por la ciudad de Valencia* (Valencia: Institució Alfons el Magnánim, 1986).

[19] Between 1910 and 1914, the "historical" parties dropped from thirty-seven seats to sixteen in the Cortes; until 1923 they hovered around this number. On the crisis of "historical" republicanism during the second decade, see the contemporary account by Alvaro de Albornoz, *El partido republicano* (Madrid: Biblioteca Nueva, 1918). (In 1929, Albornoz formed the Radical Socialist party.) See also Manuel Suárez Cortina, "La quiebra del republicanismo histórico, 1898–1931," in *El republicanismo en España, 1830–1977*, ed. Nigel Townson (Madrid: Alianza Editorial, 1994).

calling him the "sublime inspiration for regional Asturian politics."[20] Some republicans, at least, seemed to have decided that Melquíades could reinvigorate their movement without threatening its identity.

The cracks in the alliance began when, without consulting his Conjunción allies, he announced in 1912 his intention to form a new, moderate republican party. Clearly he envisioned that the Reformist party would implement the democratization that the Liberals had failed to, and thus steer the country between the Scylla of social revolution and the Charybdis of a military coup.[21] While his Conjunción comrades grudgingly accepted the new party, they could not accept the bombshell that Melquíades dropped a year later. On June 3, 1913, he declared in a speech before the Cortes that he was willing to work with the monarch to save the country:[22]

> There are some republicans who will not co-operate with the monarchy, but there is another large group that thinks as I do – that under certain conditions it would be acceptable to participate in the monarchy, that the form of government itself is transitory and unimportant. We want a monarchy that does not usurp the people's power, that is open to all ideas, however radical they are. If such a monarchy existed, we could then seriously think of accepting a monarchical regime; but it would be because the regime had moved closer to where we stood.[23]

Melquíades tried to convince his republican allies that nothing had changed, but within days, the Reformists had been expelled from the Conjunción.

In Gijón, "historical" republicans and Socialists reacted equally swiftly and uncompromisingly to what they viewed as betrayal, with a vicious campaign against their former allies that set the tone for republican/Reformist interaction throughout the rest of the decade. On the 1913–1915 city council, republicans followed a policy of pure revenge. By boycotting important votes, the seven republicans could

---

[20] January 1, 1912. See Chapter 9, note 42, for the Ferrer treason case.

[21] The ex-republican Prime Minister Canalejas, brought in after the "Tragic Week" fiasco had ousted Maura, began with calls to reform and democratize the monarchy, but caved in to the pressure of conservative forces, especially the military. For a more detailed look at the national political context of the formation of the Reformist party, see Suárez Cortina, *El reformismo*, Chapter 2.

[22] Canalejas' assassination in November 1912 left the Liberals confused and leaderless, while the Conservatives could offer only Maura, who was both unpopular and rejected by the King. In this context, Alfonso XIII made vague overtures to Melquíades that made him think there was a chance of being appointed to head a liberal/Reformist government, purged of Conservatives.

[23] *El Noroeste*, June 4, 1913.

deny the majority to the ten Reformists, who still faced thirteen monarchists. Despite Reformist pleas – "the Right is calling the shots, and all of our past effort is being wasted, as we hand over the city government to those with the same ideas of fifteen years ago" – the republicans maintained their policy of non-co-operation.[24] In 1915, even though the republicans retained only four seats on the council, the Reformists' thirteen seats still made a coalition government essential.

The low point for the "historical" republicans came in 1917, when their animosity for Melquíades kept them out of the Democratic Coalition that took a leading role in the tumultuous events of that year. As the *turno* system furiously plugged new leaks, using extraparliamentary measures and increased repression to shore up its walls, political and social tensions threatened to topple the entire fortress. Melquíades' support for striking workers and democratization helped coalesce a local electoral coalition in December 1917 that included Socialists, some dissident republicans, and even a group of anarchosyndicalists, who made their political debut.[25] The "historical" republicans watched impotently as the Reformists rode the crest of the populist wave that seemed to vault them into undisputed hegemony over the opposition.

This left alliance never solidified, however. As the Conservatives dwindled to an ever more insignificant minority, the Reformists took on more of the characteristics of an establishment party than an opposition party. Despite their rhetorical claims to the political left, by the end of the decade they were culling many of their votes from old monarchist neighborhoods. Thus, in the last parliamentary elections of 1923, the Reformist candidate Orueta won easily in Carreño and Llanera, in most of Gijón's rural districts and in the wealthy downtown areas. His Federalist opponent Barriobero took the working-class areas of Tremañes, El Llano, Cima and other urban neighborhoods. To combat this kind of evidence of their transformation, the Reformists pursued an elaborate theory of republican/monarchist con-

[24] This plea is found in one of the letters from the Reformist party to the Socialist and Federalist parties, that provide evidence for this conflict. To the Federalists: November 22, 1913, and then December 4, with the comment that they had received no response to the first letter. To the PSOE: December 14, 1913: AGS, H-29.

[25] The Parliamentary Syndicalists, as they called themselves, were led by Laureano Piñera and Ramón Martínez, members of the CNT federation. In a letter to the editor, Piñera insisted that most syndicalists voted anyway, despite the official prohibitions, and that they might as well formalize this situation with a party dedicated to their interests: *El Noroeste*, October 29, 1917. Apparently most syndicalists were not convinced by this argument, since the party never took off in Gijón.

spiracy: "Today historical republicanism lost the last sparks of life that it had managed to recover as a result of its promises to renovate and become more up to date; the republican/conservative/*maurista*/ integrist alliance absorbed the republican movement into a sacrilegious irony."[26]

Despite these attacks, in local elections the tide began to turn again in favor of the traditional republican parties. In the last municipal elections, in 1922, the republicans won eight seats, compared to four for the Reformists and three for the Conservatives.[27] Whereas in 1917 the Reformists were poised to claim uncontested leadership over the political left, by 1923 they were back in the trenches, fighting for the ground they thought they had won. The coup of October 1923 cut short this new phase in the ongoing battle. By the time all the parties emerged from the other end of the dictatorship, the battlefield had been transformed almost beyond recognition. But even with the installation of the long-desired regime in 1931, the war continued in yet another incarnation. Though so much else in the political landscape had changed, republican divisiveness remained a familiar constant.

During the 1910s, this divisiveness was one of the many obstacles that prevented republicans from solidifying a unified oppositional bloc against the elite establishment. In fact, the obstacles loomed so large that they overwhelmed the small space in which the republican/ Reformist movement could elaborate its vision of reform. It claimed to be oppositional, but what exactly was it opposed to? To make the exegetical process more difficult, the distraction provided by personal attacks and brutal policemen encouraged the recourse to vague rhetorical gestures instead of substantive programs, especially in the area of social reform. The result was an extremely general reform program that rarely focused on specific economic or social problems. This lack of specificity further weakened the potential of the republican administrations to show results. In the end, republicans relied, as they had since the beginning of the Restoration, on political and juridical battles that illuminated the illiberal nature of the old regime. Focusing on the common enemy was a much easier way to build popular

---

[26] *El Noroeste*, May 12, 1923.

[27] The new council comprised thirteen republicans, eleven Reformists, five Conservatives and one Socialist – the first time since 1909 that the republicans had the largest contingent. The obvious failure of the Reformists' collaborative strategy at the national level may have contributed to this decline. They had never managed to win more than a dozen seats in the Cortes, and had not been able to displace the Liberal party as a real governing alternative.

support than trying to hash out the details of a major social reform program.

In elections, republicans stuck to vague platitudes, often focused on the change of regime as the elixir to cure all ills: "The Republic will bring us the peace that we hard-working people desire . . . it will assure the reign of justice and liberty; it is the incarnation of democracy, and democracy is the incarnation of progress."[28] As José Alvarez Junco has noted, the republicans tended to eschew programmatic definition and rely on the more powerful if less specific manifesto:[29]

> Republican Fusion does not need a program. What more do we need to say, other than that democracy is a complete system, with its economic, political and social content? . . . Democracy implies the defense of public liberties, the demand that health and safety laws be enforced, scrutiny of the administration to root out corruption, the subordination of private interests to the general interests of the municipality.[30]

When specifics emerged, they usually corresponded to the demands of the modernizing business elites to enhance Gijón's competitive advantage in industry and tourism. A representative statement of such a program, issued for the 1905 elections, included:

1) the completion of the rail and highway network connecting Gijón to other important centers
2) the dismantling of the city wall
3) completion of the wall lining the beach front
4) a long-term sanitation campaign
5) better organization of public security
6) stimulation of tourism
7) removal of obstacles to the establishment of philanthropic foundations.

Only the Federal Republicans explicitly supported measures targeting workers' welfare, such as the eight-hour day for municipal workers and the abolition of the consumption taxes. But even these measures seem paltry next to the Socialist municipal platform, which proposed the abolition of all indirect taxes, free lunches, shoes, and coats for

---

[28] From a speech by Palacios Morini of the Juventud Republicana: *Unión Republicana*, February 7, 1897.
[29] *El emperador*, 434–439.
[30] From a 1901 election manifesto: *El Noroeste*, November 10, 1901.

working-class school children, child day-care centers for working mothers, and shelters for the homeless.[31]

In practice, too, both republican and Reformist councilors shared a classically liberal approach to government. Thus, they defended an uncompromising and expansive view of the sanctity of private property, and were reluctant to support the government's interference in private affairs. With such a hands-off attitude, the city's handling of such chronic problems as unemployment, housing shortages, poverty and public health did not undergo drastic revisions after 1909. Concern for these problems was channeled into the formation of advisory bodies that issued poignant reports but could not implement changes. Thus, for example, during the inflationary and speculative wartime years, the city formed a Subsistence Committee but it could not regulate prices or distribution of essential goods. Likewise, in response to the growing housing shortage, a Committee on Inexpensive Housing drew up an impressive list of the problems and inequities in the local housing market, but it had to rely on the voluntary co-operation of builders and landlords to find solutions. Similarly, the city council could do nothing to unblock the paralysis of the local Institute of Social Reform board, which continued to depend on the goodwill of both employers and workers. The left-wing city councilmen often complained about the lack of co-operation from financial elites, but they were unwilling to violate their shared respect for private property and coerce them.

The powerful position of the financial elites is particularly clear in the city's tax structure. With the significant exception of the abolition of the *consumo* taxes on basic food items in 1911 (due more to public protest than governmental initiative), there was no effort to introduce a more progressive tax base. The city continued to rely heavily on indirect taxes on services, alcohol and other goods, while property and commercial taxes formed a minuscule portion of city income. After the war, the city even instituted a head tax, which, though leveled proportionally, fell heaviest on the poorest workers.[32] The progressive city council was caught between a rock and a hard place. It was squeezed by a centralized system that limited its range of motion and

---

[31] *Aurora Social*, October 30, 1903.
[32] This tax information was synthesized from the city's annual budget reports, the *Presupuestos Ordinarios* (Archivo Municipal de Gijón).

its financial base, and it was resisted by a business community whose values it partly shared.

Socially and economically, most of the republican leaders came from business and professional backgrounds. The Federalists tended to include more members from the liberal professions and smaller business owners, while the Reformists attracted a few more industrialists and landlords, but the overall differences were not dramatic. Of some of the more notable local Federalist politicians, Eduardo Arizaga was a medical doctor, Eleuterio Alonso owned a glass and bottle factory, Gervasio de Riera managed a lumber and coal business, Perales owned a bakery and Balbín a printing press. The popular Benito Conde ran a private school. The only "worker" ever included on Federalist electoral slates was Fernando Suárez Acebal, who was actually an engineer. Unionist Republicans followed a similar mold. Enrique Guisasola and José de la Torre were professors at the Instituto Jovellanos. Ramón Alvarez García was a lawyer and one-time director of *El Noroeste*. In the April 1909 election, the unified republican ticket ran three landlords, one industrialist, one farmer, a lawyer and a professor.

In the same election, the *melquiadistas* offered six landlords, three industrialists, a lawyer and a farmer. The influx of many ex-Liberals after 1912 increased the elite composition of the party leadership. Thus, several of the city's biggest capitalist employers, like the Felgueroso brothers, or Donato Argüelles, a landlord and businessman who had made his fortune in America, followed this transition.[33] Nevertheless, the Reformists maintained representation from other social levels as well. In the 1915 elections, they ran two industrialists, a businessman, a professor, a rentier, a farmer, a journalist, an electrician and a clerk.

The relationship between class and political orientation is always a complex issue, but some conclusions can be drawn. It is clear that in Gijón, as in Spain at large, the lack of elite consensus fractured the political spectrum and weakened the stability of the system.[34] While

---

[33] *El Noroeste*, although admittedly a biased source, noted in 1915 (November 13) that most of the property owners who were members of the Chamber of Real Estate were followers of Melquíades.

[34] Carlos Serrano argues that the crisis that opened up in 1898 was rooted fundamentally in the elites' loss of their ability to lead civil society and organize consensus – i.e., in their declining hegemony. See "¿1900?" in *1900 en España*, ed. Carlos Serrano and Serge Salaün (Madrid: Espasa Calpe, 1991), 16. Manuel Tuñón de Lara speaks more specifically about the absence of ideological cohesion in the ruling class, as evidenced specifically by the generations of 1898 and 1914: "La Guerra Civil Española, medio siglo después,"

the fractures had existed since the beginning of the liberal revolution in the late eighteenth century, the decline of Restoration stability in the early twentieth century exacerbated the intra-elite crisis. In this sense, republicanism and Reformism in Gijón represented segments of that fractured elite who participated in the struggle to define a successful hegemonic strategy. They saw the clear failure of the dynastic parties and the Restoration system to incorporate new political and social groups into the body politic. Under the threat of social revolution or anarchy, republicans and Reformists tried to find a path that sustained some form of elite leadership over the masses, but based on voluntary support rather than repression. Their attempt to walk this fine line led them on a complex and often confused course that defies easy categorization.

Before 1931, the success of their strategy depended on their leadership of a broad political coalition against the Conservative establishment. Since they were ambivalent about using social reforms to achieve this front, they used the ammunition provided them by a repressive state and a generally intransigent corps of capitalist leaders. In this context, the republicans offered juridical and political protection but not economic. When it worked, this tactic was a powerful weapon, as the events around the assassination attempt described at the beginning of this chapter illustrate. The attempt occurred in 1910 in the context of a bitter strike in which the power and scope of the trade union movement was at stake. For the conservative community the act of violence was the final proof that the unions needed to be crushed. Furthermore, it demonstrated to them how far the city had fallen since the onset of the republican era. Thus, *El Comercio* blamed the event on the "moral collaboration" of all leftist forces: the city government for not providing protection, the republican press for always taking the workers' side, and the unions for putting the perpetrator Marcelino up to it.[35] At an employers' meeting several days after the attempt, the one hundred participants drew up a list of demands that included guns for all employers and strike-breakers, increased public security and more Civil Guards. The Civil Governor supported the employers by ordering the arrest of strike leaders and the closure of the union centers. By implication, the city council was at best incompetent and at worst an accessory.

in *La Guerra Civil Española: 50 años después*, ed. Tuñón de Lara (Barcelona: Editorial Labor, 1985), 13.
[35] June 25, 1910.

The hysteria on the part of the business community reached new heights when a second assassination attempt proved more successful than the first. The victim was Casimiro Lantero, another employer involved in the lock-out/strike. This time the employers offered a reward for the killer and demanded the use of public funds to build a monument intended "as a permanent protest by the honorable people of Gijón against the band of Anarchists and assassins who dominate it."[36] Further, it circulated a petition that gathered 1,000 signatures asking for the resignation of the city council. In its place, the petition demanded a council comprised of members nominated by the Chambers of Commerce and Real Estate, the Employers' Association (Agremiación Patronal – AP) and the Merchants' Association.[37] Clearly, the business elite hoped to use the assassination as a route to recoup their lost political power.

The extremism of the AP, the threat to political liberties, the arrest of strike leaders who had committed no specific crime: all of these factors combined to make the event an ideal platform for republicans to assert their oppositional leadership. On this level of conflict, they could pull out all the stops in the defense of civil and political rights. Republicans focused their counter-attack on the wholesale arrest of union and anarchist leaders, who were not only detained, but beaten. The image of respected anarchist leader Eleuterio Quintanilla displaying his bruises at a public rally was enough in itself to bring half the city to its feet. Republicans spoke at this rally and others, calling for all the incarcerated union leaders to be freed immediately.[38] Some went further and laid partial blame for the killing on the employers' intransigence and strike-breaking activities.[39] The larger message, though, was that the fate of the unions, the prisoners and the republican city council were all fundamentally linked. As Ramón Alvarez García put it, "It is clear that the employers are identifying with the Conservatives, and co-operating with them in an effort to conquer local political power, now in the hands of the radicals."[40]

---

[36] Ramón Alvarez Palomo, *Eleuterio Quintanilla* (Mexico: Editores Mexicanos Unidos, 1973), 60.

[37] *El Noroeste*, August 27, 1910.

[38] This particular rally, in August 1911, attracted over 6,000 people, according to *Acción Libertaria*, August 28, 1911.

[39] None of them went as far as the anarchist newspaper that argued that assassination was an "occupational hazard: to be an employer, especially a despotic and cunning one, operating against all reason and logic . . . has its inconveniences": *Solidaridad Obrera*, September 16, 1910.

[40] *El Noroeste*, July 3, 1910.

The anarchists seemed to accept this analysis, as they openly defended both individual councilmen[41] and the institution of the republican city council. When the conservatives used the occasion of Lantero's funeral to march on the city hall, anarchists were among the large crowd of people there to greet them, waving republican and trade union flags, and shouting "¡Viva!" to the city council. In turn, and true to their commitment to judicial protection, republicans followed through on their defense of prisoners. In the trial of the dozen or so defendants who were charged with complicity, the Federalist lawyer Barriobero took on all their cases *pro bono*. His eloquence and the lack of evidence in all but the case of Marcelino resulted in acquittals for nearly everyone. Marcelino, the only man to admit to the crime, was given a mere three years, instead of the life imprisonment requested by the prosecutor.[42] After this successful defense of the city's political liberties, the tension subsided and the broad left coalition dissolved until the next moment of crisis.

Placed at the end of this chapter rather than the beginning, we can see the assassination and its aftermath in its proper context. Instead of symbolizing the opening up of a new institutional politics of reform, the parameters of the campaign represented its limits. This was the small space in which republicans could define an oppositional politics that produced results. With their limited vision of social reform, they relied heavily on the defense of judicial and political rights to mobilize a popular following. In this sense, the repressiveness of the Restoration regime worked to their advantage, as they could close ranks against the arrests of political prisoners, the imposition of press censorship and the arbitrary closure of union centers.[43]

In the face of an uncompromisingly hostile Conservative coalition, these moments polarized the city dramatically and pushed the republicans out in front of a broad popular movement. While this was exhilarating while it lasted, it was also dangerous. The political polarization that the republicans encouraged in the 1910s was not so easily

---

[41] For example, on December 24, 1911, *Solidaridad Obrera* attacked the conservatives' attempts to implicate republican councilmen Conde, Acero and Eleuterio Alonso in the assassination of Lantero.

[42] *El Libertario*, September 7, 1912.

[43] Their other major avenue of mobilization, anti-clericalism, will be fully explored in Chapter 7. It has not been included here because its impact on institutional politics before the 1930s was limited. The republican city councils awarded subventions to the few non-religious schools in the city and reduced the official presence of the government at religious ceremonies, but the main thrust of their anti-clerical campaign before the Republic was carried on in the broader cultural and symbolic domain.

reversed in the 1930s, when they tried to bring the two worlds together. Moreover, while their *causes célèbres* were popular, they did nothing to promote a sense of confidence in the republicans' broader political leadership or in the efficacy of the political institutions themselves. In 1931, when the republicans desperately needed that confidence, they had to start from scratch. In fact, their main political capital at that point was the proven failure of the *turno* system and of the Dictatorship that had lasted a mere six years.

Interlude: the Dictatorship, 1923–1930

By 1923, the vices of the parliamentary system in Spain were apparent to almost everyone. The bi-party rotation between Liberals and Conservatives had collapsed into a frenzied scramble to form unworkable governments. Despite this crisis in the *turno* system, the regime refused to allow even moderate opposition parties like the Reformists into the inner sanctum. In addition to the Reformists, there were a plethora of new political forces organized in trade unions or republican, socialist and regional nationalist parties, all of whom were denied access to real power within the parliamentary monarchy. As a result, by 1923 few political forces were invested in maintaining the system. As had happened in 1898, however, it took a major military defeat to bring home its weakness to the public. When the Spanish army was thoroughly routed at Annual in Morocco in July 1921, the national outcry and call for *responsibilidades*, or somewhere to fix the blame, contributed to the atmosphere in which Primo de Rivera suspended Parliament and installed himself as a temporary dictator.[44]

In addition to his desire to protect the army, Primo de Rivera harbored a grand, if vague, mission to save the country from its deepening crisis. Primo shared the conviction of other reformers that if Spain could be rid of the corrupt administrators and *caciques* that strangled her, then the Spanish people themselves would produce real and honest leaders. Thus, the new regime was yet another attempt to "regenerate" a sluggish and demoralized nation. The discontent with the existing system was so great that many people, with a broad range

---

[44] On the Moroccan disaster, see Raymond Carr, *Spain, 1808–1939* (Oxford: Oxford University Press, 1975), 516–523. On Primo's regime, see Schlomo Ben-Ami, *Fascism from Above: The Dictatorship of Primo de Rivera in Spain, 1923–1930* (Oxford: Oxford University Press, 1983).

of political views, were willing to let him try.[45] The fact that this attempt at regeneration also failed finally opened the way for the republicans to have their chance.

In the meantime, the republicans and Reformists were pushed back to the margin of local politics. Despite Primo's intention to open the way for a new political class, his ambitious project of municipal reform was never implemented.[46] Thus, the temporary measure of appointed city councils, instituted in 1923, turned into a permanent condition of the regime. In Gijón, at least, this resulted in a return to the old monarchist establishment.[47] The Civil Governor chose the councilors from a list of major tax payers, which contained the "same established families" of which local historians Canella y Secades and Bellmunt y Traves had spoken in 1895.[48] The administrations of these years demonstrated their conservative affiliation in a variety of ways, but the tone of the era is best summed up by one particular event. When the aristocratic Revillagigedo family inaugurated a vocational charity school to be run by Jesuits, the public ceremony harked back to the years before republican city councils. The Infante Don Jaime presided over a procession that marched from the Revillagigedo palace to the Centro Católico and then to the city hall, where the city council and local dignitaries eulogized the dead Conde de Revillagigedo, and the Infante unveiled a portrait of the formidable leader of the Conservative party in Gijón.[49] The composition of the power bloc under the Dictatorship could not have been more clearly laid out.

It did not take long for republicans and Reformists to realize that there was no place for them in this setting, and they soon became implacable enemies of the regime. Nevertheless, they were in no position to launch an attack. The irony of the hated Dictatorship was that

[45] In Asturias, the only outright condemnations came from a few republicans and the anarchists. Monarchists and Catholics embraced it, the Reformist *El Noroeste* accepted it with "relative conformity" (October 3, 1923), and the Federalist party opted for a wait-and-see attitude: "we accept that there should be a revolution, since it is a national necessity, and the fact that there is a moralizing tendency among its authors causes us much satisfaction" (Juntas, Partido Federal, September 17, 1923: AGS, K-6).

[46] See Javier Tusell Gómez, *La Reforma de la administración local en España (1900–1936)* (Madrid: Instituto Nacional de Administración Pública, 1987), 177–183, for an analysis of the municipal reform project drawn up by his minister Calvo Sotelo.

[47] Raymond Carr makes the more general argument that Primo failed to see that the old political class was the only group of men capable of running the new Spain: *Spain: 1808–1939*, 576.

[48] See Chapter 1, note 31.

[49] *El Noroeste*, September 19, 1929.

it gave them a much-needed respite, in which they could concentrate all their energies on internal reorganization. When a reconstructed republican movement emerged from the other end of the Dictatorship, enough time had passed to dim the memories of the feuds and the impotence of the past. In 1930–1931, when the country was floundering in the wake of Primo's resignation, the republicans were ready with a new face and a long pedigree. The impressive electoral coalition of April 1931 was the culmination of this process.[50]

The road to this coalition was long and arduous, however. Before it could happen, Reformists and republicans first had to pass through their own internal crises and then overcome the deeply felt hostility that divided them. Perhaps the most dramatic crisis was sustained by the Reformist party, as its leader drifted ever further from the radical rhetoric of 1917. Melquíades abandoned his characteristic "indifference" to the form of regime and actively embraced the monarchy, to the chagrin of many of his followers.[51] In the years that followed, most of the party's important intellectuals, like Manuel Azaña and Pérez de Ayala, left to form or join new republican parties. Drained of its reforming impulse, as well as many of its members, the Reformist party ceased to play a national role and receded into its Asturian bastion.[52] There, his support was based more on personal loyalty than on policies. When the Dictatorship collapsed in 1929, Melquíades held firm in his new monarchism, and refused to participate in the Pact of San Sebastián in August 1930, where all the major republican groups agreed to work collectively towards a Republic. When he finally accepted the Republic, it was too late for him to play any leadership role in the new regime.[53]

In Gijón, however, the story is somewhat more complicated. From the available evidence, it appears that local Reformists did not follow Melquíades' lead. In September 1930, when CNT leader Quintanilla suggested a joint manifesto from all the anti-monarchist forces, it was

---

[50] After Primo's resignation in January 1930, a transitional regime fumbled for over a year before it attempted to hold elections under the 1876 Constitution. In early 1931, the government offered to hold municipal elections as a prelude to elections for a Constitutional Cortes, but everyone treated these elections as a plebiscite for the monarchy.

[51] In a strange demonstration of loyalty, Melquíades, in contrast to the vast majority of Spaniards, maintained that the King was not implicated in Primo's coup.

[52] For more details of this evolution, see Suárez Cortina, *El reformismo*, 280–293.

[53] Reformist journalist Antonio Oliveros called Melquíades' fall "political suicide," and expressed his desire that the party should have disbanded in 1930 instead of experiencing the humiliating eclipse that it did in the 1931 elections: *Asturias en el resurgimiento español* (Madrid: Juan Bravo, 1935; reprint, Gijón: Silverio Cañada, 1982), 86.

the Federalists, not the Reformists, who refused to participate. Likewise, in February, 1931, the Reformists initiated the campaign for a "left" coalition in the April elections. Their candidates on the unified slate called themselves "Reformistas Republicanas," apparently acknowledging their independence from the course set by their leader. According to local Reformist leader Antonio Oliveros, Melquíades strongly disapproved of the coalition forged in Gijón: "this union with Republicans and Socialists that you have made here is a crazy idea."[54] Crazy or not, this coalition undoubtedly prevented the local eclipse of Reformism.[55] As the new political spectrum sorted itself out in the first few months, the local Reformist party carved out a strong niche for itself on the conservative side of the republican forces.

The evolution of the other republican forces was, if possible, even more complicated. With the exception of the Federalists, the "historical" parties were extinguished, as republicans tried to create new vehicles less contaminated by decades of marginalization and weakness. In 1926, republican leaders in Madrid formed an organization called Alianza Republicana, for the purpose of uniting all republicans and forming a minimum program to propel them forward.[56] For three years, the Alianza managed to hold together a diverse grouping that ranged from the socialist-leaning contingent under Alvaro de Albornoz to Lerroux's Radicals. Gijonese republicans greeted the Alianza with enthusiasm and optimism: "Republican in-fighting is no longer an important factor. In fact, it is almost non-existent. Instead, republican ideas have conquered . . . the collective conscience. If the Republic should be re-established, we can affirm that there would be national consistency as to its characters."[57]

Unfortunately, they spoke too soon. During 1929–1930, the Alianza suffered a series of amputations that destroyed its original intent. On the left, the followers of Albornoz withdrew to form the Radical

---

[54] Quoted in Diego Mateo del Peral, et al., Historia de Asturias, vols. VIII and IX, Edad contemporánea I (Vitoria: Ayalga Ediciones, 1977), 222.

[55] The only two cities where the Reformists did well were Gijón and Avilés, where they formed part of electoral coalitions.

[56] The pact was signed by Manuel Azaña for Acción Republicana (formed in 1925), Hilario Ayuso for the Partido Republicano Federal, Marcelino Domingo for the Partido Republicano Catalán and Lerroux for the Partido Radical: Dardé Morales, "Los republicanos," 155. For more on the origins of Acción Republicana, see Eduardo Espín, Azaña en el poder: el partido de Acción Republicana (Madrid: Centro de Investigaciones Sociológicas, 1980), Chapter 1.

[57] El Noroeste, February 11, 1927. Local republicans took the opportunity of the annual celebration of the First Republic to publicize and gather support for the new organization.

Socialist party, headed in Gijón by the medical doctor Carlos Martínez. On the right, a prestigious group of intellectuals, among them
the Asturian novelist Pérez de Ayala, created the Agrupación al Servicio de la República. And, in the late summer of 1929, the Federalists
deserted, amid complaints that the Alianza had done nothing to
hasten the arrival of the Republic.[58]

Thus, when the Dictatorship fell in January 1930, the republicans
had to scramble to assemble a united front. In Gijón, the minutes of
the local Federalist party meetings, from late 1930 until the April
1931 elections, attest to the difficulty of this process. Personal and
political rivalries, both newly created and of long standing, hindered
the discussions. Of more recent origin was the grudge that the Federalists held against Alianza Republicana, which had absorbed some of its
prominent members.[59] More entrenched was the animosity between
Federalists and Reformists, which spanned almost two decades of
mutual recriminations. When the Reformists first suggested an electoral alliance, a stormy debate ensued in the ranks of the Federalist
party. Significantly, it was the older generation who objected most
strongly to collaborating with their old enemies. The younger generation who came of age during the Dictatorship had no such personal
resentments. Moreover, they equated the Reformists' consistent opposition to the Dictatorship with a leftist stance: one young member
insisted that the Reformist party had become "workerist and republican."[60] After many such meetings, the broad electoral coalition was
concluded, with the inclusion of all republican parties, the Reformists
and the Socialists.[61] Even the CNT gave its tacit support through the
voice of Quintanilla.[62]

---

[58] Juntas, Partido Federal, September 3, 1929 (AGS, K-6). In addition, the local branch
agreed that it was contrary to Federalist principles to engage in permanent coalitions
with any group not committed to the installation of a Federal Republic.

[59] The dispute was complicated, but two Federalists and ex-city councilors, López Fombona
and Federico Fernández, resigned in March 1930 over a dispute with the party leadership.
Soon after, they joined the Alianza Republicana: Asambleas del Partido Federal, February
23 and 30, March 21 and 23, 1930 (AGS, K-5).

[60] Asambleas del Partido Federal, March 13, 1931 (AGS, K-5).

[61] The final distribution of seats agreed upon was: eleven Federalists, twelve Reformists,
three Socialists, one for the Agrupación al Servicio de la República, and two each for
Alianza Republicana and Derecha Liberal (a conservative republican party founded by
Miguel Maura and Alcalá Zamora, future president of the Republic). The Radical Socialists decided to abstain, in the belief that fundamental changes should precede a popular
election: Actas, Partido Federal, April 1, 1931 (AGS, K-6).

[62] Quintanilla's personal role in the transition is remarkable, given his affiliation. As the
republicans squabbled, he played the role of detached elder statesman, co-ordinating
meetings and insisting on the necessity for unity. In an oft-quoted letter from Quintanilla

The effort expended by republican groups to present a united front was matched by that of the old monarchist parties, who also managed to combine their forces. No matter how casually Madrid wanted to treat this election, on the local level it was taken as a broad plebiscite on the future of the regime and the country. *El Noroeste* spoke openly of a battle between the "two Spains": the election was not a "petty fight between parties, but a fight to the death between a pharaonic Spain, with its miseries, corruptions and infamies, and the Spain that desires to join the currents of contemporary thought."[63] In the classic language of the regenerationists, the republicans would finally usher Spain into the modern world.

On April 12, 1931, an impressive majority of voters affirmed their support for the new Spain. The victory of the republican coalition was unequivocal, with all thirty candidates on the slate winning seats.[64] It seemed as if the moment had finally arrived for the republicans. Unified, backed by popular support, with the reigns of power in their hands, many of the obstacles that had constrained them for decades were apparently gone. Unfortunately, however, most of the old obstacles were only submerged, ready to rear their ugly heads once the celebrations were over. Despite the achievement of their most cherished goal, the republicans had as much trouble as ever in legitimizing and asserting their political leadership. Their failure to do so contributed to the descent into civil war barely five years after they were dancing in the streets.

to Oliveros, he promised that "the Gijonese syndicalists, who represent the majority of voters, are going to make this one time an exception to our apolitical ideals and will vote as one man for the Republic. Thus, any liberal or republican party that does not enter the Alliance will be soundly defeated." (Quoted in Ramón Alvarez Palomo, "Avelino González Entrialgo," *Ruta*, 36 (1978), 12.) Quintanilla also supported this position in the national CNT: "The CNT must proclaim its circumstantial solidarity with all the political and social forces who agree on the concrete point of demanding the convocation of a Constituent Assembly that would liquidate the past and open a channel for the currents of modern thought." (Letter to CNT Pleno, printed in *El Noroeste*, February 27, 1930.)

63 *El Noroeste*, March 29, 1931.
64 Only seven monarchists emerged victorious. On the average, the republicans pulled 74% of the vote in all of Gijón's districts, ranging from 68% in District 7 to 78% in District 6: *El Noroeste*, April 14, 1931. In Asturias as a whole, monarchist candidates won only 64 out of 1,050 seats, scarcely over 6%. Republicans took 701, Socialists 184, and Communists 15: Miguel Martínez Cuadrado, *Elecciones y partidos políticos de España, 1868–1931* (Madrid: Taurus, 1969), 998–999.

5

The republicans in power: municipal
politics, 1931–1936

∼

The municipal elections of April 12, 1931 produced perhaps the greatest show of republican unity and popular support ever seen in Gijón.
On April 13, hours before the news arrived from Madrid, the city
carried out its own peaceful revolution that culminated in the declaration of the Republic and the release of political prisoners that evening. The process began at 2 p.m., when a large crowd convinced the
newly elected republican councilors to lead a march to city hall and
demand the resignation of the monarchist city council. Later that afternoon, all of the coalition parties met and constituted a revolutionary
committee to monitor the transition. By early that evening, with still
no word from Madrid, the committee took the responsibility of
officially declaring the Republic in Gijón. In the Plaza de la Constitu-
ción in front of the city hall, an enormous crowd watched in silence
as the republicans raised the Federalist flag (the only non-monarchist
one available). Afterwards, "the enthusiasm overflowed and the shouts
of 'long live the Republic' multiplied. People embraced each other
emotionally, while many men threw their hats into the air as a sign
of jubilation."[1]

After the inaugural act, the crowd moved on to the jail, led by the
young Reformist lawyer, Dionisio Morán, who became the orator of
the transition. With approval wired from Oviedo for the release of
the mostly anarchist political prisoners, Morán and another Reformist
lawyer, Mariano Merediz, presided over their liberation. After an
emotional public reunion with family and friends, the twenty-three

[1] *El Noroeste*, April 14, 1931.

142

prisoners and their retinue began a triumphant procession to city hall, cheered on by jubilant crowds. There they appeared on the balcony of the city hall, while an estimated 15,000 people gave them a rousing ovation. Members of all the coalition parties spoke, as did anarchist Segundo Blanco. Consistent with the reigning goodwill, the crowd applauded all the speakers with equal enthusiasm.

When the rally was over, Gijón's official band played a concert in the Plaza del Carmen, renamed, by "popular will," after the republican martyr Captain Galán.[2] Into the late hours of the night, the band marched up and down the streets of the city, playing the "Marseillaise" and the "Internationale". Women of all classes displayed flags or wore cockades in republican colors, while "the common people" filled the streets "singing and carrying the flag of the Republic."[3]

For the republican parties of Gijón, this day summed up all their hopes for the future. As they had led the cheering crowds shouting "¡Viva!" to the Republic, they hoped to assert their leadership over a broad popular base that would stabilize the regime and bring about the long-awaited transformation of local and national politics. With republicans in power in both Madrid and Gijón, their moment in the spotlight had finally arrived.

The problem with the spotlight was that it exposed all the weaknesses that had been hidden in the shadows. From the opposition, the republicans had been able to hold together a broad popular coalition on the strength of a few vague phrases and the common experience of persecution. But from the seat of power, they had to construct a more substantial reform program to sustain the same coalition, a coalition that was essential to legitimizing the Republic in an industrial, working-class city like Gijón. What the spotlight exposed, in all its unforgiving brightness, however, was that the republicans had no such program on which they could agree. Instead, it revealed the same deep divisions and ambiguous attitude towards social reform that always had been characteristic of the movement. As a result, the republican establishment in Gijón lost the popular momentum of April 12th and the chance to define a reformist politics that would tie the working classes to the regime and to their leadership. Without this support, republicans were incapable of carving out a stable space for the regime from where it could fend off challenges from the left and right. In

---

[2] Shot after an aborted republican uprising in December 1930, Captain Galán became the most famous martyr for the republican cause.
[3] *El Noroeste*, April 14, 1931.

the end, the republicans lost control of their Republic, forced back to the sidelines in a polarized field where they had no place.

The rise and fall of republican politics in Gijón was part of a national pattern that ended in collective disaster, but the particular combination of political forces in the city created a distinctly local version of it. On the national level, republicans were divided between those who sought to build a socially conservative regime buttressed by solid middle-class support and those who wanted to attract a strong working-class base through social reforms. The latter, exemplified by Prime Minister Manuel Azaña, had the opportunity to implement their program in the first *bienio* (1931 to November 1933) and the Popular Front (February to July 1936), while the more conservative republicans, exemplified by the Radical leader Alejandro Lerroux, had their chance during the second *bienio* (November 1933 to February 1936). For a complex variety of reasons, both failed, leaving the door open for more extremist appeals to both the middle and working classes.[4]

In Gijón, no republicans could ignore the working classes, but two versions of the Republic still existed, one which emphasized its popular base – the "Republic of Workers" – and the other which tried to present a more integrationist vision of a Republic for all Spaniards. The main proponents of these views were the same two parties that had been competing with each other for two decades: the Federalists and the Reformists, renamed the Liberal Democrats (PRLD) in 1931. This picture already differed dramatically from the national scene, since neither of these parties played a national role after the first elections.[5] Likewise, none of the main republican parties in Madrid had much impact in Gijón until the very end of the regime.[6] This con-

---

[4] On the national republican options see Eduardo Espín, *Azaña en el poder: el partido de Acción Republicana* (Madrid: Centro de Investigaciones Sociológicas, 1980); Octavio Ruiz Manjón, *El partido Republicano Radical, 1908–1936* (Madrid: Tebas, 1976); Nigel Townson, "The Collapse of the Center: the Radical Republican Party during the Spanish Second Republic, 1931–1936" (Ph.D. diss., University of London, 1991); and Juan Avilés Farré, *La izquierda burguesa en la II República* (Madrid: Espasa Calpe, 1985).
[5] Of about eighty Federalist candidates who ran for the Cortes in June of 1931, only nineteen were elected, most of them within a republican/socialist coalition. The Reformists only ran ten candidates, of whom four were elected: Javier Tusell Gómez, *Las Constituyentes de 1931: unas elecciones de transición* (Madrid: Centro de Investigaciones Sociológicas, 1982); 121 and 124.
[6] The four main parties with national support (defined by Tusell as those electing candidates in over half the electoral districts) that emerged out of the first Cortes results were Alcalá Zamora's Derecha Liberal, the PSOE, the Radical Socialists and the Radicals: *Las Constituyentes*, 103.

figuration had important results for the political evolution of the city. Because of the local prestige of the Reformists and the weaknesses of the Federalists, the city government ended up in Reformist hands from 1931 to February 1936. Without the option of a republican-led "Workers' Republic," the local government had even less chance of stabilizing a popular base and neutralizing the political alternative of the revolutionary left.

The republican parties, 1931-1935

It took several weeks after the April elections for the euphoria of victory to wear off and for the centrifugal forces to scatter the various parties into their new pattern. The June 1931 parliamentary elections brought an end to this initial period of shuffling and readjustment, and signaled the emergence of a new political spectrum, with its local and provincial variations. The "left coalition" of April had been reduced to the Socialists, the Radical Socialists and the Alianza Republicana, which together represented the main forces of republicanism in the province. But the two main parties in Gijón, the Federalists and the Reformists, both abandoned the coalition, opening a distinct rift between local and provincial politics and setting the stage for the city's own peculiar version of the Republic.

The unusual local pattern began when the independent Federalist slate (allied with a small agrarian party)[7] won the parliamentary election in Gijón's electoral district. The victory partly reflected the historical strength of Federalism in Gijón and partly stemmed from the abstention of the PRLD,[8] which took the unusual step of endorsing its old enemy. In its endorsement, the PRLD claimed that the two old enemies represented the pure local will, matched against the power of the central government in the form of the Republican – Socialist Conjunción. This grandiose interpretation sounds more reasonable in the context of the national election results. The victory of an independent Federalist slate occurred in only one other province, and in

---

[7] The Federalists abandoned the "left" coalition because it only offered them two slots out of a provincial slate of fourteen. For the tumultuous debate over this offer, see Juntas, Partido Federal (PF), June 8, 1931 (AGS, K-5): all of the Junta citations in this chapter are found in either legajo K-5 or K-6.

[8] The PRLD withdrew from the coalition for similar reasons as the Federalists and then decided to abstain from the election after one of its rallies was disrupted by left republicans and Socialists. In fact, it may have been worried about testing its provincial electoral base. On its abstention see *El Noroeste*, June 23, 1931.

145

Oviedo most of the votes came from the city of Gijón.[9] Likewise, the Federalists received over five times as many votes as the republican/ socialist coalition in Gijón. As a result, the local set of political forces looked very different from the government coalition in Madrid (or in Oviedo) that was about to impose its mark on the first *bienio*.[10]

Thus, despite momentous political changes, the Reformists and the Federalists maintained their traditional hegemony in city politics. Even though the PRLD had abstained in the national elections, it retained its power base through the city council, where it had thirteen seats, followed by the Federalists' twelve. And despite the electoral posturing of the Reformists in June, they had not buried the hatchet with their old enemy. As vintage Federalist Eztenaga summed it up: "an abyss separates us in local politics."[11]

From early on, the PRLD defined itself as the republican party of order. In one of its first manifestos, it offered itself as the stabilizing force for the new regime; now that the revolution was over, it argued, the country needed moderate political groups to create, not to destroy.[12] By officially proclaiming the revolutionary period over, the party implied that it was essentially a political and not a social or economic phenomenon. The wording of the manifesto also revealed the party's fear that the Republic would spin out of control, in the hands of young, hot-headed radicals with no experience of the world of practical politics. As one local Reformist said ominously, "today it seems that there are no 'true' republicans except those who burn convents ... the others have neither voice nor vote. Long live Liberty!"[13] As time passed, these fears and concerns, together with a shared appeal to a middle-class audience, created a common ground with the non-republican right, with whom the PRLD would form an

---

[9] Tusell, *Las Constituyentes*, 122. The other province was Málaga, where one Federalist was elected on a minority slate with 15% of the vote. In Oviedo, all of the four Federalists on the minority slate won (with 25% of the vote), as well as all twelve of the candidates on the majority Conjunción slate: four PSOE, four Radical Socialists, one Alianza Republicana, one Derecha Liberal, and two dissident Federalists (p. 185).

[10] Nationally, the PSOE received the most votes, followed by the Radicals, the Radical Socialists, and the Derecha Liberal. In terms of numbers of deputies elected in the first round, the PSOE had 113, followed by 87 for the Radicals and 61 for the Radical Socialists. Alianza Republicana only captured sixteen seats, but gained national prominence largely because of Prime Minister Azaña. The PRLD ended up with four, and the Federalists with nineteen, most of those as part of the Republican – Socialist Conjunción: Tusell, *Las Constituyentes*, 128.

[11] Juntas, PF, October 23, 1933.

[12] Dated June 4: *El Noroeste*, June 5, 1931.

[13] *El Noroeste*, June 26, 1931.

electoral alliance in 1933 and again in 1936. In spatial terms, this common ground translated into a defense of downtown Gijón against the industrial suburbs: membership lists of the PRLD and the far right parties demonstrate that a majority of the members of these groups resided downtown, the locus of traditional elite politics in the city.[14]

In contrast to the position staked out by the PRLD, the Federalists announced a fairly radical program of social and economic reform designed to appeal to the working classes, and more specifically to the local CNT. The new platform accepted by the national assembly of the party and endorsed in Gijón included the six-hour workday as a solution to unemployment; the obligatory mobilization of unproductive capital; the possible nationalization of banks, railroads, mines, etc., under the direction of worker syndicates; the creation of a republican militia and the disbanding of the Civil Guard; and official protests against the persecution of communists and anarchists.[15] As soon as the April elections were over, the local Federalist councilors announced that they were planning for the "social labor" of the new council in creating jobs and expanding beneficent institutions.

In addition to supporting fundamental reforms, the Federalist party courted the "worker element" through direct, usually informal, relations with the CNT. Thus, while planning for their national convention in December 1930, the local Federalist party requested that the CNT send a minimum program for the purpose of establishing an understanding between the two organizations.[16] The entente was apparently successful, as the party was later informed that the CNT had so far approved of Federalist actions and programs, and could be counted on to back them up.[17] Significantly, this report was delivered by a Federalist who also belonged to the CNT. The number of overlapping memberships is hard to determine, but it seemed no secret that several ranking members of the CNT were card-carrying Federalists. When the CNT held its anti-monarchist assembly in September 1930, for example, the Federalists were represented by Gómez Fariñas, a prominent *cenetista*.[18]

Even without dual membership, there seemed to be a great deal of

---

[14] From undated lists circulated after 1936, probably for the benefit of leftist "purification" committees. For details see Table 3.2 in Appendix 3.

[15] Juntas, PF, June 3, 1931. It also included the expropriation of *latifundias*, not an important issue in Asturias.

[16] Juntas, PF, December 3, 1930.

[17] Juntas, PF, June 15, 1931.

[18] Juntas, PF, September 25, 1930.

quiet collaboration between the two organizations. Thus, the Federalists supported the CNT's efforts to free its prisoners by appointing two representatives to the "Workers' Pro-Prisoner Commission" in February 1931.[19] In return, the CNT contributed to the Federalist electoral cause by lending the car of *cenetista* leader José María Martínez to make campaign sweeps in the province.[20] Before the June elections, some Federalists even suggested that they try to enlist the CNT as silent partners: "although [they are] apolitical, we could make secret gestures to see if they would support us."[21]

With this kind of potential popular base and a hefty minority on the city council, the Federalists seemed well positioned to resist the more conservative agenda of the PRLD. But despite these advantages, the Federalist party had numerous weaknesses that prevented it from taking a leadership role in city politics. Without a majority, the Federalists needed to ally with the other left parties on the city council, but they stuck to their long-standing purist rejection of such compromises.[22] Moreover, the party was ambivalent about taking a leadership role in the "unitary" and centralized Republic that emerged after 1931. As one member said succinctly: "this Republic is not ours."[23] Thus, in March of 1932 when a local assembly again debated the party's position on collaboration with other republican forces, the majority voted to maintain their oppositional stance as long as the Republic remained "unitary, undemocratic and a defender of capitalism."[24] The policy of self-imposed marginalization not only kept the party on the perimeter of local power; it created grave internal tensions. From a perusal of reports of committee meetings and assemblies, it is clear that while some party members supported this policy, others were in favor of a more "realistic" strategy that included compromises with other republican parties and less close ties with the CNT. At a general assembly in January 1932, Alfredo Fernández referred explicitly to these two tendencies: "one rightist, conservative, which represents the outdated, the old members of the party, whose maximum goals were never more than to call themselves republican; and another leftist, liberal, advanced and worker-oriented that attracts

---

[19] Juntas, PF, February 19, 1931.
[20] Juntas, PF, June 15, 1931. Martínez was a chauffeur.
[21] Juntas, PF, June 10, 1931.
[22] With the Alianza Republicana and Socialist councilors, they could have put together a bloc of sixteen votes.
[23] Juntas, PF, June 14, 1931: councilman Súarez Inclán.
[24] Juntas, PF, March 11, 1932.

the younger elements."[25] Shortly after this assembly, Fernández and some of his supporters were expelled. They started a dissident Federalist group that remained a thorn in the parent organization's side throughout the entire period.[26]

Even after the expulsion, the existence of these two tendencies continued to weaken the party's resolve. Compounding the tension was the fact that the Federalist city councilors tended to be men of the old guard, like Ramón Fernández and Evaristo Riestra, who had been active in politics since before the First World War. On the other hand, the party's executive committee was dominated by younger, less compromising men, some of them members of anarchist unions. The result was an ongoing battle between the councilors and the party executive, with the former often flagrantly disobeying the party line. In December of 1931, for example, during the CNT's violent general strike, the councilors argued for importing more police, while the radicals protested that police only repress the people.[27] Likewise, in a discussion over whether to fire or demote two municipal workers, the radicals supported demotion on the grounds that they had families to support, and the old guard favored termination because of the threat to the principle of authority.[28] These unresolved ideological tensions helped prevent the party from playing a more protagonistic role in city politics.

The positions staked out by Federalists and Reformists constituted the basic parameters of local republican politics until the February 1936 elections. With the Federalists in permanent opposition, the PRLD dominated the city government, aided by the two Derecha Liberal councilmen and the growing co-operation of the Catholic/monarchist minority. Although the PRLD tried to maintain its populist, reformist rhetoric, in reality it presided over a fiscally conservative, pro-law-and-order city council that lasted (with a brief interregnum) from the spring of 1931 to the elections of February 1936. The parliamentary elections of October 1933, which, for national politics, mark

[25] Juntas, PF, January 29, 1932.
[26] During this period, the national Federalist party underwent a similar schism. The result was a majority Partido Republicano Democrático Federal and a minority Izquierda Federal, with closer ties to the CNT: Antonio Checa Godoy, *Prensa y partidos políticos durante la II República* (Salamanca: Ediciones Universidad de Salamanca, 1989), 122. Despite the parallel, the local schism did not seem to be institutionally derived from the national split. The general crisis of the party had its roots in the ambiguities of Federalist dogma and strategy, but it seemed as if each local entity followed its own dynamic.
[27] Juntas, PF, December 25, 1931.
[28] Juntas, PF, September 28, 1932.

the division between a reformist and a conservative phase of the Republic, only reinforced the existing pattern. The PRLD coalition with the Catholic Acción Popular (AP) confirmed its rightward migration, and the Federalist defeat confirmed the party's confusion and disarray. Thus, the distinction between the first and second *bienios* was one more of tone than of content.

When the PRLD allied with the Catholic AP in the national elections of October 1933, the party found it increasingly difficult to maintain its moderate image.[29] The eleventh-hour alliance between the PRLD and AP was only concluded after Melquíades' plans for a centrist coalition fell through, but this reluctance did not soften the impact.[30] The Reformists campaigned as the stable center but their rhetoric was belied by the AP candidates on their slate, who were at best indifferent to the Republic and at worst hostile to it. The AP candidates included José Moutas, ex-editor of the conservative Catholic newspaper, *El Carbayón*, Romualdo Alvargonzález, a politician from the old Conservative party, Bernardo Aza, a banker and industrialist from one of the richest families in the province, and Fernández Ladreda, also a wealthy businessman with roots in the Liberal party.[31] In this company, the PRLD had to do cartwheels to deny the fact that the new alliance sat squarely on the right of the political spectrum. After the revolution of October 1934, there was no doubt. The fear of working-class revolt cemented the right-wing coalition, in which the Reformists lost what remained of an independent centrist position.

As the Reformists drifted further to the right, the Federalists' internal confusion threatened to bash them against the rocks. In

[29] Acción Popular began more as a lobbying group than a political party, but it carried out a furious organizational campaign during 1932 and 1933 through churches, Catholic syndicates, rural *cacique* networks, and six of the eight daily newspapers in Asturias. Acción Popular was the main representative of Gil Robles' Spanish Federation of Independent Rightists (CEDA) in Asturias. See Manuel Suárez Cortina, *El fascismo en Asturias, 1931–1937* (Madrid: Silverio Cañada, 1981). On the national CEDA, see José Ramón Montero, *La CEDA: el catolicismo social y político en la II República* (Madrid: Ediciones de la Revista de Trabajo, 1977).

[30] Melquíades' decision to go with AP alienated what remained of the left wing of his party, including Oliveros, the editor of *El Noroeste* for sixteen years (Suárez Cortina, *El fascismo*, 131). A similar process occurred in the more prominent centrist party, the Radicals, which also concluded an eleventh-hour coalition with the CEDA that had serious national repercussions. As Nigel Townson argues, the pact gave the CEDA a foot in the door and marked the final split between the true republican parties: "Algunas consideraciones sobre el proyecto 'republicano' del Partido Radical," in *La II República española: bienio rectificador y Frente Popular, 1934–1936*, ed. J. L. García Delgado (Madrid: Siglo Veintiuno, 1988).

[31] Suárez Cortina, *El fascismo*, 215.

October 1933, the party attempted to form a left republican alliance with Alianza Republicana and the Radical Socialists, but burned bridges and the obstinacy of all parties prevented its realization. Unwilling to go it alone, the Federalists chose to form a coalition with the conservative republican parties in a so-called "center" bloc. The CNT, normally the Federalists' unspoken allies, ran an active abstention campaign in rejection of the Republic that had massacred the rebels of Casas Viejas.[32] While the Federalists were not directly implicated in Casas Viejas or the repressive policies of the first *bienio*, they could be indicted for their impotence in preventing them. Thus, their marginalization began to erode their popular base. Electoral abstention is always difficult to interpret, but the results seemed to demonstrate the success of the CNT campaign: in Oviedo, barely 18% of the electors did not vote; in Gijón abstention hovered around 32%.[33]

Following the national pattern, the disunity of the left resulted in a rousing victory for the PRLD/AP ticket in Gijón.[34] In terms of the provincial pattern, however, Gijón looks more unusual. Except for the PRLD strongholds of Gijón and Avilés, the province was divided into rural, agricultural districts that voted for the right, and urban, industrial areas that voted Socialist. The combination of CNT antipathy towards the PSOE, the special history of Reformism in Gijón and the crisis of the Federalists prevented the triumph of the "left." While this parliamentary election neither altered the composition of the city council nor signaled major policy shifts, it had a tremendous emotional impact on city politics. Simply the fact that the PRLD had allied with the non-republican right increased the level of polarization. Furthermore, the Federalist confusion and defeat in the election cast doubt on the capacity of the republican left to wrest power from an

---

[32] In January of 1933, when anarchists in the village of Casas Viejas in Andalusia decided to proclaim libertarian communism, the police forces of the Republic shot twenty-two of the participants, many of them in cold blood. The incident seriously undermined the legitimacy of the reformist administration. On the events, see Jerome Mintz, *The Anarchists of Casas Viejas* (Chicago: University of Chicago Press, 1982).

[33] Eusebio Izquierdo Fernández, "Organizaciones sindicales y conflictividad social en Asturias durante la II República, 1931–1933" (Tesina, University of Oviedo, 1985), 75.

[34] The right received 13,600 votes. The Socialists, who ran alone, received 5,500, their best showing ever in Gijón, while the Federalist coalition polled a humiliating 4,150. The PCE got 2,647 votes, while the Left Republicans barely registered with 720. If all of the non-PRLD/AP votes are tallied, they add up to over 13,000 votes, only a few hundred less than the center – right coalition received. Election results were printed in *El Noroeste*, November 21 and 25, 1933. On national republican disunity in the elections, see Juan Avilés Farré, "Los partidos republicanos de izquierda, 1933–1936," in *La II República española: bienio rectificador*. He points out that if the 1931 coalition had been maintained, it would have won two-thirds of the districts (p. 74).

expanding right.[35] In this sense, the October 1934 revolution seemed to be as much a vote of no confidence for the Federalists as a war against fascism. With everything that had happened, the non-republican left, principally the CNT, could paint a convincing picture of a Gijón in which the regime had changed only so that everything could remain the same.

City politics, 1931–1935

The concrete results provided by several years of republican rule seemed to back up the left's argument that little had changed. While all the republican parties made a rhetorical commitment to a "social" Republic in the first few weeks of the regime, little of this rhetoric translated into tangible achievements. More surprising, perhaps, not even the political symbolism connected with the old regime was convincingly overturned. As the PRLD depended more and more on its Catholic and monarchist allies, it began to waffle on issues like secularization that had always been unquestioned points of convergence for all republicans. If we add this absence of new signposts to the lack of generational renewal in the city government, the result was a picture that coincided in many ways with local politics under the monarchy. Thus, at least in Gijón, the Republic never offered a clear political alternative to the old regime.[36]

The social and economic similarities were the clearest. As in the past, the city council placed balancing the budget and protecting private property before solving the unemployment problem or reducing the gap between rich and poor. Thus, the budget allotments for public works, welfare, education, etc. were not markedly increased, and the tax structure remained as regressive as ever. As the Socialist *Avance* complained, "we haven't seen any sign of financial innovation, no proposition about the municipal budget that offers an alternative to the well-worn paths tried by the monarchy and the Dictatorship, and thus we find that the city government has made a budget as bad as or worse than those of the past."[37]

---

[35] The Federalists' disarray was demonstrated at the party assembly following the election, which wallowed in bitter recriminations about who was to blame for the state that the party was in: Juntas, PF, December 1, 1933.

[36] One of the debates about the Republic, especially the first *bienio*, has been whether it tried to do too much or too little. The impact of republican reforms cannot be judged, however, without sorting through the tremendous local diversity of implementation.

[37] *Avance*, December 27, 1933.

To be fair, it must be acknowledged that the economic problems faced by Gijón were national in scope, and that local governments had limited resources to deal with the impact of the depression.[38] Nevertheless, the city's unemployed, who numbered about 4,000 men and their families,[39] could not be aware of these complexities. And even given the structural limitations, the inaction of the city government was dramatic. Thus, the only concrete proposal implemented by the city council was the promotion of a voluntary public subscription for a no-interest loan.[40]

Other proposals, from Federalists, Socialists or CNT unions, were all rejected as too costly or threatening to business interests. Federalist councilors proposed that payment of the municipal debt be suspended and the savings funneled into public works.[41] All of the left groups also suggested that funds be raised by some form of tax on the rich: either income tax, as suggested by the Socialists, or taxes on luxury services, as proposed by the Federalists. In addition to demanding that the government help create jobs, both the CNT and the Socialists requested unemployment benefits or a daily subsidy for those out of work. Not only did the government reject all of these suggestions, it demonstrated its lack of sympathy for the plight of the unemployed by such insensitive measures as the decision to evict residents of the public "economical houses" who fell behind on their rent.[42]

The government's lack of sympathy for the popular classes was also clear in its support of a pro-employer, law-and-order version of labor relations. Whenever major strikes occurred, the hated Civil Guard were still sent in to "keep the peace" and protect scab labor.[43] One story related in the anarchist *Solidaridad* illustrates popular resentment over this set of priorities. According to the article, a poor woman whose mattress had been stolen was refused assistance by a Guard who claimed he could not help her because he was on call in case of any

---

[38] On the national economic problems, see Joseph Harrison, "The Inter-War Depression and the Spanish Economy," *Journal of European Economic History*, 12:2 (Fall 1983), and Juan Hernández Andreu, *Depresión económica en España, 1925–1936* (Madrid: Instituto de Estudios Fiscales, Ministerio de Hacienda, 1980).

[39] *El Noroeste*, January 29, 1933.

[40] The subscription raised 200,000–300,000 pts., but it was spent almost immediately: *Avance*, February 3, 1934.

[41] *Juntas*, PF, September 9, 1931.

[42] *Solidaridad*, March 1932.

[43] See, for example, the transfer orders for 100 guards to Gijón in December 1931 because of the general strike, and 150 in July 1931, in response to "intractable elements [of] this province, and principally of Gijón and Oviedo, who promise diverse acts of violence": Ministerio de Gobernación documents, AHN, 39A, núm. 18.

disturbances as a result of the ongoing telephone strike. As the author bitterly concluded, Guards were willing to protect large companies but not poor women.[44] In another example, the Socialist union of municipal workers accused the city of negligence as an employer by not complying with social legislation on such basic issues as the freedom to unionize and the right to work under a contract.[45] As to be expected, the city did not push other employers to recognize this legislation, either.[46]

In some ways, none of these economic and social attitudes were surprising, since they were consistent with the liberal, fiscally conservative principles that the Reformists had held for many years. What was more surprising was the PRLD's softening of its traditional commitment to secularization. As the party's strategy led it to depend more heavily on the co-operation of the monarchist minority, government policy lost its strong anti-clerical bent and began to adapt mildly pro-clerical positions. Thus, whereas in the first few weeks the Reformists had voted with the left coalition to expel the Jesuits[47] and to change a variety of street names from those of saints and monarchist figures to those of republican heroes, within less than a year they had done a dramatic *volte-face*. In January of 1932, when Reformist Fernando Barcía wanted votes to elect him as mayor, he promised the monarchists that the PRLD would not push the expulsion of the Jesuits or the secularization of the religious cemetery.[48]

In addition, the PRLD also compromised on religious holidays. In June of 1932, the city gave municipal workers the traditional Corpus Christi holiday, over left republican objections that this action blurred distinctions between Church and state. In an even more loaded decision, the city postponed its celebration of the anniversary of the

---

[44] *Solidaridad*, October 17, 1931.
[45] Letter written to the Ministry of Labor, April 12, 1934 (AGS, H-27).
[46] Two letters illustrate this problem, with relation to the arbitration boards that had been created by the Socialist labor ministry. One, from the Transportation Union, complained about the backlog of disputes, held up for lack of a constituted board, or *jurado mixto* (September 6, 1933: AGS, H-22). In another letter, a lawyer for naval pilots petitioned for the formation of a *jurado mixto* so they could bring up their dispute with the ship owners (May 1934: AGS, H-30).
[47] The vote to expel the Jesuits, or "social lepers," as Reformist councilor Valdés Prida called them, came on the first day of the new regime. In fact, Gijón was the first municipality to petition for their expulsion, an act either adhered to or condemned by dozens of municipalities around the country. A telegram from the Ayuntamiento of Madridejos (Toledo) to the Ministerio, on June 16, 1931, for example, adhered to the position to expel the Jesuits, "first formulated" by the Ayuntamiento de Gijón (AHN, 16A, exp.17).
[48] Juntas, PF, January 21, 1932.

Republic in April 1933, because it fell on Good Friday.[49] Well before the elections of October 1933, then, the republicans lost what had been their most stable source of unity and popular appeal. Moreover, they had lost the simplest way of distinguishing between the Republic and the preceding regimes. The lack of distinction seemed increasingly pronounced during the second *bienio*, although it was more a question of atmosphere than substantive changes in policy. The PRLD still intoned its centrist rhetoric, but the voice of the non-republican right began to drown it out. On the city council, for example, a reactionary politician like Rufino Menéndez could now freely attack a republican project like the building of a memorial dedicated to free-thinker Rosario de Acuña, whereas in July of 1932 he had been suspended from the council after calling the Republic "wretched and sterile," and praising the death of democracy in Spain's "Mediterranean neighbor," i.e. Italy. But after the 1933 elections, as *Avance* complained, "the rightists believe that their complete triumph, with the return of the Jesuits and the implantation of fascism, is certain."[50]

The image of a newly defiant right was also fueled by the first signs of Falangist or fascist activity in Gijón.[51] Posters inviting workers to join the Falange appeared on downtown buildings, and graffiti was scrawled on the wall lining the beach. Small groups of Falangists sold newspapers in the street, often provoking altercations with Communists or anarchists. Although the size of the Falangist movement in the city was still quite small, it maximized its public impact with a few well-placed activities.[52] This presence only fueled the growing fear of fascism taking shape on the left.

While the city government did not endorse this fascist activity, many leftists accused the city of a two-faced policy that consisted of a lenient attitude towards the extreme right and a campaign of persecution

[49] The Federalists expressed outrage at the way the "politics of Catholicism" had taken over the city government: Juntas, PF, April 19, 1933.
[50] *Avance*, December 9, 1933.
[51] *Avance* reported that fascism in Gijón "began to take shape" around the 1933 elections (February 10, 1934). Manuel Suárez Cortina confirms that the Falange began to organize in the summer and fall of 1933, although, as elsewhere in Spain, it remained weak until after the February 1936 elections: *El fascismo*, 153–164. On Spanish fascism and the Falange, see Stanley Payne, *The Falange: A History of Spanish Fascism* (Stanford: Stanford University Press, 1961).
[52] The size of the movement is difficult to determine. *Avance* reported that the Falange claimed to have 2,000 members in the city (February 10, 1934), but this number is hard to reconcile with the 112 votes cast for its ticket in the 1936 elections, or the undated list of 275 members that was in possession of the leftist government in 1936–1937 (AGS, F-110).

towards the working-class organizations. As one pamphlet complained: "How many reactionary centers have been closed in Gijón? How many reactionaries, fascists or true enemies of the Republic have been arrested or indicted? None that we know of."[53] In contrast, the *ateneos* and the labor unions' headquarters, the Casa del Pueblo, were subject to frequent closure, and CNT leaders were regularly thrown into jail, often as a result of anarchist activities elsewhere in Spain. Thus, even though the local CNT did not participate in the revolutionary uprising of December 1933, all of its organizations were shut down and its leaders remained in jail until the amnesty of April 1934.[54] The CNT certainly contributed to its own persecution by adopting an increasingly hostile attitude towards the Republic. Nevertheless, it was also true that the police and the city government showed much less vigor in clamping down on the equally hostile extreme right.

The impact of this atmosphere on city politics was subtle but powerful. Even before the revolt of October 1934, there was a growing sense that, not only was the city government powerless to stop the process of polarization, but it had been swept along by it. This sense was confirmed after the revolt, when the Civil Governor dissolved the elected city council and replaced it with an appointed commission of Liberal Democrats and members of Acción Popular, most of them former monarchists. Without a left republican opposition on the council, and with most of the worker centers in the city closed, the Republic of 1935 posed a grim contrast to the hopes of April 1931.

The dominant theme of 1935 was the repression of the rebels and, more broadly, of the working-class organizations in the city. In one of the only local strikes that year, called to protest against the firing of three union leaders, the government pronounced the strike illegal and threatened dismissal for all employees.[55] For the celebration of May 1st, the city also set a hard line: if public service workers did not show up to work, they would be fired.[56] This attack on the left differed from that of earlier years because it was not matched by a strong commitment to a moderate version of the Republic – i.e. to the vision that the Reformists had held since 1931. As a result, the city government of 1935, like the national

---

[53] Avelino González Mallada, "Sobre la clausura de la Casa del Pueblo," printed in Ramón Alvarez Palomo, *Avelino González Mallada: alcalde anarquista* (Barcelona: Historia Libertaria de Asturias, 1987), 231. *El Noroeste* makes a similar point: September 12, 1933.
[54] Alvarez Palomo, *Avelino González Mallada*, 239.
[55] *El Noroeste*, August 1 and 2, 1935. On August 3, the paper reported that the strikers returned to work without their three fired co-workers.
[56] *El Noroeste*, April 28, 1935.

government of that year, seemed less republican than anti-revolutionary. Thus, on the anniversary of the Republic in April, there were no official celebrations, other than the customary illumination of public buildings. Instead of official festivities, "the Gijonese republicans all celebrated the anniversary in their own way."[57] The clear implication was that the city government had ceased to be the center of republican politics in Gijón.

Perhaps the best illustration of the tone of city politics that year was a council debate over the decision to change a street name. The Acción Popular representatives proposed changing the street name "Ferrer Guardia," the founder of a "free-thinking" school who was executed after the "Tragic Week" in 1909, to "Capitán Alonso Nart," a Civil Guard killed during the October revolt. The Reformists did not object to naming a street after Nart, but they argued that an unnamed street should be chosen.[58]

Symbolically, this seemingly petty discussion revealed a lot about city politics. As the Reformists agreed that Nart should be immortalized, so they fully supported the repression of the left in Asturias, even in the broadly vindictive form that it took. And yet, they still held on to their vision of a Republic in which Nart and Ferrer could peacefully co-exist. Their inability to resolve the contradictions between these two positions left them in an increasingly untenable spot. As they floundered under the weight of these contradictions, the initiative fell more to Acción Popular, which pushed its harsher vision of a law-and-order regime. As in 1931, then, there were still two visions of the regime. But in 1935, one of the original visions, of a Workers' Republic, had been expelled from the city government. And the Reformist vision, instead of constituting the mainstream viewpoint, had been pushed to the margins. In its place was a new mainstream vision that was actually an old one, the familiar voice of the monarchist and clerical forces that the Republic had supposedly overthrown. Thus, after everything that had changed since 1931, it seemed as if nothing had changed.

The Popular Front

By the end of 1935, then, the political atmosphere in Gijón coincided closely with that of the nation at large. In Madrid, the CEDA was

[57] El Noroeste, April 16, 1935.
[58] El Noroeste, November 16, 1935.

the most powerful political voice in the Cortes, and Gil Robles openly talked about imposing a "new Constitution." Its republican allies, the Radicals, had lost control, of the CEDA, of the Republic, and finally of their own party. Although the pretext for their self-destruction was a series of financial scandals, like the PRLD in Gijón they were trapped in an increasingly untenable situation. On the one hand, they were ostracized by republicans as the party that had provided the sheep's clothing for the enemies of the Republic, but on the other hand, they were uncomfortable with the strident rhetoric of the extreme right.[59] The lurking crisis surfaced when the scandals forced Lerroux and his ministers out of government, leaving the CEDA without its republican cover. Constitutionally, President Alcalá Zamora should have appointed Gil Robles as Prime Minister, but doubting that he could trust the regime in the hands of the CEDA leader, he called an election, what would become known as the Popular Front election, for February 1936.[60]

In Gijón, as elsewhere, the election both demonstrated and reinforced the sense of political polarization in the country. Most of the parties were grouped into two opposing electoral blocs, while those that tried to hold on to the center, like the Radicals, were decimated. The right consisted of the CEDA and its local allies, like the PRLD in Gijón, while the left comprised all of the worker parties (with the informal inclusion of the CNT in some areas) and the left republicans, who had combined their forces into two major groups, the Izquierda Republicana (IR) and the Unión Republicana (UR).[61] The base of this left coalition was the feared threat to the Republic and the experience of repression which, since October 1934, had affected republicans as well as anarchists and socialists. Thus, the shared persecution that had formed one of the bases for popular coalitions under

---

[59] For the Radicals' decline, from 1933 to 1935, see Nigel Townson, "Una República para todos los españoles: el Partido Radical en el poder," in *El republicanismo en España, 1830–1977*, ed. Nigel Townson (Madrid: Alianza Editorial, 1994).

[60] For a fuller analysis of the background to these elections, see Santos Juliá Diaz, *Orígenes del Frente Popular en España, 1934–1936* (Madrid: Siglo Veintiuno, 1979).

[61] The re-shuffling of the left republican parties occurred over the course of the second *bienio*, after the disastrous showing in the 1933 elections. The Unión Republicana was formed in 1934 out of a dissident sector of the Radical party and the majority of the defunct Radical Socialist party. It occupied the right wing of the Popular Front, with its full adhesion to the legal institutions of the Republic and its discomfort with the revolutionary left. Izquierda Republicana contained Azaña's Alianza Republicana, the minority Radical Socialists of Marcelino Domingo, as well as individuals from smaller parties. See Avilés Farré, "Los partidos republicanos."

the monarchy again proved to be the left's most successful point of encounter.[62]

The defensive alliance ended in victory for the Popular Front in Gijón, as it did on the national level, but more significantly it brought an end to twenty-five years of Reformist hegemony in the city and unleashed a power struggle over who would take the reins of the Republic.[63] The Federalists were in no position to do so, as the election had only confirmed their disarray. One sector had been defeated on an independent ticket, while the other faction supported the Popular Front without being offered any spots on the list.[64] Thus, the two major parties in the April 1931 coalition were virtually eclipsed, in testament to their failure to take or maintain control of the Republic.

With the old republican forces decimated, new parties like the IR and the UR struggled to take their place, but they were challenged by the Socialists and the Communists, who were beginning to put down political roots in the city. The position of the revolutionary worker parties was enhanced by the closer relationship with the CNT that had been developing since the formation of the "Workers' Alliance" in 1934.[65] By early 1936, although the CNT still eschewed formal political participation, it was clearly moving away from its entente with the republican left and towards a united revolutionary front. The question was, would the republicans have one more chance to shape their own Republic, or would it slip out of their hands again? The coup of July 1936 decided the issue, pushing the republicans to the sidelines of the regime that they had created.

The last phase of the peacetime Republic began with the electoral

---

[62] Santos Juliá emphasizes that the resurrection of the Republican – Socialist Conjunción was due largely to the fact that both left republicans and socialists were subject to an intense persecution that temporarily reduced the profound differences between them: *Orígenes*, 10.

[63] The Popular Front coalition in Gijón received 24,746 votes, while the PRLD/AP front got 12,315: *El Noroeste*, February 22, 1936.

[64] The old Partido Republicano Democrático Federal decided not to join the Popular Front after their proposed slate that included two Federalists was ignored. In an official note published in the newspaper the party bitterly reminded the upstart new parties that in April 1931 they had graciously given eight seats to the three new republican parties that had barely more than fifty members between them. Only five years later, the note complained, they pretend they don't know us: *El Noroeste*, March 31, 1936. The new Partido Izquierda Federal supported the Popular Front.

[65] For more on this relationship, see Angeles Barrio Alonso, "Asturias en la alianza CNT – UGT, 1934–1937," in *Los nuevos historiadores ante la Guerra Civil española*, vol. II, ed. Octavio Ruiz-Manjón Cabeza and Miguel Gómez Oliver (Granada: Diputación Provincial de Granada, 1990). Also see Chapter 10 for an account of the alliance and its repercussions.

campaign in late January, which set the polarized and strident tone of the next few months. For both sides, the rhetorical center of this campaign was the October revolution, which came to represent everything that divided them. The Acción Popular newspaper, calling for a new "Reconquest," made its reading of the stakes very clear: "To be or not to be, this is the dilemma. The brutal tragedy of a Spain, submerged in barbarism. Or a great Nation, released from slavery."[66] The Popular Front was equally dramatic in its calls to save the Republic from the threat of counter-revolution. As a speaker put it at one rally, "if the Left wins, democracy will stand, if the Right wins, all is lost."[67] The Popular Front campaigned more concretely for the amnesty of the rebels of October 1934,[68] and, while there was no direct connection between amnesty and the salvation of the Republic, the constant juxtaposition of the two themes tended to conflate them. Thus, the rebels, and their champions in the Popular Front, came to symbolize the defense of the Republic against its enemies.

Significantly, the PRLD played a very small role in this rhetorical sparring. El Noroeste's reporting on the election seemed curiously flat and detached, and its editorials betrayed the sense of bewilderment felt by a once-powerful party that had lost its bearings in an unfamiliar political environment. As one editorial lamented, "either one is situated on the right or on the left. The intermediate parties, those in which there have always been the most judicious individuals, not dominated by the masses – these parties are threatened with extinction."[69] In this context, the PRLD could only watch helplessly, as "Spain . . . is engaged in a verbal civil war."[70]

The election results confirmed the PRLD's premonition of its own demise.[71] The final blow to the party came a few days after the election, when the Reformist city councilors were forced to resign. The

---

[66] Acción, February 16, 1936.
[67] El Noroeste, February 11, 1936.
[68] In the manifesto of the "Partidos de Izquierda y Obreros" the demand for amnesty included all political and social crimes committed after November 1933: El Noroeste, January 16, 1936.
[69] February 6, 1936.
[70] February 11, 1936.
[71] Melquíades was the only Liberal Democrat elected to the new Cortes: Javier Tusell Gómez, Las elecciones del Frente Popular (Madrid: Edicusa, 1971), vol.II, 82. The fate of the PRLD was only an extreme version of what happened to all the centrist parties who tried to situate themselves between the two blocs. Thus, the combined strength of the Radical party, the PRLD and the Derecha Liberal had been reduced to 10% of the votes in 1936, versus over 30% in the 1931 and 1933 elections: Checa Godoy, Prensa y partidos, 143.

conflict over the formation of a new city council demonstrated how much things had changed since 1931. In Madrid, the new Popular Front government ordered that the "left" city councils of April 1931 be reinstated, as a way of rooting out conservative local governments. But in Gijón, the April 1931 city council had comprised mainly Reformists and Federalists, while the Popular Front delegation just elected to the Cortes consisted of seven Socialists, four IR members, one Communist and an Independent. When the Reformist mayor Barcía tried to reconstitute the old city council, a commission of the Popular Front interrupted the proceedings, declaring that it was taking over the city government in the name of the "popular will." The commission appointed Socialist Angel Martínez as the new mayor and named a council made up of two representatives from each of the groups that had proclaimed allegiance to the Popular Front.[72] This act of "popular will" was sanctioned by an enormous crowd outside, which applauded the new council members as they waved from the balcony of the city hall.

The power struggle, however, was not over. The city council that resulted from this "act of popular will" consisted of ten Socialists and Communists and only six republicans, a balance that clearly made both local and national republicans uneasy.[73] To rectify the balance, the local IR party asked the Civil Governor (of the same party) to appoint a new officially sanctioned city council. When he did, it contained twelve republicans (all IR), one of them to serve as mayor, six Socialists and four Communists.[74] Not surprisingly, all of the other left political forces in the city were outraged. The Socialist and Communist deputies refused to take their seats, not, they insisted, because they objected to a republican majority, but because the distribution put all the power into the hands of a new party without sufficient weight in the city. "How can we consider that Gijonese republicanism is represented in this party with barely no roots in the city," especially compared to "other historical republican parties which, like the Federalists,

---

[72] *El Noroeste*, February 23, 1936. The council consisted of two IR, two Juventud IR, two UR, two Juventud Comunista, two PCE, two Juventud Socialista, two UGT and two PSOE. The "Juventud" is the youth group associated with each party.

[73] As Santos Juliá emphasizes, the national Popular Front coalition was clearly weighted in favor of the republican parties, so that they, not the worker parties, would be in charge. The total number of worker party candidates (PSOE, PCE, POUM – Partido Obrero de Unificación Marxista, the Trotskyists – and Partido Sindicalista) was 150, versus 193 for the republican candidates: *Los orígenes*, 145–149.

[74] *El Noroeste*, April 10, 1936.

have demonstrated their roots on many occasions?"[75] Despite the protests, the new council withstood the pressure. As a result, for the last three months of the peacetime Republic, the city was run by twelve IR councilmen, an arrangement that would have been unimaginable in April 1931.

This series of political ruptures brought Gijón more in line with Madrid, but it did not have the desired effect of galvanizing the masses behind the Republic. Manuel Azaña, Prime Minister once again, had pushed the formation of the Popular Front to give the regime another chance to stabilize around a popular base, but his party did not have the social and political network to legitimize this mission. The Federalists would have been the obvious party to lead the implementation of the workers' republic in Gijón, but they could not shape themselves into a political force that could build on their prestige and their popular roots. Thus, even without considering the challenge posed by the non-republican right, the Popular Front government in Gijón rested on a weak foundation.

In a sense, however, the republicans had few options. If there was any chance to impose a republican agenda, they had to wrest power from the "popular will" government, whose set of priorities did not match their own. On this council, the Socialists and Communists dominated the tone of city politics with their socially combative rhetoric and confrontational gestures. While the PSOE and the Partido Comunista Español (PCE) did not have strong roots in the city either, they could build on the growing common ground with the CNT. Thus, one of the highest priorities of the new government was to avenge the rebels of October 1934, a task that all the revolutionary organizations were committed to. Along this vein, one of its first acts was to set in motion the process to re-hire all municipal workers fired for political or social reasons and to root out those who had abused their power to persecute workers.[76] Although the republicans did not necessarily oppose this process, it was not their issue.

More worrisome for the republicans were the threatening gestures directed at local business. The worker party representatives made strong statements about not letting capitalists hoard their money while thousands of workers remained without jobs. As Mayor Angel Martínez warned, "We are not disposed to tolerate the capitalists hold-

---

[75] *El Noroeste*, April 11, 1936.
[76] *El Noroeste*, February 23, 1936.

ing their money in bank accounts while the people live in misery. If they do not voluntarily put their money to work creating jobs, it may be necessary to take measures against the greed which is the cause of the unemployment and the misery."[77] The council did not act on these threats, but the idea of expropriating "legitimate" private property went against everything that even the most left republicans stood for.

In this radicalizing atmosphere, the Civil Governor acceded to local republicans' request to appoint a republican majority city council. While it might seem puzzling that the Governor would entrust the leadership of this council to the untried Izquierda Republicana, in fact it made perfect sense. A mixture of republican parties would have produced the same internal bickering that had crippled the movement for decades, and although the IR was new, it was a coherent political force that might have been able to provide clear local leadership to implement the national program of the Popular Front. Despite their protests, the Communists and Socialists played a role in this power shift as well. While in February 1936 they had been enthusiastic about a worker party government, the experience of operating within the liberal republican framework obviously took its toll.[78] When a republican majority was proposed, they initially agreed, probably relieved that responsibility would be taken out of their hands. But although they facilitated the power shift, their dramatic refusal to sit as a minority force signified that the republicans were on their own.[79]

In this difficult atmosphere, the last republican-led city council attempted to chart its course. The major social problem it faced was unemployment, followed by the lack of public schools. To secure the allegiance of the masses, which was key to Azaña's and the IR's strategy, the government needed to vigorously attack if not solve these problems. But the rub, as always, was finding the money to pursue

---

[77] *El Noroeste*, March 6, 1936.

[78] For example, there were several stories like this one, where a commission of stevedores came to the city council, asking it to force an employer to accede to their demands. Mayor Angel Martínez had to say that he sympathized with them, but that "the city government has no power to oblige the Employers' Association to take the measures that you are demanding": *El Noroeste*, March 13, 1936.

[79] Withdrawing to the sidelines also put the local PSOE more in line with the national policy of the party. Although the party was divided on the question of collaboration, the left wing prevailed. Their hope was that the republican government would hang itself and pave the way for a true revolutionary workers' government. On this question, see Santos Juliá, *La izquierda del PSOE, 1935–1936* (Madrid: Siglo Veintiuno, 1977). In Asturias, once the Socialists left Gijón's city government, their newspaper, *Avance*, became a vociferous critic of its policies.

these projects when the city was in desperate financial straits. And in this sense, the IR government could offer little more than the PRLD; within the strictures of a liberal regime of private property, it was left to beg businessmen to show their civic conscience. Whether businesses were really as poor as they claimed, or whether they were deliberately sabotaging the Republic, was immaterial. In either case, the city government looked helpless, and the limits of liberal reform seemed glaringly obvious to many poorer residents.

The impotence was best exemplified in the results of a highly publicized meeting of all the "civic leaders" of the city, convoked by the city council in order to construct solutions to the unemployment problem. The meeting began with a plea from an unemployed worker who talked about hunger and begged the audience to do everything in its power to create more jobs. The city engineer followed, with a list of urban reform projects that were both pressing and ready to enter the construction phase. After political speeches by city councilmen, encouraging a united response to the city's problems, the representatives of local business got up to speak. The president of the Junta del Puerto (the port management board) blamed the government for not sending the funds it had allocated for public works. The bank representatives said they were doing what they could, but had to consult with their superiors before committing to anything. The president of the Chamber of Urban Property promised to report the aspirations of the meeting to his organization. At the end, the assembly agreed to pursue three avenues: 1) to send a commission to Madrid to increase state funding; 2) to get a loan with the lowest possible interest rate from the local banks; and 3) to open a voluntary subscription for a soup kitchen for unemployed workers and their families.[80]

Over the next couple of months, none of these avenues produced satisfactory results. The commission returned from Madrid with vague promises and empty pockets.[81] The soup kitchen did finally open in mid-June, but the money collected was only enough to feed 150 children of unemployed workers. And lastly, despite much begging and pleading, the banks refused to give the city a loan at any interest rate, claiming lack of funds. The city council was furious, but had no recourse other than to petition the central government to change the laws regulating banks' public funding.[82] A second, more emotionally

---

[80] *El Noroeste*, April 25, 1936.
[81] *El Noroeste*, June 6, 1936.
[82] *El Noroeste*, May 14 and 15, 1936.

charged, assembly of "civic leaders" at the end of June still came to nothing.[83]

For the revolutionary left, the bank loan served as the perfect symbol of the inadequacies of republican reform. In a series of editorials, *Avance* hammered away at this point: "the fundamental bases of the Popular Front cannot be implemented without running into conflict with the interests of capital." Instead of begging from its knees, the city should demand what it needed, "relying on the power of the workers' organizations to back it up." In addition to forcing the bank to agree to the loan, the city should municipalize services, both to raise money and to reduce the power of capital.[84] The lurking question behind these critiques was clear: "What meaning does the Popular Front have if it can't solve conflicts, if it can't satisfy workers' elemental needs . . . how long can workers go on sacrificing the energy they need for their own cause to a mere phantom?"[85] The republicans, of course, argued that this kind of sniping, added to the nearly continuous strike activity, only made the task of the Popular Front more difficult.[86]

As the Popular Front struggled under its internal tensions, the non-republican right used the opportunity to build its own case that the Republic was dissolving into anarchy and to plan its attack against it. The formal attack came on July 18, 1936, when the military revolt began in Morocco. While it took another fifteen months for the Nationalists to enter Gijón, the impact of the uprising was immediate and dramatic. As the worker organizations took control of the defense of the city in the first weeks of the rebellion, so they took political control from the republicans. While the government remained in the hands of the Popular Front, with the participation of left republicans and worker organizations, the balance of power had shifted to the latter groups, who had the manpower and the resources, as well as the political language of polarization, to mobilize the city for civil war. As at the national level, the republicans slipped into the background, left to support a regime that was no longer theirs.

The start of the Civil War, then, marked the definitive failure of the republican political strategy and, by implication, its hegemonic

---

[83] *Avance*, June 26, 1936.
[84] *Avance*, June 26 and July 1, 1936.
[85] *Avance*, July 7, 1936.
[86] At a tense rally of the Popular Front in early May, republican speakers asked workers not to make more trouble for the government: *El Noroeste*, May 5, 1936.

project. Even if the loyalists had won the war, the republicans' vision of peaceful political reform was dead. In the long contest between the two populist languages of empowerment that had begun in the late nineteenth century, polarization had prevailed over integration. Central to the republicans' defeat was the long-term failure of their municipal policy, which could have served the purpose of legitimating their project at the grass-roots level and creating the solid mass base that eluded them. As the last two chapters have tried to demonstrate, there were a number of obstacles working against the success of integration through municipal reform, some of which were beyond the republicans' control. But the republicans also shared responsibility for the failure of their political strategy, which suffered under the weight of its internal contradictions. While the republicans' populist rhetoric made them dependent on winning over the masses, their limited social and economic vision did not offer enough sustenance to support such a following. In the complex industrial world of twentieth-century Gijón their liberal individualism did not address the material needs and demands of "smoke-darkened" Gijón. To overcome this weakness, the republicans supplemented their formal political policy with a strategy of cultural integration (discussed in Part III), but it was not enough to secure their hegemony. Without arguing that the republican project was doomed from April 1931, the deck was clearly stacked against it.

6

The trade union movement, 1900–1936

∼

The trade union movement that burst onto the scene around the turn of the century fizzled out almost immediately, but over the next three decades it established itself as a powerful independent force in Gijón's political culture. Although it did not officially participate in elections or governmental institutions, the anarchosyndicalist-dominated trade union movement came to define a radical political alternative to republicanism. Republicanism had a great impact on the labor movement and, more broadly, on the politicization of workers, but it lost control of that process early on. As republicanism became increasingly drawn into municipal politics, the new forces of anarchosyndicalism and Socialism battled to take control of the still inchoate labor movement. This struggle continued, on and off, until the two sides negotiated the "Workers' Alliance" in 1934, but after the first decade the Socialists were relegated to minority status. In direct contrast to the balance of forces at the provincial level, Gijón became an anarchist bastion in one of the staunchest Socialist regions in the country.

The question of why anarchosyndicalism prevailed in Gijón is linked to the broader dilemma about the divided Spanish labor movement that continues to intrigue historians. The survival of an anarchist-influenced labor movement well into the twentieth century, and the relative weakness of Socialism until the 1930s, have provoked a number of explanatory paradigms.[1] Perhaps the most

---

[1] In general terms, the traditional paradigms fall into three categories: cultural, political and economic (leaving aside those that relied on some version of the Spanish "national character"). Cultural explanations saw a link between the "millenarianism" of anarchism

interesting aspect of the question has been why different versions of the labor movement flourished in certain areas of the country. Complicating this problem is the heterogeneity of the anarchosyndicalist movement, which makes it difficult to treat as a coherent phenomenon.[2] With this variety of variables, it seems unlikely that any monocausal or global explanation, from "national character" to "backwardness," could satisfy them all.[3]

Instead of over-arching generalizations, the key to interpreting the geography of the labor movement is buried in each local setting in which it took root. In this case, the key, at least in Gijón, was the local political context rather than the economic[4] and

and the intense religiosity of the Spaniards: see Gerald Brenan, *The Spanish Labyrinth* (London: Cambridge University Press, 1943) for the classic formulation of this position.

Economic arguments have been based on some version of Spanish backwardness. The classic Marxist teleology was articulated by Eric Hobsbawm in an influential essay, "Millenarianism II: The Andalusian Anarchists," in *Primitive Rebels: Studies in Archaic Forms of Social Movement in the 19th and 20th Centuries* (New York: Norton, 1959), where he connects backward economic development with the atavism of the anarchist labor movement. Within this economic paradigm there has been a separate debate about the rationality or irrationality of anarchism in the Spanish context. Thus, a variety of studies, from Temma Kaplan's *The Anarchists of Andalusia, 1868–1903* (Princeton: Princeton University Press, 1977), to Michael Seidman's *Workers against Work: Labor in Paris and Barcelona during the Popular Fronts* (Berkeley: University of California Press, 1991), have asserted that anarchism reflected a rational response to the realities of the Spanish economic context.

The political paradigm points to the unresponsiveness of the Spanish state as the origin of both the anti-statist movements of anarchism and federalism. See Pere Gabriel, "Classe obrera i sindicats a Catalunya, 1903–1923" (Ph.D. diss., University of Barcelona, 1981), and Albert Balcells, ed., *El arraigo del anarquismo en Cataluña: Textos de 1928–34* (Barcelona: Júcar, 1980). For a general review of the literature of the "causes" of anarchism, see Gabriel's bibliographic essay, "Historiografía reciente sobre el anarquismo y el sindicalismo en España, 1870–1923," *Historia Social*, 1 (1988), in which he asserts that the question of "causes" is still unresolved.

[2] On the heterogeneity of the anarchosyndicalist movement, see Xavier Paniagua Fuentes, *La sociedad libertaria: agrarismo e industrialización en el anarquismo español, 1930–1939* (Barcelona: Editorial Crítica, 1982), and for a compact version by the same author, *Anarquistas y socialistas* (Madrid: Historia 16, 1989), 93–103.

[3] "National character" has been largely discredited by historians, but "economic backwardness," despite being a slippery term with no concrete parameters, is still in current use.

[4] Applicable arguments based on economic structure were largely developed by Catalan historians for Barcelona, which, although much larger, shared certain characteristics with Gijón. Both cities were among the more industrialized of Spanish cities, and each was located in one of the economically "advanced" regions of the country, and yet anarchosyndicalism prevailed. To explain this phenomenon for Barcelona, historians have posited a connection between the shape of industrialization and the predominance of anarchism; i.e. the undercapitalization of capitalist enterprise preserved a number of small workshops and artisanal labor, and this decentralized structure mitigated against the effectiveness of the centralized unions of the Socialist UGT, and in favor of the autonomous, loose federations of the anarchosyndicalist CNT. Since Gijón shared a similar economic structure, its experience seemed to corroborate the links hypothesized for Barcelona. The classic version of this argument is found in Balcells' introduction to *El arraigo*. See Pere

social[5] structure of the city. While the inflexible and weakly reformist state provided a common political denominator, its differentiated impact spawned a variety of local political responses or dynamics. Within this spectrum, certain dynamics favored the insertion of the anarchosyndicalist, and others that of the Socialist movement. In Gijón, for example, a powerful conservative establishment and a venerable republican tradition left little room for a Socialist labor movement that depended on electoral conquest and moderate shop-floor tactics. Thus, the conservative stranglehold on the city helped legitimate the political cynicism of the anarchosyndicalists. In contrast to a mining town like Mieres, where a workers' party had a real chance of taking over the municipal government, in Gijón this possibility was unlikely even if every worker in the city voted for the Socialist party (PSOE). Further, the Socialists had to compete against an entrenched republican movement, particularly in its Federalist incarnation, that touted a similar platform of municipal reform. The anarchosyndical-ists, on the other hand, did not directly challenge the republican move-ment with an alternative political party, but maintained enough flexi-bility to maneuver within the existing system without being tainted by its failures. Furthermore, as has often been pointed out, federalism and anarchism shared a certain outlook, based on a belief in local autonomy and a suspicion of centralized authority. Thus, anarchism must have seemed more familiar to a working class weaned on federal-ist ideology.[6]

Gabriel, "Sindicalismo y sindicatos socialistas en Cataluña. The UGT, 1888–1938," *His-toria Social,* 8 (1990) for a more sophisticated version. However, this structural argument does not explain the other main anarchist stronghold in Asturias, the town of La Felguera, which contained one metallurgical factory that employed virtually all of the 5,000 mem-bers of the local CNT. Further, even in Gijón, the apparent decentralization was partly neutralized by the integration of the employers, both within and across sectors. Adrian Shubert, in *A Social History of Modern Spain* (London: Unwin Hyman, 1990), argues more broadly that the size or "modernity" of industries is not a good general predictor of anarchism versus socialism (p. 133).

[5] In terms of social structure, Balcells has argued that one of the important factors in the growth of anarchosyndicalism in Catalonia was the immigration of large numbers of illiter-ate and unskilled workers from the rural south, who were attracted to the more extremist anarchist philosophy. In Gijón, however, most immigrants came from within the prov-ince, and the population of the city was characterized by both stability and high literacy. Furthermore, in other parts of the province, similar immigrants joined the Socialist trade unions, particularly in the mining basin. More broadly, Joaquín Romero has pointed out that even the classic landless laborers did not inevitably turn to anarchism, as evidenced by the success of the Socialist farm workers' association (FNTT) in the 1930s: "The Spanish Case," *Government and Opposition,* 5:4 (1970).

[6] Angeles Barrio makes this point: *Anarquismo y anarcosindicalismo en Asturias* (Madrid: Siglo Veintiuno, 1988), 21.

Once the anarchosyndicalist movement established itself, its growing strength probably depended as much on the self-propelled tradition it created as on a fervent commitment to anarchist ideology.[7]
In simple terms, the labor movement in Gijón became identified with
anarchosyndicalism.[8] Although the Socialist movement struggled
along, joining the UGT meant living on the margin of the community
to which most of one's co-workers belonged. As new generations were
born into the city, this tradition would also be passed on from father
to son, as it was from Juan Bartolomé, who helped found the labor
movement, to his son Acracio, who became a CNT leader in the
1930s. By this point, the CNT (Confederación Nacional de Trabajo:
the anarchosyndicalist labor federation) stood as much for a way of
life as it did for a specific ideology.

Thus, the anarchosyndicalist movement inserted itself into the available political space and became one of the major players in a complex
local dynamic. Even though it claimed to remain aloof from all political activity, its presence had important repercussions for local politics.
In fact, its "anti-political" ideology gave the anarchosyndicalist movement a great deal of flexibility. At times, it could offer itself as the
pure alternative to a bankrupt republican reformism. At other times,
however, the anarchosyndicalist federation could quietly co-operate
with the republicans in ways that the Socialists, with their own exclusive political party, could not. Thus, in some contexts, the labor movement confined itself to purely syndicalist activity, the day-to-day struggle to improve working conditions and build a powerful front against
the employers. During these periods, the republican movement could
act as the unofficial political arm of a broad populist front, carrying
its battles beyond the workplace. But at strategic points of republican
weakness, the anarchosyndicalist movement could emphasize its independence and its revolutionary credentials.

The result was a complicated set of political relationships and networks that could have evolved in a number of ways, depending in part
on the success of the republicans' reformist strategies. Instead of a
clear distinction between political and anti-political, or reformist and
revolutionary, there existed a fluid boundary that changed according
to circumstances. Only after 1931 did this boundary begin to solidify.

---

[7] In any case, the degree of adherence to anarchist, anarchosyndicalist or syndicalist principles is difficult to determine, but this chapter is more concerned with political practice
than ideology.
[8] Juan Pablo Fusi makes this argument about socialism in the Basque country: *El país vasco,
pluralismo y nacionalidad* (Madrid: Alianza Editorial, 1984), 62–63.

After years of republican promises about the magical benefits of the Republic, the limitations of the new regime, especially in its local incarnation, reinforced the strength of a radical alternative. In this context, the anarchosyndicalist federation in Gijón, unaffected by the fratricidal war in the Catalan CNT, posed a formidable challenge to the local republican regime. To tell the story of how it developed into a powerful force is the task of this chapter.

The construction of a solid anarchosyndicalist organization was a long and slow process that culminated in the 1930s, when the local CNT reached the height of its powers. As elsewhere in Spain, its development was hindered by waves of repression, which periodically broke or crippled the organization. Likewise, the ongoing confrontation between Socialists and anarchosyndicalists often prevented the labor movement from presenting a united front. But these weaknesses were also countered by considerable advantages. The flexibility of the anarchosyndicalist movement resulted in an adaptive strategy that was well suited to the dramatic changes in political climate. At the same time, the movement maintained an unusually high level of continuity, in its leadership and in its basic philosophical stance, which tried to balance the mundane tasks of trade unionism with the aspirations of anarchist revolution. While it is always difficult to interpret how all of this filtered through the rank and file, the organization's membership levels certainly demonstrate a basic degree of unwavering loyalty that provided yet another element of continuity. By the 1930s, then, the long and slow process had produced a coherent organization backed by a solid mass base, a combination unmatched by any other political force in the city.

Laying the foundations, 1901–1916

During the first decade of the century, however, the weaknesses of the labor movement were much more apparent than its strengths. With little tradition or experience to sustain it, the movement simply collapsed after the disastrous general strike of 1901. The 5,500 unionized workers of 1900 dwindled to a few hundred by the years 1903–1904, and notices of meetings or strikes were replaced by complaints of inertia and pleas to re-establish communication.[9]

Anarchists and Socialists naturally blamed each other for the

[9] For example, *Tiempos Nuevos*, December 1, 1905; *El Noroeste*, June 18, 1904; *El Socialista*, July 31, 1908.

collapse, and invested much of their energy during these years in venting this hostility.[10] The battle lines acquired physical as well as rhetorical dimensions, as Socialists and anarchists retreated into separate union centers that became the loci of several violent confrontations. In April of 1904, for example, when anarchist hecklers shouted down the speaker at a Socialist propaganda meeting, the ensuing mêlée ended in the fatal stabbing of Socialist Modesto Costales.[11] Amid conflicting accounts of what had happened, the one clear conclusion, as the prosecutor at the trial pointed out, was that anarchists and Socialists "loathed each other."[12]

Despite the destructiveness of this rivalry, it also had positive effects. The clear ideological and strategic stance of the Socialist movement forced the anarchists to come to terms with their own identity as a mass movement. By 1909, when the unions reappeared, they had developed the emerging ideas of anarchosyndicalism into a clear alternative.[13] Crucial to this evolution was a new generation of leaders formed under the tutelage of Ricardo Mella, one of Spain's prominent anarchist theorists, who lived in Gijón during these years of reflection. The most important of the new leaders was Eleuterio Quintanilla, whose influence on the local anarchosyndicalist movement extended through the 1930s.[14] Also among this group were Pedro Sierra, who would represent Asturias at the CNT congress of 1918, and José María Martínez, architect of the Workers' Alliance (Alianza Obrera) and martyr of the October 1934 revolution.

The basic theoretical and strategic framework that emerged from this process of self-definition clearly opposed that of the Socialists.[15]

---

[10] In 1901, a verbal polemic on this issue was carried on between Manuel Vigil in *El Socialista* and Rogelio Fernández in the anarchist *La Revista Blanca*.

[11] *El Noroeste*, April 28, 1904.

[12] *Aurora Social*, August 12, 1904.

[13] Angeles Barrio makes this point in *Anarquismo y anarcosindicalismo*, 49. For a more detailed discussion on the theoretical development of this period, see pp. 49–67.

[14] Quintanilla was born in Gijón, the son of a concierge and a cigarette maker. A *chocolatero* by profession, he later helped found and run the Escuela Neutra, a free-thinking private secondary school. His politicization process began when his federalist employer encouraged him to read the worker press and attend classes at the Ateneo Obrero. He met Mella in 1903, when the latter was giving a lecture on "The Great Works of Civilization" at the Instituto de Jovellanos. On his life, see the political biography by his fellow *cenetista*, Ramón Alvarez Palomo, *Eleuterio Quintanilla* (Mexico: Editores Mexicanos Unidos, 1973).

[15] On the Socialists' strategic and theoretical orientation during this period, see Manuel Pérez Ledesma, *El obrero consciente: dirigentes, partidos y sindicatos en la II International* (Madrid: Alianza Editorial, 1987), Chapter 7 and Paul Heywood, *Marxism and the Fail-*

Anarchosyndicalism combined the revolutionary and anti-political orientation of the old Bakuninist anarchist movement with the economic organization of syndicalism. Whereas the Socialists pursued a strategy of electoral conquest, the anarchosyndicalists supported what they called direct action, which meant "that the workers deal directly, without intermediaries, whether they are workers or politicians, or bourgeois or authorities, with those with whom they have a conflict."[16] This contrast drew a clear line between those who accepted the possibility of the state as intermediary and those who did not. The most powerful weapon in the direct action arsenal was the general strike, which was to be used to destabilize the capitalist state. In contrast, the Socialist unions were to employ the strike only as a method of last resort, and only in the pursuit of limited, attainable goals. These opposing perspectives on the role of the trade union resulted in two types of organizational structures as well. To build a solid structure, the Socialists employed paid bureaucrats and charged membership dues, which were used to pay salaries and fill the coffers of strike funds. In contrast, the anarchosyndicalists rejected this regimentation as both useless and dangerously authoritarian.

The development of these two versions of the labor movement reached a crucial point at the end of the decade. The Socialists expressed their commitment to political gradualism when Gijón's branch joined the national PSOE in forming an electoral coalition (the Conjunción) with the republicans in 1909. In the same year, the anarchosyndicalists constituted their first local federation, and in 1910 they enthusiastically promoted the creation of the National Confederation of Workers (CNT), as an independent syndicalist alternative to the path chosen by the PSOE/UGT.[17]

Both movements had a chance to put theory into practice when a

---

ure of Organised Socialism in Spain, 1879–1936 (Cambridge: Cambridge University Press, 1990), Chapter 1.

[16] As defined by Catalan anarchosyndicalist Angel Pestaña, when trying to explain that the concept meant more than going into the street and beating up scabs. Quoted in Pérez Ledesma, *El obrero consciente*, 261.

[17] The founding congress of the CNT explicitly defined an organization that would be both anarchist – anti-political, decentralized, and anti-authoritarian; and syndicalist – organized by trade, employing the weapons of the general strike and direct action, and working for the economic emancipation of the workers. However, the balance between these two aspects of the organization would be constantly contested over the next three decades. For a fuller description of the founding of the CNT, see Antonio Bar, *La CNT en los años rojos: del sindicalismo revolucionario al anarcosindicalismo, 1910–1926* (Madrid: Akal Editor, 1981). The organization was formally established in 1911 with about 30,000 members.

new phase of associationism opened in Gijón in 1909, probably connected to the political ferment of that year, which produced the
"Tragic Week" in Barcelona and the first republican city council in
Gijón. As suddenly as had occurred a decade earlier, workers again
flocked to join the unions, this time divided into two centers. By the
end of 1909, the anarchist and Socialist press was overflowing with
enthusiasm:

> As can be seen by what we have said . . . the seed sown before 1901
> is finally producing its fruits. The old plant, withered and dejected for
> so many years, has been reborn, vigorous and verdant. The enthusiasm
> and the perseverance of a handful of believers has made possible this
> miracle . . . the reorganization of the Gijonese proletariat has proceeded
> so rapidly that even these believers see it as a miracle.[18]

The one sour note in all this activity was the unabated competition
between Socialists and anarchosyndicalists. "It would be difficult to
find a city in Spain where the battles between factions of the militant
proletariat are as vicious as they are in Gijón," admitted one anarchist
editorial, and another cited the trade union movement's inability to
overcome its internal ideological feuds as one of its greatest weaknesses.[19] Moreover, according to membership statistics in 1910, no
clear victor had yet emerged (see Table 10). The anarchosyndicalist
federation had the highest membership, but Socialist, federalist and
independent trade unions still claimed an important share.

Over the next few years, however, the tide clearly turned. One of
the decisive events in this evolution was the bitter labor conflict of
late 1910 and 1911 that encompassed nine months of constant confrontation, a general strike, and the assassination of an employer.
While the Socialists again complained about anarchist imprudence, the
hysteria and extremism of the Employers' Association helped legitimate the more combative stance of the anarchosyndicalist federation.
In this polarized atmosphere, the Socialists' credo of moderation
seemed out of place. The failure of the Conjunción to produce tangible results for the Socialists only enhanced this image of helplessness,
which the anarchists fully exploited. As *El Libertario* argued, the Conjunción "could not even manage the repeal of the draconian laws,
prevent the repression following the events of last September [i.e. the

---

[18] *Solidaridad Obrera*, December 11, 1909.
[19] *El Libertario*, August 17, 1912 and *Solidaridad Obrera*, November 27, 1909.

Table 10 *Union organization, 1910*

	1/1910	?/1910
Centro calle Casimiro Velasco (anarchist)		
"El Progreso," masons	510	584
"La Prevenida," carpenters and cabinet-makers	270	280
"El Reflejo," painters	110	110
"El Espátula," molders	115	100
"La Constructiva," boilermakers	120	122
"La Mecánica," turners, blacksmiths, fitters	120	120
"El Sindical," various trades	40	34
"La Primera," bottle makers	115	115
"La Fraternidad," glassmakers	70	70
"El Despertar," stonecutters	16	16
"Unión Obrera," mechanical sawyers	360	312
"La Progresiva," engravers	115	144
"Estrella del Arte," carriage makers	40	40
"La Prosperidad," barbers	40	50
"La Aurora," bakers	80	80
Total	2,121	2,177
Centro calle Anselmo Cifuentes (UGT)		
"La Terrestre," railroad workers	100	?
"El Primero de Mayo," Musel port workers	215	268
Agrupación Socialista, Tremañes	22	20
Agrupación Socialista, Gijón	41	?
"La Chispa," bronze- and tinsmiths	40	25
"La Cerámica," potters	50	40
"El Fieltro," hat-makers	30	27
"El Trabajo," metalworkers	155	140
"La Organizadora," various trades	210	180
"La Conciencia," packers	147	116
"La Velocidad," streetcar workers	87	80
"Luz y Fuerza," electricians and gas workers	70	70
"La Minerva," typesetters	105	65
"La Legal," municipal workers	165	157
"La Unión Asturiana," waiters	70	56
Socialist Youth, Gijón	28	36
Total	1,547	1,364
Casino Federal		
"La Cantábrica," dockworkers	368	365
"La Dársena," carters	125	126
Total	493	491
Independent		
Fishermen	480	480
Farmers' Association	1,306	1,306
Business clerks	115	115
Total	6,062	5,933

Sources: *El Noroeste*, January 7, 1910; *Boletín del Instituto de Reformas Sociales*, 8 (1911).

strike], or institute one law that has benefitted the working class."[20] Whether as a result of the anarchist attacks or of Socialist frustration at the party's impotence in Gijón, the local PSOE branch had been reduced to a handful of militants by the middle of the decade.[21]

There are no complete statistics for the trade unions during these years, but it appears as if the UGT fought its last major battle in Gijón in the metallurgical industry in 1913. Over a period of almost nine months, the Socialists worked to get Gijón's metalworkers to join a common regional syndicate that would belong to the UGT.[22] If it had succeeded, this campaign would have kept their foothold in the city and established a link with the powerful regional organization.[23] The defeat of this campaign seemed to break the back of the local Socialist movement.[24]

As the Socialists lost ground, the anarchosyndicalist federation began to build a permanent infrastructure. Although the mass union movement collapsed again after the general strike of 1910, in the quieter years before the world war the federation began to focus on longer-term organizational goals that would pay off in the long run. As one article summed up, "the present period of calm, in terms of worker/employer conflicts, greatly favors the work of professional and corporative organization."[25] Thus, while the movement kept a low profile in terms of open conflicts, membership quietly surpassed its pre-strike levels by mid-1912. The contrast with the much slower

[20] September 21, 1912.
[21] In 1914, the local party counted thirty members; by 1915, the number had dropped to twenty-one. The much smaller towns of Sama and Mieres had three times as many active socialists: seventy-four and sixty-four, respectively: letters from the Asturian Socialist party to the local branch in Gijón, February 10 and September 11, 1915 (AGS, H-29).
[22] Correspondence between the Sindicato Obrero Metalúrgico Asturiano and a federation of Gijonese metal unions, May to December, 1913 (AGS, K-20).
[23] The Asturian Socialist miners' union alone had 10,000 members in 1913, and almost 13,000 by 1915, about a tenth of the national membership of the UGT: Adrian Shubert, *The Road to Revolution in Spain: The Coal Miners of Asturias, 1860–1934* (Urbana: University of Illinois Press, 1987), 112. For statistics on the national UGT, see Miguel Martínez Cuadrado, *La burguesía conservadora, 1874–1931* (Madrid: Alianza Editorial, 1974), 487. In 1915, the UGT had 121,550 members, while the PSOE had 14,332. In contrast, the Asturian anarchosyndicalists had failed in their attempt to form a regional federation in November 1913 (*El Noroeste*, November 21, 1913), and the national CNT had been outlawed and pushed underground by the government in 1911.
[24] Defeat was apparent in declining membership in the metal syndicate: according to a membership list covering the period from January 1913 through 1916, the number of new members registered in the Socialist metallurgical syndicate in Gijón declined from 165 in 1913, to 70 in 1914, and to 90 for both 1915 and 1916. In 1916, the total membership of 289 was only a fraction of the number of metalworkers in the city.
[25] *El Libertario*, October 5, 1912.

recovery after the 1901 strike seems to indicate that members were developing a longer-term perspective on what the struggle entailed.

In accord with this longer-term perspective, the federation opened its first libraries and cultural centers (see Chapter 8), and laid the groundwork for a broader organizational framework to link workers in different trades.[26] Perhaps the most important symbolic initiative in integrating the union movement was the project to construct a Casa del Pueblo.[27] Quintanilla and other leaders were convinced that the Casa would provide a sense of continuity that would help the movement survive periodic defeats like 1901 and 1910 and keep the workers from scattering.[28] The Casa was not completed until 1928, but the process of raising money, getting city approval, picking a design and finally constructing it provided an important focal point for the movement over the next two decades. Moreover, it helped the anarchosyndicalist federation to establish itself as the voice of the labor movement in Gijón. While the Socialists remained aloof, local republicans donated money, the city architect contributed the design, and the city council approved its request to buy the land. When the Socialists later tried to submit a request to build a separate Casa del Pueblo, the republican city council turned it down on the grounds that the city only needed one.[29] Thus, even before it was completed, the Casa del Pueblo stood as a visual symbol of Socialist marginalization in Gijón.

Completing the infrastructure, 1917–1923

Over the next few years, before the Dictatorship imposed another hiatus on the development of the anarchosyndicalist movement, the local federation succeeded in building a solid structure on the ground

---

[26] Thus, the painters, carpenters and masons discussed forming a "local federalist pact between the construction guilds" that prefigured the industrial syndicates formed after the war (*El Libertario*, October 5, 1912). Likewise, workers in the chocolate and pastry-making industries agreed to form a society integrating all trades connected to the food industry (*El Noroeste*, October 14, 1913).

[27] "Casa del Pueblo" literally means "house of the people," but there is no effective translation into English. "Union center" is too narrow, because the Casa was meant to be more than a place where each union held its meetings.

[28] From a retrospective article on the history of the Casa del Pueblo: *El Noroeste*, August 17, 1930.

[29] When the one Socialist city councilman argued that the workers' movement was irreconcilably split and could not unite under one roof, the republicans responded (disingenuously) that the federation (CNT) intended to admit workers of all political persuasions into its Casa del Pueblo: minutes of the city council meeting, *El Noroeste*, March 28, 1913.

that had been prepared. These last years of the constitutional monarchy were fraught with conflict, from the general strike of August
1917 to the spiraling violence of political assassinations (*pistolerismo*)
in Barcelona and other cities, but the CNT in Gijón managed to
remain largely intact.[30] Its ability to steer a stable course through these
rough waters can be attributed largely to the development of a flexible
moderation that would become the hallmark of Gijón's CNT. Once
the Socialists had been marginalized, the federation concentrated on
the practical tasks of solidifying its roots in the city and of transforming
its organizational structure. At the same time, it trained a new generation of union leaders who would be prepared to take over in 1931. By
1923, then, the movement's continuity and stability had established it
as a permanent force in local politics.

The new path of flexible moderation was evident in the events leading up to the August 1917 strike. The strike movement was part of
a nationwide attack on the political system, but in Asturias, an alliance
of CNT and UGT unions and republican and Reformist politicians
gave it a greater transcendence. As a result, the strike lasted three
weeks longer in Asturias than anywhere else. Gijón's anarchists were
among the first and most vigorous proponents of this surprising rapprochement between the two union movements.[31] As Quintanilla
argued,

> We wish for a reconciliation of all the worker elements of Spain, if only
> to deal with the machinations of businessmen and profiteers, as well as
> to let the government know how displeased we are with its criminal
> conduct . . . afterwards, it would be easier to make an effective syndical
> unity that would bring so many benefits to the Spanish proletariat.[32]

While at first glance this conciliatory attitude seems inexplicable, given

---

[30] The basic text on the social and political unrest of this period is Gerald Meaker, *The Revolutionary Left in Spain, 1914–1923* (Stanford: University of Stanford Press, 1974). Nationally, the CNT at first benefited from the politicization of the period by ballooning from 30,000 members in 1915 to several hundred thousand (as many as 800,000, but the figures are uncertain) by 1919, but violence and repression led to its collapse only a couple of years later. See Bar, *La CNT*, 339–341, 492.

[31] At a national level, this rapprochement led to the Pact of Zaragoza, signed between the CNT and the UGT in July of 1916, for the purpose of co-ordinating a series of joint actions that culminated in the political strike of August 1917. The pact agreed to pursue joint action for the purpose of controlling prices, solving the work crisis and releasing political prisoners. Nevertheless, the anarchosyndicalist movement was not integrated enough for this pact to have uniform impact, so that UGT/CNT relations depended very much on local conditions.

[32] *Renovación*, May 1916.

178

the local history of enmity, at a deeper level it makes sense. After years of jockeying for position, the local anarchosyndicalist movement was finally strong enough to reach out without fear of losing its identity or its status.

However, the hopes for syndical unity never materialized, and the Socialists and anarchosyndicalists retreated into their opposing corners, from where they continued their customary attacks. The August 1917 strike had represented a kind of middle ground, where the Socialists moved towards revolutionary direct action and the anarchosyndicalists participated in a movement demanding the democratization of the political system. After it collapsed, however, Socialists interpreted this as a sign of the danger of revolutionary action, and reaffirmed their faith in moderation and electoral reform. The anarchosyndicalists took the opposite message from the strike, and strengthened their anti-political rhetoric with direct attacks, not only on the Socialists, but on the Reformists, with whom they had had a cordial relationship.[33]

And yet, while the local CNT used the political chaos of the declining monarchy to reaffirm its anti-political ideals, in other ways it was clearly open to change. Thus, the anarchosyndicalist federation ended up accepting many of the organizational strategies first adopted by Socialists and once rejected by anarchists as authoritarian and bureaucratic. In addition to embracing more complex forms of organization like the industrial union, the federation also agreed to the necessity of membership dues, paid bureaucrats and strike funds. Apparently, the anarchosyndicalists had come to the conclusion that a strong and stable organization was as important as the Socialists had always insisted. From this point on, they attempted to balance the need for a stable organization with the fighting mentality of a revolutionary force.

Industrial unionism was adopted officially by the CNT at the 1919 national congress, with Gijón's enthusiastic adherence. The old

---

[33] Angeles Barrio (*Anarquismo y anarcosindicalismo*) remarks on this relationship, although there is little concrete evidence for it aside from the fact that Quintanilla belonged to a masonic lodge where many prominent Reformists, including Melquíades, were members (p. 180). The breakdown of this relationship came after August 1917, when the Reformists turned their attention to achieving power within the system (pp. 255–256). In the last few years, attacks on the Reformists in the anarchist press became more frequent, such as the article in *Solidaridad Obrera* (June 22, 1923) in which Quintanilla lashed out against the *caciquismo* of the Reformists, even more odious, he insisted, than that of the *pidalistas* (followers of Conservative politician Alejandro Pidal y Mon) whom they replaced.

"societies of resistance" were to become "sections" of broader units that would incorporate all the workers of a particular industrial sector. Since, by its very nature, a section is not an autonomous unit but a part of a greater whole, the new organization encouraged both centralization and the social homogenization of the working class. From 1919 to early 1920, *sindicatos únicos* in Gijón were formed in the food industry, the building trades, the glass industry, the clothing industry, maritime and terrestrial transport, metallurgy, and a mixed syndicate for miscellaneous trades. The need for the new organizational structure was justified by reference to the more complex capitalist world:

> because of the cohesion of the employers, which often leads to a generalization of labor struggles, and because of the increasing specialization within the trades of each industry, spurred on by developments in machinery and in industrial technique, and because of the growing overlap of issues that require solidarity.[34]

However the new strategy was explained, it was consistent with the evolution of the movement towards a greater investment in organizational cohesion and away from the early reliance on spontaneity and raw enthusiasm.

Another sign of this evolution was the acceptance of "reformist" practices that only a few years ago the movement had condemned. As one Socialist pointed out, most of the syndicates at the anarchist center had opened permanent strike funds, and the administrative committee had created a central bank for the accumulation of dues. Furthermore, he added, most of the strikes waged by these syndicates made limited quality-of-life demands that differed little in content from those of the Socialists.[35] In another reversal, the young José María Martínez admitted that the unions had to face the reality of paid staff positions, even though they should guard against their abuse.[36] Discussion of the increasing sophistication of the organization continued up to the last local congress, in June of 1923, where some delegates argued for the formation of a single "Workers' Syndicate" that included all workers.[37]

---

[34] Report of a local congress, *El Metalúrgico Asturiano*, April 6, 1920.
[35] *El Noroeste*, December 28, 1917. The author, Ramón Martínez Peón, used this evidence to argue that there were no fundamental differences between the two trade union federations.
[36] *El Noroeste*, August 4, 1919.
[37] The themes debated at the congress ranged from organizational matters to the integration of non-workers, from wives to technical personnel, into the movement: *Solidaridad Obrera*, June 15 and 22, 1923, and *El Noroeste*, June 23, 1923.

As always, however, the process of consolidation was not a smooth one. Whereas in earlier years inter-federation rivalry had posed the biggest obstacle, now it was repression. Increasingly abandoned as a lost cause by the national and regional Socialist federations, Gijón's small core of Socialist militants were no longer a threat.[38] In contrast, the government's nationwide clampdown, provoked by violent labor unrest in Andalusia and Catalonia, made life more difficult for the local CNT, even though its primary impact was elsewhere.[39] The fledgling regional federation (CRT), formed in 1920 with over 18,000 members, was reduced to 1,000 by 1922, and the national federation was decimated. In addition, the combination of employer and government pressure forced the local federation to dismantle the new industrial unions in 1921 (see Chapter 10).

Nevertheless, the setback was temporary. When the government eased back on its restrictions in late 1922, Gijón's federation began a dramatic recovery. Before the coup of September 1923, several of the *sindicatos únicos* had been reconstituted, as well as the provincial CRT, which had regained 6,590 of its members.[40] Another sign that the organization was alive and well was the local congress of June 1923, where the enthusiastic tone expressed the conviction that it was in a period of expansion and development rather than contraction. While this promise was cut short by the coup later that year, it is important that Gijón's organization had not been decapitated and demoralized, as had its counterpart in Barcelona and elsewhere. While

[38] From the extant correspondence, it appears as if the PSOE had written off Gijón as a lost cause. In 1919, Gijón's Socialists requested funds for a massive propaganda campaign, given the city's industrial importance, but the provincial committee refused, advising it to rely on its own resources (letter from the local branch to the executive committee, expressing outrage at its neglect: February 11). Likewise, during the 1923 electoral campaign the executive committee tactfully informed the Agrupación that the PSOE had made an electoral deal with the republicans, giving up Gijón so that the republicans would support Socialist candidates elsewhere (letter, executive committee to local branch, suggesting that the latter drop its candidate in the upcoming election) (AGS, H-29).

[39] In 1918–1920, Andalusia was a hotbed of rural insurrection; in Catalonia the infamous "Canadiense" strike that lasted for almost six months during 1919 brought the city of Barcelona to a standstill, and the war of *pistoleros* waged by employers and the CNT resulted in the loss of 1,500 lives, 900 of them in Barcelona, according to Murray Bookchin, *The Spanish Anarchists: The Heroic Years, 1868–1936* (New York: Harper and Row, 1977), 191. On events in Catalonia, see León-Ignacio, *Los años de pistolerismo* (Barcelona: Planeta, 1981), and on rural Andalusia, see the classic work of Juan Díaz del Moral, *Historia de las agitaciones campesinas andaluzas: Córdoba* (1929; reprint, Madrid: Alianza Editorial, 1973) and Antonio Barragón Moriana, *Conflictividad social y desarticulación política en la provincia de Córdoba 1918–1920* (Córdoba: Publicaciones del Ayuntamiento, 1990).

[40] In September 1923, the CRT held a regional congress: *El Noroeste*, September 4, 1923.

activity was severely limited during the Dictatorship, the Gijonese anarchosyndicalists had an essentially sound and coherent organizational structure that was ready to re-launch whenever the political circumstances changed.

A pause: the Dictatorship, 1923–1930

The success in holding the local federation together before September 1923 also helped it weather the next six years better than most of the other *cenetista* federations. The government did not categorically outlaw the CNT, but its attempt to impose strict regimentation on union organizations put it in an uncomfortable position.[41] Those federations that refused to collaborate with the state were suppressed, and those that accepted had to operate in a narrow legal sphere that drained them of any revolutionary content. This dilemma opened an internal debate within the CNT that exacerbated the underlying tension over its identity and eventually ended in the schism of the 1930s. Gijón's anarchists participated in this debate as well, but the local leadership united behind an intermediary position between revolutionary anarchism and pure syndicalism, a position they held through the 1930s.[42]

Essential to this balance was the commitment to a mass base, which led Gijón's anarchist leaders to argue that the CNT should maintain as much of a legal profile as the regime permitted. As Quintanilla argued, the organization should operate "in the light of day," since "clandestineness is counterproductive to its efficacious labor."[43] This strategy of moderation drew support from a tolerant Civil Governor, who fomented an environment in which the federation could maintain at least a reduced existence.[44] In the first few years of the Dictatorship,

[41] On the regulations, see B. Olías de Lima Gete, *El derecho de asociación en España, 1868–1974* (Madrid: Instituto de Estudios Administrativos, 1977), 69–74.
[42] On the theoretical controversy within the CNT during the 1920s, see Antonio Elorza, "El anarcosindicalismo español bajo la Dictadura, 1923–1930," *Revista de Trabajo*, 39–40, 44–45, 46 (1972–1974). From the Asturian perspective, see Barrio, *Anarquismo y anarcosindicalismo*, Chapter 4. On the CNT in Catalonia, see Susanna Tavera, "Els anarcosindicalistes catalans i la dictadura," *L'Avenc*, 72 (1984). The controversy led, in 1927, to the formation of an independent anarchist federation, the FAI (Federación Anarquista Ibérica), that would work for pure anarchist revolutionary goals.
[43] *Solidaridad Obrera*, September 27, 1925. During its 1925–1926 stint, the newspaper carried on a wide-ranging debate about tactics, strategy and orientation, but there was general agreement that the future of the movement lay in an open, mass-based organization.
[44] Angeles Barrio points out that the policies of each Civil Governor differed enormously, and that the one in Asturias was among the most tolerant. In Barcelona, for example, the CNT was outlawed in May of 1924: *Anarquismo y anarcosindicalismo*, 264.

most of Gijón's unions kept their legal status by submitting their statutes and their activities to the Civil Governor for approval.[45] The relative freedom of movement permitted the re-appearance of *Solidaridad Obrera* in 1925, the only local edition to survive after 1923, and it attracted the national committee of the CNT, which resided in the city until 1926. In addition, it permitted ongoing work on the Casa del Pueblo, which became the official headquarters of the federation in 1927, and was formally inaugurated in 1930. The result was not by any means a booming and vigorous movement, but the maintenance of an organizational shell that provided, along with the old generation of leaders, an impressive degree of continuity. Thus, *Solidaridad Obrera* reported in late 1925 that the glassmakers' union existed but was going through hard times, the transport workers were slowly reconstituting, the food industry syndicate contained only bakers, waiters, pastry makers and a few others, and the textile and graphics arts syndicates had been reduced to their executive committees. Of the two largest syndicates, the metalworkers' had disappeared, but that of the construction workers still listed 800 affiliates in 1925.[46] While the newspaper saw nothing to boast of in this motley collection, in many other areas of the country the CNT existed only in its theoretical polemics.[47] Even the bare survival of the trade union structure, combined with the unusual continuity of leadership in the local federation, put it in an excellent position to take advantage of the fall of the Dictatorship in 1930.[48]

The Republic, 1931–1936

The ground had been so well prepared that by the municipal elections of April 1931 the CNT federation had completely reconstituted

---

[45] On October 11, 1923, for example, the Sindicato Metalúrgico de Gijón submitted its statutes (cited in Barrio, *Anarquismo y anarcosindicalismo*, 265). Further documentation of these requests is sparse, but other clues exist. For example, on December 12, 1925, the Construction Syndicate was indefinitely suspended because it refused to drop the word "único," but the memo indicates that it had survived for over two years (AHN, legajo 58A, núm.34). Also, in November 1925 *Solidaridad Obrera* complained about the eight days' advance notice that unions had to give when they scheduled meetings, but this implies that the unions existed and complied.

[46] *Solidaridad Obrera*, November 27, 1925; Registro, Sindicato de Construcción (AGS, K-104).

[47] Raymond Carr, *Spain: 1808–1939* (Oxford: Oxford University Press, 1975), 570: "the movement ceased to exist for seven years."

[48] In addition to the familiar faces trained under Mella, like Quintanilla, Martínez and Sierra, there were younger men like Avelino Entrialgo and Avelino Mallada, who first joined the movement in the last years of the monarchy and became prominent during the 1930s.

and established itself as a leading force in the transition to a new regime.[49] After the declaration of the Republic, the CNT emerged as one of the most powerful players on the local political scene, with its control of the labor movement, its solid mass organization and its informal ties with the Federalists. Moreover, instead of experiencing a decline over the course of the Republic, as it did in many other regions, the CNT in Gijón increased its influence and status.[50] Through a combination of factors, including the collapse of the Federalists, the avoidance of a schism between anarchists and syndicalists and the conclusion of the "Workers' Alliance" that ended the long feud with the Socialists, by 1936 the CNT was the most formidable political force in the city.

The federation's political role in the Republic had its roots in the uncertain months after the Dictatorship had collapsed but before the fall of the monarchy. In December 1930 the CNT participated in the monumental popular mobilization against the monarchy, and from this point until after the establishment of the Republic it acted almost as an unofficial guardian of the political transition. As a manifesto issued on April 14 declared,

> Although [the anarchosyndicalists] have not participated officially in the revolutionary movement, nor entered into its directing organisms, we have taken to the streets in support of it, as we did for the December movement, and we affirm our RESOLUTION TO KEEP OUR GUARD UP AGAINST ANY POSSIBLE REVOLUTIONARY ATTEMPT that tries

---

[49] According to records from the October 1930 CNT congress in Barcelona, Gijón's federation contained 3,000 members (Alvarez Palomo, *Eleuterio Quintanilla*, 75). At the July 1931 congress, it claimed 11,416 members: Confederación Nacional de Trabajo, *Memoria del Congreso*, 1931; reprinted in *Revista de Trabajo*, 53 (1976).

[50] Asturias was the only other region besides Madrid (because it began with such a small *cenetista* movement) that did not experience a membership decline between 1931 and 1936. In Gijón, the number of members declined slightly, from its peak of 14,713 in 1932 to 11,397 in 1934, but the peak is skewed by the temporary creation of the Syndicate of Public Interests in 1932, which added 1,500 members that disappeared after the syndicate was dissolved (because it was so successful, according to an oral interview with Ramón Alvarez). In contrast, the Catalan, Andalusian and Levantine federations lost as much as 45% of their members. As a result, the CNT never regained its 1919 level of membership before the Civil War: David Ruiz, "Clase, sindicatos y partidos en Asturias, 1931–1934," in *Estudios de Historia Social*, 31 (1984), 94. A good local study of decline is José Manuel Macarro Vera's *La utopía revolucionaria: Sevilla en la II República* (Sevilla: Monte de Piedad y Caja de Ahorros, 1985). Whereas the CNT began the Republic as the majority force in the province, its decline from 26,000 to 18,000 between 1933 and May 1936 made it a minority force in the working-class movement for the first time (p. 62).

to return us to the undignified regimes condemned by universal conscience.[51]

A leaflet distributed a month later went even further, openly proclaiming the CNT's instrumental role in the establishment of the new regime:

> There was no choice but to end the monarchy, using whatever means possible, and since the moment of the social revolution has not arrived, the CNT paused its anti-parliamentary campaign so that the liberal bourgeois political parties could carry out their historic mission – long neglected by them in our country.[52]

After the declaration of the Republic, the federation continued its tone of moderation in its official press. One writer cautioned that the newly revived union movement should start slowly, beginning with the recuperation of wages and benefits and the improvement of workers' moral characters.[53] In another editorial, José María Martínez expressed the hope that the interaction between workers and the middle classes would bring them into a closer understanding as "brothers in a great family that human society has converted into slaves."[54]

The concrete agenda laid out by the federation was equally devoid of maximalist claims. The themes discussed at the local congress of October 1931 give an indication of this orientation: from achieving the six-hour work day to lobbying the city for improved sanitation, health care, and help for the unemployed, none challenged the limits of a reformist Republic.[55] Likewise, the statutes of the metallurgical syndicate stated that its primary objective was "to improve the moral and material condition of its associates."[56] In line with this focus, the federation showed considerable restraint in its

---

[51] *El Noroeste*, April 14, 1931; emphasis in original.
[52] Distributed throughout the city and printed in *El Noroeste*, May 19, 1931. Although it is difficult to interpret abstention rates, the percentage of non-voters in the April 1931 election was lower than it had been for the last elections of the monarchy in Gijón: 30% in 1920–1922, and 23% in 1931 (Barrio, *Anarquismo y anarcosindicalismo*, 317).
[53] *Solidaridad*, July 18, 1931.
[54] *Solidaridad*, September 19, 1931.
[55] An account of the 1931 congress is found in *Solidaridad*, October 10, 1931. The regional congress of September 1932 was similarly moderate in tone, concerned mostly with solving the unemployment problem (*El Noroeste*, September 28, 29, 30, 1932).
[56] Reglamento, Sindicato Metalúrgico, CNT, April 21, 1930 (AGS, K-46). The statutes of the UGT Federación de Construcción express a similar goal: the "improvement of the situation and conditions of workers through economic action" (AGS, H-24).

2

use of destabilizing weapons like the general strike[57] or terrorist violence.[58]

The pragmatism of the federation is also clear in the position it took in the internal ideological dispute that became public in August 1931 through the challenge issued in the so-called "Manifesto de los Treinta." The *treintistas* criticized the conspiratorial and ultra-revolutionary stance of the anarchists in the FAI, and argued that the CNT needed time to build up its strength and prepare for a more distant revolution.[59] The ensuing battle for control over the CNT culminated with the victory of the FAI position within the CNT and the expulsion of the moderates in the summer of 1933. The latter formed a dissident federation until their reinstatement in May of 1936.[60] The basic position expressed by the *treintistas* and their most prominent spokesperson, Angel Pestaña, was shared by most of Gijón's *cenetista* leaders, who agreed that the radicals took an overly confrontational stance. However, despite this agreement, the Gijonese refused to provoke an open split in the CNT.[61] Instead of publicly confronting the radicals, the federation in Gijón quietly followed its own route, never allowing the anarchist cadres of the FAI to mold it into a pure revolutionary

[57] For example, in May 1933 Gijón's CNT criticized a general strike called by the national federation as inopportune, although it participated to show its solidarity. Then, at the regional congress in July, the more radical metalworkers of La Felguera tried to pressure Gijón's federation into joining their general strike against Duro Felguera, but the Gijonese offered instead to take in the children of the strikers (Pleno Regional, July 1933: AGS, K-46).

[58] A few isolated terrorist acts occurred, mostly after the elections of December 1933, but it is difficult to know the relationship between the perpetrators and the federation. A bomb was found in an empty trolley car, another in the window of a Dominican monastery, and a third exploded at the port, where a guard was killed. Another bomb went off in the Teatro de Jovellanos, and police caught three others with bomb in hand (Audencia Provincial de Oviedo, caja 78:325, caja 79:132,249).

[59] On *treintismo* and the ideological split in the CNT, see E. Vega, *El Trentisme a Catalunya. Divergències ideològiques en la CNT (1930–1933)* (Barcelona: Curial, 1980); Susanna Tavera, "La ideología política del anarcosindicalismo catalán a través de su propaganda" (Doctoral Thesis, University of Barcelona, 1980), and Antonio Elorza, *La Utopía anarquista bajo la Segunda República* (Madrid: Ayuso, 1973).

[60] The size of the dissident federation was small – about 70,000 rejoined the CNT in May 1936 at the congress of Zaragoza, bringing the total membership of the CNT to half a million. Nevertheless, it had a concentrated impact on certain areas in Catalonia. A classic study of one of the dissident federations is Albert Balcells, "La crisis del anarcosindicalismo y el movimiento obrero en Sabadell, 1930–1936," in *Trabajo industrial y organización obrera en la Cataluña contemporánea, 1930–1936*, ed. Balcells (Barcelona: Editorial LAIA, 1974).

[61] Pestaña even made direct appeals to Avelino Entrialgo and the executive committee in Gijón, explaining his position and asking their support: November 19, 1932, June 22, 1933, July 28, 1933, August 19, 1933 (AGS, J-12).

weapon.[62] Through following this pragmatic "third way," the Gijonese kept their organization and their identity intact, thus further strengthening their position in the city.

Nevertheless, in one area the CNT federation refused to use restraint or moderation – against its old enemy, the Socialists. With their entry into the political establishment, the Socialists posed a new threat to anarchosyndicalist leadership of the labor movement. Thus, in Gijón as elsewhere in Spain, the CNT continued to resist the formation and growth of Socialist unions using every weapon at its disposal to prevent the UGT from gaining a foothold in the city, including waging war against the new legislation created by the Socialist labor minister, Largo Caballero. The complex dynamic set in motion by this opposition to Socialist labor legislation put the CNT in conflict with the Republic, whether or not it actively intended to overthrow it.[63] Further complicating the picture is that the "pure" anarchists did intend to overthrow it, believing that "libertarian communism" should be established immediately, while others, like the majority in Gijón's federation, felt that the time was not ripe. In the case of Gijón, then, the CNT helped destabilize the Republic, but more through its war with the Socialists than through its revolutionary ideology.[64]

With this framework in mind, the vigorous strike activity, what the Socialist *Avance* called "the CNT's war on the Republic," can be better understood. Many of the important strikes were aimed at

[62] The FAI had a presence in Gijón, but it was minoritarian and did not alter the basic practice of the CNT (Barrio, *Anarquismo y anarcosindicalismo*, 363–364). One of the more prominent members of the FAI, or *faístas*, in Gijón was Segundo Blanco, but even he agreed that the CNT should maintain its independence. In a meeting of local militants, Blanco and Quintanilla argued about whether they should maintain a dialogue with the *treintistas*; for Blanco communication amounted to disloyalty. But despite the angry rhetoric, both agreed on the fundamental points: the FAI should not control the CNT, and the *treintistas'* provocation of a schism should not be supported: minutes, September 17, 1933 meeting (AGS, J-12, E-1).

[63] José Manuel Macarro Vera makes this point in *La utopía revolucionaria*, 469–470. Historians have argued about how much the CNT should be blamed for destabilizing the Republic: some have argued that the repression of the government turned the CNT against the Republic (see, for example, Elorza, *La Utopía anarquista*, and Antonio Bar Cendón, "La CNT frente a la II República," in *Estudios sobre la II República*, ed. Manuel Ramírez (Madrid: Editorial Tecnos, 1975)), and others that the CNT set out to wage a war against it from the start (Macarro Vera's book is one of the most sophisticated versions of this position). The reality probably lay between the two positions, in a dynamic that unfolded differently in each local context.

[64] In contrast, the radical wing of the CNT launched an open offensive against the Republic that began in late 1931 and lasted through the attempted revolution of December 1933 (see Bar Cendón, "La CNT").

preventing the Socialists from organizing.[65] In addition to campaigns directed against local Socialist organizations,[66] the first general strike of December 1931 was called in solidarity with Barcelona dockworkers who had been fired for refusing to work with UGT members. Beyond this evidence of the war against the UGT, the entire wave of strikes in some sense constituted an indirect attack on the government's labor institutions. By continuing to refuse mediation in labor disputes, the CNT legitimated its methods of direct action and ensured that the new labor regime would not function in Gijón.

The hard line taken against the UGT did not seem to hurt the federation, as even *Avance* admitted that few *cenetistas* defected.[67] In 1930, with the local UGT virtually starting from scratch, only twenty-seven workers joined the organization.[68] Even though the local branch grew slowly over the next few years, most of its members came from either independently or newly unionized sectors rather than from old CNT territory. Thus, the transport, construction and metallurgical industries remained fairly impregnable to the UGT. Its section of metalworkers contained a measly sixty-five members in 1931 (dropping to sixty-one by 1934), the construction syndicate only appeared in September of 1932, and it never established a section of transport workers.[69] In contrast, the CNT metallurgical and construction syndi-

---

[65] The distribution of the labor movement in the province did not change much during the Republic. The Socialists remained the majority force, with their stronghold in the mining basin and in Oviedo, and the CNT maintained its hold over Gijón and La Felguera. The regional Socialist organization (Federación Socialista Asturiana) claimed 30,000 members in 1932, and about 40,000 in 1934, compared to 32,000 for the CRT in July 1933. The Communist unions complicated the picture somewhat, but they did not make much headway in Gijón. One historian estimates the Communist nucleus at about 120 to 140, with some influence in the transport syndicate until they were expelled in 1932. In the province, they managed to capture the 9,000-member anarchosyndicalist miners' union, which constituted their provincial base of support: Paco Ignacio Taibo, *Asturias 1934* (Gijón: Júcar, 1984), 60–61.

[66] One example was a vicious battle in the construction industry in 1932, when the CNT called a series of strikes to demand that UGT workers on construction sites be fired: *El Noroeste*, June 21, 1932; *Avance*, May 20 and 27, June 11 and 22, 1932.

[67] An article of July 7, 1932 expressed frustration over the apparent blindness of Gijón's workers.

[68] During the same year, 1,500–1,700 members joined in Asturias, Galicia and Santander as a whole: from a membership register (AGS, J-37).

[69] For the Sindicato Metalúrgico, Sección Gijón, there is a membership list (AGS, K-4). For the construction syndicate, there are no figures, but at a general meeting on June 2, 1933 only fourteen people voted, with "various" abstentions, which indicates that perhaps twenty to twenty-five members were present: minutes, Junta General, Federación del Ramo de Edificación (AGS, J-28). For the period after July 1936, there are more complete records on UGT syndicates, which confirm the earlier pattern. Thus, whereas the UGT and CNT maintained parallel organizations in metallurgy, maritime transport, petroleum, the entertainment industry, the sugar industry and railroads, and amongst port workers and municipal workers, with two exceptions the UGT lagged behind in all

cates each contained about 3,000 members, and the transport syndicate grew from 800 to 1,500 in 1934 (see Table 11).

The only area where the UGT finally carved a niche for itself was in the organization of clerical and low-level professional workers (see Table 12).[70] A professional breakdown of the Agrupación Socialista in January 1937 reinforces this picture.[71] It lists fifty professionals, fifty-eight white-collar workers, eighty-four skilled industrial workers, ten skilled service workers and twenty-eight semi- or unskilled workers. The UGT's success with these intermediate groups contradicts the economic model that purports to explain Socialist/anarchist distribution by reference to industrial structure, with the argument that the UGT appealed only to the "modern" mass proletariat. Although the UGT in Asturias did control the mining and railway industries, in Gijón its role was to provide a more moderate and less proletarian alternative for skilled groups who felt out of place in the CNT Casa de Pueblo.[72] By the end of the Republic, then, the UGT played an instrumental role in broadening the base of the labor movement beyond the traditional working class. The combination of this division of labor and the increasing co-operation between the UGT and CNT after the "Workers' Alliance" of May 1934 brought the labor movement in Gijón to its peak in 1936 behind the undisputed leadership of the CNT.[73]

As a result, the Alianza Obrera initiated a new phase, not only

the competing unions, even at its peak during the Civil War. The two exceptions were railroad workers (UGT, 392; CNT, 140), and port workers (UGT, 411; CNT, 69): from a Delegación de Trabajo list of the forty-one syndicates in Gijón, undated, probably from early 1937 (AGS, H or J-30), and a questionnaire distributed to all UGT syndicates in December 1936 (AGS, K-266).

[70] Unfortunately, the UGT statistics compiled during the Civil War may not accurately portray the pre-war situation, but we can assume that most of the UGT advances date from the February 1936 elections at the earliest. The information in Table 12 is taken from the December 1936 questionnaire and the Delegación de Trabajo list.

[71] The list contains 378 names, but 103 specified no profession, and 45 called themselves soldiers (AGS, F-90).

[72] Interestingly, this is exactly the conclusion reached by Pere Gabriel about Barcelona. The UGT grew to about 86,000 members in 1936 (vs. 180,000 for the CNT), with strength in the service sector, education and banking, as well as in railways and maritime transport. Many of these professions had previously been organized in independent, neutral guilds or unions, but found the UGT a hospitable refuge from the more radical CNT: "Sindicalismo y sindicatos socialistas," 59–69.

[73] The co-operation began with the pact that culminated in the revolution of October 1934, but deepened after February 1936, when Socialist and CNT unions in the same industries began to form alliances. The municipal workers were the first, followed by the entertainment workers, the brewery workers, and the education workers. Reports of these alliances appeared in El Noroeste, in June of 1936. A broader proposal to unite with the UGT appeared on the agenda of the CNT regional congress in April 1936, but this was not resolved until well into the war (El Noroeste, April 19, 1936).

Table 11 *Union organization, 1931–1934: Confederación Nacional de Trabajo (CNT)*

	6/1931	9/1932	7/1933	9/1934
Graphic arts	250	310	300	350
Food industry	1,235	1,932	709	747
Communication	250			
Metallurgy	3,000	3,031	3,000	3,000
Port workers	400	250		
Tram workers	95	(Transport)	(no report)	
Chauffeurs	183	(Transport)		
Transport	800	1,600	2,100	1,500
Gas workers	130	90	120	100
Railroad workers	130	(Transport)	130	70
Glassmaking	550	550	600	650
Municipal workers	280	250	200	160
Construction	2,548	3,295	3,300	2,800
Ceramics	250	260	272	286
Sugar industry	50	432	400	
Domestics	70			
Various trades	140	95	65	30
Hat-makers	110	114	114	114
Clothing	403	617	600	660
Dockworkers	227	(Transport)		
Textile	315	317	(no report)	
Mercantile		70	120	150
Defense of public interests		1,500		
Public spectacles (e.g. cinema)			(no report)	80
Fishing			800	700
Petroleum			80	
Total	11,416	14,713	12,910	11,397
CRT (regional)	24,881	25,403	30,803	
La Felguera	3,400	3,992	3,630	

Sources:
1931: Confederación Nacional de Trabajo, *Memoria del Congreso*, 1931; reprinted in *Revista de Trabajo*, 53 (1976)
1932: *El Noroeste*, September 28, 1932
1933: AGS, K-46
1934: Eusebio I. Fernández, "Organizaciones sindicales y conflictividad social en Asturias durante la II República (1933–1934)" (Tesina, University of Oviedo, 1985)

Table 12 *Union organization of clerical and low-level professional workers (December 1936)*

	UGT	CNT
Telegraph workers	130	none
Casino clerks	60	none
Teachers	1,009	50
Technicians	35	none
Salesmen	249	30
Notary clerks	11	none
Motorists and machinists	105	10
Credit and finance workers	114	few
Pharmacy helpers	152	none

Other UGT unions (1936–1937)
Naval machinists
Naval pilots
Commercial clerks

within the labor movement but in the local balance of power. After this point, the CNT, with the support instead of the antagonism of the UGT, consolidated a radical alternative to the republican-led regime in Gijón. The first manifestation of this alternative was the failed revolution of October 1934, whose repression temporarily suppressed the movement. With the election of the Popular Front, and the lifting of repressive measures, however, the labor movement quickly re-organized and continued to pursue means of closer collaboration. Thus, by July 1936, the labor movement was approaching a united front, while the other republican political forces were weaker and more divided than ever. From one of the powerful players in the city, the CNT had emerged as the strongest.

In order to reach this point, of course, the CNT and UGT had to overcome a long history of mutual antagonism. While a number of political changes made this evolution possible, it is significant that only Gijón's CNT, with its history of pragmatism and flexibility, took advantage of the opportunity for rapprochement.[74] The ground was

[74] Elsewhere, the CNT rejected the Alianza Obrera, and the national federation harshly criticized the Asturians in 1934 and 1935. Only in May 1936, at the national congress

191

prepared in a number of ways, beginning with the Socialists' withdrawal from the government, the rightward shift of the regime that culminated with the elections of November 1933, and the rise of fascism in Europe. From their position within the regime, the Socialists had moved by the end of 1933 to alienated opposition.[75] The CNT federation in Gijón shared the Socialists' alienation from the regime, and had given up its initial benevolence. But what pushed it into seeking an alliance was its disapproval of the course set by the radicals who dominated the CNT. A series of failed revolutionary attempts, culminating with the disastrous December 1933 uprising, convinced Gijón's leaders that the CNT had to rethink its strategy of launching spontaneous and unco-ordinated uprisings:

> [given the threat of fascism,] we are agreed in proposing that the CNT, without any confusion, and preserving its collective personality and doctrinal and tactical orientation, should form a revolutionary worker alliance with all the proletarian organizations which have as their goal the abolition of capitalism by means of the social revolution.[76]

From this point, through the initial signing of the pact in March 1934[77] to its approval at the regional congress of September,[78]

---

in Zaragoza, did the CNT finally decide to pursue an alliance with the UGT, but discussions dragged on through the entire Civil War. See Angeles Barrio Alonso, "Asturias en la alianza CNT – UGT, 1934–1937," in *Los nuevos historiadores ante la Guerra Civil española*, vol. II, ed. Octavio Ruiz-Manjón Cabeza and Miguel Gómez Oliver (Granada: Diputación Provincial de Granada, 1990). For a broader view of the Alianza, see Victor Alba, *La alianza obrera: historia y análisis de una táctica de unidad en España* (Gijón: Júcar, 1977).

[75] For this process in Asturias, see María José Baragaño Castaño, "La radicalización del movimiento socialista asturiano en la Segunda República, 1931–1934" (Tesina, University of Oviedo, 1986). For a national picture, see Santos Juliá Diaz, *La izquierda del PSOE, 1935–1936* (Madrid: Siglo Veintiuno, 1977).

[76] From a letter written from the local jail in December 1933, and signed by Avelino González, Segundo Blanco, Avelino Martínez, J. M. Martínez and several others. They had been arrested as a result of the insurrection, even though Gijón had not participated. Quoted in Taibo, *Asturias 1934*, 17–18.

[77] On March 31, 1934 the new provincial executive committee of the Alianza Obrera announced the pact, describing it as a "fraternal embrace" to better wage the war against fascism, but gave no details: "Nota redactada para dar a conocer la creación de la Alianza Obrera: al proletariado asturiano," *Avance*, April 1, 1934.

[78] At the regional congress, the Gijonese had to face some heavy opposition from the metalworkers' syndicate of La Felguera, which was more heavily influenced by the FAI. The vote was close: thirty-nine to thirty-five for an alliance with the UGT, and numerous abstentions in a vote of twenty-one to sixteen for a pact with the PSOE (the thorniest issue in the debate). Gijón's syndicates provided twenty-four of the pro-alliance votes and none of the "anti" votes: *El Noroeste*, September 18 and 20, 1934.

the Gijonese *cenetistas* became its tireless champions.[79] The pact committed its signatories to collaborate in launching the social revolution against the bourgeois regime, with the goal of setting up "a regime of economic, political and social equality founded on federalist principles." To this effect, the executive committee was empowered "to construct a plan of action that will assure the triumph of the revolution," while local committees of the alliance would direct the transition to the new regime. The immediate result of this agreement was the October 1934 revolt, which, despite its intended national scope, was essentially a regional phenomenon. At the last moment, the Asturian Communist party joined in the Alianza and participated in the revolt,[80] over a year before the Third International began to move towards its Popular Front stance.

For a variety of reasons, including its isolation, the revolt was a failure. Moreover, its repression succeeded in shutting down both Socialist and CNT activity in the province for the next sixteen months. Nevertheless, when the Popular Front government inaugurated the last, liberal phase of the Republic, Gijón's federation completed the familiar rebuilding process with little effort. Through the confused final months of the peacetime Republic, as the left republican parties tried to establish their leadership, the CNT reconstituted its mass base and built on the ties established with the UGT. When the uprising of July 19th disrupted the political scene once again, the left republicans had neither the resources nor the popular support to defend the Republic against its enemies. As a result, power effectively shifted to the CNT, as the strongest leftist organization in the city. After decades of operating on the margin of the political establishment, the CNT finally entered the arena as a direct participant.

With this moment, the formal working-class movement in Gijón completed its long evolution from a divided and weak entity in the

---

[79] The details of the negotiations can be found in the report submitted to the regional congress in April 1936, which includes a copy of the alliance and an account of the process (AGS, J-12, "Informe" of the Comisión de Alianza al Comité de CRT, Asturias y León, April 10, 1936). See also Eusebio I. Fernández, "Organizaciones sindicales."

[80] For details on the PCE's role, see "Informe al Comité Central del Partido Comunista de España de los sucesos desarollados en Asturias durante el movimiento revolucionario de octubre 1934," printed in J. A. Sánchez y García Sauco, *La revolución de 1934 en Asturias* (Madrid: Editoria Nacional, 1974), 178–179. Up until then, the Communists had taken the standard party line of pushing for a "united front from below" in which the CNT and UGT would be dissolved, and co-ordination would be handled by the only true workers' party, the PCE. See editorials published in *El Noroeste*, February 2 and 12, April 3, 10 and 25, 1934.

early twentieth century to the major political force in the city in July of 1936. Despite the fact that the anarchosyndicalist ideology of the movement kept it on the margin of official political activity, in practice its presence had a dramatic and evolving impact on local politics. The success of Gijón's federation in striking a workable balance between the radical critique of society and the task of making workers as comfortable as possible within the present system helped consolidate its presence as an oppositional force, both under the monarchy and during the Republic. But it was only during the latter years of the Republic that it came to constitute an independent alternative to reformist republicanism. With the inability of the Republic to live up to the myriad hopes placed on it, the CNT, particularly in Gijón, came to embody a more powerful image of change. After July 1936, it was able to infuse this image into the identity of the Republic in Gijón, thus transforming the local incarnation of the regime in its own image. The fact that the CNT was in a position to do this attests to the reality of the city's polarization by the end of the peacetime Republic.

PART III

Defining an oppositional culture: the struggle over the public sphere

~

The struggle to define an oppositional movement that could tear down the fabric of the old regime extended beyond the realm of formal political and economic institutions and into the broader domain of the public sphere, where the limits of hegemony are tested. Outside the coercive structures of formal political and economic control, the public sphere provided a relatively open space of contention, where the ruling elites had to demonstrate their claim to moral and intellectual leadership and win the consent that marks the distinction between hegemony and domination.[1] Once Gijón began to develop the infrastructure of a thriving public sphere, with its institutions and networks of voluntary associational life, contending forces tried to shape and channel this associational life, to "structure attention" towards their own hegemonic agendas.[2] Thus, the public sphere developed as the central arena in which the competing systems of power fought for legitimation.

As all the contending forces seemed to understand, successful legitimation depended on the reflexive acceptance of a universe of cultural values and practices that situated the population in a broad hegemonic framework of authority. Thus, both the republi-

---

[1] As Jackson Lears defines it, consent does not necessarily indicate deep belief in the hegemonic vision, but the inability to articulate an alternative: "The Concept of Cultural Hegemony: Problems and Possibilities," *American Historical Review*, 90 (1985), 569.

[2] Craig Calhoun argues that the public sphere is always shaped by the "structuring of attention" by the dominant power and/or by challenging social movements: "Introduction: Habermas and the Public Sphere," in *Habermas and the Public Sphere*, ed. Craig Calhoun (Cambridge, MA: MIT Press, 1992), 37.

195

can and labor movements perceived that their assault on the old regime required the destruction of a traditional cultural universe in which most Spaniards were still embedded in 1900. To undermine this world view, republicans and trade unionists each sought to create an alternative, counter-hegemonic culture that would both displace the existing one and prepare the humble residents of "smoke-filled" Gijón to participate in the future society as they imagined it. While at one time this struggle over the "dominant symbolic paradigm"[3] would have been viewed as marginal to the "real" political struggle, scholars have increasingly acknowledged the centrality of cultural manifestations in political contests.[4] Accordingly, the following two chapters will analyze the role and impact of the contest for hegemony in the public sphere.

The reigning hegemonic culture derived its legitimacy from the glorious heritage of the Reconquest and the Catholic Kings, when the alliance of Church and state defeated the Moors and forged a great imperial nation. Even though the political and economic power of the monarchy and the Church had declined since the sixteenth century, their cultural authority had not. The hegemonic vision of the Spanish nation in 1900 still derived from the prominent position of these two institutions and the value system they implied: a hierarchical society with God and King at the top and sinful man humbled before them. The implications of this hierarchy were simply expressed in an article in Gijón's first populist Catholic newspaper: "for everyone to live together in harmony, it is necessary that each one fulfills the role that corresponds to him; some must lead and some must obey, with charity from above and humility from below."[5]

This hierarchical framework contrasted sharply with the democratic and communitarian goals of republicans, socialists and anarchists. To prepare Spain for a new regime based on these goals, each movement sought to promote a cultural transformation that would prepare for and accompany the political one. As introduced in Chapter 1, for republicans this meant turning a nation of subjects into a nation of citizens capable of intelligent participation in the democratic process. Essential to this transformation was cutting the individual loose from the authority of

[3] David Kertzer, *Ritual, Politics and Power* (New Haven: Yale University Press, 1988), 175.
[4] Lynn Hunt makes this point in the introduction to *Politics, Culture and Class in the French Revolution* (Berkeley: University of California Press, 1984), citing the work of Maurice Agulhon and Mona Ozouf as examples (p. 15).
[5] *El Obrero Católico*, October 17, 1897.

the Church, which taught obedience and blind faith instead of independent thinking. Also essential to the creation of a nation of citizens was the minimization of class conflicts that could divide and fragment the citizenry. Thus, the cornerstones of the republican cultural alternative continued to be: education, the secularization of society and cross-class harmony.[6] The anarchist cultural vision overlapped in certain ways, notably in the importance of "free-thinking" education and in the secularization of society. Where the anarchists diverged was in their rejection of cross-class harmony, at least in the version propagated by the republicans. Thus, they accepted and adopted the originally republican themes of education and anti-clericalism, but sought to incorporate them into a culture based on work and class identity and the solidarity of a brotherhood of workers.

The result of these overlapping and divergent visions was a cultural struggle for the hearts and minds of the Spanish people. The parameters of the struggle were laid out in the late nineteenth century, but as in the formal political realm, 1900 proved an important hegemonic turning point. By the 1930s, the republicans had managed to articulate the strongest cultural alternative, based on the secularization of public symbols and education, and on the creation of competing civic rituals, practices and associations. In contrast, only in the last years of the Republic did the labor movement even approach a full-fledged alternative, a separate proletarian culture in the style of the German Social Democrats. Even then, the influence of republican culture was strong within the labor movement. And yet, the republican alternative culture never attained hegemonic status, certainly not in Spain as a whole, but not even in Gijón, where the remnants of a public Catholic culture competed with republican and proletarian cultures in a fragmented public sphere that epitomized the fragmentation of Spanish society.

The upshot was that the oppositional forces in Gijón, as in Spain at large, were never able to form a common culture that could provide symbolic unity for the Republic.[7] There were

---

[6] For a more in-depth look at what Manuel Tuñón de Lara calls the "grand cultural currents" that fed into the republican cosmos, see the collection of articles *Los orígenes culturales de la II República*, ed. Tuñón de Lara *et al.* (Madrid: Siglo Veintiuno, 1993). The term is from his introduction.

[7] I am taking "common culture" from Raymond Williams' concept of a democratic participatory culture, rooted in the experiences of the majority, which would replace the imposed culture of a minority: "The Idea of a Common Culture," in *Resources of Hope: Culture, Democracy and Socialism* (New York: Verso, 1989).

aspects of a common culture, particularly in the realm of public anti-clericalism, but, in contrast to France, for example, they never congealed into a counter-hegemonic force that could unite the common people in a definitive attack on the Spain of the Catholic Kings.[8] Before the Republic, this weakness was often disguised, because the heterogeneity of the oppositional culture gave it a flexibility that could work to its advantage. The combined assault of the labor and republican movement cultures, with their associations, their symbols and their communal rituals, often succeeded in choking off the cultural expression of the old regime. But the fissures within the opposition, between the nation of citizens and the brotherhood of workers, prevented either vision from prevailing and left the Republic mired in cultural confusion. Ironically, the combination of a weakened traditional hegemonic culture and a confused replacement only hastened the descent into civil war. On the one hand, it hindered the legitimation of the Republic, and on the other, it compelled the traditional elites to resort to force to restore their domination. What could not be resolved through formal political channels or in the public sphere spilled over into the more lethal domain of naked force.

---

[8] One could argue that one of the great strengths of nineteenth-century French republicanism was its powerful cultural idiom, drawn from the revolutions of 1789, 1830 and 1848. Although different groups contested its meaning, most of the positions were located within a common symbolic and cultural universe based on the nation of citizens.

7

Republican culture: a nation of citizens

~

The outlines of republican culture, which drew its inspiration from the eighteenth- and nineteenth-century liberal revolutions, were clearly demarcated by the onset of the twentieth century, and changed little before the Civil War. This culture was dedicated, at least in theory, to the democratic participation of an educated public, to the secularization of society, and, in a more general way, to the modernization of a "backward" country. Republicans were not the exclusive guardians of this broad democratic agenda, but they were its main proponents, especially in Gijón.[1] Moreover, they saw themselves as its primary agents, the leaders who would mold the ignorant *pueblo* into the rational citizenry of the future. When the future became the present, in 1931, the republicans had to continue the process of transforming the public sphere while simultaneously creating and implementing new political institutions.[2] The success of the Republic depended on both foundations: on sound institutions and on a republican public that understood and accepted them.

In Gijón, the bulk of a republican public had to be culled from the large working-class population, which was uneducated but ripe for change. As argued in Chapter 1, republican groups and individuals began this task in the late nineteenth century, with institutions like

---

[1] José Alvarez Junco defines what he calls a lay intellectual milieu, which included non-republican figures who shared most of this basic agenda: "Los intelectuales: anticlericalismo y republicanismo," in *Los orígenes culturales de la II República*, ed. J. L. García Delgado (Madrid: Siglo Veintiuno, 1993).

[2] For a national view of the republicans' cultural agenda in the 1930s, see Sandie Holguin, "The Conquest of Tradition: Culture and Politics in Spain during the Second Republic, 1931–1936" (Ph.D. diss., University of California, Los Angeles, 1994).

the Ateneo and the University Extension, but it intensified in the twentieth century as republicanism enhanced its local political power and the competing labor movement strengthened its challenge. The Ateneo continued to be the model for organizations designed to civilize and educate the lower classes, and it even enhanced its impact with the creation of several branches, located primarily in the working-class *barrios*. These were joined by other organizations which promoted a similar civic education agenda among workers, the most important of which were the Workers' Musical Association (Asociación Musical Obrera – AMO) and the Association for Culture and Hygiene (ACH). One more crucial institution, the Escuela Neutra, a private secondary and primary school, rounded out the formal network created by republicans to mold their new citizens.[3]

Central to the republicans' concept of citizenship was the secularization of the relationship between the individual and the nation. In addition to promoting secular ideals in their formal associations, the republicans pursued this goal through a broad effort to dislodge the omnipresent Catholic Church from its position as the "sacred center" of the community.[4] The Church's cultural role was a threat, both because Catholicism had become absorbed into an antagonistic political framework, and because of its domination of the collective ritual life of the community. As long as the Catholic symbolic universe dominated communal life, the republicans could not create an alternative "cultural frame" in which to legitimate their authority.[5] In other words, the conflict was not over religion, *per se*, but about dueling cultural systems. In this duel, anti-clericalism became a key weapon in the republican arsenal, as well as a central ingredient in Spanish political life.

The ambitious republican cultural agenda met with mixed results in Gijón. It was clearly successful in promoting respect for education and literacy among sectors of Gijón's working-class population. And

[3] The University Extension program dropped out of the network by the end of the first decade, because of the dispersal of its founders: Jean Louis Guereña, "Las instituciones culturales: políticas educativas," in *1900 en España*, ed. Carlos Serrano and Serge Salaün (Madrid: Espasa Calpe, 1991), 80.

[4] According to Lynn Hunt, the "sacred center" lies at the heart of a society's "cultural frame": "it gives the members of a society their sense of place. It is the heart of things, the place where culture, society and politics come together" (*Politics, Culture and Class in the French Revolution* [Berkeley: University of California Press, 1984], 87).

[5] As Lynn Hunt argues, a "cultural frame" is crucial in ordering social reality (*Politics, Culture*, 88). She borrows the term from Clifford Geertz, "Centers, Kings and Charisma: Reflections on the Symbolics of Power," in *Culture and its Creators: Essays in Honor of Edward Shils*, ed. Joseph Ben-David and Terry Nichols Clark (Chicago: University of Chicago Press, 1977).

the kind of free-thinking education it promoted permeated the curriculum of every alternative course offered in the city, no matter what the political orientations of the founders. Furthermore, the religious underpinnings of public life yielded dramatically to the secular republican onslaught, so that by the outbreak of the Civil War the Church barely held on to its once impregnable position. Equally important, the republicans were able to use secularization as a powerful bridge to the labor movement, which adopted the ethic of anti-clericalism and often joined in republican-led campaigns. Thus, the cultural impact of the republican movement was profound, both in terms of its own organizations and activities and in terms of its influence on the labor movement, which accepted many of its central precepts. As a result, and in contrast to its impact on the national level, in Gijón and other cities republicanism posed a serious cultural threat to the hegemony of the old regime.[6]

On the other hand, republican culture was still too weak to deliver the final blow. Catholic influence remained strong, particularly in education. Even during the Republic, the regime did not have the resources to replace the Catholic educational establishment. Perhaps more important was the growing challenge from the labor movement, which created parallel institutions and worked to infiltrate republican ones. By the end of the Republic, radical working-class elements appear to have co-opted the organizations designed to civilize workers under republican guidance. Thus, the Ateneo ended its long life closer to the labor movement than to its republican founders. In fact, the fate of the Ateneo epitomizes the irony of republicanism in Gijón. The strength of the Ateneo illustrates the power of republican cultural ideals, many of which were widely absorbed and diffused. But its co-option by other political agendas demonstrates that republican culture was too porous to use as a foundation in the republicans' drive for power. Culturally as well as politically, the republicans lost control of their working-class audience as they lost their bid for hegemony.

Secularizing public life

The secularization of public life in Gijón, particularly in the realm of communal ritual practices and symbols, was perhaps the greatest success story of local republicanism. Over the course of thirty-six years,

---

[6] A similar process transpired in other urban centers, but most of rural Spain remained embedded in a traditional Catholic culture. At the national level, then, the impact of secularization was much more uneven.

the anti-clerical movement constructed a solid framework of secular public symbols and rituals that constituted the rudiments of an alternative civic culture. Moreover, this civic culture managed to displace many of the traditional manifestations of public Catholic culture and, more broadly, to undermine its secure position as the "sacred center" of the society. In the process of uprooting the Church from the center of public life, the republicans forged a broad mixed coalition that incorporated under their leadership everyone to the left of the monarchists. Thus, in this battle, the republicans managed to assert their leadership and focus the oppositional forces in an effective and concerted charge on the old regime. While they could not keep this coalition together behind a broader acceptance of republican hegemony, the results achieved in the anti-clerical campaigns often disguised this weakness, especially before 1931.

In 1900, the task of secularizing public life was monumental. The Catholic Church maintained a virtual monopoly on public ritual and symbols, from baptisms and marriages to street signs and festivals.[7] Half the streets of the city took the names of saints or sacred institutions, and most of the traditional festivals originated in doctrines and practices of the Church. The important Holy Week procession followed Jesus to the cross and Christmas celebrated his birth. Even Carnival, which probably had its roots in the pagan Roman Saturnalia, had been at least partially co-opted into the Christian calendar as a symbol of the purification of the body and soul in preparation for Lent.[8] The summer cycle of *romerías*, originally pilgrimages to saints' shrines, got its timetable from their birthdays. The *romerías* provided a balance of worship and entertainment over the course of a full day's activities that included both a solemn mass and a kind of "May day" frolic in the country:

> The first event of the day is the reveille, when the musicians with tambourine and *gaita* wander through the streets, playing their instruments, as the people reciprocate by offering them sweets and fine wine. The religious ceremony, which occupies the midday hours, is well

[7] As Carlos Serrano put it, "in 1900 a Spaniard most probably had his life arranged by a calendar, both social and festive, regulated by the Catholic Church: Christmas, the Festival of the Three Wise Men, Holy Week and Easter, Marian and patron saint festivals, and above all the sacraments (baptism, marriage and death); a daily schedule accompanied by the multiple tolling of bells from multiple bell towers": "1900 o la difícil modernidad," in *1900 en España*, 201.

[8] On Carnival as an essentially Christian festival, despite its origins, see Julio Caro Baroja, *El Carnaval* (Madrid: Círculo de Lectores, 1992), 40.

attended and full of pomp, including a priest brought from outside
Gijón, the dissonant clashing of bells, and cut branches that have been
transported processionally to their resting place in the church at the
foot of the saint. The climax of the morning is the solemn procession,
presided over by the saint hoisted on shoulders, and accompanied by
the celebrants and the local authorities, followed by the entire town.
The mass concludes with the auction of the branches, which serves as
a clear gesture that the public wants to support the *fiesta*. The afternoon
begins with a family banquet, more magnificent than any other celebrated during the year, attended by all the relatives. The rest of the
afternoon is dedicated to profane pursuits, and among these dancing
plays a primary role.[9]

The *romerías* had their roots in peasant culture, but in urban Gijón
they were generally celebrated in the rural *aldeas*, to where special
trolleys shuttled people from all over the city.

Rituals like these could carry multiple meanings, but at one level
they acted as a powerful legitimation of the Church and the monarchy,
and of the public links between the two.[10] In addition to their obvious
function of encouraging public piety, these rituals illustrated the central role of the Church in the social structure and underscored its
official relationship to the state. As the description of the *romería* indicates, public authorities routinely participated in religious celebrations,
not simply as individuals but in an official capacity. Moreover, the
municipality subsidized some of these events, as evidenced by the
1903 budget allocation for the religious festivals of the main parish
church of San Pedro. Whatever participants felt about these events,
they articulated a powerful narrative of Church authority and presence
in everyday life.[11]

In order to deconstruct this narrative, republicans tried a variety of
tactics, from imposing new meanings on old events to inventing new
traditions.[12] Most simply, they tried to sever the official links between

[9] E. Gómez Pellón and G.Coma González, *Fiestas de Asturias: aproximación al panorama
festivo asturiano* (Oviedo: Caja de Ahorros de Asturias, 1985), 13.
[10] On rituals as arenas for contested meanings, see Temma Kaplan, *Red City, Blue Period:
Social Movements in Picasso's Barcelona* (Berkeley: University of California Press, 1992),
especially Chapter 1.
[11] As Steven Lukes put it, political ritual "helps to define as authoritative certain ways of
seeing society": "Political Ritual and Social Integration," *Sociology*, 9:2 (May 1975), 301.
Thus, Lukes sees political ritual as playing more of an argumentative than a simplistically
integrative function.
[12] The useful concept of "inventing traditions" comes from Eric Hobsbawm's and Terence
Ranger's collection, *The Invention of Tradition* (Cambridge: Cambridge University Press,
1983). As they define in their introduction, "invented tradition is taken to mean a set

local government and religious events. Before the era of republican majorities on the city council, they staged demonstrations to embarrass and discredit public officials who took part in religious ceremonies. Thus, before the *jubileo* procession in October of 1901, federalists called a meeting, for all "republicans, socialists, anarchists, freethinkers and any democrats who want to attend" to plan such a protest. On the day of the event, several thousand protesters showed up to heckle the marchers, drowning out their chanting by singing the "Marseillaise" and shouting "Long live the Republic," "Long live the revolution" and "Long live anarchy." By the time the procession reached the church, a crowd of eight to ten thousand booed the Cortes representative Domínguez Gil with sneers about his "hypocritical" liberalism: "¡Vaya un senador liberal!"[13]

Once republicans controlled the city council, they worked from the inside to withdraw government support from religious activities. Thus, in 1910 the city dropped its subsidy of the festival masses at San Pedro. More publicly, official city presence at religious ceremonies declined significantly. The change was so dramatic during Holy Week in 1910 that it prompted a newspaper piece called "Breaking with Tradition." The article noted that for the first time the city government absented itself from the celebration of the Easter Mass, delegating only one councilor as a token representative. At the Holy Burial, the Catholic city councilmen attended, along with members of the military units stationed in Gijón, but they were allowed to do so only in a private capacity.[14] After 1910, this diminished participation became routine, except during the Dictatorship when the conservative elites briefly returned to power.

Putting an end to the official sanction of religious activities was the simplest part of the republican anti-clerical agenda. A more complicated task was to wean the public from their dependence on the religious calendar. One strategy was to keep the old calendar and its events intact, while attempting to drain the religious significance from them. Two different versions of the traditional celebration of the birthday of St. James illustrate this tack. In 1919, organizers announced

of practices, normally governed by overtly or tacitly accepted rules and of a ritual or symbolic nature, which seek to inculcate certain values and norms of behavior by repetition, which automatically implies continuity with the past" (p. 1).

[13] *El Noroeste*, October 14, 1901 and *Aurora Social*, October 19, 1901.

[14] *El Noroeste*, March 26, 1910.

the successful laicization of the *romería* customarily held in the barrio of Ceares, apparently in the face of stiff opposition:

> The residents [of Ceares] vocalized their protest against the ecclesiastical authorities, who understood yesterday that in these days it is impossible to go against the will of the entire people. As a result, yesterday the religious function was completely cut out, and instead, the secular events were more magnificent than ever.[15]

In the 1930s, the paper reported that the new version of the *romería* was flourishing, "none the less anticipated for its recent origins."[16]

In the other case, the Ateneo began organizing its secular version of the *verbena*, the soirée held the night before the *romería*. At the first *verbena* in 1906, the program included an original monologue by local writer Joaquín Dicente, called the "Lion of Bronze," a comedy skit, and a one-act play, "There are no women."[17] Without St. James, the *verbena* would not have existed, and yet the program was geared more to enriching the audience's artistic appreciation than to feeding its piety. As part of the Ateneo's packed schedule of lectures, performances, festivals and exhibitions, the saint's day would be gradually incorporated into a secular cultural universe, not obliterated but no longer part of a religious calendar. In transforming the old culture, both the Ateneo's *verbena* and Ceares' *romería* could make the connection between the old Spain and the new, using familiarity with the old to draw the public into the new. And in the new Spain, the Church had a greatly diminished presence: for some extinguished altogether; for others, only as a place for private worship.

Carrying this process even further, opponents of the old Spain went beyond manipulating existing rituals: they attempted to create new ones to establish their own secular calendar. Dissidents picked other dates to commemorate, like the anniversary of the Federal Republic (February 11th), the Paris Commune or local philosopher Jovellanos' return to his birthplace on August 6, 1811. Significantly, however, the new celebrations often utilized the structure of the traditional *romería*. Stripped of the mass, the *romería* evolved into a recognized festival form applicable to any situation. Thus, it always began with the roving street band that gathered participants for the evening *verbena*, which

---

[15] *El Noroeste*, July 26, 1919.
[16] *El Noroeste*, July 7, 1933.
[17] *El Noroeste*, July 23, 1906.

was followed by the next day's picnic and dance. Sometimes, it even included a transformed procession, as in the annual homage to Jovellanos of the Farmers' Association, when they carried various agricultural products from their headquarters to the old folks' home.[18] Again, by incorporating a familiar ritual into a subversive enterprise, anticlericals could undermine religious authority while demonstrating their roots in local culture and tradition.

One of the important dates in the new secular calendar was the homage to Jovellanos, hero of the liberal revolution and native son of Gijón. Especially during the Republic, Jovellanos came to epitomize the moderate republican vision of modernization and social reform. Not coincidentally, one of the most effusive celebrations of the yearly tribute took place in 1935, when the moderate republican vision was under serious attack from left and right. All the forces of republican culture were gathered together and put on display in an event that was both a statement of power and a plea for support.[19] The participants included all of the Ateneos and Associations of Culture and Hygiene, as well as the republican parties and various small business associations. The homage began with a civic procession, with members of outlying organizations marching into the city center to join in. Young people wearing crowns of flowers and traditional dress followed by the local band brought up the rear. The route started in the Plaza de la República and passed in front of Jovellanos' house, to end in the Plaza 6 de Agosto, where local officials draped his statue with the customary wreath. Afterwards, everyone went to celebrate with a picnic and dancing in the country.

Even without the impetus of a special homage or holiday, organizers sometimes sponsored a *romería* whose only purpose was to display anti-clerical sentiment. The first "anti-clerical *romería*" was held in the *aldea* of La Guía, in 1910, apparently drawing a large crowd.[20] Bands playing the "Marseillaise" and other tunes entertained picnicking families, while hundreds of couples danced. *El Noroeste* even reported that women "in elegant summer suits" outnumbered the men. Aside from the absence of religious accoutrements, the festival

---

[18] *Avance*, July 14, 1936.
[19] The main speaker began by saying, "In our present circumstances, it would do us good to look back to Jovellanos . . . to help us comprehend that a strong and wealthy region like Asturias cannot consume all its energies in epileptic convulsions that will be its ruin": *El Noroeste*, August 6, 1935.
[20] *El Noroeste* reported that attendance matched that of any of the traditional grand festivals: September 5, 1910.

was distinguished by the presence of various political symbols, notably the flags of republican and worker societies. A crowning speech by republican orator Melquíades Alvarez left no room for confusion between the old *romería* and the new.

Perhaps the most dramatic example of the anti-clerical *romería* came in 1919, after a broad-based coalition led to the election of Socialist deputy Teodomiro Menéndez to the Cortes. To celebrate, the "Democratic Women of Natahoyo" organized a *romería*, and, inspired by the example, leftist elements in La Calzada and in Cima scheduled their own democratic *romerías*. The series of festivals created what amounted to an abbreviated secular version of the traditional summer cycle.[21] In contrast, the newspaper reported that the classic Noche de San Juan, commemorating the birth of John the Baptist, which "in other times was celebrated with great fanfare, this year one could say that it passed unnoticed."[22]

Although evidence is spotty, it appears that the perceived decline of St. John was part of a trend, a trend that accelerated after the declaration of the Republic. The combination of a hostile atmosphere and republican refusal to recognize sacred holidays chased religious processions off the streets and into the protection of the churches. In fact, when the traditional procession for the Virgin of Carmen actually took place in July 1935, the newspaper noted that it was the first one since the advent of the Republic.[23] Even during Holy Week, the customary activities were curtailed by the fact that Maundy Thursday and Good Friday were normal working days. The power inherent in a public calendar was acknowledged by one writer who noted that "without processions, and with the calendar of *fiestas* approved by the Republic, these days are considered ordinary working days and end up passing without any of their classic meaning."[24] In the festive battle for the occupation of the streets, the Church had clearly lost most of its territory.

The symbolic occupation of the streets took yet another, more literal, form. One of the first tasks that the new republican city council undertook in April of 1931 was the visual transformation of the city, from the removal of monarchist shields and crowns on public buildings to the changing of street names that commemorated heroes of

[21] *El Noroeste*, June 5 and 6, 1919.
[22] *El Noroeste*, June 24, 1919.
[23] *El Noroeste*, July 16, 1935.
[24] *El Noroeste*, April 18, 1935.

the old regime. Within the first couple of weeks, the city council had already authorized a dozen substitutions, and more trickled in throughout the next few years. Several of the new streets were named after warrior heroes of the liberal revolution, like General Riego (leader of the 1820 revolution) and Captains Hernández and Galán, martyrs of the 1930 uprising. Others were named after political heroes, like Pablo Iglesias, and others after local artists known for their reformist sympathies, like Leopoldo Alas or Ventura Alvarez Sala, a realist painter in the tradition of Courbet. As significant as the new pantheon of heroes were those exiled by the re-naming: St. Lawrence, St. Doradía, Alfonso XII, the Virgin of Carmen and St. Anthony.

Of all the ritual battles in the city, perhaps the most intensely contested was the sacred territory of burial grounds. The city had both a civil and a religious cemetery, but while the conservatives controlled city hall they allowed the tiny civil cemetery to suffer complete neglect. According to a group of freemasons burying one of their members in the 1890s, "it is a filthy place, full of garbage thrown maliciously over the wall from the Catholic cemetery."[25] Whether its followers threw debris over the wall or not, the Church did everything it could to prevent bodies from being buried in the civil cemetery, and the law normally supported its authority. Thus, in 1901, the Church managed to get permission to bury the body of Eladio Carreño, one of the founders of local republicanism, in the religious cemetery, despite his wishes.[26] Where individuals circumvented or ignored Church authority, there were even cases of priests "stealing cadavers from the civil cemetery," according to an article in *Aurora Social*.[27] A full account of such a ghoulish act came in 1909, when the wife of a Socialist party member died. She requested a civil burial, and her husband applied to the municipal judge for permission. In a story reminiscent of Peter's denial of Jesus, the husband related how the Jesuits called on his wife three times before her death, and each time she firmly refused extreme unction. Nevertheless, when he arrived at the civil cemetery for his wife's burial, he discovered the body had been stolen. The parish priest

[25] Letter to the Director of Los Dominicales del Libre Pensamiento from two members of the lodge, Amigos de la Humanidad, quoted in Victoria Hidalgo Nieto, *La masonería en Asturias en el siglo XIX* (Oviedo: Consejería de Educación, Cultura y Deportes, 1985), 93–94.
[26] *El Noroeste*, August 29, 1901.
[27] July 29, 1904.

had ordered that it be removed to the Catholic cemetery, where she was buried immediately.[28]

The battle raged well into the Republic, even after the Cortes passed a law secularizing all cemeteries in January of 1932. Many places were slow to enforce the law by tearing down the wall between the two cemeteries, and Gijón, despite its republican credentials, was no exception.[29] In April of 1933, the continued division provoked another incident of corpse-stealing, this time of an already-buried body. A local priest instigated the exhumation of a worker buried in the civil cemetery at his family's wishes. Two municipal policemen assisted him in the unsavory task, and the municipal judge agreed that the priest still had ultimate authority over the body.[30] In this atmosphere, the civil burial was a powerful cultural statement, perhaps the most courageous public stance an individual could take against the domination of the Church over everyday life. As Socialist Angel Martínez once intoned, during a solemn civil burial, "I dedicate a moment of silence to all those who, free of religious prejudice – be they anarchist, socialist or free-thinkers – were buried in the civil cemetery; this act does not represent one man's privilege, but is dedicated to all of us who, being lovers of liberty, desire to go to our tomb without rendering homage to any religion."[31] For both sides, the act of burial was obviously much more than an individual act; it was part of a hotly contested public culture.

Despite the Church's spirited defense of its ritual space, the republican and labor movement anti-clerical coalition had clearly shattered its monopoly of public ritual. Moreover, it had created credible alternatives to the religious calendar that were patronized by large numbers of people. Generating credible alternatives was much harder, however, in the educational arena. The Church's powerful presence in primary and secondary education required enormous financial and political resources to counteract. The woefully inadequate public

---

[28] *El Noroeste*, April 8, 10, 13, 1909; *Aurora Social*, April 16, 1909.
[29] The reason for the delay was most likely the growing co-operation between the majority Reformists and the Catholic minority on the city council, over the objections of Federalists and Socialists (see Chapter 5).
[30] *El Noroeste*, April 14 and 15, 1933.
[31] *El Noroeste*, October 26, 1914. Martínez spoke at the dedication of a mausoleum to Socialist founding father Eduardo Varela, who died on December 26, 1912. It would be nice to know how many people followed his example, but the municipal death records provide no clues to the incidence of civil burial.

school system made the task of providing alternative secular education even more intractable. Even if republicans gained control over the public schools, thousands had to be built to accommodate the population. In Gijón as elsewhere, the lack of funds hampered republican efforts to build a credible secular public school system, even after the advent of the new regime.[32]

Some strides were made after 1931. The 1932 city budget allocated money for primary schools in El Llano, Natahoyo, La Calzada and Santa Olaya (beyond La Calzada).[33] To improve conditions for the poorest students, the city council voted to implement free lunch programs, the first of which was inaugurated with great fanfare in El Humedal. In a more direct attack on religious education, Gijón was one of the first cities to carry out the edict expelling the Jesuits, which included the closure of their prestigious secondary school.[34] In the confiscated building, the council opened a municipal secondary school, which was already full six months later. Before a full-time staff could be hired, volunteers from the ranks of Gijón's republican teachers apparently took up the slack.[35]

Still, the republican administration found it difficult to revolutionize the system overnight. With the chronic shortage of funds, it was nearly impossible both to exorcize religious influence and take better care of its underprivileged students. In 1934, for example, the teachers' union complained that the council had reneged on its subsidy for the free lunch program in El Humedal, not to mention its promise to expand the service.[36] The union went even further in its complaints, painting a bleak picture of the state of primary education in the city:

> The problem could not be more frightening: thousands of children, hungry and without schools; a city government for whom educational issues have been completely marginal; a local school board that does

---

[32] On education policy and problems under the Republic, see Mercedes Samaniego Boneu, *La política educativa de la segunda república durante el bienio azañista* (Madrid: CSIC, 1977).

[33] *Avance*, November 22, 1931.

[34] The Colegio de la Inmaculada was founded in 1889. One local commentator described the school's importance: "This school has educated children from the most renowned families of Asturias and the surrounding provinces, and who are today distinguished by their high social position" (Felipe Portola, *Topografía médica del concejo de Gijón* [Madrid: El Liberal, 1918], 175).

[35] *Avance* (November 21, 1931) reported that the Comité Federal in Gijón had offered their members' services, since so many of them were certified teachers.

[36] *Avance*, February 10, 1934. None of the other lunch kitchens had even opened. The government took refuge in its "unfavorable economic situation."

not act . . . and through it all, an infinity of children exposed to the pernicious influences of the street, without the benefits of education.

In support of this claim, the author referred to statistics compiled by the *ad hoc* "Committee on the Replacement of Religious Orders and Congregations," stating that 8,035 children remained without schools.[37] By 1934, the teachers' union belonged to the political opposition, so its critique should be taken with a grain of salt.

Nevertheless, it seems clear that the republican agenda of establishing a complete network of public secular schools faced formidable obstacles. Between the back-pedaling of the Reformists, the strapped budget, and the strength of Catholic opposition to educational reform,[38] the city government proved an ineffective weapon in implementing the republican educational agenda. In the spring of 1936 the Ministry of Education devised a radical plan to help the city establish new public schools by confiscating the property and buildings of religious schools, but there was no time to pursue this option before the outbreak of war.[39] At that point, one educator estimated that about half of Gijón's children were still receiving religious education.[40]

While public education struggled, there were few private, secular alternatives. One of the most prominent of these, the Escuela Neutra, was another product of the republican and labor movement anticlerical alliance. The idea originated with a public subscription opened by two anarchists, José Machargo and shoemaker Rogelio Fernández. Several wealthy men, most of them prominent republicans and Reformists, responded with generous donations, including a basement in which to house the school.[41] At the school's inauguration in 1911, free-thinker Rosario de Acuña and politician Melquíades Alvarez gave keynote speeches. The school opened with one teacher, added a

---

[37] *Avance*, February 28, 1934.
[38] The Asociación Católica de Padres de Familia, a national organization formed in 1931, opened a branch in Gijón in February of 1933 that attracted 500 or so members (a petition sent to the Cortes protesting against the expulsion of the Jesuits gathered 500 signatures). They worked to halt the laicization of schools by the Republican government, "who want to tear our children from Catholic schools, founding a unified lay school": *Memoria* (Gijón: Imprenta Palacio, 1933).
[39] The Catholic newspaper *Acción* was outraged at this offer and advised religious schools to fight what they called illegal confiscation of property (April 25, 1936).
[40] *Avance*, July 16, 1936.
[41] Among them were Laureano Suárez, president of the Reformist political club, Dionisio Cifuentes and Marcelino González (who donated his basement), also prominent Reformists.

second in 1913, and in 1914 anarchist leader Eleuterio Quintanilla quit his job as a *chocolatero* to join the teaching staff.[42] In later years, he became its director. Over 100 students matriculated for the 1913 academic year, and by 1930, enrollment in the combined primary and secondary institution was over 200, most of them "children of laborers."[43]

The goals of the school issued straight out of the "free-thinking" or "rationalist" educational movement.[44] In a 1913 speech the director explained that the school was committed to religious and political neutrality, concentrating only on providing what he called an "integral education": "that is to say, a concern with mental development, the purity of emotions, the discipline of the will in the formation of character; and at the same time, the harmonious development of the whole organism."[45] This agenda met the requirements of both republicans and anarchists, neither of whom believed education required direct ideological indoctrination. Thus, throughout the school's history, republicans and anarchists co-existed peacefully within its walls, pursuing their common enterprise.

This enterprise generated strong conservative opposition. Thus, rightist forces did what they could to undermine it, from attempting to link it to anarchist violence to blocking the city subsidies proposed by republican councilors.[46] Its symbolic presence was great enough to provoke a terrorist bomb attack in 1936, probably engineered by one of the fascist groups in the city.[47] The attacks against the Escuela Neutra are the best evidence of its perceived effectiveness in the secularization campaign. Although it reached only a small proportion of the city's children, we can assume that many of these grew up to be

[42] Ramón Alvarez Palomo, *Eleuterio Quintanilla* (Mexico: Editores Mexicanos Unidos, 1973), 78–79.
[43] Quote is in a letter (April 26, 1930) from the Escuela Neutra to the Sindicato Metalúrgico, requesting a donation: AGS, K-20.
[44] On this movement in general, see Pere Solà, *Las escuelas racionalistas en Cataluña, 1900–1939* (Barcelona: Tusquets, 1978).
[45] Gregorio Sánchez Díaz in *El Noroeste*, February 22, 1913.
[46] As a result, the school survived mainly on private funding – from wealthy liberals, republican groups and labor unions. In one of its annual reports in the 1920s, for example, it thanked "the increase of members who compensated for the lack of official protection that followed the city's withdrawal of its customary subsidy": cited in Ramón Alvarez Palomo, *Avelino González Mallada: alcalde anarquista* (Barcelona: Historia Libertaria de Asturias, 1987), 65.
[47] *Avance*, July 9, 1936. The bomb went off at 3:30 a.m., and did extensive damage, breaking windows and destroying tables, books and maps.

212

future oppositional leaders – whether republican or anarchist.[48] Despite this subversive power, however, it was only one school in a city where thousands of children attended religious schools and thousands more attended no schools at all. The goal of molding new generations of citizens could only be hindered by the inability to reach so many of them.

Molding a republican public

To close the gap, reformers also targeted working-class adults, offering them the alternative education they might have missed as children. In institutions like the Ateneo, the Association of Culture and Hygiene (ACH) and the Workers' Musical Association (Asociación Musical Obrera – AMO), republican mentors strove to turn adults away from the religious indoctrination of their youth, as well as from the vices of illiterate popular culture.[49] The Catholic Church operated its own adult cultural centers to lure workers away from the twin evils of alcoholism and atheism, but the majority of workers clearly rejected them. Thus, in contrast to the Church's control of juvenile education, the secular organizations dominated adult education and cultural training. Over the course of thirty-six years, several thousand workers, mostly men, took advantage of courses, lectures, excursions, and the opportunity to entertain and be entertained, all provided in an atmosphere that stressed democratic citizenship and sobriety.

Nevertheless, despite the obvious success of these institutions, they did not ultimately fulfill their founders' hopes of creating a loyal republican public. Instead, they became battlegrounds where some of their working-class members directly challenged their mentorship and their principles of social harmony. In the rapidly polarizing atmosphere of the 1930s, the eroding middle ground on which republican culture built its foundation could not hold. Thus, although many of the pre-

---

[48] For example, Ramón Alvarez Palomo, a member of the revolutionary government in 1936–1937, and the author of several books, including Quintanilla's biography, considered his tutelage under Quintanilla at the Escuela Neutra to be the first step on his road to political consciousness (from an oral interview).

[49] In this sense, these institutions fit into the late-nineteenth-, early-twentieth-century international crusade to "moralize" the working classes. See Robert Bezucha, "The Moralization of Society: the Enemies of Popular Culture in the Nineteenth Century," in *Popular Culture in France: the Wolf and the Lamb: from the Old Regime to the Twentieth Century*, ed. Jacques Beauroy et. al. (Saratoga: Anma Libri, 1977), 175–187.

cepts of republican culture survived, by 1936 they no longer constituted a coherent, republican-led alternative to the old regime.

The heyday of the republican-led educational movement was the
two decades before the First World War, the period of greatest initiative and least competition. After the establishment of the Ateneo and
the University Extension, two more organizations emerged out of the
sense of mission that energized turn-of-the-century reformers: the
AMO and the ACH, both founded in 1904. Both fit the pattern of
bourgeois patronage set by the Ateneo, in which the elite supporters
seemed equally compelled by the desire to help and to mold.

The AMO evolved from an *ad hoc* singing group of several dozen
youths who gathered in the house of republican schoolteacher Benito
Conde during the 1890s.[50] It was formalized in 1904 when engineer
and social reformer Suárez Acebal made a plea for donations to build
its own center, and several wealthy "protecting members" responded.
It was inaugurated soon after, with one hundred male participants
under the presidency of Valdés Prida, a republican and one of the
"protecting members." The members received music lessons and performed in the AMO choir, which gave public concerts, played at local
benefits and festivals, and even did extensive tours in northern Spain.[51]

The creation of a choral society targeting workers was not unique
to Gijón. In Spain, the tradition originated in Catalonia on the
impulse of Catalan composer Anselmo Clavé in the mid-nineteenth
century.[52] The first choirs in Asturias appeared in the 1860s, *ad hoc*
groups to perform at Carnival, followed by permanent associations in
the 1880s. As in Catalonia, the choirs seemed to be a direct response
to industrialization, an attempt to channel the associational opportunities of workers newly congregated for factory or mine work into
"respectable" avenues. As such, all of them maintained ties with, and
depended on, the patronage of Asturias' grand industrialists, intellectuals and businessmen.[53]

In many ways, the choral society was the perfect vehicle for republi-

---

[50] Benito Conde was one of the most respected of the federalist mentors. Belarmino Tomás, a provincial Socialist leader and ex-student of Conde's, called him "a man full of heart and idealism": *El Comercio*, November 29, 1936.

[51] On its founding, see *El Noroeste*, January 23, 1904. In 1907, Juan Teófilo Gallego Cata-lán reported that the organization was thriving, after overcoming many difficulties: *La educación popular en Gijón* (Gijón, 1907), 58.

[52] On Anselmo Clavé (1824–1874), see Enric Olivé i Serret, "Els Cors de Clavé i l'obrer-isme," *L'Avenç*, 104 (1987).

[53] Ramón García-Avello Herrero, "La música coral," *Ritmo*, 54 (1984), 20.

can reformers. Much more than a mere distraction for workers, the choir epitomized the values that republicanism tried to promote. The beauty of synchronized and harmonized voices expressed the reformers' own image of a co-operative society smoothed of social tensions, or the smaller scale of a disciplined factory workforce. According to proponents, music did more than just symbolize such harmony; it could actively promote it. As Clavé said, "[we want] to restrain and instruct the workers, to awaken in their lethargic souls a feeling of love and admiration for beauty . . . the regeneration of the proletariat, of the youth of the factory; to strengthen the sacred bonds of fraternity between those of all social classes."[54] Gijón's AMO echoed a similar philosophy when it articulated its intention to "fight vice, elevate the moral level of the proletariat, and propagate the spirit of positive associationism."[55] Music was not simply a form of entertainment, it was a route towards moral salvation and civic participation.

Despite its early success, the AMO slowly declined in the years after the world war, undermined, no doubt, by competing labor movement musical groups. As the labor movement became increasingly institutionalized, it could offer its own version of musical harmony, tuned to the key of class solidarity. With musical events staged in the union halls, workers no longer had to accept the patronage of the elites and the inferior status that this conferred. A description of the first AMO concert in 1904 unwittingly throws this relationship into bold relief:

> A numerous and distinguished public packed the Teatro de Jovellanos. In box and orchestra seats one could see the most elegant members of Gijón's high society, come to render homage and support for the Asociación Musical Obrera. In the balconies, compact groups of workers applauded their friends with great enthusiasm, in a notable display of solidarity.[56]

While the AMO faded away, an apparent victim of rising labor movement consciousness, the ACH, Suárez Acebal's other brainchild, followed a different line of evolution. Instead of being displaced, it underwent an internal transformation that subverted the original integrationist agenda of its founder. The ACH was launched to promote

---

[54] Quoted in García-Avello Herrero, "Música coral," 18.
[55] Quoted from a pamphlet entitled *Gijón Clavé*, in García-Avello Herrero, "Música coral," 20.
[56] *El Noroeste*, February 12, 1904.

"culture and hygiene" to those disadvantaged for whom normal channels were closed. It began with 300 members in a modest room on
the Paseo de Begoña, furnished with a few magazines, a small library
of 400 books, a lectern, and a wash basin for those who came directly
from work. Like the Ateneo, the ACH sponsored lectures on a variety
of topics, from negro funerals in Cuba to the origins of Carnival.
Suárez Acebal insisted that "the masses" were capable not only of
discussing serious social problems, but of contributing to their practical solution. If the ACH could get manual workers together with the
"intellectual workers" who had much to teach them, then everyone
could work collectively towards a more rational future.[57] With these
ideas, the new ACH followed closely in the footsteps of its model,
the Ateneo.

But more than the Ateneo, the ACH functioned as a mutual aid
society to shield individuals from the brutality of urban life. While it
devoted part of its energies to principles of general education, a growing proportion was directed towards improving workers' lives, and
especially the urban environment in which they suffered more than
most. The organization provided support in case of sickness and
calamity, as in the benefit performance for Manuel Toscano, partially
blinded in a work accident. The audience was regaled by the ACH
chorus, a play by Pachín de Melás, and music performed by the blind
orchestra, "The New Light."[58] On a larger scale, the ACH also com-
batted government neglect of the working-class *barrios*, pushing the
adoption of improvement projects from sewers to playgrounds.[59] For
those who participated in the association, the material and spiritual
aspects of culture were inseparable. If unhealthy environments sapped
workers' energies, then it was useless to expect them to be productive
citizens.

Probably as a result of the ACH's involvement in the quality of
urban life, much of the important work of the organization took place
in its branches, located mostly in the poorer neighborhoods. By the
end of the First World War, the ACH had opened over half a dozen
branches: in Natahoyo, El Llano, La Calzada, Calzada Alta, Barrios
Nuevos/Ceares, Tremañes, Pumarín/Roces, and Arenal. Last but not
least came the ACH Cimadavilla, in 1924. Of these, only two were
not situated in worker neighborhoods or mixed agricultural/worker

[57] *El Noroeste*, June 10, 1909.
[58] *El Noroeste*, October 22, 1921.
[59] On the ACH as a neighborhood advocate, see Chapter 3.

216

areas: the one in Arenal and the parent association on the Paseo de Begoña. As opposed to the Ateneo, whose status and activities always overshadowed those of its branches, the life of the ACH revolved around its subsidiary spokes. For the ACH, the neighborhood was the microcosm of the nation.

While most of the members of these branches came from the lower classes, their executive committees often included wealthy men, businessmen or property owners who lived or worked in the neighborhood and had their own stake in its improvement. In addition, the ACH depended on the patronage of wealthy donors, including prominent conservative figures. Thus, at the inauguration of La Calzada's children's playground in 1915, the presiding dignitaries were the parish priest of Jove, conservative city councilman Tejeras, and the military commander of Gijón's regiment. The land for the playground had been donated by two wealthy landlords.[60] Likewise, in 1917, La Calzada's ACH built its own center and started a library thanks to the generosity of the Chamber of Commerce, Ernesto Bachmaier, director of the beer factory, and José Navia Ossorio, Catholic politician and noble.

The ACH made no effort to hide this patronage, as it fit the organization's agenda of social harmony and inter-class co-operation. Thus, when pursuing a project, the ACH's goal was to forge an agreement that local businessmen, residents and the city could all stand behind. In fact, few of the ACH projects that challenged business interests succeeded. For example, the ACH of El Llano complained in 1917 that it had tried unsuccessfully for two years to force warehouse owners to clean up deposits of bones and dirty rags. The local health commissioner had agreed that their presence was a health menace, but the owners used their influence with higher authorities for a ruling in their favor.[61] By the 1930s, the problem was still not resolved.

The ACH was at its best when the project secured the goodwill of all parties. The process by which it worked to install a sewer system in Natahoyo is a good illustration. The president of the ACH Natahoyo was wealthy landowner Dionisio Cuervo, who initiated the project by arranging a meeting of his fellow landlords to discuss the problem. Cuervo convinced them to open a sewer fund that he would present to the mayor with a request for the immediate approval of the

[60] *El Noroeste*, July 30, 1915.
[61] *El Noroeste*, May 31, 1917.

217

project. As a result of this pressure, the city agreed, and the ACH continued hounding local officials until the first shovelful of dirt was turned over.[62]

Despite the importance of elite negotiations in the process, victory was celebrated as a community achievement. The ACH Natahoyo entertained all of its members at a *verbena*, and then organized a solemn ceremony to which representatives of all the other branches were invited. The event, replete with the flags of each subsidiary, paid tribute to what a united and well-organized community of citizens could accomplish. The image seemed to stick, as the ACH established itself as the primary intermediary between an indifferent city and its poorer citizens. The respect earned by the ACH is demonstrated in one letter to the editor from a group of workers living in Natahoyo, who were lodging a complaint about unpaved sidewalks. They suggested that the ACH of Natahoyo and La Calzada should take up the campaign, since they had often demonstrated what a well-organized population could achieve.[63]

Nevertheless, this letter may have been written just as the tide was about to turn, not against the organization, but against its integrationist philosophy. It was composed in 1929, at the end of a six-year period during which most political and labor organizations had been shut down or demoralized. In contrast, as a "non-political" association, the ACH thrived during the decade, filling the newspapers with announcements that projected an enthusiasm lacking in other areas of local life. Despite, or perhaps because of, the apparent health of the ACH, there is evidence that its control and direction were beginning to be contested. In 1925, an anarchist journal referred to a debate within the ACH Natahoyo that appeared to revolve around patronage. The article threatened that many members would quit if the organization went "back to organizing dinners for the well-heeled" instead of fulfilling the aims for which it was created.[64] The oblique description of the conflict leaves us with more questions than answers, but the fact that the anarchists thought it worth while to wage a struggle for control of the organization is intriguing in and of itself.

The evidence of such a struggle becomes clearer during the 1930s, as labor movement/republican co-operation declined. Thus, during the 1932 strike at Moreda y Gijón, the largest factory in Natahoyo,

[62] *El Noroeste*, March 22 and May 15, 1915.
[63] *El Noroeste*, January 23, 1929.
[64] *Solidaridad Obrera*, November 27, 1925.

the ACH branches of Natahoyo and La Calzada each organized a benefit to raise money for the metallurgical strikers.[65] Such a gesture seemed to indicate closer ties to the CNT unions than to the Reformist employers. The revolution of October 1934 revealed more links between the ACH and the labor movement. At the trial of four youths accused of participating in the uprising in La Calzada, a sister of one of the boys insisted that his only organizational affiliation was the ACH La Calzada.[66] In another trial, prosecutors accused the president of the ACH Pumarín of leading the revolutionary committee in that *barrio*. Furthermore, they accused him of using the ACH headquarters to distribute food during the insurrection. For this crime they requested a fifteen-year sentence and the dissolution of the ACH.[67] Another link comes from the correspondence between an anarchist living in exile after October 1934 and his wife in Gijón; at one point, she thought it important enough to send him a newspaper article on the Junta Vecinal de Jove, an affiliate of the ACH.[68]

The presence of radical activists in the ACH is clearest during the last months of the Republic, when radical political activity exploded again after sixteen months of repression (October 1934 to February 1936). At a benefit by and for the ACH La Calzada in March 1936, the centerpiece was the recitation of Rafael Alberti's tribute to the October revolution, "El alerta del minero: Asturias 5 de octubre." The evening was to end with "the magnificent proletarian hymn," the "Internationale."[69] Other special lectures reflected a similarly strong political message. At the ACH Tremañes in May 1936, Gonzalo López spoke on "How Workers Live and Work in Russia," and Avelino González Mallada held forth on "State Communism or Libertarian Communism."[70] One final piece of evidence supports a hypothesis of radicalization within the association. Among a group of questionnaires filled out by applicants to the Communist party during the Civil War, seventeen belonged to one of the ACH branches, and of these all had been long-time members of either the CNT or UGT.

---

[65] From a strike balance sheet, April 1932: AGS, K-46.

[66] *El Noroeste*, May 4, 1935.

[67] *El Noroeste*, November 8, 1935.

[68] The Junta was founded on April 6, 1930 by the ACH La Calzada, as an umbrella group to deal with urban problems in La Calzada, Calzada Alta, Jove, Musel, Veriña and Las Cabañas. On its history, see the retrospective article in *El Noroeste*, May 31, 1935, which was the one sent to A. González Mallada on June 5, 1935: AGS, K-46.

[69] *El Noroeste*, March 15, 1936.

[70] *El Noroeste*, May 22 and 29, 1936. González Mallada was an anarchist, and it appears that Gonzalo López was a communist.

In other words, these dedicated radicals had not only joined the ACH but proudly listed it on their Communist membership application.[71]

Without more information, it is difficult to reach a firm conclusion on the evolution of the ACH. And yet, whatever it had become by 1936, it was clearly no longer the civilizing instrument of middle-class reformers. Radical voices competed for control over the association, arguing implicitly that its goals could be better fulfilled from a position of proletarian autonomy and elite confrontation. Significantly, these voices did not disparage the existence of an association that attacked urban problems and provided educational and cultural skills for an illiterate working-class populace. They simply argued that the long-term goal of these projects should not be social integration into a nation of republican citizens, but the creation of an autonomous proletarian force, dedicated to advancing the interests of its class.

The trajectory followed by the ACH is even more clearly marked in the history of the Ateneo, once the model for all republican cultural institutions. The Ateneo entered the twentieth century at the height of its prestige, with a grand new locale and an exhausting array of activities, from art exhibitions to lecture series, to groups for playing chess, learning Esperanto, planning excursions and understanding photography. The Ateneo's success and the horizontal expansion of Gijón's boundaries led to the creation of two branch Ateneos, in El Llano and La Calzada, around 1905. In 1906, the Ateneo celebrated its 25th anniversary in an atmosphere of universal praise. A letter written by an admirer expresses some of the sentiments that many apparently felt:

> That in Spain an Ateneo Obrero should exist and prosper for twenty-five years is a cause for celebration in itself. One could argue that the workers of Gijón have been among the first to recognize the importance of culture and education for their class, and to utilize the powerful tool of association to achieve it. This force of will and persistence are not, unfortunately, qualities that are characteristic of our people. The past is a guarantee that, if the Ateneo maintains its commitment to neutrality and tolerance, it will endure for the good of all.[72]

The peak of this early florescence came in 1911 with the commemor-

---

[71] 135 questionnaires survive, and obviously do not offer a representative sample of ACH membership. Nevertheless, long-term membership in either the UGT or CNT indicates that none of these ACH members was part of the wave of opportunists and newly politicized people who flooded the Communist party during the war: AGS, K-264, K-269.
[72] Letter found in the Biblioteca Asturiana of the Jesuit school in Gijón, signature illegible.

ation of the 100th anniversary of the death of Jovellanos.[73] The fact that such an important event was taken on by the Ateneo signified its stature as one of the prominent centers of culture in the city, and not simply as a dispenser of remedial learning.

There was, however, a certain flaw to this triumph. As the Ateneo tried to broaden its appeal and its programs, its mission became more vague. While it never reneged on its commitment to working-class enlightenment, this commitment became diffused into grander goals. At the same time, the Ateneo was exposed to mounting competition from other cultural organizations, especially those sponsored by the trade unions, that made direct political appeals to workers. As a result, membership dropped in half during the 1910s, from 800 to less than 400. The Ateneo's leaders understood that workers were going elsewhere, but they did not fully grasp why: "the workers, following the currents of modern thought, are moving towards the centers of resistance and withdrawing from the institutions of culture."[74] However, workers did not have to make a trade-off between "resistance" and "culture." Members who participated in union life could pursue both goals. While the Ateneo tried to keep cultural life separate from politics, the union centers integrated the two into a coherent vision of the new worker.

The short-term consequence of this decline was a wrenching identity crisis that exploded during the tumultuous post-war years. One group, led by industrial magnate Secundino Felgueroso, argued that the Ateneo should drop its worker image and pursue its role as a premiere cultural center.[75] Opposing this group of reformers was the old guard, led by a professor at the Instituto Jovellanos, who argued that the Ateneo should stick to its roots and continue providing basic education and culture for the working class.[76] Significantly, both of these men were elite patrons of the Ateneo, not humble members. This fact, even more than the content of the debate, revealed the organization's true orientation as an elite-led instrument. From this perspective, the debate turned on the question of audience; should

---

[73] Patricio Aduriz, "Centenario del gijonés Ateneo-Casino Obrero," *El Comercio*, July 26, 1981.

[74] Quoted in Aduriz, "Centenario."

[75] Felgueroso was a Reformist who made his fortune in the mining industry. The proposal included dropping the word "worker" from the title, inviting highly qualified artists to visit, holding specialized seminars instead of remedial reading courses, and so on: *El Noroeste*, December 8, 1917.

[76] *El Noroeste*, December 11 and 13, 1917.

the progressive elites continue to focus on drawing in the working class, or should they turn their attention to the burgeoning class of white-collar employees, who sought to distance themselves from the working class?[77] The outcome of the battle seems to have been a stand-off, since the Ateneo continued to call itself "worker" and to teach basic education courses, while doubling its membership dues.

Despite the stand-off, the Ateneo's fortunes reversed over the next decade. From a membership of 897 in 1921, it ballooned to 2,400 in 1933. Without more information on the members, it is difficult to interpret what this revival meant. Most likely, the Ateneo continued to perform its balancing act between a working-class and a lower-middle-class audience, but this act was more suited to the 1920s than it was to the 1910s. In the post-war years, when the labor movement's cultural organizations took off, the Ateneo must have seemed staid and old-fashioned to many workers. In contrast, during the repressive 1920s, when the labor movement largely shut down, the Ateneo was an outpost of accessible culture in a wasteland of associational life. Thus, it offered one of the few legal associations where men of modest means could gather to socialize, educate themselves and discuss current issues. Furthermore, it provided an outlet for the energies of labor movement activists waiting for the Dictatorship to end. Thus, anarchist Ramón Alvarez highlighted the inauguration of a new home for the Ateneo La Calzada as one of the major events of the 1920s, because it was "one of the tribunals through which the most important militants of the CNT passed," including Avelino González Mallada and Avelino González Entrialgo, both leaders of the October revolution.[78]

The delicate balance continued during the early years of the Republic, when relations between republicans and anarchosyndicalists were still cordial. But as the glow of co-operation faded, the Ateneo became the center of another identity crisis, this time between its elite leaders and some of its radical working-class members:

> We are ending this period at a time when the direction of the Ateneo is being debated, not rationally but clouded by passions and confusion. The situation is so tense that many sincere members are unsure of what to do. The passions and the fighting that are escalating in the street

[77] The reform proposal of Felgueroso argued that there were few authentic "workers" in the Ateneo, and that most were white-collar employees who needed "spiritual nourishment," not remedial reading.

[78] Alvarez Palomo, *Avelino González Mallada*, 87.

have penetrated the heart of our center, disturbing its equilibrium . . . Here, in a center where harmony through study has always been a fundamental principle, even the elections of directors are becoming battles between the forces of the left and the right.[79]

As occurred with the ACH, the Ateneo became a prize contested by various political groups wanting to control it. Instead of abandoning the Ateneo as an elite-led, reformist institution, labor movement activists obviously valued the organization enough to fight for its soul.

By 1934, the radicals had established a powerful presence in the Ateneo, despite its technical neutrality. The pages of the monthly bulletin, which contained reviews, notices and informational articles, was increasingly caught up with the search for a proletarian cultural identity. One of the manifestations of this concern was an avid interest in current Russian literature, both fiction and non-fiction. In the 1934 survey of what members were reading, the report noted a predilection for it, especially the new generation of writers "who have added their voices to the new hopes that are springing up around the globe, putting their art at the service of the humble classes." The article went on to defend the library's purchase of the revolutionary literature against critics who had accused the library of ideological bias: "It is very natural and just that those who are searching should find satisfaction in these authors who help them and teach them to understand their own problems. It seems hypocritical to us to try and keep them away from these books."[80]

Like literature, theater also had to meet the demands of a new politicized proletariat. According to one writer, the bourgeois theater, designed only to distract the public from the contradictions of its society, could be compared to the rotting body of Louis XIV in his last days – still in power and unwilling to face its imminent demise. In its place, a new theater was budding, a theater that would accompany the proletariat on its revolutionary journey and provide it with a new cultural ethos.[81] A reflection of this new ethos is visible in the expositions and performances featured by the Ateneo. Revolutionary artists like Juan José Moreno, whose work depicted the misery of proletarian life, often displayed their work in the main gal-

---

[79] *Boletín de la Biblioteca Circulante*, February – March 1934.
[80] *Boletín*, February – March 1934.
[81] *Boletín*, May 1936.

lery. In addition, the Ateneo sponsored several productions performed by the Compañía de Arte Proletario under César Falcón, a socialist journalist.

The radical bid for power burst into the open in July 1935, when the Ateneo's secretary, Rufino García, was expelled by the board of directors for inappropriate political activity, including harboring two fugitives of the October revolution.[82] The next month, however, the general assembly of the Ateneo voted for his reinstatement after a heated two-and-a-half-hour debate, by a vote of 233 to 79. The vote prompted the board of directors to resign and the Civil Governor to close down the Ateneo, on the assumption that it was now "dominated by communists."[83] However, those who disapproved of the reinstatement convinced the Governor to hold yet another assembly where the non-radicals could show their force. He agreed, and in September this assembly elected a new board, made up of prestigious ex-presidents, including Secundino Felgueroso and Ramón Fernández (republican city councilor). The recapture of the Ateneo by its elite patrons was brief, however. After the Popular Front election, the new board contained several members of radical workers' organizations, including Rufino García and *cenetista* Pedro Sierra.

The Ateneo, then, like the ACH, found its original goals of moral education and integration contested and subverted. Wealthy reformers created the organizations with the implicit goal of drawing members into a political and social world that they controlled. The members, however, were able to take advantage of the associations' benefits without necessarily accepting their web of hegemonic assumptions. Likewise, although republican leaders built a powerful anti-clerical network that broke the Church's domination over public culture, a shared anti-clericalism did not always translate into political credits for them.

This failure of the republicans to capture the loyalty of Gijón's workers with its cultural and educational net and to assert its hegemony in the public sphere had larger political implications. Republicans needed the working-class population to give their bid for power the necessary muscle and depth, to supply the republican public that would breathe life into their formal institutions. They also needed a republicanized public sphere that could provide a "cultural frame" in

[82] *El Noroeste*, August 2, 1935. The paper, a hostile source, called Rufino a "Trotskyist communist."
[83] *El Noroeste*, August 12 and 13, 1935.

which to embed the political institutions of the new regime. Without them, republican Gijón was a mere formality, a regime imposed from city hall upon a passive population. In fact, although the city acquired certain symbols of republicanism, from the calendar of holidays to the new flag, it never united under the republicans' vision of their new Spain. Instead of unity, the Republic struggled with a confused and weak cultural identity that undermined not only the republicans but the Republic itself.

Moreover, the failure of a republican city like Gijón to achieve this kind of cultural unity provides some indication of the obstacles faced by the national government in its attempt to create a republican public. In a country where at least half the population still lived within the cultural rhythms of traditional Catholic Spain and without even the infrastructure of an oppositional culture, the Republic's symbolic power was even more tenuous. A regime that could rely neither on strong political institutions nor on a solid cultural idiom had little firm ground to stand on.

8

Labor movement culture: the brotherhood of workers

~

Like labor movements elsewhere, Gijón's Socialist and anarchist federations sought to create an alternative culture that brought their political ideals to life and instilled them into their working-class members.[1] In addition to offering workplace protection, the trade union federation was to serve both as a training ground for the new society and as the nucleus for it. It was where workers experienced the basic principles of Socialist or libertarian philosophy. Here also, workers learned to rely on each other instead of on their bosses or the political elites, including sympathetic republicans. Mutual aid and reliance were fundamental building blocks of the future society, particularly for the anarchists, who envisioned a new order of independent communities. The labor movement's vision of an alternative culture can be encapsulated in the image of the brotherhood of workers, a family purged of its subordinate and authority figures, in which all were equal as they were bound together in the fraternity of their class. The contrast between the brotherhood of workers and the nation of citizens sums up the different orientation of republicans and labor militants, who defined identity through one's relationship to work.

Although fraternity began at the workplace, it was supposed to extend into all areas of public life. At the workplace, the union attempted to protect its members from unacceptable working conditions. When members fell ill, lost their jobs, or were evicted from

---

[1] For more extended analyses of this project, see Vernon Lidtke, *The Alternative Culture: Socialist Labor in Imperial Germany* (New York: Oxford University Press, 1985), and Helmut Gruber, *Red Vienna: Experiments in Working-Class Culture, 1919–1934* (Oxford: Oxford University Press, 1991).

their homes, they could turn to the union for support. Moreover, the union houses were not simply crisis centers. As the labor movement solidified during the second decade, it began to offer a range of activities designed to meet members' needs for entertainment and education and hopefully to establish itself as the focal point of workers' lives. While working, learning and playing together, members could enhance their sense of collective identity and of belonging while reducing their dependence on the outside world.

If realized, the ideal of a pure proletarian public sphere[2] growing up in the belly of capitalism would have been a powerful weapon against the hegemonic culture. In fact, it was only imperfectly implemented, even at its peak in the 1930s, and even in labor movement strongholds like Gijón. One major obstacle to creating such an environment was the ongoing division between the CNT and the UGT, which produced animosity instead of brotherhood between the competing organizations. Repression also took its toll, making it difficult to establish a coherent, ongoing structure that could be absorbed into the members' daily lives. Thus, in the decade after the general strike of 1901, and again during the Dictatorship of the 1920s, and finally between the October 1934 revolt and the Popular Front election, most of the labor organizations, whether overtly "political" or not, closed or had their doors closed. Another more subtle obstacle to achieving the brotherhood of workers was implicit in the term itself: the unions' ambivalent inclusion of women.[3] In this sense, the proletarian version of a public sphere differed little from the republican, since both were based on gendered assumptions about women's "paradigmatically private" role.[4] Finally, the existence of a competing

---

[2] Starting from the premise of multiple and competing, or subsidiary public spheres, labor historians have used the term "proletarian public sphere" to denote an autonomous worker space within capitalist society, designed by and for workers, with the primary goal of preparing the way for the post-bourgeois society. See Donald Bell, *Sesto San Giovanni: Workers, Culture and Politics in an Italian Town, 1880–1922* (New Brunswick: Rutgers University Press, 1986), 66. Habermas acknowledged a "plebeian public sphere" distinct from the "bourgeois" public sphere, but he assumed it was derivative and subordinate: *The Structural Transformation of the Public Sphere: An Inquiry into a Category of Bourgeois Society* (1962; reprint, Cambridge, MA: MIT Press, 1989), xviii.

[3] For an extensive analysis of the gendered implications of fraternalism and brotherhood, see Mary Ann Clawson, *Constructing Brotherhood: Class, Gender and Fraternalism* (Princeton: Princeton University Press, 1989).

[4] Carole Pateman, "Feminist Critiques of the Public/Private Dichotomy," in *The Disorder of Women: Democracy, Feminism and Political Theory* (Stanford: Stanford University Press, 1989), 119. Pateman provides a careful analysis of the theoretical development of this paradigm.

republican culture limited the space in which a separate proletarian culture could flourish.

Because of these constraints, Gijón's labor movement could not build an inclusive world that would unite all of the working people of the city within a common culture. Furthermore, it never even achieved the level of coherence attained by the great European socialist movements, particularly in Germany, where the Sozialistische Partei Deutschlands provided a cradle-to-grave subculture for those who participated.[5] As a result, the labor movement offered only one of several cultures competing for hegemony in the city. Thus, even in 1936, when the CNT had finally become the most powerful political force in the city, it could not displace elements of the republican cultural milieu. The upshot of this situation was a heterogenous and fluctuating oppositional culture, in which different elements emerged dominant in certain situations. In one sense, this heterogeneity added to the power of the opposition, by making it more diverse and flexible. On the other hand, in Gijón as in Spain at large, it made it more difficult to launch a focused attack on the old hegemonic culture whose deep roots held fast, even in the political soil of the Republic.

Solidarity and mutual aid: on the job and off

Within these limitations, the labor movement in Gijón established its cultural parameters, weak in some areas and strong in others. It was weakest where it faced the most competition from the republican movement, in the areas of education and voluntary leisure associations. It was also weak, as indicated earlier, in the organization and inclusion of women. In contrast, it was strongest in promoting its mutual support system, which came to its members' aid in times of crisis, such as death, illness or work problems, and reinforced the sense of belonging in normal times. Since the government provided few programs or safety nets to deal with these problems, and the republi-

---

[5] Other work on labor movement culture in Spain has yielded similar results. Thus, Francisco de Luis Martín argues that the Socialists never developed an educational project of their own, instead relying on republican and anarchist formulations and, more generally, that they did not systematize their cultural project. See "El Cuento en la cultura Socialista de principios del siglo XX: approximación a la obra de J. A. Melía," *Sistema*, 93 (November 1989), "La cultura en la Casa del Pueblo de Barruelo de Santullán: el cuadro artístico, 1918–1936," *II Congreso de Historia de Palencia*, 1989, and "Un proyecto educativo-cultural socialista: la Fundación Cesáreo del Cerro," in *Historia de la Educación*, 7 (1988).

cans were more interested in the moral than the material salvation of the working class, the labor movement had this terrain all to itself.

In the early years, the labor movement had to fight first for the acceptance of its existence, and then for an acknowledgment of collective bargaining.[6] By the 1930s, however, the CNT in particular had achieved a significant degree of control over the workplace, which made it the best advocate a worker had, even with the new labor legislation of the Republic.[7] Because the CNT denied the legitimacy of government arbitration boards, it set up its own mechanisms for settlement of disputes. When a worker complained of unjust termination to his union, for example, the union would send an inquiry to the employer, who responded with his version of the story.[8] An unsatisfactory explanation could lead to a strike or boycott. Thus, when the construction syndicate put pressure on a particular contractor, it asked the metallurgical syndicate to forbid its members to complete any smelting jobs ordered by him.[9] From the tone of employers' letters, it is clear that they feared the power of the CNT. As one manager wrote to his boss in Madrid: "they spend their days making inspections in which they take note of the behavior of the managers, foremen, etc., in order to take it into account when the occasion presents itself, which they are convinced will be soon."[10]

If a worker was unemployed, the union also did everything it could to secure a job. While in most cases the scope of the economic crisis made this impossible, especially in the 1930s, the union federation made its presence felt by controlling access to the jobs that did open up and by negotiating with employers for other stop-gap measures.

[6] Laws protecting the right to association existed from the late nineteenth century, and the first collective bargaining legislation appeared in 1909. As Benjamin Martin points out, however, almost none of the labor legislation was implemented before the Republic, so that each local federation had to fight for its own recognition. On labor legislation from the Restoration through the Republic, Martin's is the best general survey: *The Agony of Modernization: Labor and Industrialization in Spain* (Ithaca: ILR Press, 1990).
[7] Unfortunately, the documentation on union activities is irregular at best; almost nonexistent before the First World War, occasional between 1917 and 1930, and modest for the Republican period. What exists is contained in the Civil War archive in Salamanca (AGS).
[8] Two examples are a letter from the owner of a mechanical workshop, December 8, 1930, and one from a marine yard, June 26, 1931. Both insisted that the fired worker had been negligent or unqualified, and the latter employer reminded the syndicate that he had uncomplainingly accepted the recent wage scales proposed by the local federation for the metallurgical trades: AGS, K-46.
[9] Letter, September 15, 1931: AGS, K-46.
[10] In reference to the factory committees roaming his chemical factory, January 7, 1936: AGS, K-44.

229

Thus, some employers agreed to a rotating workforce, where everyone worked two or three days a week in order to minimize lay-offs.[11] In addition, most unions forbade their members from taking two jobs or extra free-lance work.[12] Most importantly, the union centers served as clearing houses through which jobs were processed.[13] Employers would sometimes send their hiring requests directly to the syndicates, as in the case of a small businessman who wanted to hire a master polisher.[14] Syndicates also maintained an informational network with parallel unions elsewhere in Spain, in case shortages in one area could be filled by those unable to find work in another.[15] In one case, a conflict arose when a pastry maker from Salamanca arrived in town and found a job without first presenting himself to the syndicate. When his presence was discovered, representatives from the syndicate insisted that he be fired, since he had circumvented the normal hiring procedure. If the man wanted to work in Gijón, he was advised to register at the Casa del Pueblo, where his name would be put on the waiting list.[16]

As this story indicates, control over the workplace also implied the power to discipline workers who broke the ranks of the brotherhood. Lists of workers who refused to join a union, or those who fell behind in their dues, were often posted in the workers' center or published in *El Noroeste* to incite public humiliation. A particularly vehement curse was laid upon the handful of non-union members at the Primitiva Indiana chocolate factory in 1919:

> These poor workers have obstinately refused to answer the fraternal call of their companions, and have rejected unionization; in other words, they have renounced outright any idea of collective improvement,

[11] In the Acts of the Construction Syndicate, CNT, and of the Workshop Section of the Metallurgical Syndicate, there are several references to the *turno* system, as it was called, with debates on how work should be organized in each case: AGS, K–107, K-21.

[12] One example is a notice from the electricians' union to Sección Laviada (metal workers) advising members that they are only allowed one wage per day: AGS, K-46.

[13] The archives of the Construction Syndicate Bolsa de Trabajo contain 1,740 files for unemployed members, including their profession and whether or not they had secured employment: AGS, K-7, K-8.

[14] Letter, Robustiano Fanjul, of Industrial Artística, to Sección Talleres, Casa del Pueblo, May 13, 1931: AGS, K-46.

[15] A letter from the Metallurgical Syndicate in Zaragoza to the same syndicate in Gijón, September 25, 1931, sent because of the work shortage in Zaragoza, and in order to maintain close relations among all metalworkers in Spain, as well as to exchange information on the state of the industry: AGS, K-20.

[16] Letter from secretary of local CNT, April 27, 1936, to federation in Salamanca, explaining why their compatriot had not been allowed to work: AGS, K-6.

moral elevation, and civic and social virtue. With their attitude, they have become both accomplices in, and victims of, social injustice. They are voluntary slaves, a condition they sadly deserve. The Food Industry Syndicate has to treat these workers as what they are: rebels against worker organization and a threat to it.[17]

Direct pressure from working companions could also be applied, as in the case of Eduardo Díaz, a truck driver who finally joined the union when the loaders systematically refused to load his vehicle.[18] While coercive tactics like these must have alienated some people, they also commanded fierce loyalty. There was no middle ground between inclusion and exclusion, and the high price of the latter made belonging even more attractive.

For those who belonged, the rewards of inclusion in the brotherhood were great. No one had to face the oppression of the powerful employer alone, and members could count on their union to back them up in both personal and group disputes. The unions also provided a safety net of insurance for illness and death, which filled the gap left by a decidedly non-welfare state. The first report of such a service was in 1909, when metalworkers approved the statutes of a mutual aid fund for sick pay.[19] In 1918, the CNT federation broached the topic of a comprehensive insurance package that transcended the boundaries of individual trade unions.[20] While it seems doubtful that this program was fully implemented until the Republic, if then, the union federation provided a significant service for its members since it offered more than the government did.[21]

The concept of mutual aid extended beyond formal workplace funds to cover the tribulations of daily life. The existing evidence suggests that both members and unions accepted this relationship. Thus, when a widow had trouble collecting her dead husband's pension, she asked the union to intercede.[22] And when a street hawker had his

---

[17] Notice published in *El Noroeste*, March 6, 1919.
[18] Actas, CNT Construction Syndicate, April 3, 1934: AGS, K-107.
[19] *El Noroeste*, May 22, 1909. Without union records for this period, all information must be gleaned from the press. We must assume that other unions followed the metalworkers' lead, but only a few instances were reported, as in 1919, when the union of textile workers at Gijón Fabril announced the opening of a sick fund (June 30, 1919).
[20] As a CNT spokesman argued, "To limit the action of organized workers only to struggles against employers is a mistake": *El Noroeste*, April 7, 1918.
[21] In the 1930s, several letters refer to a formal CNT commission to deal with all workplace accidents (AGS, K-46, July 12, 1933 and October 28, 1933), but no documentation on how the system operated exists.
[22] Letter to local UGT federation, September 5, 1934: AGS, H-22.

home sacked by municipal policemen, his union ran a request for aid in the newspaper. The notice admitted that the problem did not fall under normal trade union jurisdiction, but averred that members should show solidarity in all aspects of business and private life.[23] In the 1930s, the CNT created a Syndicate for the Defense of Public Interests that formalized this solidarity. Acting as a kind of citizens' rights group for the poor, the fifteen-hundred-member organization handled complaints about basic survival problems:

> This syndicate is ready to stand in the way of those who, appealing to might instead of right, try to play games with the survival of the people. Since we are in no way disposed to let this happen, we have created this syndicate, for all those manual or intellectual workers who are affected by the capricious increase in their rent or in the cost of basic foodstuffs.[24]

When the worker reached the final crisis of his life – death – the union was also there to send him off with a great show of solidarity. At the minimum, all those who worked in the same shop or belonged to the same union attended the funeral of one of their comrades or even of his wife or mother. At these moments, the "great family of workers," or at least the separate families of Socialists and anarchists, became a reality, as illustrated in this description of a cabinet-maker's funeral:

> On the next day, we held the procession carrying the body to the civil cemetery, with numerous people following, nearly all of them workers ... The resulting procession was impressive, due to the large numbers of people who lined the route, along several of the city's major streets. On the casket, covered by the flag of the Agrupación Socialista, were three wreaths: one from his family, one from his work companions and one from the Agrupación. He was carried on the shoulders of four of his fellow workers who were closest to him.[25]

Of course, funerals like this were staged as much for the benefit of the living as the dead. To the outside world, they demonstrated the power and presence of the labor movement, as it occupied the streets. To union members, they provided a visual reminder of the community to which they belonged. Furthermore, the procession itself acted out a new theory of social relations by overturning the traditional hierarchy of the cortège. In the past, employers had often paid for their

---

[23] *El Noroeste*, October 14, 1913.
[24] *El Noroeste*, April 22, 1932.
[25] *Aurora Social*, February 26, 1909.

workers' funerals, giving them a place of honor with the priest at the head of the procession, while the deceased's co-workers brought up the rear. In the union funeral, workers both led and followed, in a ritual overturning of the old "syntax of social order."[26] Thus, the simple gesture of the union funeral communicated a complex array of principles, from mutual aid for the individual to the solidarity of the whole to a glimpse into the new society in which all would be equal.

At the heart of this array of principles was the notion of a union identity, which defined the relationship of a worker to his job, his fellow workers, and the world around him. If he fulfilled the expectations of that identity, he was a "buen compañero," a good comrade; if he transgressed he was an outcast, a man without a family. Furthermore, the reputation and the identity followed him wherever he moved. A letter of introduction from the union back home could welcome him into any Socialist or anarchist circle in the country. Conversely, a good communication network tracked the transgressors. One letter from a waiters' union in the Basque region warned the Gijonese federation of two waiters of "doubtful conduct" due to arrive in Gijón with false documentation.[27] If exposed, the waiters would be expelled and stripped of all their documentation, including the *carnet*, a membership booklet with the rules and regulations of the organization, a photo of the individual, and a statement asserting affiliation in the "great family of workers." By the 1930s, it was increasingly difficult to do without this membership in Gijón; after July 1936, it was impossible. At this point, the labor movement had become the indispensable source of economic and social solidarity and mutual aid.

Leisure time and the labor movement

The networks of social and economic solidarity were designed to help workers negotiate the unfriendly capitalist world in which they had to survive temporarily. But they also contributed to a more ambitious project: the creation of a broad fraternal structure that could carve

[26] In her article on civic parades in nineteenth-century America, Mary Ryan argues that the parade line-up represented the "syntax of social order": "The American Parade: Representations of the 19th Century Social Order," in *The New Cultural History*, ed. Lynn Hunt (Berkeley: University of California Press, 1989), 139.

[27] Letter to the Waiters' Section of the Restaurant and Hotel Syndicate, August 17, 1934: AGS, H-21.

out an independent space free from the demands of the capitalist world; that is, a proletarian public sphere. The sphere was to be both autonomous and oppositional, promoting self-containment as it undermined the hegemonic culture.

To complete the sphere, the labor movement needed to draw workers into a web of activities that engaged the worker during the leisure time when he was not at work or at home. This web would then envelop him in a cultural milieu that stood in opposition not only to elite institutions, but to elements of the popular working-class culture that, in the minds of union leaders, inhibited workers' growth. Evidence of these kinds of activities began appearing in the early 1910s, and then again in the 1930s, following the more general pattern of union activity.[28] Nevertheless, they never succeeded in enclosing the working class in an alternative public sphere or counter-hegemonic culture that was exclusively proletarian.

One reason for this partial failure was that workers (as elsewhere) did not always co-operate by giving up their old habits and adopting those sanctioned by the union movement. Union leaders often shared the moralizing tone of bourgeois reformers in their admonitions to workers not to drink too much, to gamble, to waste their time at soccer games or drown their sorrows in the undignified revelries of Carnival. The frustrated edge to these criticisms makes it apparent that many workers refused to give up these pleasures. Thus, one Socialist pleaded with his readers to reconsider their attachment to Carnival, a traditional festival that was both too Catholic and too bacchanalian for the labor militants' tastes: "let us think, workers, of how ridiculous we look, foolishly dressed, objects of derision for all the rest."[29] Another, anarchist, writer tried to convince his audience that Carnival was a symptom of the sickness of the present social system; because "people are accustomed to prejudice, falsity, and lies, when the moment arrives that they can break out of these customs, they do it brutally, and with violence."[30] Militants worried even more about the increasing popularity of soccer in the 1920s, which they feared was dissipating the energy of young working-class men:

---

[28] Elsewhere in Spain, with the exception of Barcelona, the chronology appears to be similar. Francisco de Luis Martín dates the Socialist movement's interest in educational and cultural issues from the first decade of the twentieth century, and sees the period from 1915 to 1920 as that during which union centers and *casas del pueblo* began seriously fomenting such activities: "La Cultura en la Casa," 1.

[29] *Aurora Social*, February 19, 1904.

[30] *El Libertario*, February 8, 1913.

The soccer plague has taken away a great contingent of union supporters; the youthful enthusiasm that used to be directed towards the
unions is today disseminated in soccer clubs . . . if you ask our youths
what newspapers in Spain promote ideas of liberty and justice, no one
will answer you, but if you look in their bags you will find them full
of the sporting and bullfighting magazines that are published in our
horrid country.[31]

Another writer grumbled that soccer, bicycling and boxing would
probably provide the spiritual direction that neither politics nor work-
erism would be able to give to working men.[32]

To counter the noxious influence of activities that at best distracted
and at worst dissipated energies, the union federations presented a
range of alternatives to fill workers' leisure time. Their purpose was
both educational and recreational, although the labor movement did
not make a sharp distinction between the two. All union activities had
a didactic purpose, if only to reinforce community strength. Education, then, was at the core of the labor movement and particularly
the anarchist project, as it was for the republican. In the words of
Eleuterio Quintanilla,

> Certainly, the just man is not born, he is created; he is created by the
> force of tenacious will and constant introspection, by implacable self-
> evaluation, by attentive observation and cool criticism of external realit-
> ies. With these qualities we can shake off the dust of established conven-
> tions and liberate ourselves from ancestral obligations.[33]

The only issue was whether education was transmitted directly, in
classrooms, libraries and lecture halls, or indirectly, through the means
of enjoyable pastimes.

The goal of molding the just man was lofty but confusing, since it
overlapped considerably with the republican educational project, as
expressed in the Ateneo and, of course, the Escuela Neutra. The overlap is not surprising, since many labor leaders, including Quintanilla,
first imbibed these principles from republican mentors. In many ways,
the labor movement simply carried on this tradition in its own educational programs. Thus, the unions offered night classes in technical
training and elementary education, in which they taught basic subjects

---

[31] *Solidaridad Obrera*, June 15, 1923.
[32] *El Noroeste*, March 18, 1927.
[33] "The Education of the Worker," *El Noroeste*, February 4, 1926. For a fuller treatment
of the anarchist educational agenda, see José Alvarez Junco, *La ideología política del
anarquismo español (1868–1910)* (Madrid: Siglo Veintiuno, 1976), Chapters 3 and 9.

like grammar, arithmetic and geometry. In addition, they sponsored informational lectures and encouraged recreational reading through the creation of libraries in the union centers. Finally, the labor movement even co-opted the Ateneo's name, with the formation of nine libertarian *ateneos* in Gijón's neighborhoods. This cultural borrowing created a powerful "free-thinking" educational milieu, which crossed class and political boundaries. On the other hand, the influence of republican culture made it difficult for the labor movement to define a completely independent cultural space.

The labor movement did attempt to fuse its own identity into these borrowed programs and institutions, but it never cut loose entirely. Thus, while the basic education courses covered the same curriculum, their format sought to promote a different set of ideals. For example, courses offered at the anarchosyndicalist Escuela Sindical were taught by union members instead of by licensed professionals.[34] According to Quintanilla's explanation of the rationale for such a format, workers needed to know that they could learn from each other, instead of from patronizing literati. Furthermore, this format helped the teachers as well as the students, by giving them practice in oral presentation and pedagogy.[35] The message was that basic education courses could teach much more than the "three R's."

The message was even blunter in the regular lecture series sponsored by the labor movement. In this case, content rather than format distinguished them from their Ateneo counterparts. Instead of lectures aimed at informing good citizens, these focused on teaching workers to be useful and loyal union members. They informed listeners of the history of the labor movement, as at the inauguration of the Escuela Sindical, when the featured speaker talked about the First International.[36] On a more practical level, the Socialist federation staged a series of talks in Natahoyo in November 1910 "in order to instill an associational conscience in the workers." The first of these speakers expounded on the benefits of solidarity and mutual aid across trades.[37] Other lectures spoke directly to anarchist or Marxist theory, such as "Surplus Value," by shoemaker Manuel Paredes, or "Logical Foun-

[34] In contrast, a non-political guild like the Association of Commercial Clerks recruited professors from the Escuela Superior de Comercio: *El Noroeste*, November 2, 1919.
[35] *El Noroeste*, November 27, 1913. The Escuela Sindical was to alternate adult elementary classes with general lectures designed for the whole family.
[36] *El Noroeste*, December 6, 1913.
[37] *El Noroeste*, November 4 and 7, 1910.

dations of the CNT," delivered at the Ateneo Libertario in 1933. Other than these categories, speakers covered a variety of topics, from female unionization to education to the Casa del Pueblo's informal conversations on "Life in the society of the future."[38]

The unions went one step further and encouraged workers to learn about these things through the written word. To facilitate this process, they created an independent network of reading material and sources, some of which were unavailable in regular libraries and bookstores. The union centers stocked the radical press, either for sale or in-house perusal, and they offered cheap pamphlets not sold in mainstream publishing houses.[39] To provide a firmer institutional base for a reading culture, both federations opened their own libraries. The Socialist library contained 500 volumes at its inauguration in March of 1913, while its anarchist counterpart held 300 when it opened in September 1912. Over the next couple of years, both libraries claimed an extraordinary reception, with the number of readers surpassing the capacity of the small collections.[40] The libraries apparently continued to prosper, even remaining in service during the Dictatorship, according to one CNT circular.[41] If this is true, the union library may have been one of the few public outposts of anarchist culture during an otherwise repressive decade.

These libraries provided a space where a union reading culture could develop, but their collections were not uniquely dedicated to proletarian culture. Thus, they appeared to contain a broad mixture of titles not dissimilar to the Ateneo's selections. No complete inventories exist, but acquisition notices point to this conclusion. Certainly, classic revolutionary texts were prominent among the new arrivals. One donation to the Socialist library included Marx's *Capital*, Jean Jaurès' *History of Socialism* and Alfredo Oppiso's *The Great Revolutionaries*.[42] Likewise, in 1913 the anarchist library added Peter Kropotkin's *The*

---

[38] *El Noroeste*, September 18, 1931.
[39] *Acción Libertaria* (December 9, 1910) announced its book service with the following titles: "Practical Measures for Avoiding Large Families," 10 pts.; "The Death Penalty and Education," Elie Reclús, 10 pts.; "The General Strike," Francisco Ferrer, 15 pts.; "The Bourgeoisie and the Proletariat," José Prat, 10 pts; "The Population Problem," Sebastián Faure, 10 pts.; "Solidarity," Anselmo Lorenzo, 15 pts.
[40] On the Socialist library, see *El Noroeste*, October 19, 1914; on the anarchist, see *El Noroeste*, January 16, 1915.
[41] On March 4, 1926, the CNT issued a circular asking for volunteers to reorganize the library and regularize its services: AGS, K-20.
[42] Letter from donors, the Agrupación Socialista, to the Circulating Library, June 1, 1916: AGS, H-29.

Conquest of Bread and issues of *La Revista Blanca,* while in 1929 they acquired selected works by Bakunin and Rocker.[43] Nevertheless, in addition to these revolutionary works, both libraries included a broader spectrum of reading material, from the natural sciences to social novelists like Victor Hugo, Pío Baroja, Emile Zola and Vicente Blasco Ibáñez. As was true in most union libraries in Spain, the collections fit into the broader mold of what José Carlos Mainer calls "democratic culture."[44] Thus, the libraries exemplified the hybrid nature of the labor movement's educational agenda.

A different kind of hybrid can be found in the unions' entertainment offerings. Theoretically, entertainment was a subset of education. As one anarchist put it: "Propaganda can be made anywhere: in the workshop or in the theater."[45] And yet, the federations understood that they needed to provide enjoyable distractions that could attract workers and their families, reinforce basic principles and hopefully dissuade members from participating in more harmful pastimes, like gambling and drinking. To fulfill all of these requirements, the unions had to do more than translate doctrine into dialogue or music; they had to entertain. In search of this balance, the labor movement's entertainment activities incorporated elements of direct propaganda, popular religious and folk traditions, and elite culture. The fact that all of this activity occurred under union auspices gave it a unique flavor, but it was not enough to constitute a pure proletarian sphere, that is, a milieu created especially to prepare workers for the society of the future.

The earliest form of labor movement entertainment was the literary – musical *velada,* an *ad hoc* format borrowed from the world of elite culture that fit the resources of a budding organization. Like the republicans, the unions staged cultural celebrations to coincide with the important events of the revolutionary calendar: November 11th (for the Chicago martyrs), May 1st and the anniversary of the Commune. The centerpiece of the *velada* was usually a play, sandwiched between a variety of other performances and speeches. As Pachín de Melás described: "[there would be] the reading of an article, a short discussion about it, the recitation of some poetry, then a story, an aria,

---

[43] *El Noroeste,* January 4, 1913, and May 16, 1929.
[44] On labor movement libraries, see Mainer's *La Doma de la quimera* (Barcelona: Universidad Autónoma, Escola Universitária de traductors i intèrprets, 1988).
[45] *Fraternidad,* August 26, 1900.

a duo, ending with a discourse given by a distinguished worker."[46]

One of the first such events recorded in the local press commemorated the anniversary of the Commune in 1900, before the union movement split. The program opened with a piano solo, followed by a speech by Sacramento Lafuente, anarchist and president of the carpenters' union. Next, several people recited poetry, including a female tailor who read her own work on the history of the Commune. The anarchist shoemaker Rogelio Fernández sang a selection from the *zarzuela* (akin to musical theater) "El Juramento," and an Asturian song was performed by Francisco Meana, son of Socialist activist León. More speeches and readings followed, including an original poem by a republican typesetter, Ricardo Serrano, dedicated to the new worker center. The program ended on a grand note with a revolutionary hymn composed by a printer from Barcelona.[47]

By the 1910s, the union federations began to regularize this type of production with the creation of permanent "artistic sections." The first mention of such a section in the Socialist center came in 1910;[48] in the anarchist center it appeared in early 1913.[49] In addition to the artistic sections of each federation, some individual unions formed their own groups, like the cigarette makers' theatrical troupe and the fishermen's choral society. The proliferation of artistic groups and spaces culminated during the 1930s, with the creation of the nine libertarian *ateneos*.[50] At this point, the union movement boasted a complex local network of entertainment centers and performers that could service the needs of the large union community.

Programs followed the model of the Commune *velada*, with mixtures of all forms of artistic and literary production. Social themes predominated, from the singing of the "Internationale"[51] to the subject matter of theater pieces like "The Great Struggle" and "Anarchy

---

[46] Pachín remembering the early days of the union movement, in "El Hijo del Herrero," *La Prensa*, November 18, 1934.
[47] *El Noroeste*, March 18 and 19, 1900; *Aurora Social*, March 24, 1900.
[48] *El Noroeste*, January 24, 1910.
[49] *El Noroeste*, February 18, 1913.
[50] Unfortunately little is known about these *ateneos*, other than their location. Of the ten in Asturias, nine fell inside Gijón's township: two were located downtown, one in Cimadavilla, and the rest in outlying areas – La Calzada, El Llano, Ceares, Avda. Oviedo, Frontón and Veriña: Martín Rodríguez Rojo, "Los Ateneos en Asturias durante la II República, 1931–1936" (Tesina, University of Barcelona, 1985), 51.
[51] According to Vernon Lidtke (*The Alternative Culture*, 128), although the "Internationale" was known in Germany in the 1890s, its saturation of union halls around Europe did not occur until after the First World War.

in Action." Referring to the latter play, a Socialist reviewer could not resist a little biting sarcasm: "during the performance, a chorus of anarchists will light a myriad of sticks of dynamite, and at the end will sing the Te Deum."[52] All of these pieces were probably written and performed by local amateurs, since there was little national touring in the anarchist or socialist movements.[53] One of the few exceptions was the Teatro Proletariado, which brought its repertoire of revolutionary works from around the world: "Hinkemann," by Ernst Toller, on the evils of war, "At Rojo," by an Irishwoman Carlotta O'Neill, on the exploitation of dressmakers, and an anti-imperialist piece called "Ruge, China!," by a Russian, Tretiakov.[54] Though we know little of the content of most of the plays, according to Lily Litvak most anarchist theater was simple in form and message, full of archetypal characters, like the Capitalist and the Priest, and delivered in melodramatic language.[55]

However, the artistic spectacles put on by the unions consisted of more than ideology adapted for the stage. In addition to revolutionary plays, classical works and comedies were also performed. Thus, for example, one program featured a comedy called "Your Excellency," while another offered the recitation of a humorous monologue, "My First Boyfriend," by a young female militant. Likewise, although no show was complete without a rousing rendition of the "Internationale," the other musical selections were quite diverse, ranging from classical composers to Asturian folk music. Without more information, it is difficult to tell what the organizers had in mind when constructing these hodgepodge programs, but the most likely answer is that they had no systematic artistic plan for a completely new proletarian culture. Folk music may have been included because it linked the movement to a traditional popular culture, or because it created a comfortable and familiar environment for the learning of new principles, but on some level it made no doctrinal sense.

The lack of a systematic plan is also apparent even in that epitome of labor festivals, May 1st. Despite the specific new symbolism brought to the celebration, its practice definitely borrowed from older tra-

---

[52] *Aurora Social*, December 28, 1901.
[53] According to Lily Litvak, most anarchist plays and performers stayed local: *Musa libertaria: arte, literatura y vida cultural del anarquismo español (1880–1913)* (Barcelona: Antoni Bosch, 1981), 246.
[54] Rodríguez Rojo, "Los Ateneos," 120–121.
[55] For more on anarchist theater, see Chapter 7 of Litvak's *Musa libertaria*.

ditions, in this case Catholic. At the first major demonstration, in 1900, the day began to the sounds of street musicians roaming the streets with their bagpipes (*gaitas*) and tambourines, in clear imitation of the *romería*, or saint's day festival. After all the workers gathered at the union center, they began the procession, following a red flag instead of the hoisted body of the saint. In lieu of the banners of confraternities, the flags of different parties or societies of resistance were sprinkled through the crowd. The march proceeded to the city hall, where delegates presented a petition of general grievances to the mayor, who promised to relay them to Madrid. In the afternoon, the participants made an excursion to one of the *aldeas* for a fraternal picnic and dance, in another parallel with the traditional *romería*.

Not everyone in the labor movement accepted this ecumenicism. In particular, many anarchist militants viewed it as pure pandering, a replacement of one type of illusion for another. For them, it was no different from a real saint's day or Carnival; yet another distraction to keep workers from the good fight. As one editorial said grimly, "While the workers only show their teeth to smile, the employers can rest easy."[56] Another piece expounded on this theme with bitter sarcasm:

> May 1st is your day. You have your *fiesta* and your barbarism. Have fun, laugh, drink, dance, sing; march in correct and tight formation as you are told. Your heroes in front, marching behind your banners; you arrive at the door of the authoritarian church, dedicate your annual prayer, and go back to dancing, drinking, laughing, talking, having fun. You have your *fiesta* and your barbarism.[57]

When the Republic declared May 1st a national holiday, this act only confirmed anarchist suspicions of the event. As Quintanilla wrote in 1934, the step completed the process of co-option by bourgeois governments. From a revolutionary statement, May 1st had sunk to the level of a secular Sunday, without the mass but replete with official sermons and Riego's "Hymn."[58] Only in 1936 did the CNT treat the holiday as anything but a normal work day (see Chapter 10).

Some of the CNT's hostility to May 1st stemmed from its feud with the Socialists, who were closely identified with the holiday. But part of the issue was stylistic. It is almost as if the anti-clerical roots of each

---

[56] *Acción Libertaria*, April 7, 1911.

[57] *Acción Libertaria*, April 28, 1911.

[58] *El Noroeste*, May 1, 1934. Riego's "Hymn" was the battle song of the liberal revolution of 1820.

group manifested themselves in opposite reactions; on the one hand, the Socialists strove to imitate and replace the rich public ritual of the Catholic Church; on the other hand, anarchists preferred a puritan-like rejection of "immoderate" display and empty ritual. Whatever the reason, the upshot was that after 1900 May 1st never took root as a proletarian festival in Gijón. With a few notable exceptions, including May 1936, the CNT either ignored it, or celebrated it with a solemn event, as in 1913, when they held an open debate on how "to enter into a new period of frank and decisive struggle that will accelerate the coming of the social state that socialists of all schools commend."[59] Because of the CNT's clout in the city, its attitude predominated. In 1917, one observer commented on the "indifference" of local workers to the event, and in 1919 another noted "a certain disdain" with which they referred to it.[60]

It is hard to know whether the CNT's hostility to the "feel good" entertainment of a May 1st celebration weakened or strengthened the movement in the eyes of its constituency.[61] Either way, however, its absence reduced the number and visibility of public proletarian celebrations in the city. Whatever its limitations, May 1st was the only city-wide labor celebration that regularly occupied and filled the city streets. As such, it was the most dramatic opportunity to bring together all of the elements of a proletarian culture into one coherent narrative. The fact that the dominant union federation in Gijón was unable or unwilling to turn May 1st into a visual manifestation of a proletarian public sphere diminished the presence of that sphere. The gap left by May 1st was, in fact, the perfect illustration of the holes in Gijón's proletarian culture. For a variety of reasons, from the feud between Socialists and anarchists, to the influence of republican culture, to the competition from other forms of popular culture, the labor movement in Gijón did not construct an independent, alternative culture that was powerful and coherent enough to replace either the existing hegemonic culture or the older republican culture.

---

[59] *El Noroeste*, April 27, 1913.
[60] *El Noroeste*, May 3, 1917, and April 29, 1919.
[61] Elsewhere in Europe, May 1st had also come to symbolize accommodation to the system or, as Eric Hobsbawm described it, "basically a good-humored family occasion": "Mass-producing Traditions: Europe, 1870–1914," in *The Invention of Tradition*, ed. Hobsbawm and Terence Ranger (Cambridge: Cambridge University Press, 1983), 285. The question is whether there is some trade-off between the comforting ritual that attracted more people into the movement and the hard-edged radicalism that the European Socialist movement lacked. I would argue that there is no such inherent dichotomy:

The sisterhood of workers?

There was yet another weakness built into the framework of the labor movement's alternative culture. Simply put, it attracted more men than women, and those women who did join played a marginal role in the movement. Conversely, it failed to incorporate the activist women who continued to practice a largely autonomous consumer-based politics. Thus, looking back fifty years, *cenetista* Ramón Alvarez could not remember any individual female militants who stood out as leaders or personalities.[62] The labor movement made various attempts to organize working women, largely in response to Catholic unions, but their appeals were confused by contradictory pronouncements about the role of women. In fact, their own assumptions about the division between public and private spheres, which contrasted the male community of producers with the female household, made it difficult to imagine an inclusive proletarian public sphere. Both structurally and psychologically, the union federation was a brotherhood, constructed around an ideal of work and male companionship that put women in, at best, an auxiliary role.[63]

As befitted their private role, women's auxiliary status derived from their membership in the worker's family. As wife and mother, the woman had tremendous power to influence her husband, educate her children, provide support during strikes or, alternatively, to undermine her husband's participation. The labor movement especially feared the latter possibility. Commonly assumed to be dupes of the priests, women could use their influence to keep men from their union duties. Thus, one author pleaded: "we say to the worker's wife: do not prevent your husband, in the name of vain terrors, from coming to us if that is where his conscience pulls him. Innumerable are the frightened

different cultural forms can be linked with a number of different political stances, depending on the context.
[62] From an oral interview, November 1987.
[63] Of course, these ideas were not confined to the Spanish labor movement, but were common throughout the industrialized world. On Spain, see Temma Kaplan, "Women and Spanish Anarchism," in *Becoming Visible: Women in European History*, ed. Renate Bridenthal and Claudia Koonz (Boston: Houghton Mifflin, 1977), and Martha Ackelsberg, *Free Women of Spain* (Urbana: University of Illinois Press, 1991). For Europe, see Richard Evans, "Politics and the Family: Social Democracy and the Working Class Family in Theory and Practice before 1914," in *The German Family: Essays on the Social History of the Family in 19th and 20th Century Germany*, ed. R. J. Evans and W. R. Lee (Totowa: Barnes and Noble, 1981), and the essays in *Socialist Women: European Socialist Feminism in the 19th and Early 20th Centuries*, ed. Marilyn J. Boxer and Jean H. Quataert (New York: Elsevier, 1978).

women like you who have retarded the march of the greatest and most beautiful ideas."[64] The problem was serious enough to provoke a vigorous debate on how to blunt the impact of Catholicism on wives and daughters at the local CNT congress in 1923.[65] If women could be kept out of the clutches of the Church, they were not, however, asked to join the union, but, as Quintanilla advised, to stand aside while their men carried out the public struggle. Accepting fashionable notions of the complementarity of men and women, his major recommendation to women was that they sacrifice themselves for the education of their children.[66]

If women signed on as auxiliaries, they received conflicting ideas about what their lives would look like in a socialist society. There was a lot of talk about free love and the liberation of each party from the chains of bourgeois marriage,[67] but would it really improve their lives and help them take care of their children? One amusing anecdote from the Republic illustrates that they perhaps had good reason to be suspicious. In a report to his cell, a Communist party member accused one of his comrades of trying to seduce his wife while he was in prison. When the woman demurred, the comrade explained that the Communist party was working for a society in which women could sleep with whomever they desired. He assured her, and the other two women living in the building, that their husbands would readily approve of the liaison. The women still refused, apparently sensing more than a little opportunism in the offer. The author of the report was incensed that such a man was a fellow Communist, despite the fact that he expressed legitimate party views.[68] More importantly, his wife must have been incensed or even terrified at the indignities that a communist society might bring.

Long after the unions had begun their courtship of women as auxiliaries, they finally targeted women workers for membership, but it seems clear that this effort only came in response to the Catholic Church's success in this area. In the early 1910s, the Church formed its first "yellow" syndicates, in traditional female occupations.[69] The

[64] *Solidaridad Obrera*, February 19, 1910.
[65] *Solidaridad Obrera* covered the congress in its issues of June 15 and 22, 1923.
[66] *El Noroeste*, September 21 and October 20, 1913.
[67] Some early discussions of free love are found in *Fraternidad*, December 1, 1900, and *Aurora Social*, October 28, 1899.
[68] From José Alvarez of La Calzada, March 9, 1936: AGS, F-57.
[69] The *Reglamento* of the Sindicato Católico de Sirvientas was approved in 1913, according to the 1925 edition (Gijón: La Reconquista).

actual number of women members was in dispute, but there appear to have been several hundred, distributed in three major associations: for cigarette makers, servants and dressmakers.[70] By the end of the decade, the radical union movement began to see these associations as serious threats. An article written in early 1918 sounded the alarm, and urged all brothers, fathers and husbands to root out and destroy the yellow seed before it bore more evil fruit.[71] Barely a week after this article appeared, an organizational committee announced the first general meeting for a dressmakers' society of resistance. Significantly, the non-Catholic cigarette makers initiated the drive that attracted 200 women to the first meeting.[72] During the same period, the Socialist party created its first female youth group, which set itself the task of attacking "clerics and yellow organizers who are underhandedly entering female organizations in order to destroy the beautiful spirit of solidarity."[73]

Unfortunately, lack of evidence prevents us from judging the success of these early appeals to women workers.[74] It seems clear, however, from the paucity of debate about female unions, that the federations developed no coherent program designed to meet the special needs of women workers. Instead, their primary function was defensive, as a parry to the rival Catholic unions. The one female union that stood outside this pattern was La Constancia, comprised of cigarette makers from the tobacco factory. The cigarette makers founded their union in 1915, and in 1917 they joined the National Federation of Tobacco Workers, a "non-denominational" trade federation. Instead of a union created by male activists for women, La Constancia emerged out of a long tradition of solidarity and corporate identity among the workers in the industry. The result was an independent union that maintained connections with the anarchist and Socialist

---

[70] In 1919, Catholic Action claimed a total of 1,258 women, a figure *El Noroeste* said was inflated (March 12, 1919). In the IRS census of 1920, only the "Needle Syndicate" is mentioned, with a membership of 500 (*Boletín Oficial de Oviedo*, July 3, 1920). Finally, in the 1930 IRS census, three unions are listed, with 194 cigarette makers (compared to the 700 in the independent union), 322 servants and 337 dressmakers (*Boletín Oficial de Oviedo*, March 11, 1930).

[71] *El Noroeste*, January 25, 1918. Significantly, the author held the male relatives of the women directly responsible, since presumably the women had been seduced by the priests.

[72] *El Noroeste*, February 2, 1918.

[73] *El Noroeste*, July 9, 1919.

[74] In the 1919 local congress, there were syndicates from the clothing and food industries, both of which employed large numbers of female workers, but there is no gender breakdown in the membership lists.

federations but never became absorbed by them. As such, it represented one of the few female voices in the world of organized labor in Gijón.[75]

The male outreach to women workers intensified during the Republic, and this time the CNT succeeded in organizing the 300 textile workers of La Algodonera and the 200 women who worked in the metallurgical factory of Laviada.[76] The CNT also made its first foray into a completely female sector of the economy – domestic service – with its Sindicato de Obreras del Hogar. Despite an intense propaganda effort, however, the organization claimed only seventy members in June 1931 before it disappeared from CNT records. One author blamed the rural origins of these workers for the failure of the syndicate, but he also recognized that servants' long hours (up to twenty per day) sapped their energy and left them little time to attend meetings.[77] In fact, lack of time may have been one of the primary barriers to women's unionization in general. There is little indication that the union federations concerned themselves with women's double burden or understood the demands on their time. The only response to this excuse was that they should stop making it. As one author insisted, once women made the effort to come, they would find out that living was more than just eating, sleeping and working.[78]

If women did make the effort to come, however, they were not always satisfied with what they found. The experience of one activist group of women – the members of the anti-fascist women's groups – illustrates some of the frustrations they faced in a male-dominated organization.[79] During the war, these women ran collective workshops, organized brigades that washed the militiamen's clothes, raised money for Red Cross activities, operated night schools, co-ordinated neighborhood clean-ups, and organized reserve brigades to assist the army in emergencies like civilian evacuation. Despite the essential services they performed, they expressed dissatisfaction with their marginal

---

[75] For a more detailed treatment of the cigarette makers, see Pamela Radcliff, "Elite Women Workers and Collective Action: The Cigarette Makers of Gijón, 1890–1930," *Journal of Social History*, 27:1 (September 1993).

[76] Register, Metallurgical Syndicate, December 1930–1931. In the Sección Laviada, there were 200 women out of a total of 447 members: AGS, K-21.

[77] *Solidaridad*, August 1, 1931.

[78] *Solidaridad*, September 19, 1931.

[79] The anti-fascist women's groups were formed before the war by the Communist party, but after July 1936 they expanded to include women of all political orientations on the republican side. Nationally, they claimed 50,000 members in July 1936, after which they established groups in 255 localities: Mary Nash, *Mujer y movimiento obrero en España, 1931–1939* (Barcelona: Fontamara, 1981), 244.

role. In one manifesto, they demanded that the syndicates pay more attention to their potential, and suggested that women be trained to replace skilled male workers to free them up for active duty.[80] Another circular complained of the "deficient treatment on all issues relating to women."[81] Thus, even women who committed themselves to the labor movement felt excluded and marginalized.[82]

It appears that what most women saw in the labor movement was the brotherhood and not the sisterhood, or even the family of workers. A few women may have chosen to fight this restricted identity from inside the movement, as the anti-fascist groups did, while others, like those in the cigarette makers' union, carved out their own space on the margins of it, while still others may have joined their CNT or UGT union and remained passively marginalized. The majority of working-class women, however, lived outside the world of the labor movement and looked inside only through the eyes of their husbands, fathers and sons. An alternative proletarian culture that left out almost half of the working-class population could not help but be weakened by the loss.

Thus, the gendered character of the labor movement milieu limited the inclusiveness and appeal of its alternative culture within the female half of the family of workers. Most working women had to turn elsewhere for solidarity, probably to the family and neighborhood networks that focused on their daily concerns. By assuming that women's interests were identified with the private sphere of the family, the labor movement missed the opportunity to expand its vision of the public sphere into the spaces that women occupied. Thus, what could have been a more integrated proletarian public sphere remained intersecting "clusters of communication" divided along gender lines.[83]

The labor movement's alternative culture was also weakened by the

---

[80] Manifesto to the syndicates, April 14, 1937: AGS, H-21. Towards the very end of the Civil War in Gijón, a few such training programs for women were initiated, but resistance was great.

[81] Circular, June 4, 1937: AGS, F-86. Resolutions included in the circular were (1) to create schools to train women for necessary wartime jobs; (2) to teach them how to lead, preside over assemblies and draft documents; (3) to make sure that all party branches have corresponding female sections.

[82] Martha Ackelsberg (*Free Women of Spain*) defines this problem as one of the central motivations for the organization of the "Mujeres Libres," an independent women's group within the parameters of the anarchist movement. During the Civil War, the group claimed 20,000 members.

[83] The term is coined by Craig Calhoun as a way of articulating the existence of different discourses within a heterogenous public sphere: "Introduction: Habermas and the Public Sphere," in *Habermas and the Public Sphere*, ed. Craig Calhoun (Cambridge, MA: MIT Press, 1992), 38.

other factors detailed in this chapter. The war between Socialists and anarchists made any unified display of proletarian culture problematic, as exemplified in the withering of May 1st. Unified public display was curtailed in another way by government repression, which made it impossible to establish ongoing, coherent traditions over the entire period. Finally, and most subtly, the labor movement culture could not displace the competing republican culture, which fought to define its version of an oppositional culture in the city. The republican culture interfered both through head-on confrontation, with its *ateneos* and its choral societies, and through the more subtle influence of cultural borrowing. The combination made it impossible for the labor movement to secure the boundaries of its own independent space.

To balance these weaknesses, the labor movement created an environment of solidarity and mutual aid among its members that generated loyalty and strengthened the movement. The power that the CNT had achieved by the outbreak of the Civil War was rooted as much in its complex social organization as in its political flexibility and this achievement should not be underestimated.

Nevertheless, because of its limitations, the labor movement never articulated an independent oppositional culture that could unite working-class Gijón in the battle against the hegemony of Church and monarchy. To rephrase Helmut Gruber's question about Vienna, there were important ways in which Gijón fell short of being "a workers' city observable in real and symbolic forms in its workaday, public and private life."[84] While the labor movement gained considerable political and economic leverage in Gijón by the 1930s, it never constituted a complete hegemonic alternative, partly because of its comparative weakness in the public sphere. Although the republicans carved out a stronger presence in the public sphere, their political and economic weaknesses and the competition from the labor movement limited the coherence of their own hegemonic project. The result was a heterogenous oppositional culture that wavered between flexible cooperation and internecine warfare. Either way, neither the labor nor the republican movement was strong enough to stand alone. Together, they seriously weakened the existing hegemonic culture of Church and monarchy, but independently they could not offer a coherent replacement. The result was a hegemonic stand-off that led to civil war.

[84] Gruber, *Red Vienna*, 16.

PART IV

The urban battlefield: conflict and collective action, 1901–1936

∽

Jesus, what a city! If there isn't a strike, then it's raining, and usually there are both at once!

Police Inspector, January 1910[1]

As the two Gijóns acquired economic, political and cultural shape over the decades, the process of polarization took its most visible form in the increasingly endemic contentious collective action for which the city became renowned.[2] This conflict was both the cause and the result of a polarizing society; it acted out the drama of opposing interests in a way that both illustrated and reinforced existing divisions. Equally important, the conflict was both the cause and the result of solidifying community networks, which provided the necessary resources and linkages to sustain such action.[3] Thus, the collective action demonstrated the capacity for

---

[1] This much-loved quote is often cited as an illustration of Gijón's character. Since it was uttered by an Andalusian police inspector who came to the city to write a report on the 1910 general strike, quoting it also offered the opportunity of poking fun at sloppy southern accents: "¡Jozú! ¡Qué pueblo ezte: cuando no hay güergaz yueve, y cazi ziempre tojunto!" Related by E. Quintanilla in *El Noroeste*, August 17, 1930.

[2] The idea of contentious collective action borrows from Charles Tilly's extensive theorizing on popular mobilization. As he defines it, collective action is the means people employ to act together on shared interests; this action becomes contentious when it bears directly on the interests of some other acting group. See *The Contentious French* (Cambridge, MA: Harvard University Press, 1986), 381.

[3] Once again, this "resource mobilization" approach to collective action owes much to Charles Tilly's work. For other examples of this approach, see Ronald Aminzade, *Class, Politics and Early Industrial Capitalism: A Study of Mid-Nineteenth Century Toulouse* (Albany: State University of New York Press, 1981), and Michael Hanagan, *The Logic of Solidarity: Artisans and*

mobilization as it generated ever higher levels of mobilization. As a result, the city developed its urban battlefield long before the official outbreak of hostilities in July of 1936.

The precise source of conflict varied widely, from workplace conditions, to public services, to consumption issues, to political ideology. The groups and organizations that launched and participated in these conflicts also varied, from permanent political associations like the CNT, to formal interest groups like the Association of Tavern Owners, to informal coalitions like the women of a neighborhood. The wide range of issues, participants and strategies demonstrates the inadequacy of traditional class models of mobilization, which privilege only certain institutional players like the trade unions and specific kinds of "worker" concerns that were labeled "class consciousness." It also illustrates the deficiency of evolutionary models of collective action based on the "modernization" of protest. Most obviously ignored in these accounts has been the female-dominated neighborhood- and consumer-based activism, which continued to provide a vibrant outlet for poor women's political energies and was never subsumed within male-dominated institutional politics.[4] When a single narrative is no longer privileged, the full dimensions of the urban battlefield are revealed, a battlefield that penetrated virtually all the public spaces of the city and included a full range of male and female actors. The result is a re-visioning of the political landscape that both overcomes the gender biases of narrower definitions of politics and provides a more convincing portrait of the diverse strength of Gijón's radical tradition.

The diversity of the community did not mean, however, that there were no ideological linkages drawing them together. While the traditional narrative would be constructed around the concept of an emerging class consciousness, the limited connotations of the term do not capture the parameters of community mobilization. Instead, I would argue that the protests that emanated from "smoke-darkened" Gijón were linked by a populist commitment to the little man's/woman's right to a decent life, as against

Industrial Workers in Three French Towns, 1871–1914 (Urbana: University of Illinois Press, 1980).
[4] For a broader argument about the continued strength of this form of activism as one of the best avenues for poor women to participate in local politics, not just in Gijón, but throughout Spain in the early twentieth century, see Pamela Radcliff, "Women's Politics: Consumer Riots in Twentieth Century Spain," in *Contested Identities: Women in Modern Spain*, ed. Victoria Enders and Pamela Radcliff (Binghampton: State University of New York Press, forthcoming).

the exploitation of employers, landlords, speculators, and the government. In more global terms, they demanded that the rhythms of the urban industrial city that Gijón had become be geared to the needs of its ordinary residents instead of its owners. This common agenda defined the general parameters of a tradition of popular protest that set the "people" against the city's elites and that often linked apparently unrelated struggles. Implicit in this confrontation was the underlying struggle over who the city belonged to: the "people" or those who held the purse strings. Not until the Civil War was this question finally resolved.

Within this general configuration, individual players waxed and waned and sometimes switched sides. The "popular community" was a fluid entity that coalesced and dissolved around different issues and protagonists. As a result, neither the participants nor the border separating popular from elite were fixed. Activists belonged mainly to the lower socio-economic stratum of society, but not exclusively to the working class. They included factory workers, artisans, farmers, fishermen, housewives and small businessmen. Different sub-groups moved to the foreground for their particular struggles, and then retreated. Significantly, however, despite the multiple origins of conflict, individual struggles often fed into a larger pattern. At moments of critical mass, issues spilled over into one another and the outlines of a broad popular community emerged. Moreover, these moments became increasingly sustained as time went on, creating the perception of an endemic culture of mobilization as well as the consolidation of an activist populist voice.

Although conflict emanated from a variety of sources, different groups sought to lead and channel it towards their own version of the people-in-arms. As in other areas of the city's public life, the two main contenders for this role were the anarchosyndicalist federation and the republicans. Most often they competed for this position, but some of the most dramatic conflicts in the city's pre-republican history, such as the August 1917 general strike and the December 1930 anti-monarchist riot, featured their combined leadership. Nevertheless, the republicans' leadership in popular protests suffered from the same contradictions that limited their government policy. Because of economic links to the city's elites, they were often torn between the maintenance of law, order and private property, and the assertion of populist ideals. In addition, their theoretical commitment to principles of liberal individualism clashed with the communitarianism of the populist

251

radicalism. After their entrance into the political mainstream in 1931, the republicans fell increasingly on the side of law and order.

In contrast, the anarchosyndicalists became more adept at both expressing and organizing popular discontent. By taking on the broader problems of urban life, in addition to workplace concerns, the CNT tried to make itself into an advocate for the larger popular community as well as the corporate defender of its members. The result of these contrasting patterns was a clear shift of power from the republicans to the CNT, which accelerated during the Republican years, although the CNT still never absorbed the entire oppositional culture under its leadership. However, the shift was enough to set the stage for the radicalization of conflict that exploded on the barricades of October 1934. Without the mediating influence of the republicans to soften the lines of opposition, the city's polarization appeared in stark relief for the first time. After October 1934, there was no middle ground.

These final two chapters will complete the portrait of Gijón's political culture by charting the evolution of popular protest in the city, from the general strike of 1901 to the Civil War. Chapter 9 will focus on the diverse protest tradition of the pre-republican period that first gave Gijón its notorious reputation. Chapter 10 deals with the evolution of this tradition under the new conditions of the Republic, and its contribution to the increasingly inevitable Civil War.

9

Conflict and collective action, 1901–1930

~

Social conflicts in Asturias go on forever.
Editorial, *El Noroeste*, September 12, 1919

In December of 1900, the dockworkers' union, La Cantábrica, took the initial step in what would snowball into Gijón's first general strike. The three-hundred-member union, which included all of the city's dockworkers, demanded that their employers adopt the eight-hour day and agree to hire only from union ranks. Through their organization, the Agremiación Patronal (AP), the employers not only rejected the terms, but they refused to negotiate with the union. In response, La Cantábrica struck on January 15th, while the AP counter-attacked by importing scab workers from Castille to replace them.

Under this challenge to the principle of unionization, the rest of the 6,000-member local federation joined in the struggle by voting to launch a general strike in support of the dockworkers. In retaliation, the employers fired back with a lock-out. Two sets of government mediators could not get the two sides to budge, and the strike/lock-out dragged on until the first week of March, when the intransigence of the employers, internal divisions between Socialists and anarchists[1] and the exhaustion of their resources forced the strikers to capitulate.

---

[1] The sub-plot of internal dissension revolved around the anarchosyndicalists' desire to push the struggle further versus the Socialists' fear of destroying the new union movement. The Socialists' version of the story is contained in participant Manuel Vigil's bitter post-mortem articles printed in *El Socialista* between March and May 1901. The details of the strike can be found in *El Noroeste* and *El Socialista*, January through March 1901.

253

The terms of the armistice were harsh for the unions, which lost most of the gains they had made in the previous several years. The AP demanded a return to nine- and ten-hour work days, no salary increases, and the freedom to hire and fire at will. The ultimate humiliation was that La Cantábrica had to accept the permanent employment of the scab crew that had crossed picket lines.

The disastrous general strike brought a crashing halt to the flurry of activism that followed the Cuban war.[2] As the unions buckled under employer and government pressure, the infant movement collapsed along with the sense of optimism and possibility that permeated the boom years. Nevertheless, the strike was an important turning point, the first large-scale protest that mobilized the city and divided it in two. Moreover, it reached this level after a rapid escalation from a relatively minor conflict, in which both sides refused to back down. Although both the mobilization and the division faded in the short run, they constituted a pattern that would be repeated, reinforced and sustained over the next thirty-six years.

During the remaining two decades of the Restoration monarchy, this pattern of conflict was definitively established, securing Gijón's reputation as one of the most turbulent cities in the country. What made this pattern especially dramatic was that it extended beyond the realm of institutional labor conflict. Where the 1901 general strike established the dichotomy between employers and workers, other protests posited the antagonism between consumers and speculators, small businesses and the government, poor residents and the police. The most powerful moments of conflict occurred when these parallel oppositions converged in a kind of snapshot that captured the underlying process of polarization. It was in the convergence of these various movements that we can see the true dimensions of the city's emerging political culture.

Significantly, these moments were increasingly sustained as time wore on and periodic outbursts evolved into a culture of mobilization. The next moment of combustion was sparked in 1909 by a tax revolt, followed by a series of unrelated protests, including a major series of strikes in 1910. For almost two years a combination of groups sus-

---

[2] Gijón's general strike fit into a national wave of activism after the war: after a decade of relative quiet, there were eighty-one in 1900, and 1901–1902 were equally contentious. As in Gijón, the mobilization dropped off after 1903 until the "Tragic Week" in 1909: José Alvarez Junco, *El emperador del paralelo: Lerroux y la demogogía populista* (Madrid: Alianza Editorial, 1990), 269–70.

tained a high level of mobilization that included significant co-operation across issues between tavern owners, fishermen, farmers, republican politicians, consumers and trade unionists. At this point, the outlines of a broad popular community first surfaced. After the defeat of the strike movement in the fall of 1910, these outlines faded again until the impact of the war, inflation and a disintegrating political system sparked a new wave of protests. This "moment" lasted several years, from late 1914 to 1921, until the combination of repression and the withdrawal of the republicans restored relative tranquility to the city for the last year of the monarchy. But by this time, the tradition of protest had been too deeply rooted to snuff out permanently. When the political situation changed again in late 1930, the mobilized and divided population sprang to life once again, ready to participate actively in the creation of a new political order.

1909–1910: a popular community takes shape

The wave of conflict that enveloped the city at the end of the first decade began with an apparently minor protest over a consumption tax levied on milk in January of 1909. *Consumo* taxes had always been controversial, as the 1898 riot demonstrated, but local governments found it difficult to replace this revenue, especially given the business community's unrelenting pressure against increases in property taxes.[3] Under financial strain, the city government voted to increase consumption taxes in the 1909 budget to the maximum allowed by law.[4] Included in this increase was a five-*céntimo* tax on a liter of milk, to be charged to farmers when they brought their produce into the city to sell. This tax set off a groundswell of protest that broke the apathy of the previous several years and established the first links in what would become by 1910 a formidable popular alliance.

The protest began when the Asociación de Agricultores (Farmers' Association) refused to pay the tax and declared a boycott on milk

---

[3] In *El Noroeste*, October 30, 1908, an editorial complained about the lack of money-raising options open to local governments. Property taxes were nominal, about 13% of the 1908 budget, compared to consumption taxes, which made up 66% of local income (statistics quoted by republican councilman Ramón Alvarez González, *El Noroeste*, July 3, 1910). On business lobbying, see the petition in *El Noroeste*, December 3, 1909, signed by 200 prominent businessmen arguing that even these property taxes should be replaced by the "fairer" consumption taxes. See Chapter 1, pp. 54–6, on the *consumo* riot of January 1898.

[4] *El Noroeste*, October 30, 1908.

sales inside the city limits. Although they were producers, the farmers attracted wide support by pitching the struggle in populist terms, aligning their interests with those of ordinary consumers. Workers and housewives, in addition to other small businessmen saddled with similar taxes, responded sympathetically, as did the labor unions and republican parties that claimed to represent them. By mid-January, this sympathy had taken form in a loose coalition dedicated not only to revoking the tax, but to lowering food prices and the cost of living. Perhaps more importantly, the protest came to symbolize a larger awakening: "the symbol of a great social force rising up, a rebirth of life, an awakening, that promises to blow fresh air through the city, and to inject new sap into the old and worm-eaten trunk."[5]

The coalition was loose because it pursued a single goal through diverse channels of action. The republicans, labor unions and Farmers' Association worked through the legal system, drawing up manifestos, negotiating with city officials and running electoral campaigns. In their first joint statement, a coalition of these organizations devised an alternative budget that would replace the milk tax revenue by cutting public funds for the summer tourist festivities and the municipal band, items that held few benefits for humble residents.[6] When the city council ignored the proposal, these groups staged a rally that attracted some 1,500 people, the largest public demonstration since 1901. The speakers included farmers, Socialists like León Meana and Eduardo Varela, the young anarchist Eleuterio Quintanilla, and federal republicans like Casimiro Acero and Benito Conde. In addition to these tactics designed to influence the conservative city council, republican politicians also used the milk conflict to launch their own local electoral campaign. In fact, those candidates who supported the abolition of *consumos* did especially well, and the issue helped create a republican-dominated city council for the first time.

While these groups operated through official channels, others pursued direct action tactics to enforce the boycott. As in the consumer riot of 1898, women played a prominent role in this type of spontaneous, often neighborhood-based activism where they could rely on their own networks. On the first day of the boycott, a lone farmer who defied the ban and brought her milk to market under armed guard returned home after being subjected to violent verbal harass-

[5] From an enthusiastic article in *El Noroeste*, January 29, 1909.
[6] *El Noroeste*, January 12 and 19, 1909.

ment by other farm women.[7] A few days later, a dozen farm women from the rural suburb of Roces were arrested for blocking the road to Gijón and smashing the milk bottles of those who refused to turn back.[8] As soon as word of the arrests reached the outskirts of the city, other women from the farm communities converged on the city. After marching with banners that protested against both the arrests and the taxes, they gathered in the stadium with other women from the city who had joined them and held an informal discussion, "each one commenting on how they understood the question under debate." However, when they appealed for support from the Farmers' Association, the president advised them to calm down and go home, advice that the republican newspaper fully endorsed.[9] As in 1898, the specter of unruly women was threatening even to those who sympathized with their agenda.

Nevertheless, the impact of the combined pressure finally induced the city government to partially concede by halving the milk tax and absorbing the deficit.[10] More interesting than the resolution was the rift that the debate revealed in republican ranks. On the one hand, federalists like Benito Conde and Casimiro Acero supported the populist stance of the protesters, expressed in the new newspaper *El Productor*: "It is not that we do not want festivals, nor that the city should stop supporting them. Nothing of the kind. It is just that it seems brutal to us that the city is willing to build the grand festival stage on the shoulders of innocent babies."[11] On the other hand, republican businessmen, while they sympathized with the workers' plight, would not support a solution that forced the business community to take up the slack. As republican politician Valdés Prida insisted, the city needed the band and the festivals to attract tourism, "that virtual vein of gold that we can exploit . . . few appreciate how much it contributes to increasing the city's wealth."[12] At the heart of this simple debate was the permanent tension that would plague republican policy for the next twenty-five years.

---

[7] *El Noroeste*, January 2, 1909.
[8] *El Noroeste*, January 2, 1909.
[9] *El Noroeste*, January 12, 1909.
[10] This resolution came after a stop-gap compromise on February 1 that put a moratorium on the milk tax collection for five months while other options were researched. The final decision to halve the tax came in early July, after a new round of negotiations.
[11] June 25, 1909. Few issues of the newspaper survive, but it seems clear that its life was short.
[12] *El Noroeste*, January 20, 1909.

As the milk crisis reached its peak, two more disputes added fuel to the populist fire. Like the *consumo* issue, both concerned the problems of urban life, but each from a different angle. The first conflict focused on the issue of intra-city transportation costs for workers. After initial complaints, the streetcar company offered a discount rate for workers, but it only applied to those commuting during restricted hours from the city center to the industrial suburbs.[13] The offer only increased the anger of those who lived in these suburbs, since it seemed like one more example of their permanent marginalization from the city.

When the company published the restricted discounts, residents and workers of the outlying neighborhoods fought back, again through the use of a diverse range of tactics. At first relying on informal workplace and residential ties, they formed a coalition to pressure the company to include all workers and even clerks under its discount rate.[14] They began with petitions and public meetings, which escalated to boycotts and intimidation when management denied their requests. After a month of fruitless protests, the coalition invited the formal trade union federation to join in, which it did. The republicans, once again, were divided. While *El Productor* stood firmly behind the protesters, the more moderate *El Noroeste* dropped the cause after the adoption of more extreme tactics, fearing an adverse affect on the summer tourist industry.[15]

At the same time that farmers, workers and clerks struggled to reduce the cost of living, yet another combatant entered the fray. In June 1909, the city's tavern owners launched a campaign to repeal the law mandating Sunday closure for all drinking establishments.[16] At first glance, this issue might seem unrelated to the sober protests over the cost of living and the populist alliance they inspired. However, protecting the right to drink and socialize at the corner bar on his day off was at least as important as the price of milk to the average working-class man. Thus, the law united owners and customers in a

---

[13] *El Productor*, May 30, 1909.

[14] *El Noroeste*, June 6, 1909, and *El Productor*, June 7, 1909.

[15] *El Noroeste*, June 28 and July 15, 1909. No issues of *El Productor* survive for this stage of the protest, but *El Noroeste* refers to the other newspaper's attack on the streetcar company. Unfortunately, *El Noroeste* refused to publish anything else on the transit protest after this, so we do not know the outcome.

[16] The law was passed in late 1904, with the support of both Catholics, who wanted respect for the holy day, and Socialists, who represented many clerks and waiters in service establishments.

defense of Spain's public bar culture. More specifically, it activated neighborhood networks of male sociability.

Before 1909, individual bars had triggered these networks by opening surreptitiously on Sundays, despite the threat of fines. In one case, a group of locals in Cimadavilla roused the owner from his Sunday dinner to open the bar, which was next door to his house. As they were drinking *sidra*, a second group came by, and, angered by the owner's refusal to serve them, the interlopers went to the police. The quick-witted owner took all of the drinkers into his house, passed out sets of rosary beads, and set them all to praying on their knees. When the police arrived at the "tabernacle," there was nothing they could do.[17]

After several years of scattered protests like these, the tavern owners' guild, La Liga, decided to confront the government head on. Its president, Restituto García, publicly opened his bar in order to be arrested, and then appealed for popular support. The response was overwhelming. A coalition comprised of the Farmers' Association, the Unión de Gremios (small commercial enterprises), the butchers' guild, the fishermen's union and La Cantábrica (the dockworkers), among others, organized a campaign for his release. Meeting in the Farmers' Association headquarters, the coalition agreed to call for a half-day shutdown of the city's small businesses. Significantly, only the cafés and luxury establishments of the Calle Corrida remained open, as several thousand people marched to the city hall to present their demands to the mayor.[18] García was freed soon after, and several weeks later La Liga published an open letter of thanks to all the businesses, trade unions and farmers who had helped the tavern owners publicize their plight.[19] After several more months of pressure, the city finally agreed to amend the law, permitting bars to open on Sunday if they gave their employees another day off.[20]

The campaign to repeal the Sunday bar closing law, like the protests over the milk tax and the streetcar fare, demonstrate how urban networks of solidarity could form the basis for protest movements. All of these protests resulted from essentially *ad hoc* coalitions of those affected both directly and indirectly. Although unrelated in both origins and goals, the overlap of participants indicates that broader net-

---

[17] *El Noroeste*, March 6, 1908.
[18] *El Noroeste*, June 22, 1909.
[19] *El Noroeste*, May 6, 1909.
[20] *El Noroeste*, April 23, 1910.

works were being tapped. In all cases, the disputes revolved around the consumption of goods and services, either the consumers united against the company, as in the case of the streetcar campaign, or consumers and producers allied against the government, as in the other two situations. What linked these protests, and makes their sum greater than the individual parts, was the acknowledgment of the "little man's/woman's" right to a decent life and livelihood. Through the accumulation of small conflicts like these, the city was erecting a tradition of defending popular rights against elite hegemony.

The most dramatic example of this evolving tradition occurred at the end of 1909 in the venerable neighborhood of Cimadavilla, over a dispute in the fishing industry. As the most cohesive of Gijón's working-class neighborhoods, Cima provided the most powerful example yet of how neighborhood and workplace networks could mobilize a community to action. At issue was the traditional monopoly over fish distribution exercised by the fishing guild, Germinal, which represented 500 fishermen, sailors, vendors, small boat owners and their families. Germinal received a 4% commission for the fish it sold, which went into pension and life insurance funds. In addition, its auction house, or Rula, provided jobs for many of Cima's women, who worked as wholesale buyers and sellers.[21] Threatening the monopoly were a handful of wealthy fleet owners who, in the name of free trade, decided to open a competing Rula in early December.

Germinal responded to this challenge with a public campaign branding the project as a destroyer of the community that depended on the Rula for its survival. In validation of this interpretation, the people of Cimadavilla banded together behind the organization in defense of their community integrity. As a result, the dispute between the "humble" people of Cima and the fleet owners transformed every nook and cranny of the neighborhood, from the docks to the local taverns, into a battlefront.

Germinal took charge of the legal side of the battle, lobbying city hall, borrowing boats from neighboring ports and soliciting support from other fishing guilds. One of their greatest successes was to convince provincial fishermen to bring their fish to the old Rula.[22] While the official delegation argued its case, the residents of Cima mounted

---

[21] An article in *El Productor*, June 12, 1909, describes the workings of the Rula, with its benches filled with buyers, the noise of buzzers signaling bids, and the smell of boxes of fresh fish.

[22] *El Noroeste*, December 11, 1909.

their own direct action campaign. Whenever the fleet owners' boats attempted to unload their shipments, crowds of men and women miraculously appeared to harass the employees. During the first confrontation, a group of women wrestled one of them to the ground, dumping the box he was carrying in the process. The newspaper reported that the police pulled them off "with difficulty," and had to call in seven pairs of Civil Guards to disperse the excited throng. The next day a woman who dared buy one of these fish was treated for head wounds at the hospital, after having been beaten by another group of women.[23] The fleet owners finally brought a suit against eleven people charged with issuing death threats; seven of these were women fishmongers.[24] During their arraignment a large, mostly female, crowd waited outside the courtroom all day. As in the milk tax protest, women seemed to be prominent in these direct assaults launched at the physical site of the problem.

To organize this kind of action, participants had to rely on the existence of dense neighborhood networks that could draw people out of the woodwork at a moment's notice. For example, after three fleet owners' boats docked one morning with an especially large load, the fishmongers set in motion a chain of events that culminated in a massive demonstration and near riot. Since they worked on the docks, they first noticed the boats and passed on the news to the fishermen's wives, some of whom were cigarette makers. Together, the women planned a demonstration to take place during the lunch break, when the fishermen would return home for their midday meal. The crowd gathered in front of the cigarette factory and marched first to city hall, where they presented their demand that the old Rula be granted an official monopoly. Then, they headed for the docks where they threw rocks, turned over boxes of fish and verbally harassed the loaders. When police tried to arrest the perpetrators, they simply melted into some nearby bar, where no one would denounce them. By implication, both customers and owners once again colluded against the authorities.[25]

In the face of this community revolt, the organized populist forces were slow to respond since the issue did not fit neatly into either the republican or the union movement agendas. Republicans were divided between their theoretical support of free trade and their loyalty to

[23] *El Noroeste*, December 3 and 4, 1909.
[24] *El Noroeste*, December 5, 1909.
[25] *El Principado*, January 5 and 6, 1910.

Cima, a republican stronghold. As a result, even the republican-dominated city council could not agree on a solution.[26] The union federation at first viewed the conflict with suspicion since, as the anarchist journal noted, "Because the fishermen's guild possesses business interests in the catch and its distribution, it is not essentially a worker or syndicalist conflict."[27] Nevertheless, the federation eventually decided to ignore the technical class distinctions and throw its weight behind the hundreds of families in battle against a handful of magnates.[28] Although the federation's pressure failed to convince the government to sanction Germinal's monopoly, its flexibility in accommodating the populist struggle in Cima laid the groundwork for future collaboration. In contrast, the republicans demonstrated once again the limits of their populist rhetoric. What the union federation seemed to recognize was that Germinal's corporatist protest, like that of the farmers and the tavern owners, had broader implications. At these moments, they all shared a populist sensibility of the rights of "the people" fighting back against the impersonal and elitist forces that dominated their environment. For this reason, all of them could draw inspiration from the apparently unrelated actions of each separate group, and feed off the collective energy that transformed the city into a breeding ground of conflict in 1909 and 1910. In fact, the union federation took advantage of this fertile context, reinforced by such outside events as the "Tragic Week" in Barcelona, to launch its own comeback, which consisted of at least twenty strikes and a dozen boycotts over the two-year period.[29] Significantly, the employers also responded to this atmosphere by pushing their intransigence to the limit.

The labor troubles began in the spring and summer of 1909 with a series of grassroots wage and hours demands issued by the reconstituted metal and construction workers' unions that escalated into a major confrontation over the principle of union recognition when the

---

[26] The Commission appointed to find a solution advised that the two Rulas should share the market, and even when this was rejected some republican councilmen argued that a monopoly was illegal, while others insisted that it was morally justified in this case. See debates, *El Noroeste*, March 6 and 27, 1910.

[27] Fishermen were paid a proportion of their catch – 7/15 for the crew, and the remainder for the fleet owner: *Solidaridad Obrera*, February 19, 1910.

[28] In mid-February, it appointed a commission to lobby the city government and threaten a worker boycott of the new Rula: *El Noroeste*, February 18, 1910.

[29] Instituto de Reformas Sociales, *Informe acerca del conflicto obrero-patronal de Gijón* (Madrid: La Sucesora de M.Minuesa, 1910), 6.

employers refused to negotiate with them.[30] From the workers' point of view, the bourgeoisie was trying to "destroy our organization,"[31] a charge which the employers at least implicitly acknowledged: "In these union centers, the worker learns only to hate the employers, to shirk his responsibilities, and to provoke strikes when possible. The union leaders do not teach workers about the merits of saving, or anything that will be useful to them."[32] Eight years after the first round in 1901, employers and unions lined up to resume the battle over hegemony in the workplace.

The most serious phase of the conflict began when the Langreo railroad company fired the two top officials of the Socialist La Terrestre union on February 14, 1910, after the union submitted a list of demands. The union struck in support of its leaders, but the company, under its president, the *cacique* Alejandro Pidal y Mon, refused to budge.[33] From this modest beginning, the conflict gathered speed. In what was becoming a familiar pattern, the dispute escalated as other employers and unions refused to break ranks, even indirectly. First, the dockworkers of La Cantábrica, the naval pilots of La Defensa, and the carters of La Dársena, all federal republican trade unions, agreed to boycott goods shipped by the company. Then, the Employers' Association (AP) entered the fray by hiring scab labor for the docks to break the boycott. La Cantábrica responded with a strike, which set off a domino effect in related industries. By the middle of April, the carters (La Dársena), the warehouse loaders, the cartwrights and sawyers in the carpentry shops, and even the bakers of La Aurora had all joined the strike.[34] When the employers responded with a lock-out in sections of the construction industry, the total number of workers directly affected was over 1,000.

Behind these 1,000 workers stood the entire labor movement, which marshaled its resources in a stunning display of solidarity. All of the unions put their strike funds at the disposal of the strikers, and each federation (the anarchist, Socialist and Federalist) appointed a

---

[30] *Solidaridad Obrera*, November 13, 1909, gives an overview of the increased activity. *Acción Libertaria*, in an analysis of the entire strike wave, noted that the activism issued from the workers themselves rather than the militants, who were caught off guard: December 2, 1910.

[31] *Solidaridad Obrera*, January 8, 1910.

[32] *El Noroeste*, January 9, 1910, interview with an employer.

[33] In April, the Institute of Social Reform sent a committee to gather information about the origins of the strike, and much of the following account is taken from its report: *Informe acerca del conflicto.*

[34] *El Socialista*, April 15, 1910, explains the intricate unfolding of solidarity.

commission to raise voluntary funds. The Socialists' artistic section put on a benefit play, entitled "The Great Struggle," in the Teatro Jovellanos, that attracted a sell-out crowd. An especially moving gesture came from the dozens of families who offered to provide daily meals for strikers' children.[35] As the strike dragged on into the summer, contributions flowed in from outside Gijón, where local anarchist and Socialist newspapers opened subscription funds.[36]

Moreover, several familiar groups outside the labor movement reciprocated the solidarity they had experienced in their recent struggles. Thus, the links forged with farmers, fishing people, and tavern owners over the course of the past tumultuous year proved durable. The fishermen of Germinal demonstrated their support by refusing to undertake the naval pilot tasks of mooring and directing boats into the harbor. The women fishmongers played a prominent role in crowds that harassed scabs on the dock.[37] The Farmers' Association agreed to provide free forage for the horses of the carters and, finally, the tavern owners proclaimed their adhesion to the workers' cause and sent them money.[38] La Liga's published declaration of support illustrates nicely the awkward yet sincere populist connections that had been made:

> This society, made up largely of manual laborers who work in factories and workshops in order to cover the taxes that the government levies on their modest establishments, and thus who are companions in your labors, cannot ignore this titanic struggle . . . Remembering the noble and sincere support that the workers' centers and other entities . . . gave to us in our struggles, a debt of gratitude obliges us to offer our unconditional support.[39]

The widespread support received by the strikers could not match the determination and resources of the employers, who were bent on proving their authority. As *El Noroeste* (March 29th) stated, "The Employers' Association has decided that it is time to deal a definitive

---

[35] *El Noroeste*, April 21, 1910, printed a list of the names of each family and how many children they could feed. On April 26th it reported on the constant flow of people offering their services to the strike welfare committee.

[36] *El Socialista*, June 3, 1910, reports on this national fund-raising.

[37] *El Noroeste*, April 2, 1910. In one incident, a fishmonger was arrested for calling a strikebreaker "scab," which provoked a demonstration by her companions outside the jail. She was freed the same day.

[38] Reported at the general strike meeting on April 20th, at which thirty unions were represented: *El Noroeste*, April 21, 1910.

[39] *El Noroeste*, February 14, 1910.

blow to these conflicts which, because of the war between capital and labor, are occurring with increased frequency in Gijón, to the detriment of both workers and employers." The strike began to unravel on August 13th, when La Cantábrica capitulated on terms that "are far removed from a felicitous solution," including the employers' right to give permanent jobs to scabs.[40] The last of the strikers returned to work in October, on more favorable terms, but the underlying issue of union recognition remained unresolved.[41]

As a result, the strikes elevated the level of tension between unions and employers. The AP's willingness to push every conflict into a showdown over employer prerogatives had created a pattern of escalation that was and would be difficult to stop. Furthermore, it transformed even the most niggling economic disputes into principled confrontations that emphasized the opposition between two monolithic forces. In turn, the hard line taken by the employers reinforced the more intransigent position of the anarchosyndicalist federation in its turf battle with the Socialists and the Federal Republican unions. After the 1901 and 1910 strike waves, the Socialist and Federalist strategies of limiting major conflicts grew increasingly untenable, with the resulting erosion in their local status.

While the wave of protests and strikes in 1909 and 1910 created the impression of a city divided, national political events also played their part. The crisis of the Conservative government, faced with the unpopular Moroccan war and the "Tragic Week" in Barcelona, put the regime in its most vulnerable position since the Cuban – American war. In this climate, republicans, socialists and anarchists took the opportunity to hammer home their political interpretation of the crisis. Through local political demonstrations, they claimed, at least implicitly, the connection between the local and the national, the economic and the political. On the one side were those who backed the oppressive government and the AP, while on the other side were those who opposed the government and stood up for the common people in their everyday struggles.

This juxtaposition was reinforced by a number of joint rallies that united the opposition groups under a vague but powerful populist rhetoric. In October 1909, for example, when the anarchist federation organized a demonstration to express outrage over the impending execution of Francisco Ferrer, it turned into a broad vote of no

---

[40] *Solidaridad Obrera*, August 20, 1910.
[41] *Solidaridad Obrera*, October 15, 1910.

confidence for the government that attracted several thousand people, including representatives from all the trade unions, the Socialist party, the republican parties, the left-wing newspapers and radical emissaries from around the province.[42]

The same groups united again in February of 1910 in protest against the government's policy in Morocco. They issued a joint list of demands, which included amnesty for prisoners, the repeal of the hated law of jurisdictions, and the end to compulsory military service. Together, they marched to the city hall, accompanied by the republican city councilmen, the flags of all the unions and progressive parties, the local band, which played the "Marseillaise," and five to six thousand people. After the customary presentation of their demands, the anarchists sponsored a rally in their center which featured speakers from all the opposition groups.[43]

These sweeping political protests were especially crucial for the republicans, who needed issues on which they could take an uncomplicated populist stance. Although individual republicans supported and participated in the various economic conflicts of 1909–1910, the movement could never give its unqualified endorsement. However, in more universal attacks on the monarchist regime, the republican movement could assert a leadership role and try to stake out its position at the head of the city's growing oppositional force. As long as they remained outsiders themselves, this balancing act worked fairly well, but as they penetrated first the local, then the provincial and finally the national political establishment, it began to falter. In 1910, however, this process had only just begun. As a result, the emerging oppositional community appeared at this moment in its broadest and most catholic form, stretching from middle-class politicians to small businessmen and farmers, down to the humblest workers.

1914–1923: the opposition takes root

Despite the diversity of forces that came together in these two years, the collapse of the strike movement in the fall of 1910 dissipated the

[42] *El Noroeste*, October 23, 24, 25, 1909. Ferrer was a "free-thinking" educator who founded a rationalist school in Barcelona. Without any proof, except for his vague ties to the anarchist movement, he was convicted of planning the uprising that led to the "Tragic Week," and was executed in November. On the "caso Ferrer," see J. C. Ullman, *The Tragic Week: a Study of Anti-Clericalism in Spain, 1875–1912)* (Cambridge, MA: Harvard University Press, 1968), 298–304, and Alvarez Junco, *El emperador*, 379–385.
[43] *El Noroeste*, February 13 and 14, 1910.

converging energies. The defeat did not extinguish all activity, as had occurred after 1901, but over the next several years conflicts remained isolated. Only when the outbreak of the First World War exacerbated existing tensions in Spanish society did the momentum for a broad popular opposition gather steam again. This opposition addressed similar issues to those that emerged in the first decade, but circumstances had intensified them. Thus, the problems of urban living standards were magnified by the shortages and inflation provoked by the war, while political disgust increased as the ruling parties' hegemony further deteriorated. Finally, replacement of craft unions by industrywide syndicates added new muscle to the battle over workplace control. Contributing to the process of intensification were the increased linkages between consumer, political and workplace struggles.

As conflicts shifted into a higher gear, the moderate republicans began to lose ground to the anarchosyndicalists, who were increasingly adept at organizing and channeling popular outrage, both at the workplace and in the city at large. Through its flexibility in defining the parameters of its interests, the CNT was able to build on the diversity of the city's rich oppositional culture while the republicans floundered in their own internal contradictions. As a result, these years of intensified strife witnessed a subtle shift in popular leadership, whose consequences were not fully apparent until the Republic. Other more informal groups still figured prominently, but the CNT staked out an increasingly central role.

Signs of these trends appeared in the first major wartime conflict, which erupted in September 1914 over rising food prices. The spark issued from the city's bakers in mid-August, when they collectively mandated an increase in the price of bread. This action ignited widespread complaints and eventually a city-wide general strike, the first use of this tool for a consumer protest. Taking the lead in the dispute was an association formed under the auspices of the anarchosyndicalist federation but dedicated entirely to consumer and tenant issues: La Analítica.[44] Through this organization, the CNT made its first attempt to extend its institutional leadership over broader oppositional movements.

La Analítica held its first public assembly in August, which attracted an overflow crowd of both men and women. The assembly asked the local government to intervene in capping the bread price,

[44] On the formation of La Analítica, see *El Noroeste*, February 7 and 8, 1913.

267

but the republican city council was once again paralyzed by its divisions over economic policy. Analítica then held a second assembly that urged a general strike to force the bakers' hand.[45] Two days later, a grass-roots general strike unfolded, without having been put to a vote of all the unions.[46] It began with the port workers, who sent commissions to other factories in the outlying neighborhoods, asking others to join. As they marched towards the city center, more workers left their posts, and many women and children joined in, adding their voices to the cry of "Down with the hoarders!" By the time the marchers arrived at the city hall, most of the major factories had been deserted.

The crowd that gathered in the plaza was so hostile that the mayor (a Conservative) decided to forego the customary acknowledgement from the city hall balcony. When police tried to disperse the protesters, the crowd began to throw rocks, the police ordered a charge, and a violent street battle ensued. In the course of the fighting, which moved through the city as cavalry charges dispersed groups only to have them reappear elsewhere, several workers were wounded, including two who were hospitalized with gunshot wounds. This violence triggered further protests, including a joint anarchist/Socialist petition demanding the resignation of the mayor and punishment of the police officers who decided to use violence against the protesters. When the city refused to take action, the joint union committee organized a "social" boycott that aimed at isolating the police officers from their community.

The anarchosyndicalists' role at the center of this unfolding conflict demonstrates their multiple strategies for asserting hegemony over the city's popular forces. In the process, the CNT helped formalize the links between populist issues. Nevertheless, the CNT's high profile in this protest rested partly on forces that it had tapped but could not control. Through its consumer association, it activated traditional networks and concerns and attempted to channel them into an orderly general strike.[47] But the actual event was more of a hybrid that incorporated elements of the food riot, the march to the city hall, and the general strike. Thus, although the union federation sponsored this consumer campaign, the drama unfolded according to a number of

---

[45] *El Noroeste*, September 3, 1914.
[46] The narrative of the events is taken from *El Noroeste*, September 6, 1914.
[47] After the riot, the union federation went to great lengths to convince people to stay off the streets and let it negotiate with the authorities.

scripts, only one of which was written by the union movement. While this diversity limited union control over the result, it also explained the power of the protest. Even in its expanding role, the CNT was only one player in a broader cast of characters.

This broader cast of characters included the poor women who had responded to La Analítica's call to action but were also capable of proceeding on their own initiative. The most dramatic instance of female protagonism occurred in November of 1917, when frustrated women rioted over the scarcity of coal for domestic use. The crisis activated the same network as the protest three years earlier, but in this case the trade union movement played a supporting role as housewives took the lead. The unions' participation in the conflict demonstrated their efforts to identify themselves with consumer issues, but their secondary role illustrated the diversity of forces that fed into the city's oppositional tradition.

The domestic coal crisis had been building up since the outset of the war, when the unusually high demand for Asturian coal created a profitable export market. Unable to compete, the domestic market was increasingly neglected, despite the basic cooking and heating requirements of the population. From the end of 1914, the tension around coal distribution and sale in the city sparked regular disturbances during which the police had to be called in to restore order.[48] By 1917, women complained that half the coal outlets in the city had shut down, and that they waited all day in lines for coal that never appeared.[49] The tension was exacerbated by the fact that the population regularly observed truckloads of coal en route from the mines to the city docks, where it was loaded for export.

In early November, female consumers began to mobilize. A delegation of working women approached the CNT federation, requesting its formal intervention with the city government. The CNT submitted their petition to requisition coal, but the city council waffled, despite a republican councilman's warning that the women would carry out their own requisitioning if nothing was done.[50] After several weeks of waiting for action, on November 26th they fulfilled

---

[48] Joaquín Bonet, *Biografía de la villa y puerto de Gijón*, vol. II (Gijón: La Industria, 1968), 67.
[49] *El Noroeste* published a letter from a "humble" *vecina*, or female resident, giving a full account of the situation (February 2, 1917).
[50] *El Noroeste*: the women's request to the CNT was reported on November 9th, and the councilman's warning on November 20, 1917.

the councilman's prediction. Following a discussion among them-selves, female shoppers marched to the docks and began looting trucks of coal. When the police arrived, the crowd simply dispersed and reap-peared on another dock. Finally, around midnight, the looters returned home of their own accord. By a remarkable coincidence, the very next day a large shipment of coal arrived in the city, and the crisis temporarily subsided.[51]

In many ways, the unfolding of this riot followed an old pattern of poor consumers challenging the authorities to uphold the moral economy. As had occurred in the general strike-turned-riot in 1914, this old script helped set in motion a powerful protest that resonated with both protesters and authorities. But although it evoked the past, it also had contemporary significance. Whereas the consumer riot had once been a major defensive weapon of a poor community, by 1917 more permanent organizations employed other weapons, like strikes and rallies. However, the consumer riot still provided one of the best avenues for poor women, rarely organized in unions or political par-ties, to participate in local politics in a way that linked them to other groups while setting their own agenda.[52] Through this route, activist women continued to shape and contribute to a broader oppositional community that included but surpassed formal organizations.

One of the formal groups that still played a major role in defining this community was the republican movement. In contrast to the other principal formal player, the CNT, which pursued its strategy of linking worker and consumer concerns, the republicans continued to rely on calls for political reform that exploited the weakness of the decaying regime. The apogee of this strategy came in 1917, when provincial and local republicans tried to lead a broad coalition of forces in favor of the democratization of the regime. But just as the CNT could not control all of the forces it unleashed, neither did the republi-cans. When the republicans realized this, after a nearly revolutionary strike in August 1917, they began backing down from the ambiguous position that gave them power but not control. The August 1917 strike thus marked an important turning point in the gradual decline of the republicans' populist leadership.

---

[51] *El Noroeste*, November 27, 1917.

[52] For a more extensive version of this argument, see Pamela Radcliff, "Women's Politics: Consumer Riots in Twentieth Century Spain," in *Contested Identities: Women in Modern Spain*, ed. Victoria Enders and Pamela Radcliff (Binghamton: State University of New York Press, forthcoming).

As in 1909–1910, the local events of August 1917 took place in a context of mounting national crisis. The economic strains sharpened by the European war aggravated the political situation, pushing the country to the edge of open rebellion in the summer of 1917. A number of different groups, from Catalan nationalists to junior army officers, to disgruntled republicans, anarchists and Socialists, raised their voices in an initially unanimous cry for national political reform.[53] In this movement, Gijón, and more broadly Asturias, played a prominent role, its first moment of stardom on the national stage. The combination of national pressures and the local oppositional tradition created a combustible mix unrivalled anywhere in the country.

The reform movement culminated in August of 1917, when the national Socialist and anarchosyndicalist federations agreed to launch a nation-wide general strike for the benefit of the "bourgeois" political revolution.[54] As a result of a series of mishaps and misunderstandings, this co-ordinated strike never occurred. Instead, isolated strikes erupted around the country, most notably in Valencia and Catalonia. Of all the strikes, however, the most dramatic and effective transpired in Asturias, where republicans, Reformists, Socialists and anarchosyndicalists co-operated in a peaceful political general strike that lasted two weeks. While the trade unions organized the strike, Reformist and republican politicians defended the strikers' actions and transmitted joint demands for the regime's democratization. In addition, the offices of *El Noroeste*, the Reformist newspaper, acted as a communication center for the province, distributing information and printing clandestine manifestos.[55]

In Gijón, the strike completely shut down the city for the first six days, causing the Civil Governor to declare a state of emergency. After the first six days, the strike gradually petered out, and by September 3rd everyone had returned to work. The open-ended political nature of the demands made it difficult to determine the right moment to

[53] On 1917, see Gerald Meaker, *The Revolutionary Left in Spain, 1914–1923* (Stanford: Stanford University Press, 1974) and Juan Antonio Lacomba, *La crisis española de 1917* (Madrid: Ciencia Nueva, 1970).

[54] Afterwards, Eleuterio Quintanilla emphasized that the strike had a reformist political agenda rather than a social revolutionary one: *El Noroeste*, December 2, 1917. Also see Ramón Alvarez Palomo, *Eleuterio Quintanilla* (Mexico: Editores Mexicanos Unidos, 1973), 201.

[55] As related by the paper's editor, Antonio Oliveros, in *Asturias en el resurgimiento español* (Madrid: Juan Bravo, 1935; reprint, Gijón: Silverio Cañada, 1982), 116. The paper itself honored the strike by shutting down production for two weeks, from August 13th through August 30th.

end the strike, especially when it was clear that Asturias stood alone. Despite the uncertain finish, the strike constituted the city's most spectacular joint protest. Furthermore, it demonstrated what happened when the city's oppositional forces united behind a single goal that transcended narrow corporatist interests. In this sense, August 1917 built on the linkages established in 1909–1910 while strengthening them. The result was another snapshot in the process of polarization, the clearest image yet of congealing oppositional communities.

This interpretation is reinforced by the strike's aftermath, when employers prolonged the confrontation by deciding to "select" which workers they would allow to return to work. Thus, the giant metallurgical plant Moreda y Gijón and the railroad and streetcar companies fired dozens of employees they considered troublemakers. The government joined in the persecution by closing union centers for several months and hounding their leaders, in addition to bringing in extra troops to enforce social order.[56] The employers' actions are especially significant, since they went out of their way to declare their loyalties in a dispute that did not directly involve them. In this way, they contributed to the sense that all conflicts flowed from a similar source: the opposition between two monolithic sides, the elites versus the people. For those who missed this connection, El Noroeste hammered home the theme of the "two Spains" in the weeks and months after the strike.[57]

In this atmosphere, the unions had no trouble mobilizing support in the campaign on behalf of the seleccionados. The most dramatic event in the campaign was a rally held on November 25th that amassed the largest crowd of demonstrators ever seen in Gijón, according to the newspaper. It was jointly sponsored by the two workers' federations, the Reformist, Radical and Republican parties, the Jovellanos masonic lodge, the Association of Clerks (dependientes) and the Farmers' Association. As the marchers wound their way from the Plaza Begoña to the city hall, thousands more lined the streets to cheer them on. At the city hall, Quintanilla read the joint statement from the balcony: "The people of Gijón, represented by the immense majority of all social classes, asks the public authorities to grant full amnesty for all those accused and convicted of political and social

---

[56] In two telegrams from the Civil Governor, dated November 14 and 15, 1918, he requested "more troops from other regions, since those that guard the province are locals," and "seven battalions and three squadrons": AHN, Legajo 53A, núm.1.
[57] For example, September 5, 1917.

crimes, and to order the re-hiring of the 'selected' workers."[58] While Quintanilla's invocation of the "people" was a stock phrase, there was clearly more to this event than the welfare of several dozen workers. In the wake of the political campaign against the government, thousands of residents turned out to express their displeasure with a government that was only effective in repressing its people.

In this context, the coal riot that exploded only two days later provided further evidence of the depth of this sentiment. Voicing their indignation at the government's inability to supply basic goods to its people, these ordinary housewives implicitly articulated the link between the political crisis and their pocketbook crisis at home. Adding to the voices of the anarchists, republicans, workers, farmers and clerks who sponsored the rally, they reinforced the impression of a pervading dissatisfaction that encompassed both economic and political concerns.

During the same tumultuous month of November, yet another voice joined the oppositional chorus, in the form of a new tenants' organization called the Liga de Inquilinos (LI). Following the apparently defunct Analítica, the LI announced its intention to fight for reasonable rents and decent housing for the urban poor. Although its direct targets were the landlords, the LI pointedly blamed the government for failing to guarantee this basic need, either through protective legislation and/or public housing. It also explicitly made the connection with other consumption issues, by including demands for better regulation of food prices, restrictions on exports and punishment of hoarders in all of its public declarations.[59] Thus, it carried on the attempt begun by Analítica to institutionalize and focus consumer opposition. As the speakers at the first meeting insisted, tenants had to unite under their common class oppression.[60]

Unlike Analítica, however, the LI proclaimed its independence from other political or syndical organizations. Its first president was Laureano Piñera, a dissident *cenetista* who argued that anarchists should drop their apolitical stance.[61] Piñera's presence linked the organization

---

[58] *El Noroeste*, November 26, 1917.
[59] For example, see the accords of its first regional assembly in 1920: *El Noroeste*, November 12, 1920.
[60] *El Noroeste*, November 5, 1917.
[61] Piñera helped found the Grupo Sindicalista Parlamentaria after the August 1917 strike, but unfortunately there is little information on the group. Presumably this silence indicates its lack of impact on local politics. For a report on its formation, see *El Noroeste*, October 23, 1917.

with the anarchosyndicalists, but his unorthodox views probably ensured its formal independence. Whatever its relationship with the CNT, the LI's agenda followed the broader strategy of linking the consumer and the worker, the economic and the political.

The LI obviously hit a nerve, as its modest office was besieged by men and women pouring out their private horror stories of rapacious and greedy landlords. It registered individual complaints and eventually organized campaigns to counter what many perceived to be the owners' rent-raising conspiracy. In April of 1919, for example, the LI called a rent strike. When a judge ordered the eviction of one female participant, the LI mounted a boycott on the entire building. To pressure its owner to submit, the LI encouraged other tenants to vacate the building, convinced union members not to work on building repairs, and lobbied the local health board to inspect for violations of health regulations.[62]

Not surprisingly, the powerful Property Owners' Association fought back. During the April 1919 rent strike, it called a meeting of the city's business and financial interests to complain about what it termed the attack on private property. While the convocation produced no concrete resolutions, it symbolized once again the interconnectedness of local conflicts, which rarely stayed within the bounds of the original issue. On the familiar plane of the struggle between the "free market" and community rights, the LI aligned itself on one side, with rioting housewives, while the city elites huddled on the other.

The activation of these larger networks brought another familiar player into the struggle. In response to the Property Owners' complaints, the League of Tavern Owners issued a statement in support of the LI and its aims. The statement declared that rents should be fixed at 1914 levels, that the government should intervene more directly in the prices of necessities, and that taxes should be removed from meat and alcohol.[63] While the alcohol tax obviously touched their own corporate interests, the tavern owners convincingly bound their own concerns to those of the larger community that sustained their modest businesses. As in 1909–1910, the common problems of urban living could cross corporate boundaries.

On the other hand, it was precisely these types of issues that posed the most serious dilemmas for republicans. A few gave their unquali-

---

[62] *El Noroeste*, April 1, 1919.
[63] *El Noroeste*, April 15, 1919.

fied support to the LI, such as the young lawyer Mariano Merediz, who represented the organization in court. But the majority tried to paper over the conflict between tenants and landlords with ambiguous declarations. Thus, *El Noroeste* ran a story in which it insisted that "the fact that a league of tenants has arisen in opposition to the Property Owners' Association need not indicate a bitter class struggle, but a healthy harmony of interests."[64] In another context, this statement might have been plausible, but in Gijón it was wishful thinking.

The newspaper's attempt to contain the opposition between the two organizations within controllable boundaries ran counter to the prevailing pattern of dissolving borders. The fact that small conflicts escalated into citywide showdowns, and that the same players regularly turned up to participate in these disputes, belied the image of compartmentalization that *El Noroeste* clung to. Narrow issues were increasingly transformed into struggles over the nature and structure of power in the city. In the process, the abstract idea of fighting for control of the city took on concrete meaning in the lives of ordinary people.

Perhaps the most dramatic illustration of this process can be found in the events surrounding two instances of alleged police brutality in the fall of 1919. Through a series of mishaps, Civil Guards shot and killed two apparently innocent young workers, aged nineteen and twenty-six. Exactly what happened was never clarified, but the public assumed the police were at fault. As a result, thousands of people, including all the familiar participants, poured into the streets to demonstrate once again against the government that offered its citizens nothing more than repression. In this way, these tragic but isolated events became part of a larger narrative about local power relations.

The first victim was the son of a bartender, "Manín el cervecero," whose family lived in Natahoyo. When he and some friends, who earned money carrying passengers' luggage, were waiting at the railway station for the next train, Civil Guards chased them, shooting the youth in the back as he fled. His friends contended they had only run out of fear, while the Guards insisted that they had stolen goods stored at the station. In the process of chasing the thieves, they had fired into the air but somehow accidentally hit their human target.

Whatever the true course of events, popular sympathy with the boys and deep distrust of the Civil Guards pointed to only one

[64] April 5, 1919.

interpretation. The cry was first raised by forty women who sent a letter of protest to *El Noroeste*, signed by "mothers from Natahoyo and La Calzada."[65] In support of their position, they offered testimony from "all the neighbors," who vouched for the honesty of the boy. By writing the letter in this way, the women made the event into a community issue in which the neighborhood was closing ranks to protect its children. In contrast to the police narrative of cops and robbers, their letter clarified the victim's status as son and community member. The killing was thus an attack not on a marginal thief, but on the community at large.

From the neighborhood, the protest spread outward. The CNT federation held an assembly, with special invitations to those who either witnessed the crime or knew the victim. The assembly agreed unanimously that if the Guards were not brought to justice, "the citizens will be forced to repel this class of aggressions by appointing ourselves guardians over each other's personal security." They also agreed to leave work if necessary to attend the funeral scheduled for the next day at five in the afternoon.[66] In addition to the CNT, the Socialist party, the masonic lodges, the LI, the republican city council and the Farmers' Association all issued strong statements of protest. Once again, a small event had activated a broader set of networks that stimulated these familiar faces to register their identification with the popular cause.

The authorities tried to derail this growing movement by rescheduling the funeral for 3 p.m., but word of mouth foiled the strategy. With thousands lining the street by the appointed hour, police delayed the release of the body from the public hospital for two more hours, as mourners waited in the driving rain. Finally, after a failed attempt to storm the hospital and steal the body, the procession began at 5:30, slowly winding past an estimated 16,000 thousand people. Their massive presence sent a clear message that the boy's death transcended the level of individual tragedy and implicated the entire system.

A few weeks later, Guards shot and killed a second young man, also during a chase from an ambiguous crime scene. In this case, however, the shot hit a completely innocent third party, a cabinet-maker named Cándido, who happened to be walking by. In this case, the protest

---

[65] October 24, 1919.
[66] *El Noroeste*, October 25, 1919.

was launched from the workshop where Cándido had been employed, but, as before, the original cry was taken up by a full spectrum of groups and organizations with no direct connection to the victim. Even Cándido's membership in the Socialist party and the draping of its flag over his casket did not prevent the rival CNT from giving its full support. The result was another massive funeral cortège. The combined impact of the two events, in which people implied that they needed protection from their own government, must have been dramatic. This powerful criticism reinforced economic and political discontent and fed into a broad indictment of a city run by the few for the benefit of the few.

In addition to consumer issues and calls for political reform, the other major arena of struggle revolved around the control of the workplace. As before, the union federations took the lead in this battle over the rights of worker association, but after 1918 they were pushing for recognition of the newly formed industrial syndicates. Employers objected that the syndicates allowed "outside agitators" to control what went on in their factories, and they responded with powerful campaigns to force their dissolution. Although many individual labor conflicts ostensibly erupted over bread and butter issues, they were rarely resolved without touching on these larger principles. As an official CNT notice put it in January 1920, "We are going through a period of incredibly intense agitation, in which our dignity is on the line."[67] Thus, even the smallest labor disputes became part of the big picture of a polarizing city.

The evidence for this pattern of escalation is abundant. For example, in August 1918 metalworkers at the port of El Musel declared a strike over the lack of proper construction parts.[68] However, when the strike finally ended in April of 1919, employers had conceded an eight-hour work day, wage increases, and the obligation to hire through the metallurgical syndicate.[69] Another strike provoked by hat-makers in La Calzada over inferior machines was quickly transformed into a showdown over the authority of the Textile and Clothing Syndicate.[70] Likewise, metalworkers at Moreda y Gijón struck for better wages and a

---

[67] *El Noroeste*, January 12, 1920.
[68] Information included in a letter to the Secretario General of the Sindicato Metalúrgico Asturiano, from the local union, Primero de Mayo, dated August 31, 1918: AGS, Legajo K-44.
[69] *El Noroeste*, April 23, 1919.
[70] *El Noroeste*, April 6, 7, 17, 1919.

shorter work day, but their demand that the company negotiate with the Metallurgical Syndicate turned the strike into a six-month stand-off. In the final settlement, arbitrated by Quintanilla, the workers won nearly all their demands. Most importantly, the company agreed to the election of shopfloor stewards, who would monitor the workplace as representatives of the Syndicate. As an added bonus, Moreda finally agreed to re-hire the *seleccionados* from the 1917 strike.[71] Conflicts such as these abounded throughout 1919 and 1920, when there always seemed to be a minimum of four or five strikes going on simultaneously. Furthermore, the syndicates appeared to be making headway in their drive for recognition.

The culmination of this period of intense labor conflict came at the end of 1920, when the employers finally forced a victorious showdown over the syndicates. The opportunity for a direct confrontation arose when, in December, the CNT ordered a work slowdown to protest against government repression of anarchists in Catalonia. The Employers' Association (AP) responded promptly with a lock-out, and the CNT followed on December 9th with a general strike, which shut down the city for an entire week.[72] Thus, what had begun as a commentary on events outside Gijón quickly activated the deep animosities between employers and workers. When the CNT opted to return to work on December 15th, the AP launched a full-scale war on the syndicates. It announced that members would no longer negotiate with any syndicate, that shop stewards would be relieved of their representative duties, and that they reclaimed the right to hire and fire at will. The CNT rejected the ultimatum, and the strike continued for several more weeks, as each side held firm, despite the mediation of the Institute of Social Reform.

After nearly six weeks of this stand-off, the AP's resolve forced the syndicates to cave in. On January 21st, a worker assembly agreed "to disband the Sindicatos Unicos and to remove the delegates in each factory, resolving that each guild should negotiate separately with its employers, making it clear to them that we accept all of the terms proposed by the employers if they will re-admit the workers to their jobs."[73] The decision was reached after laborious and agonized dis-

---

[71] *El Noroeste*, October 13, 1919.
[72] Since *El Noroeste* was unable to publish from December 10th through 15th, its account of the strike is in the December 16th issue.
[73] AHN, 53A, núm.5. The syndicates were temporarily banned by the government in March 1921.

cussion, but the majority admitted that they could not resist indefinitely the combined resources of the AP.

Thus, the employers achieved their goal of effectively dismantling the syndicates. Although a skeletal structure remained, the industrial syndicate no longer functioned as a force in labor relations. More importantly, the defeat had broken the back of the union movement. The combined impact of this defeat and demoralization over events in Catalonia put the CNT on a defensive slide that culminated with the coup of September 1923.

Although the Dictatorship forced a temporary hiatus in political activity, Gijón's tradition of activism was too embedded to be permanently erased. The pattern of polarized mobilization that surfaced in 1901 repeated itself in ever stronger cycles of confrontation over the following twenty years. In opposition to repressive and unresponsive government and business elites, a tradition of protest in the defense of popular interests took shape. The power of this tradition lay in its diversity, in the heterogeneity of participants and specific issues, but also in the capacity to create links between them. The same diverse cast of characters appeared time and again, mounting their own corporate struggles and identifying themselves with the struggles of others. What tied them all together was a populist sense of the rights of the common residents of the city, as contrasted to the elites who ran the city for their own benefit. Although national issues often intruded, sometimes in dramatic ways, the conflict centered on the structure of local power relationships. Thus, at the heart of the matter was the question of who the city belonged to, the Gijón of lights or its smoke-darkened counterpart. When the Republic was declared in 1931, this fully formed question resurfaced, challenging the new regime to declare its popular loyalties. With this challenge, a new cycle of opposition was set in motion that carried Gijón and the rest of the country towards civil war.

10

Conflict and collective action during the Republic, 1931–1936

~

On December 15, 1930, the city of Gijón erupted in the first major conflagration since the 1923 coup. The spark was provided by the execution on December 14th of Captains Galán and García Hernández, who had led an unsuccessful republican uprising in the town of Jaca.[1] Ironically, the defeat at Jaca helped revitalize the anti-monarchical forces, which swept into power several months later. Thus, in Gijón, the massive protest against the executions confirmed the widespread lack of confidence in the struggling monarchy and the popular demand for political change. Republican candidates rode the tide of this popular mandate in a broad coalition that won an overwhelming victory in the April 1931 elections. In the optimism of the moment, it seemed as if "smoke-darkened" Gijón had finally seized the reigns of power and taken over both the city and the country from the economic and social elites.

What soon became apparent, however, was that the inauguration of the Republic marked a new phase in, rather than the end of, the ongoing battle for control of the city. When the republican government failed to demonstrate its clear loyalty to "smoke-darkened" Gijón, the republicans lost what was left of their ambiguous leadership of the popular community. Set adrift from the moderating republican

---

[1] The uprising at Jaca was to have been part of a nationwide *pronunciamiento* (military-led coup) on December 15th to establish a Republic but, for reasons that are unclear, the revolution was launched prematurely in Jaca on December 12th and therefore easily suppressed. See Graco Marsà, *La sublevación de Jaca: relato de un rebelde* (Paris: Durant, 1931) for a contemporary account and José María Azpiroz Pascual and Fernando Elboj Broto, *La sublevación de Jaca* (Zaragoza: Guara Editorial, 1984).

influence, the remaining oppositional forces pursued their unmediated war against the elite forces of the city, which also refused to trust the government with their interests. With the Republic caught helplessly in the middle, the polarization of left and right, popular and elite, continued unabated, directly contested in the streets and in the workplaces as it had been for several decades, and culminating in armed confrontation in October 1934 and July 1936.

In the radicalization of conflict that followed April 1931, the CNT was the clear beneficiary. The CNT had already proved its populist credentials in several decades of labor and consumer struggles, leaving it perfectly positioned to assert a broad leadership role among those disappointed with the achievements of the Republic. As the legislative reforms were churned out slowly, if at all, the CNT took its familiar position in the streets, neighborhoods and workshops, fighting the enemy in public spaces where everyone could bear witness. To a populace that had long learned to be skeptical of government, this was where politics had always been located. Consequently, the CNT's continued commitment to direct action, which was viewed as irresponsible and disruptive by the authorities, must have made perfect sense to a popular community nurtured on this type of contestation. In turn, the broader popular community could use the CNT's organization to pursue traditional forms of mobilization.

For these reasons, the Republic never managed to absorb or deflect the city's endemic strife into legal and peaceful avenues. Instead, Gijón under the Republic was as tumultuous as the previous three decades had been, perhaps more, because of the expectations that had been raised and dashed. The result of such unchanneled conflict was, of course, lethal for the regime. The fact that the republican government was unable to channel or absorb this popular mobilization was one of the clearest signs of its inability to establish its own legitimacy. As long as political discourse remained primarily in the streets, the republican regime was powerless to mediate the growing polarization of a mobilized population. Under these conditions, civil war became virtually inevitable.

The first bienio, 1931–1933

At first glance, the December 1930 protest seems a long way from the Civil War. And yet, on closer examination, the event set the stage for the next five-and-a-half-year cycle of conflict. The protest began when the CNT declared a forty-eight hour strike to denounce the executions in Jaca, a measure endorsed and seconded by all the city's anti-monarchist forces.[2] In customary fashion, strikers from the outer boroughs converged on the city center. However, as thousands of residents of the poor neighborhoods occupied the central streets and plazas of the city, for the first time in several years, resentment apparently boiled over. What had started as an orderly strike escalated into a full-scale riot that went far beyond the CNT's original plan.

The spark issued from someone in the crowd milling around the Plaza del Instituto Jovellanos, who shouted that "the first thing to do was get rid of this plaque." The offending plaque proclaimed the street name "Calle Primo de Rivera," renamed from "Calle Instituto" in 1923. To compound the symbolic outrage, it was affixed to the wall of the Jesuit church. A more powerful image of Church and state united against the people could not have been invented. After the call to arms, the crowd erupted. Some people began throwing rocks at the plaque, and others headed, following another familiar ritual, to the city hall, where they demanded the mayor's permission to remove the sign. When he demurred, insisting he lacked the authority, people began to throw stones at the city hall, breaking several windows before the police regained control.

In the meantime, those left in the plaza stormed the doors of the church, pulling out benches, chairs, banners, and even one of the sacred statues, which they used to light a bonfire in the street.[3] At this point, several shots were fired and a young worker named Carlos Tuero was fatally wounded. Since it was unclear who fired the shots, the rumor spread that Jesuits barricaded in the church had perpetrated the assassination.[4] At the time, Tuero's death literally added more fuel to the fire, as the entire church was soon enveloped in flames.[5] The

---

[2] The following narrative was extracted from *El Noroeste*, when it began publishing again after the strike, on December 19, 1930.

[3] This anti-clerical violence preceded a larger wave of such church burnings in May of 1931 and later in July and August of 1936. For descriptions, see Vicente Carcel Orti, *La persecución religiosa en España durante la Segunda República (1931–1939)* (Madrid: Ediciones Rialp, 1990). For an intriguing analysis of the phenomenon, see Manuel Delgado, *La ira sagrada: anticlericalismo, iconoclastia y antirritualismo en la España contemporánea* (Barcelona: Editorial Humanidades, 1992).

[4] Ramón Alvarez Palomo notes that the rumor was later codified in a popular song: *Eleuterio Quintanilla* (Mexico: Editores Mexicanos Unidos, 1973), 292.

[5] Conservative historian Joaquín Bonet paints a graphic picture of terrorists pouring gasoline on the organ and the holy statues: *Biografía de la villa y puerto de Gijón*, vol. II (Gijón: La Industria, 1968), 104.

combination of more police and the onset of darkness finally restored order.

Violence erupted again the next day, this time at the "Primo de Rivera" primary school in La Calzada, where residents tore down the sign with its name. To avoid more confrontations, authorities forced the family of the slain worker to bury Tuero at dawn the following day, accompanied by Civil Guards. In addition, they followed the usual procedures of arresting union leaders and shutting down the Casa del Pueblo, at which point the CNT retaliated by prolonging the strike. Finally, on the fourth day, the CNT and the authorities negotiated a return to work on the condition that all the prisoners be released.

Although *El Noroeste* applauded the strike, it nervously observed that the labor movement should not be activated lightly. Indeed, the strike launched to protest the deaths of two unknown heroes had clearly set in motion a world of frustrations that had little to do with them or even with the organizers' limited agenda. Instead, working-class Gijón enacted the traditional ritual of descending on the elite city center to physically present and enforce its demands. This time, their demands harmonized with those of the republican politicians, but in October 1934 this same ritual would be repeated in a more aggressive manner against the legal authority of the Republic. In this sense, the regime itself was incidental to the ongoing crusade to capture the city from its elite owners, a fact never quite grasped by the majority of republicans. Thus, the republicans accepted the December 1930 riot as ammunition against the existing regime, but assumed that they could prevent such "activation" under the Republic, simply because it was the Republic.

In fact, the inauguration of the Republic signaled the intensification of such mobilization, particularly in the case of the CNT. It was not that the local CNT actively sought to overthrow the regime. Nevertheless, it refused to back off on its demands and, more importantly, refused to allow even a reformist government to take over its role as advocate and defender of the workers. Thus, the CNT clung to its direct action tactics and its attempts to mobilize not only its own members but the larger community. Furthermore, as evidenced by continued auxiliary support for CNT actions, many people from the city's popular classes seemed to accept the need for direct mobilization in the streets. Thus, while republicans and Socialists tried to discredit the CNT during the first *bienio*, their accusations never stuck. The

283

CNT employed its direct action tactics against a number of targets but most often in ways that kept popular sympathy on its side. At times it challenged the government over the repression of *cenetista* workers throughout Spain, as exemplified in the most famous incident in Casas Viejas in January of 1933.[6] In these protests, the CNT claimed that it was simply exposing the betrayal of the workers that the "Republic of Workers" was supposed to represent. In addition to challenging the government, the CNT also continued to contest the employers' hegemony in the workplace. The large number of CNT strikes helped make Asturias, along with Barcelona, the most strike-ridden province in the country over the next couple of years.[7] In July, for example, *El Noroeste* reported on the status of seven ongoing strikes, involving municipal workers, metallurgists from Moreda, dock-workers, port construction workers, ceramicists, gas and electric workers and women textile workers. And perhaps the most dramatic challenge to the employers occurred in December 1932, when the local federation declared a week-long general strike protesting against the lay-off of 500 metalworkers in La Felguera.[8]

While the large number of strikes was seen by its enemies as evidence of the CNT's bad faith against the Republic, most were rooted in conventional workplace conflicts and involved moderate demands. Furthermore, in many cases, the employers shared equal responsibility for the strikes by treating all demands as challenges to their basic authority. The textile strike at La Algodonera in July of 1931 is a good example. According to *El Noroeste*, the conflict began when management punished one of the operators for requesting a glass of water, and her fellow workers protested with a sit-down strike.[9] Apparently such Dickensian regimentation was not unusual, as workers reported that foremen followed them to the bathrooms to time their visits, and refused to let them go home to warm up the midday meal. The strike escalated when the company retaliated by revoking its recognition of the union's authority to bargain, and the women in turn authorized their union to add wage increases to their demands. The

---

[6] Two examples were strikes called on May 29, 1931 and May 10, 1933. See *El Noroeste*, May 31, 1931 and May 11, 1933 for details.
[7] *Anuario Estadístico de España*, 1934, 758–759.
[8] The workers were laid off to help improve the financial problems of the company (Duro Felguera). The conflict in La Felguera dragged on until August 1933, when it was resolved largely in favor of the employers, but Gijón's federation struck only for a week to show its solidarity.
[9] July 8, 1931.

company defended the low wages by arguing that the women were "supplemental" wage earners, and refused to budge.[10]

To deflect its own responsibility, the company tried to blame the strike on Gijón's contentious atmosphere: "we know that we suffer greatly for being located in Gijón, since in any other locality in the north or northeast of Spain, we would not have this conflict."[11] While there was a grain of truth in this familiar litany, this strike, as many others, followed a long-established dynamic of direct confrontation over control of the workplace that required the active participation of both sides.

The most controversial of the CNT's strikes, and those that most rankled the government, were launched against the rival Socialists. But even in these conflicts, which had the potential to make the anarchosyndicalists look like fratricidal spoilers, the CNT managed to link its struggles to larger populist issues. The first general strike of the Republic is a case in point. It evolved out of a decision by local transport workers to support their *cenetista* comrades in Barcelona, who had been fired for refusing to accept Socialist co-workers, but the local conflict was soon transposed into a familiar issue of workplace control.[12] As the general strike unfolded, the UGT found itself on the side of the employers and the police, helping them bust the unions.

The drama began when CNT port workers were fired on November 10, 1931 for refusing to unload a ship staffed by UGT scabs in Barcelona. The ship owners replaced the workers with a local scab crew of *ugetistas*, and, after several weeks of stand-off, the CNT responded on December 4th with a transport boycott on all merchandise arriving at the port. With this escalation, the Employers' Association (Agremiación Patronal – AP) entered the fray, threatening to fire any of their workers who upheld the boycott. The first to do so were the haulers employed by the metallurgical factory, Moreda y Gijón, who lost their jobs when they refused to transport supplies from the port to the factory.

In an apparently spontaneous act of solidarity, the remaining 1,100

---

[10] The strike was finally resolved towards the end of August, with a settlement that, in the opinion of the anarchist *Solidaridad*, fell far short of the workers' demands, but did grant significant concessions: raising the minimum wage from 2.20 pts. to 4 pts., and agreeing to recognize the union (August 22, 1931).

[11] *El Noroeste*, June 27, 1931.

[12] The following narrative has two basic sources: the Socialist *Avance*, which was hostile, and the more measured reports of the Civil Governor, contained in telegrams sent between November 11 and December 23, 1931: AHN, Legajo 7A, núm.8.

workers of Moreda and the 600 men and women at another large metallurgical plant, Laviada, locked themselves in the factories in a sit-down strike.[13] Workers in a few smaller plants followed suit, so that by the afternoon of December 9th, over 4,000 workers were participating in the occupation. Furthermore, outside the barricaded factories, female supporters literally surrounded the buildings in order to prevent the police from storming them. Thus, the conflict spilled out of the workplace and into the community. And in doing so, it activated another populist issue, the animosity between the police and the people.

The animosity flared up when 150 Civil Guards were called in to evict the strikers, and the occupation ended in a bloody confrontation that left one worker dead and ten others wounded. Typically, there were conflicting accounts of its origins. The authorities claimed that after the strikers agreed to vacate the building, a hostile crowd fired them up and everyone began throwing rocks at the police. In this version, the police fired some twenty-five shots in self-defense. In contrast, the version that spread like wildfire through the city depicted an unprovoked "massacre." Whatever the true story, it was this one that resonated with popular beliefs.

The strike committee distributed pamphlets calling for a general strike, and thousands of angry witnesses and supporters milled in the streets demanding justice. Because the dead worker had been a Federalist as well as a *cenetista*, the Federalist city council members withdrew from their seats in protest. The next day, the general strike was broken only by the city's UGT workers, backed up by *Avance*, which grumbled that the strike served only to enforce tyranny at the workplace. But the Socialist newspaper missed the point entirely. The UGT had backed itself into a position that was completely out of step with community opinion and that implicitly endorsed police brutality. In other words, through guilt by association, it became identified with elite Gijón.

This association was neatly symbolized by the day's only violent encounter, which transpired outside the venerable Café Dindurra. As was often the case, the luxury cafés on the downtown boulevards were

---

[13] The issue of who instigated the occupations was later debated in court, as the government tried to convict *cenetista* leaders of this charge. A federal agent insisted that he had witnessed an assembly pass by acclamation a motion to occupy the factories, while the defendants insisted there was no such vote. They were acquitted. Lawyers for the defense were Federalist politician Barriobero, Reformist Mariano Merediz, and Communist José Loredo Aparicio: *El Noroeste*, November 19, 1932.

among the few establishments to ignore general strikes. Thus, on this day of mourning, it was packed with its usual prosperous clientele. Moreover, this elite clientele was being served by UGT waiters who, coincidentally, serviced most of the elite cafés. In the language of the two Gijóns, the image of café, clientele and UGT waiters communicated a potent message. As working-class Gijón banded together to protest against the massacre of its own, the Socialists apparently demonstrated which master they had chosen to serve.

And thus, the Café Dindurra became one of the major targets of popular anger. As the Governor's report described it, the "public" that filled the Plaza de Begoña in front of the café spontaneously assaulted the establishment, wounding two policemen who tried to prevent them. When the crowd followed the officers to the hospital, attempting to pull them out into the street, police began shooting and another worker was killed, while four more were seriously wounded.

After this explosion, the violence died down, but the strike dragged on for another ten days, stuck on the issue of scab labor. Although the CNT asked for little more than a return to pre-strike conditions, the employers refused to put the replacement crew on the negotiation table. When they rejected even a compromise solution that featured a rotation between UGT and CNT port workers, the CNT federation was finally forced to capitulate on December 21st. Although the CNT had provoked the strike, the federation came out of it looking like the victim of an aggressive employer strategy. The AP had clearly used the opportunity to flex its muscle and demonstrate that it still ruled the workplace, even under the new Republic.

In addition to waging strikes, the CNT reinforced its populist image by continuing its direct consumer campaigns. Some of these were organized through the federation's Anti-Unemployment Committee, which sponsored numerous rallies and marches in favor of "bread and work." While they focused on the issue of jobs, they also addressed more general concerns about the cost of living for poor families. In a May 1933 rally, for example, demonstrators asked that families of unemployed workers not be evicted from their homes, even if they fell behind on the rent.[14] Furthermore, the organizers made a special appeal for women to attend these events:

> To you, *compañeras*, who are closest to the immense tragedy of your humble homes; who see how hunger and sickness are slowly consuming your lives and those of your children; it is to you that these

[14] *El Noroeste*, March 31, 1933, and *Avance*, March 26, 1933.

demonstrations are principally dedicated, and thus we hope that you will turn out in force for today's event.[15]

In this way, organizers made the connection between home and work and tried to draw the entire family into the struggle.

The CNT's most concerted attempt to bring in the larger community was the formation of a new syndicate, in the spring of 1932, for the Defense of Public Interests (SDIP). In contrast to a conventional union, which comprised groups of workers, the SDIP was organized through neighborhood committees. Its specific purpose was to enforce a generous renters' rights law of December 1931 that had not been vigorously implemented. Following anarchosyndicalist strategy, the SDIP utilized various forms of direct action, from rent strikes, to mass demonstrations, to the reversal of evictions. *Cenetista* Ramón Alvarez described this latter action: when someone alerted the SDIP to an eviction, a group went to the home and broke off the judge's official eviction seal. Then, they carried the furniture back in from the street and left their own sign, "opened by order of the CNT."[16]

The public impact of these kinds of tactics contrasted with the quieter methods of the older Liga de Inquilinos. Over the course of the Dictatorship, the Liga had acquired a new president, the right-wing Socialist Germán de la Cerra. Under his leadership, the organization dedicated itself almost exclusively to judicial challenges. Thus, it sought enforcement of the renters' decree by bringing some 800 cases to court.[17] While these cases may have gotten some results, they did not draw in the community, in particular women, in the way that the SDIP's tactics did. Housewives could fit into the neighborhood structure of the organization, and the SDIP's direct assaults resonated with the patterns of traditional consumer protests.

In one of the mass demonstrations sponsored by the SDIP some 3,000 people, most of them women, marched from the outer neighborhoods to the city center behind a banner proclaiming "The SDIP asks for justice in enforcing the renters' decree." Another sign

---

[15] *El Noroeste*, May 31, 1932: from the Comité Pro-Parados (Anti-Unemployment Committee).
[16] From a discussion with Ramón Alvarez, November 1987.
[17] *Avance*, April 17, 1932. Unfortunately, there seems to be no more information on the evolution of the Liga. Cerra also advised the fishermen's collective organization, the Pósito de Pescadores, in their conflict with the ship owners, but he was later expelled from the Socialist party for his evolutionary views, after the party radicalized (from a letter defending his actions to the head of the government, Alejandro Lerroux, November 24, 1934: AGS, Legajo J-50).

announced: "We want a healthy and economical home." The only violence erupted when, at the city hall, officials refused the customary reading of the accords from the balcony of the city hall. The revocation of this traditional participatory right evoked shouts and hisses from the crowd, which eventually forced its way into the building and convinced the mayor to change his mind.[18] The entire event drew on a traditional repertoire of popular mobilization, which allowed the SDIP to harness the energy of the streets behind it.

It was this capacity for popular mobilization, and not the CNT's revolutionary ideology, that posed the greatest threat to the regime, and in particular the reformist *bienio*. The CNT's direct action strategies helped keep political discourse in the street, and encouraged people to pursue the same extra-legal channels of activism that they had developed under the monarchy. In the context of a regime slow to enact reforms, and an Employers' Association quick to push confrontation, these methods remained an effective way to conduct politics. But of course they also sapped legitimacy and energy from a government trying to establish itself as the mediator of a polarized society. On one level, then, it was the failure to win acceptance as the binding arbitrator of disputes that brought down the reformist coalition of 1931. And in this failure, the popular mobilization chronicled in this chapter played a complex role: on the one hand, it helped weaken the reformist government, but, on the other hand, it provided evidence of its weakness. Thus, intense conflict was both cause and result of the breakdown of the regime.

The second bienio, 1934–1935

When the reformist parties lost the November 1933 elections, the Republic entered its second, more conservative, phase. With the shift to the right, visible at the local level in the victorious alliance of the Reformists and Acción Popular, the nature of popular opposition also shifted. While earlier protests had been staged as appeals to the progressive government to live up to its promises, now they seemed like defensive maneuvers against a hostile ruling power. This shift had commenced before the election, as disillusionment with the "Republic of

---

[18] The accords were: (1) a strict reading of the new decree; (2) rent reductions retroactive to January 1932; (3) a slow-down of the eviction process to allow renters to pay "in their own time"; and (4) the firing of most of the municipal judges (who were property owners themselves) for partiality: *El Noroeste*, May 27, 1932.

Casas Viejas" started to turn the tide, but it accelerated afterwards. The result was an increasing edge to the otherwise similar strikes and demonstrations that filled local newspapers.[19]

The new tone was set by the first major conflict of the period, another general strike that broke out within a month of the elections. In contrast to the previous two major general strikes, in 1931 and 1932, this one sought the overthrow of the government – not the Republic, but the more conservative administration that had taken power. In fact, the strike in Gijón was part of what was intended to be a nation-wide rebellion, planned by the radical wing of the anarchist movement. Reflecting the local federation's ambivalence towards this radical wing, it called a general strike instead of mounting an armed rebellion. Confused in its intentions, the strike was a strangely lifeless affair that lasted only a few days.[20] Despite the confusion, it represented an important transition in the nature of the local CNT's challenge to the regime.

The strike is usually seen as a transition for other reasons. It was when the leaders were sitting in jail for their role in the strike that they wrote their famous appeal to end the feud with the Socialists. For them, the December revolution proved the inefficacy of isolated anarchist revolts and, implicitly, the course set by the radical leadership of the national federation. At the same time, of course, the November elections had demonstrated to many Socialists the fickleness of the legal road to revolution. And thus the road to convergence and eventually the Alianza Obrera (Workers' Alliance) began.

While the reconciliation of once bitter enemies was a dramatic move, its impact on collective action and conflict before the October revolution was more symbolic than substantive. The small size of Gijón's UGT meant that it could add few bodies or resources to local movements. The symbolic impact was most visible on the picket lines, where UGT workers no longer crossed them to serve as scab labor. Thus, although they added little to potential mobilization, they also stopped detracting from it. In fact, the only conflict in which their

[19] In Gijón alone there were thirty-seven strikes between December 1933 and October 1934, out of ninety-five in Asturias as a whole: statistics compiled by Eusebio Izquierdo Fernández, "Organizaciones sindicales y conflictividad social en Asturias durante la II República, 1933–1934" (Tesina, University of Oviedo, 1985), 119.

[20] The nationwide rebellion was a failure as well. It never got off the ground in most places, and where it did, as in parts of rural Aragon, it was quickly and easily suppressed. On the uprising in Aragon, see Enrique Montañés, *Anarcosindicalismo y cambio político: Zaragoza 1930–1936* (Zaragoza: Institución Fernando el Católico, 1989).

presence played a crucial role was in the municipal strike of August 1934, where UGT and CNT unions combined forces to win a marginal victory. Although everyone in the labor movement hailed the united strike as the wave of the future, the proof of the Alianza's potential, in fact it was an anomaly.[21] Any local mobilization, revolutionary or otherwise, would rise or fall on the presence of the CNT and the broader popular community.

However, the strike did illustrate the rising political temperature of the spring and summer of 1934. Oppositional activity erupted from a variety of corners, including the poor neighborhoods. Thus, on May 30th, a delegation of women from El Llano marched to the mayor's office to protest against the rise in bread prices and followed up with a well-attended demonstration to emphasize their displeasure with the government's economic policy.[22] Consumer protests led by disgruntled wives and mothers were not new, but the fact that the women judged they were still necessary under the Republic implied that institutional politics had changed little. Furthermore, the women's direct style of politics must have reinforced the conviction of the CNT and now of the UGT/PSOE that they had chosen the right path of resistance.

On a smaller scale, this conviction was further bolstered by evidence of a virtual guerrilla war in the streets of Cimadavilla, where members of the fishing community literally came to blows with supporters of the ship outfitters. This was, of course, Cima's own version of the struggle between popular and elite hegemony, a struggle that prepared it to participate with the other more "modern" poor neighborhoods in the upcoming rebellion.

The surviving records of two court cases offer a glimpse into this intimate conflict.[23] In one instance, a street fight erupted between two women, a fishmonger who was also President of the women's section of the Pósito, and a daughter of a manager of the fleet owners' Rula. The weapons were improvised: a set of knitting needles and a casserole dish, the latter proving the more effective instrument. Both women denied starting the fight and, significantly, each had their own

---

[21] Co-operation had dramatic effects in this case because the CNT and UGT shared control over the 400-member municipal workforce; in most cases, one or the other federation dominated the entire sector or industry: see Chapter 6.

[22] *Avance*, May 31, 1934.

[23] Most of the judicial records for this period were destroyed, either in October 1934 or during the Civil War, but those few that remain (including those cited here) are kept in the Archivo Histórico Provincial, Sección Audencia Provincial.

witnesses who swore to their story.[24] Another case involved a knife fight between two men, a fisherman named Salustino and an employee of the fleet owners named Cristóbal. The two got into a heated argument on the docks, just as the boats were unloading their daily catch, and Cristóbal ended up dead. Just as in the case of the women, each side and its witnesses told contradictory stories. As one witness admitted: "this question involves a rivalry between those who belong to the Pósito and those who work for the Rula of the ship owners, since Salustino belongs to the first and Cristóbal the latter, and since there are very bitter relations between the two groups."[25]

While the specific details of these two fights are murky, the broad outlines are quite clear. In Cima's narrow streets and crowded public squares, confrontation between the two Gijóns occurred on an intimate, face-to-face level. The enemy was not an abstract concept but a woman with a casserole dish. The Pósito organized its share of mass demonstrations and marches to city hall, but these casual confrontations in the street capture more dramatically the depth of hostility between the two sides. Furthermore, they add another dimension to the picture of a regime unable to contain the unmediated conflict breaking out from every corner.

This unmediated conflict set the stage for the open rebellion of October 1934. The thirty years of street politics and the direct confrontation between elite and popular communities provided the foundation on which the formal revolution unfolded. The result was a mixture of long-term patterns and short-term planning, of local and national politics. Without the context of Republican politics, the transition from a hopeful first *bienio* to a disillusioned second, and the formation of the Alianza Obrera, an armed revolt never would have been launched. More specifically, Prime Minister Lerroux's appointment of three ministers from the right-wing CEDA party on October 4th signaled the point of no return for the left, a point at which, in their minds, they had to forcibly reclaim the Republic for the workers.[26]

[24] The fight took place on June 9, 1934. The woman of the Pósito was tried and convicted in August of 1939, after waiting in jail since the fall of Gijón to the nationalists in November 1938: Sumario 130/34, caja #96.
[25] The incident occurred on July 31, 1934, and is found in Sumario 165/34, caja #96.
[26] The left viewed the CEDA as a crypto-fascist organization that was planning a coup d'état to overthrow the Republic. Historians and partisans of one side or another have debated the justification of this fear, but for the purposes of understanding October 1934, it is important only to acknowledge its intensity. For two opposing views, see Paul

However, after organizers in Madrid sounded the call to battle, the rebellion unfolded on the familiar terrain of the "two Gijóns." Thus, residents of the outlying neighborhoods first launched an attack on the city center and then retreated back to their home territory to defend against counter-attack. Not surprisingly, the barricades went up in the same neighborhoods that had been struggling to overcome their marginal status for decades: El Llano, La Calzada, Cimadavilla. Likewise, residents of these neighborhoods used their networks of solidarity to construct a support system for the few hundred armed men who actually manned the barricades.

In other words, behind the relatively small fighting force lay the resources and energies of "smoke-darkened" Gijón. These energies made the revolution in Gijón something more than an unbalanced military encounter between the "Workers' Alliance" and the army. Instead, they demonstrated a degree of popular disappointment with the Republic that could not be suffocated as easily as the armed rebellion. On the other hand, the rebellion illustrated the limitations of these resources, which were geared toward a very local and intimate level of politics. Thus, residents could provide warm support behind the barricades, but little resistance against the national government's troops. The result was a hegemonical stand-off that was not resolved until the next round of fighting commenced in July 1936.

The rebellion was launched on October 4th, hours after the swearing-in of the three ministers. Socialist parliamentary deputy Teodomiro Menéndez carried the orders by train to Asturias, hidden in the brim of his hat.[27] Similar orders went out to other provinces, but Asturias was the only place that heeded the call in a massive and effective manner. The rebellion cut a swathe through Asturias' central industrial region, from the mining towns in the interior through Oviedo and Gijón (see Map 7). The fighting was unusually sustained; it took national troops about two weeks to suppress the last of the opposition.

Despite the image of a provincial revolt, in fact, the fighting took

Preston, *The Coming of the Spanish Civil War: Reform, Reaction and Revolution in the Second Republic* (London: Routledge, 1978) and Richard A. H. Robinson, *The Origins of Franco's Spain: The Right, the Republic and Revolution, 1931–1936* (London: Newton Abbot, 1970). For a more detailed (sympathetic) account of the revolt in a national perspective, see David Ruiz, *Insurrección defensiva y revolución obrera: el octubre español de 1934* (Barcelona: Editorial Labor, 1988).

[27] Diego Mateo del Peral *et al.*, *Historia de Asturias*, vol. VIII: *Edad Contemporánea I* (Vitoria: Ayalga Ediciones, 1977), 234.

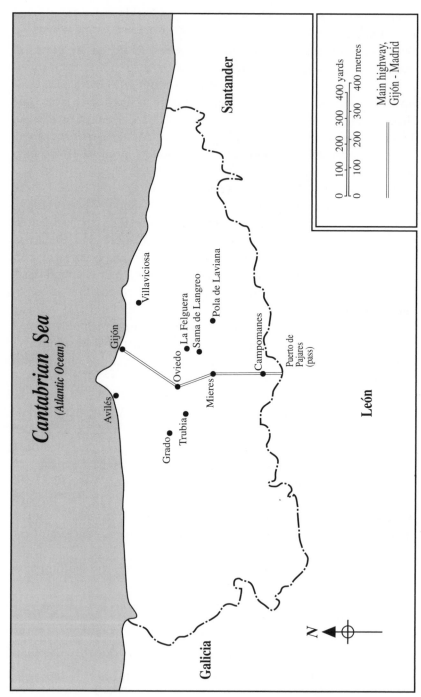

Map 7 Industrial Asturias

place on several virtually independent fronts. Local miners armed with dynamite quickly overpowered the small mining towns of the central basin. They then combined forces and opened two fronts, the first in Oviedo, and the second in Campomanes, at the southern periphery of the region. In Oviedo, columns of miners descended on the city and engaged in a twelve-day battle with the besieged forces of order within. In Campomanes, they fought a fourteen-day pitched battle to keep reinforcements from entering the province. The last front was the city of Gijón, which, ignored by the Socialist miners, carried on its own urban rebellion, the city at war with itself.[28]

Partly because of its isolation, and partly owing to a number of other obstacles, Gijón was the weakest of the military fronts. In fact, it fell in a mere six days, overwhelmed by lack of arms,[29] the size of the police and military presence in Gijón[30] and the vulnerability to reinforcements arriving from the sea. In this sense, the rebellion in Gijón was a sideshow, and has usually been treated as such by historians. And yet, on another level, Gijón's rebellion disclosed more about the complex forces of polarization that were pulling the country apart than did the dramatic pitched battles in the rest of the province. Thus, while the latter revealed how well the labor movement could mount a militia force, the revolution in Gijón bared the reality of a mobilized and divided population.

The military weakness of the rebellion in Gijón was apparent from the outset, when the paucity of arms delayed the uprising until midnight on the 7th, after most of the mining towns had already fallen. Until then, the city moved into general strike mode. By the afternoon

[28] The account of the revolution in Gijón was taken from the following sources: Paco I. Taibo, *Asturias 1934* (Gijón: Júcar, 1984); N. Molins i Fabrega, *La insurrección proletaria de Asturias* (1935; reprint, Gijón: Júcar, 1977); *El Noroeste*, October 17, 1934; Manuel Villar, *El anarquismo en la insurrección de Asturias* (Valencia: Ediciones Tierra y Libertad, 1935); Comité revolucionario, "Informe al Pleno Regional de Sindicatos de Asturias, León y Palencia sobre los sucesos revolucionarios en Gijón" (AGS, Legajo J-12); José Canals, *Octubre rojo en Asturias* (1935; reprint, Gijón: Silverio Cañada, 1984); Guzmán García Alvarez, unpublished written testimonial (BCUO); and *Región*, October 19, 1934 (HMG).
[29] The mining towns had access to dynamite, and there were major munitions factories in Oviedo and Trubia. Few of these arms ever made it to Gijón, both because of lack of communication, lingering distrust between anarchists and socialists, and the all-out effort made to take Oviedo.
[30] In contrast to mining towns, which contained a single Civil Guard post, Gijón had five, distributed among the working-class neighborhoods of the city. In addition, there was a company of Guardias de Asalto (150 soldiers), 24 *carabineros*, 60 municipal guards and a battalion of army regulars (200–300 soldiers) – altogether over 500 armed professionals: Taibo, *Asturias 1934*, vol. I, 110 and 194.

of the 5th, everything was closed down, but the streets were teaming: "Nothing is operating in the city. The regular rhythms of normal life have been interrupted. The excitement of the workers is enormous. Enthusiasm is overflowing. The groups that form in the streets, numerous and dense, discuss the events with passion."[31]

After the second day, with the province up in arms, and rumors of Oviedo's imminent fall, local militants decided to launch the attack and gamble on the expectation that reinforcements would arrive soon. After dark, militants and residents put up barricades in El Llano and La Calzada, where they prepared their assault on the center. With several dozen rifles, groups of rebels stormed the Guardia Civil post in downtown Gijón, but after several hours of fierce resistance, both from the Guards and from residential balconies, they withdrew to their neighborhood strongholds. The choreography of this opening scene followed patterns set long ago. Working-class Gijón invaded the center in a symbolic and physical attempt to take the city from its elite owners. When the combined defiance of police and inhabitants repulsed the attempt, the rebels retreated within the walls of their own community, where the police dared not follow without reinforcements.

The only place where the police did follow was Cimadavilla, because of its proximity to the city hall. However, the combined efforts of residents and militants succeeded in expelling them after a night of fierce fighting. Residents helped with the process of building barricades, throwing mattresses out of windows, piling up planks and dragging light boats from the harbor. By 10 a.m. on the 7th, Cima was in the hands of the rebels, with its four narrow access streets sealed off.

Victory was short-lived, however. While Cima was ideally situated for urban guerilla warfare, its position near the harbor made it a perfect target for naval bombardment. On the night of the 7th, the battleship *Libertad*, anchored off the coast of Gijón, began shelling the neighborhood. By the following afternoon, residents were ready to surrender, and women waved white sheets from their windows to signal the authorities. The kind of conflict they understood was no match for heavy artillery. Panicked residents tore down the barricades that now trapped them inside and began streaming out of the neigh-

---

[31] Villar, *El anarquismo*, 135–136. Villar was a Catalan anarchist paid by *Solidaridad Obrera* in Barcelona to visit Gijón and write an account of the revolution.

borhood. But this time the narrow entrances worked against them, as the authorities were there to arrest all the men and hold them for questioning.[32] They were later moved to Gijón's oldest church until combatant and civilian could be properly distinguished, apparently through the use of torture.

After the fall of Cima, the rebels consolidated their forces in El Llano and La Calzada, waiting for the arrival of the troops, but they had virtually no ammunition. The CNT had sent a messenger to Oviedo three days in a row, trying to get a promise of arms and reinforcements, but to no avail. The only help that arrived was an armored truck with forty men from La Felguera on the night of the 8th. Otherwise, Gijón was told it had to wait until Oviedo fell into the rebels' hands.

Government troops arrived by sea on October 9th, and began marching from the port of El Musel through Pumarín and La Calzada, carrying out a house-to-house search where they met resistance (pillaging and terrorizing, according to rebel accounts), and using prisoners to protect their flanks. The final battle occurred in El Llano, which became one of the oft-repeated heroic myths of the revolution:

> It is quite possible that those fields had never witnessed such a sight: a small group of poorly armed men, exhausted by three days of ceaseless fighting, and, besides, disillusioned by their comrades who had not kept their promises in sending reinforcements . . . how these men contained and even pushed back, again and again, that enraged army, made up for the most part of mercenaries recruited from the lowest ranks of society.[33]

With no ammunition, five dozen fatigued militants held off an entire company for several hours until the rest of their comrades, and eventually they themselves, could retreat. Those who made it out joined the fight elsewhere in Asturias.[34]

At 4 p.m. on October 10th, the revolution ended, although the

---

[32] One witness who lived near the entrance later described this process, in which hundreds of men were herded into a corner, exposed to the rain and cold, until they were brought to the parish church for questioning: in a letter (undated) written by Adolfo M. Martínez to the Comité Regional of the CNT: (AGS, Legajo K–225).

[33] Molins i Fabrega, *La insurreción*, 111.

[34] Eleven men were found dead on the barricades in El Llano after this final battle, and some fifty people, rebels, soldiers and non-combatants, died during the October events in Gijón. This number was a small percentage of the estimated 1,600 to 2,000 deaths in the province, over half of them in Oviedo: Mateo del Peral, *Historia de Asturias*, vol. VIII, 255.

strike lasted until the 23rd. As the regiment marched from El Llano into the center, the "good citizens" came out onto their balconies to applaud the soldiers.[35] In fact, most of these citizens knew little of what had happened since that first night when the rebels were pushed back across the tracks. As a result, they had the impression that the situation had always been under control, and that "Gijón" had not been seriously affected by the rebellion.[36] Their version of the story revealed much about the physical and psychological divisions between the "two Gijóns."

To explore this division further, it is necessary to go beyond the bare-bones narrative of the fighting and focus on the support system behind the barricades in the other Gijón. Aside from building barricades, workers who did not carry arms helped organize the production and distribution of food and vital services. Thus, employees kept electricity flowing, even after managers fled the plant in El Llano. Likewise, fifty-six bakers from the Sindicato de la Alimentación rotated to keep a steady production of bread to dispense free to the neighborhood, made with flour requisitioned from warehouses by neighborhood committees.[37] When bread became scarce in other parts of the city, residents could get it in El Llano "without any other requirement than to verify their status as workers."[38] One worker corroborated this stipulation when he testified to being hired by a wealthy woman from downtown Gijón to go into El Llano and get bread for her. Apparently, she was both afraid to venture into the neighborhood and convinced that the trip would have been fruitless.[39]

Women also contributed, feeding and bandaging the men on the barricades, delivering messages, and keeping their own families nourished. Several women testified to having directly assisted the revolutionaries: one woman brought a pot of coffee to the temporary headquarters in the Guardia Civil post in El Llano, another lent dishes for the makeshift kitchen. Another woman volunteered her services as a cook and two more gave up their dinner to some hungry armed

[35] "la gente bien," in the words of conservative historian Bonet, *Biografía*, 107–108.
[36] Conservative accounts like Bonet's and *Región* tell the story this way.
[37] One baker/owner complained in his deposition that his employees had taken over his bakery and kept it operating without his family's presence until the troops entered El Llano: deposition of Ricardo Menéndez León, taken by Juzgado Eventual de Plaza núm.13, Gijón (AGS, Legajo K-270).
[38] Villar, *El anarquismo*, 148–149.
[39] Deposition of José Díaz Villanueva, a sailor who lived in one of the downtown districts: AGS, Legajo K-270.

men who happened to be passing as they sat down to eat.[40] Another account related that the cigarette makers brought cigarettes from the factory and distributed them to those on the barricades in Cima.[41] Yet another remembered some women smuggling ammunition from El Llano to Cima.[42] Commenting on the important role played by women throughout Asturias, one participant admitted his surprise at their heroism and usefulness. Before the revolution, he believed women would not actively participate, but afterwards, he realized they were just as crucial as men.[43] Some women participated in ways not so welcomed by the committee, as in the case of those who assaulted businesses in El Llano, La Calzada and El Musel for food and supplies.[44] The neighborhood committees tried to keep all transactions under their orderly control, but apparently these women decided to take matters into their own hands, following a version of the traditional consumer riot. In a sense, these women used the revolution to carry on their own private battle with the businessmen who pushed up their cost of living.

One of the most dramatic stories of popular participation that involved both men and women revolved around the disembarkation of soldiers from one of the battleships. While the captain prepared to unload his troops, he left sixty men to guard the dock, but they ended up fraternizing with residents from La Calzada and planning a mutiny. The details narrated by different chroniclers are confusing, but all versions highlight the central role played by the crowd on the docks.[45] In both stories, the mutiny ended when the *Libertad* fired on the hundreds of excited men and women on the dock, wounding an indeterminate number. Twenty-four women and thirty-six men were later arrested for instigating a riot.

Perhaps the most convincing evidence of popular support came after the rebellion ended, when residents had multiple opportunities to

---

[40] Depositions of Azmerinda Vega Cueto, a cigarette maker who lived in El Llano, Consuelo Cuesta, Rafaela González, a shop assistant, and María Luisa Casares Quidiello: AGS, Legajo K-270.

[41] Molins i Fabrega, *La insurrección*, 107.

[42] From an oral interview with Ramón Alvarez Palomo, who was twenty-one when he participated in the revolution.

[43] Manuel Grossi Mier, *La insurrección de Asturias* (1935; reprint, Madrid: Crónica General de España, 1978), 101.

[44] A number of women were arrested on December 5, 1934 for this crime: Taibo, *Asturias 1934*, vol. II, 134.

[45] For two slightly different versions, see Comité revolucionario, "Informe" (AGS, Legajo J-12), and Molins i Fabrega, *La insurrección*, 108–109.

display their sympathy for prisoners.[46] Thus, in February 1935, when open political opposition was dangerous, hundreds of women from Cimadavilla filled the courtroom where the combatants from their neighborhood were being tried.[47] Then, on February 4, 1936, when a trainload of Asturian prisoners was being transferred from Pamplona to Gijón, residents (again mostly women) jammed the station platforms and filled the streets en route to the prison. As the prisoners walked from the trucks through the prison doors, they and the crowd broke into a rousing chorus of the "Internationale," punctuated by "¡vivas!" to the revolution.[48] In these events, women, as before, seemed to play a special role in caring for society's victims and in shaming the government that was depriving families of breadwinners.

The largest demonstrations of support for the prisoners came with their release after the amnesty declared by the Popular Front. On February 20th, the local government notified the population that it would free the 900 October rebels held in the local prison. Crowds again packed the plaza in front of the prison and then marched through the streets with them, dropping them at their front doors or accompanying them to the railway station for departure to other points in Asturias. The festive atmosphere turned to mourning the following day when the body of another prisoner, CNT leader Avelino Alonso, arrived from the prison where he had died at the moment of amnesty. News of his return provoked a spontaneous strike, and by the time his casket arrived, a "mountain of people" had packed the route from the station to the cemetery, more than had turned out for anything since the inauguration of the Republic.[49]

These outpourings of support demonstrated that the October rebellion had tapped into deep popular resentments that could not be capped by putting a few thousand men behind bars and closing down

---

[46] The exact number of prisoners was never clear, since the authorities didn't want to publicize the extent of their repression. Paco Taibo estimates that between 15,000 and 18,000 people were processed throughout the whole province, most of them beaten and tortured. Of these, about 3,000 passed through the improvised prison in the Jesuit school in Gijón. Between 3,000 and 4,000 were sentenced to one year or more in prison: *Asturias 1934*, vol. II, 159.

[47] *El Noroeste*, February 25, 1935.

[48] *El Noroeste*, February 4, 1936.

[49] *El Noroeste*, February 21 and 22, 1936. Alonso's cause of death was not given, but the paper noted that he had had an accident at work at the Fábrica de Laviada a few days before the October rebellion.

the worker centers.[50] Moreover, the issue widened the gulf between the Republican government and the popular community, which always closed ranks over political prisoners. Thus, while the popular classes expressed their sympathy for the prisoners, the government received congratulations from the city's traditional elites.

For example, when government ministers visited the city on October 17, 1934 to decorate soldiers and restore morale, representatives of the city's business and professional interests[51] presented a petition that requested punishment for the guilty, an increase in troops and Civil Guards for Asturias, and aid to those whose property had been damaged. It also praised the army for saving Asturias from "total ruin," and asked that everything possible be done to prevent a replay of "these barbarous events." Among the signatories were the Employers' Association, the Association of Ship Owners, and the Property Owners' Association, all organizations that had been engaged in ongoing struggles with the city's popular forces for decades. In addition, a long list of contributors donated money to the "army of repression in Asturias." The list included all of Gijón's large industries, religious and charitable organizations, professional associations, educational institutions, and a host of small businesses.[52] The fact that the Republic was now comfortably associated with these groups was a telling sign of how far things had moved from April 1931.

Even the Popular Front city government could not erase this impression. In the confused final months before the Civil War, it did little to win back popular confidence in the regime. Furthermore, it delivered some openly mixed messages about its intentions. In particular, the staging of the last celebration of the anniversary of the Republic, on April 14th, presented a provocative narrative of local power relationships.[53] The centerpiece of the celebration was a military parade, in which troops stationed in Gijón since the revolution

---

[50] The labor movement was effectively shut down between October 1934 and February 1936, after which it began to rebuild its formal structures.

[51] The organizations represented included Agremiación Patronal, Unión de los Gremios del Comercio e Industria, Comité Local de Iniciativa, Asociación de Navieros, Asociación de Consignatarios de Buques, Defensa de Propiedad Urbana, Cámara Oficial de la Propiedad, Cámara de Comercio: *El Noroeste*, October 17, 1934.

[52] This copy of the list seems to have been the property of workers' organizations, which used it to determine political loyalties after July 1936: AGS, Legajo F-110.

[53] For accounts of the preparations and the festival, see *El Noroeste*, April 10 and 15, 1936.

marched from the statue of Reconquest hero Menéndez Pelayo to the Plaza de la República. At the plaza, their provincial commanding officer, Colonel Aranda, presented them with a republican flag and speakers called on "Asturias, cradle of the Reconquest" to defend against the "enemies of Spain." In addition to the fact that most of the rhetoric and the symbolism derived from the conservative vision of Spain, the honored guests consisted of the same group of *fuerzas vivas* that had donated money to the "army of repression." Thus, the "army of repression" marched triumphantly through the re-captured downtown streets to the applause of the city's elite representatives.

The symbolic response to this event came two weeks later, when the worker organizations staged their own show on May 1st. More than a festival, it was a collective display of strength on the part of the labor movement. For the first time since 1900, the entire union movement combined its efforts to create a powerful labor day ritual that expressed its place in the community. And in doing so, the event visualized an alternative identity for the Republic that clashed with the one presented by the regime itself. Moreover, both participants and observers seemed to understand the stakes involved. Organizers went to great lengths to plan a demonstration that transcended the traditional May 1st celebrations of the past, and observers nervously commented on the new seriousness of what was once just another holiday.[54]

The serious tone was set by the declaration of a complete general strike, which applied not just to industries but to all service businesses, including bars and cafés.[55] With this decision, the union movement made sure that the day could not devolve into a commercial celebration. In fact, *El Noroeste* criticized it on precisely those grounds, when it complained that the closure of entertainment establishments deprived this May 1st of its traditional glitter and joyfulness. Its great mistake, according to the paper, was to "prevent the general population from enjoying itself as it normally would on days of rest."[56] Of course this was exactly the point. The "general population" would be

---

[54] Thus, *El Noroeste* described its impressions: "In truth, yesterday was a unique day in Gijonese life ... because it didn't seem like a Sunday, although it was a holiday, nor did it seem like a general strike, although no one worked, and neither did it seem like any of the previous May 1sts, because it went far beyond what had been achieved before": (May 2, 1936).

[55] The joint CNT/UGT organizing commission published the plans for the event in *El Noroeste*, April 30, 1936.

[56] May 3, 1936.

forced to either join in the worker celebrations or stay inside their houses as the workers took over the city. Despite the criticism, the shutdown of economic life was a success, partly through intimidation and partly through the co-operation of groups like the Tavern Owners' Association, which published a notice urging their members to comply with the unions' request.[57]

Furthermore, the shutdown created the desired effect. Since everything was closed, the only people on the streets were the tens of thousands of workers and their families, "an impressive multitude," walking to the day's events. Their presence was further dramatized by recurrent outbursts of the "Internationale," the frequent use of the proletarian salute and the colorful red handkerchiefs worn by many. As the newspaper reported disconcertedly, this made the city look like it did during the October revolution. In other words, it represented a dramatic, if temporary, occupation of the streets by the city's poor residents. At the city hall, the marchers presented a series of resolutions, defined as the minimum aspirations of the proletariat under the Republic.[58] Consisting of a broad range of issues, most of which were included in the original goals of the "first *bienio*" coalition, the demands constituted one last challenge for the Republic to live up to its promises. The day ended after a celebratory picnic when, in contrast to a normal holiday, all the participants went home early.

More than anything else in the last months of the peacetime Republic, these two events, the anniversary of the Republic and the May 1st commemoration, demonstrated the distance between two versions of the regime that were essentially mutually incompatible. Over the course of five years, the middle ground between these two versions had eroded almost to the point of extinction. On the one hand was the "Asturias of the Reconquest" and on the other an increasingly aggressive interpretation of the "Republic of Workers." The tragic irony was that the flesh and blood Republic could neither satisfy either of these visions, nor create a compelling alternative. In this context,

---

[57] Printed in *El Noroeste*, on May 1, 1936.

[58] The full list was printed in *El Noroeste*, May 3, 1936, and included (1) punishment of those who put down the October 1934 revolution; (2) confiscation of noble lands and recovery of common lands; (3) the forty-hour week; (4) worker control in industry; (5) establishment of minimum wage; (6) nationalization of banks and basic industries; (7) re-establishment of the social legislation of the Constitution; (8) submission of banking industry to the needs of the country; (9) a serious effort to end unemployment; (10) the creation of new primary schools; (11) approval of fishing reform; and (12) access to university and professional education for working-class youths.

it was no surprise when the dueling festivals gave way to another round of armed confrontation, although no one could have predicted the unprecedented scale of violence that would ensue.

This round began when the army instigated what it expected would be a clean coup d'état, using as its rationale the assertion that the country was sliding into chaos. In particular, Asturias was singled out as a primary example of this danger. Thus, Calvo Sotelo, the CEDA deputy whose assassination provided the catalyst for the revolt, pronounced in parliament two weeks before his death that Asturias was "two steps away from anarchy."[59] In Gijón, the Reformist *El Noroeste* complained on July 10th that "here we have been living with constant strikes for months, with no end in sight and the possibility of another general strike on the horizon. Isn't it time for some reflection?"

In fact, although there were a good number of strikes in Gijón in the spring and summer of 1936, neither the quantity nor the demands were unusually intense.[60] Rather than anarchy, the strikes, along with the impressive May 1st demonstration, signified a high level of mobilization. This cycle of mobilization, based on the previous thirty years of activism, had begun with the protest in December 1930 and continued throughout the Republic, with a hiatus between the October revolution and the Popular Front election of February 1936. If they had correctly labeled the significance of the activity, the rebel officers might have thought twice in planning their coup. If the country was truly slipping into anarchy, they would have met little resistance to their revolt. But the fact that it was deeply mobilized turned an attempted coup into civil war. With this act, the mobilized and divided population entered the field of battle to directly settle the hegemonic struggle once and for all, while the Republic stood helplessly watching from the sidelines.

---

[59] Reported in the conservative newspaper *Acción*, June 27, 1936.
[60] Of the most important, several were fought over the issue of scab labor, several others over the demand to re-hire "selected" workers, another to impose the forty-four-hour working week, and another to force employers to implement new conditions agreed on before the October 1934 revolution.

Conclusion

~

After years of hegemonic struggle, the outbreak of civil war in July 1936[1] finally gave "smoke-darkened" Gijón the opportunity, albeit briefly, to wrest power from the hands of the elites and embark on a revolutionary experiment in popular empowerment. The experiment was constrained by political infighting, by the exigencies of the war and by lack of resources. Aborted before it reached maturity and crippled by problems outside local control, it is impossible to predict how it would have continued to evolve. What is clear, however, is that the aspirations of the regime echoed those articulated over several decades of mobilization by a variety of popular groups and organizations. The revolution that unfolded contained elements of anarchism, socialism, republicanism and even communism, but what seemed to drive it was not any specific ideology but the familiar struggle for community empowerment and the little man's/woman's right to equal citizenship and a decent life. From this perspective, the political

---

[1] The rumors of the uprising in Morocco arrived in Gijón on the night of the 18th. City authorities and trade union federations met to form a defensive plan, and notified the rest of the city by setting off the sirens of all the factories and the boats in the harbor. Two days later, on July 20th, several of the military units stationed in the city left their barracks to seize the city for the rebels, thus marking the official start of the Civil War in Gijón. The delayed local rebellion favored the republican loyalists, who had time to organize their defense, but the last of the rebels were not defeated until August 21st. From that date until October 20, 1937, the city was in the hands of the anti-Francoist forces. For a basic account of the uprising and its initial defeat, see Diego Mateo del Peral *et al.*, *Historia de Asturias*, vols. VIII and IX: *Edad Contemporánea I* (Vitoria: Ayalga Ediciones, 1977), 274–277. On the war in Asturias, see Juan Antonio Cabezas, *Asturias: catorce meses de guerra civil* (Madrid: G. del Toro, 1975).

experiment of 1936–1937 was both the culmination of and the response to a long tradition of popular mobilization.

Taking the lead in this experiment was the CNT, whose rhetoric of polarization captured the mood of a city and country at war with itself.[2] Once the military uprising opened the floodgates of political change, the already weak republican legitimacy collapsed and the more powerful leftist forces pushed forward with their urgent vision of change. *De facto* power shifted immediately, when the trade unions organized the physical defense of the city from the military rebels, and even after the surrender of the rebels on August 21st, the republicans never regained more than an auxiliary status in the regime. Signaling the bankruptcy of the politics of integration, the revolutionary regime embraced the politics of polarization as the route to popular empowerment.

However, the political dominance of the CNT did not translate into a broader anarchist hegemony over the revolution in Gijón. Instead of an anarchist utopia, the "home front" policies of the new regime reflected the eclectic agenda that had fueled popular protests for decades. Thus, where the war allowed it, the government focused on improving the quality of life for the city's poorer residents and on ensuring a fairer distribution of goods and services, both economic and cultural. From entertainment to education, to urban planning and

---

[2] The other revolutionary forces – the Socialist party and the Communists – also competed for control, which produced some of the factional infighting that proved so debilitating to the republican cause. However, in Gijón this jockeying for position never consumed the home front as it did, for example, in Barcelona, where the Communists and their allies became strong enough to provoke and win a showdown in the streets. The classic accounts of this showdown, which culminated in May 1937, are George Orwell, *Homage to Catalonia* (London: Secker and Warburg, 1938), and Burnett Bolloten, *The Grand Camouflage: The Communist Conspiracy in the Spanish Civil War* (London: Hollis and Carter, 1961). Both accounts are highly critical of the Communists. In Asturias, the Communists lobbied for their national agenda of the unification (read "absorption") of the Socialist and Communist parties, as well as the fusion of the CNT and UGT into a great "Central Unified Syndicate of the Working Class" (the first issue of *Asturias*, July 22, 1937 lays this out), but were extremely cautious in criticizing their powerful rivals. See, for example, the vague rhetoric of the Communist mouthpieces, *Asturias* (July 1937) and *Boletín del Norte* (August through November 1937). The CNT thus remained the most powerful player in local politics, in apparently close co-operation with the Socialists: in December 1936, local UGT and CNT federations signed a pact that guaranteed "freedom of association" in either camp, and that promised maximum courtesy in their interactions (*El Comercio*, December 13, 1936), months before the signing of a similar national pact in Valencia in July 1937. Then, in 1937, both regional federations took up the question of a deeper alliance. In April, the UGT congress voiced its approval for such a union, and in June the CNT congress did the same, at an emotional session where invited UGT speakers were warmly applauded and everyone embraced (*Avance*, June 1–3, 1937). Apparently no formal agreement was signed before the war ended in Asturias.

the production and consumption of goods, the regime experimented with ways to overcome the marginalization of the masses and move them from the periphery to the center of local power relations.[3] For the city's popular residents, the Civil War represented the culmination of this struggle, not the abstract stand-off between revolution and counter-revolution.[4]

The intimate stakes of the Civil War were reinforced by the isolation of Asturias during most of the fifteen months of revolutionary control. By the end of August 1936, the Asturian front had stabilized, into a western nationalist zone and an eastern republican zone that included the mining basin and the cities of Avilés and Gijón. The only ground still hotly contested was Oviedo, where victorious rebel troops successfully resisted efforts to recapture the city. With Oviedo in the enemy camp for the duration of the war, Gijón became the *de facto* capital of an Asturias that was isolated geographically and thus institutionally from the bulk of loyalist territory in the south and east, and even politically from the neighboring governments in Santander and the Basque provinces. Thus, the Civil War comprised a number of local and regional conflicts that only nominally added up to a national civil war. As in the peacetime Republic, the fragmentation of political life in Spain enhanced the importance of local political boundaries and dynamics.

Despite the deep roots of Gijón's oppositional tradition, in the end the popular community was overwhelmed by the invasion of nationalist armies from outside the province. At that point, the political culture

---

[3] The ambitious goals of the city government included a comprehensive urban renewal plan to provide the working-class neighborhoods with sanitation services, paved streets and parks; the completion of new schools; a unified cultural policy that aimed to provide free access to a wide range of entertainment and public art; and a visual symbolic transformation of the city through the creation of new official seals, coats-of-arms, and, of course, street names. The economic policies of the regime concentrated on ensuring universal consumption of basic goods, depending on need rather than ability to pay, and, in the realm of production, on the twin goals of worker empowerment and productivity. None of these plans or policies conformed with any coherent ideological framework: the economy combined private ownership with public or union control and distribution, public culture included the same mix of revolutionary polemics, local folklore, anti-clericalism and international mass culture that existed before the war, and political culture in general reflected elements of both the workerist revolutionary culture and the republican civic culture. The result was a heterogeneous political culture that shared a vague commitment to "modernity," "progress," and the "people," as well as a violent rejection of "tradition."

[4] Evidence about popular concerns can be found in accounts of numerous delegations of private individuals and groups who visited the mayor's office and registered their requests and demands. Petitions covered a wide range of issues, but tended to cluster around two areas: neighborhood improvement and consumption.

that drew its strength from the intimacy of the urban nucleus proved no match for an enemy that relied on the discipline and efficiency of its troops, not from its community rootedness. Thus, it was finally military prowess, unmediated by the subtleties of hegemonic persuasion, that put an end to the long power struggle. By September of 1937, after the Basque country and Santander had fallen and the Nationalists were marching through republican Asturias, Gijón became increasingly preoccupied with the war, with refugees pouring in from the east, and finally with evacuation. On October 17th, the provincial authorities in Gijón decided that further resistance was useless and prepared the final evacuation of government officials and militia. Those who did not leave on the 20th fled to the mountains, where some of them fought as guerrillas for more than a decade. On the next afternoon, the conquering army entered without firing a shot.

The significance of the conquest was immediately apparent. In the first issue of the restored *El Comercio*, the editors announced the victory in the language of polarization: "One of the Spains is now finished: that of trade unions and of sterile partisan politics. The other Spain, with its unified political strength, is now beginning."[5] Over the next several weeks, a constant stream of well-wishers stopped in at the city hall to affirm their allegiance to this Spain, including representatives from the Urban Property Owners' Association, the Chamber of Commerce, the Merchants' Association, the Employers' Association, the Bank of Bilbao, the Union of Ship Outfitters, and all the prominent local businessmen. To celebrate the victory of the "true" Spain, the authorities staged a series of military parades and public masses, the most dramatic of which paid tribute to the Nationalist soldiers who held out until August 1936. It began with a mass in the square outside the building, followed by a military parade, several thousand strong, and a solemn dedication of a poem written for the heroes: "From heaven they watch, on their knees, worshipping Jesus at his altar, the army of fervent crusaders."[6]

And thus, the monarchist/clerical elites reasserted their domination in Gijón, executing with the sword what they could not do in more than three decades of hegemonic struggle. Instead of accommodating to the world of mass politics, they imposed a forty-year dictatorship that successfully demobilized the population. Even with the transition

---

[5] November 7, 1937.
[6] *El Comercio*, November 18, 1937.

308

to a democratic regime, the demobilization has not been effectively reversed, either in Gijón or in Spain at large. While this situation has, somewhat ironically, made the elite-dominated transition a smoother process, it has been at the cost of sapped political energy and a decline in direct participation. In contrast, Gijón through the Civil War reminds us what it is like when ordinary people are passionately involved in the ongoing political struggles of everyday life.

The demobilization imposed by the Franco regime thus ended a cycle of mobilization that was triggered by the hegemonic break of 1898 and culminated in the Civil War. In stark terms, the Civil War signified Spain's failure to channel or incorporate this mobilization into an institutionally viable form of mass politics. Instead of achieving political integration, the country developed an increasingly polarized political culture that resisted all efforts at stabilization until military force imposed an authoritarian solution. Understanding the progression from initial mobilization to Civil War – from the perspective of an expansive model of political culture – has been the central focus of this case study.

To this end, the first chapter began in 1900, against the backdrop of a stagnant Restoration regime, in which popular participation had been effectively stifled for twenty-five years. The rest of the chapters then explored the mechanisms of mass mobilization and the various attempts to organize that mobilization around specific hegemonic projects. On the one hand, the republicans attempted to transform an elite liberal parliamentary system into a democratic polity in which all the citizens would feel a legitimate stake in the political order. On the other hand, the labor movement offered a class-based revolutionary politics that operated through direct mobilization instead of parliamentary government. While the exact combination of republican and anarchist forces was specific to Gijón, some version of these two projects defined the counter-hegemonic options in early-twentieth-century Spain.

For either political force to succeed, it had to capture the loyalty of the urban working classes, who suffered from economic, physical, political and social marginalization in the elite power structure of the old regime. While these concrete forms of exploitation did not dictate any particular political formation, as predicated by the traditional Marxist model of class consciousness, they were not irrelevant either. In fact, in Gijón and presumably other urban centers, they provided the building blocks of a popular community that emerged out of a mix of common urban problems, segregation, and networks rooted in the daily realities of a segregated culture. Without addressing or at least seeming to address some of the real problems of this community, no political group could hope to win and maintain a mass constituency.

Thus, as Chapters 4 and 5 argued, the republicans' inability to turn the municipal government into an instrument of social and economic reform, even during the Republic, seriously limited their credibility as populist democrats. Historians have often argued about whether the Republic was weakened by too much social reform or too little, but the debate usually revolves around national legislation. As this study demonstrates, however, the variation in local implementation makes such categorical positions problematic. Whatever was planned in Madrid, in Gijón there were few concrete reforms that could have legitimized the democratic government.

Furthermore, this failure increased the appeal of the anarchosyndicalists, who claimed to practice a form of direct democracy that bypassed corrupt institutions. Despite the CNT's avowed apoliticism, however, it played a complex political role that perfectly suited the available political space in the city. Instead of challenging the republicans for governmental control, the CNT alternated between quiet co-operation with the republicans and declarations of principled opposition to all forms of government. In this way, the anarchosyndicalist labor movement kept access to legal channels open while avoiding responsibility for political failure. In contrast, the Socialists shared none of these advantages. They were forced to compete with the republicans for electoral supremacy and faced the burden of justifying participation in a system that delivered few benefits to their followers.

Significantly, because of the decentralization of Spanish political culture, the dynamic between republicans, anarchosyndicalists and Socialists took different forms depending on the local political context, making it hard to generalize about the larger impact of each political force and the role it played in Spain's political crisis. Thus, for example, global arguments that blame or acquit the anarchists for the failure of Spanish democracy have little substance at the level of grassroots politics. What is true, however, is that where anarchosyndicalism took root, it encouraged – although did not create – the kind of direct mass mobilization that has been difficult to contain within the institutional framework of representative government. It was this capacity for direct action, more than its revolutionary ideology, that the CNT contributed to the political culture of early-twentieth-century Spain. The struggle between republicans and the labor movement for popular affirmation extended beyond the realm of formal politics and into the public sphere, especially in the growing urban centers like Gijón where an independent civil society was taking shape. Both groups attempted to "structure attention" in the public sphere by channeling the energies of an emerging urban sociability towards their broader political goals. Thus, through voluntary associations, a partisan press, and a secularization campaign, the republicans sought to instill their values and create a republican public capable of responsible democratic citizenship. Likewise, the labor movement endeavored to construct a proletarian public sphere, in which workers would participate in a range of educational and leisure activities that reinforced their political class identity and prepared them for the future seizure of power. Neither the republicans nor the labor movement, however, succeeded in transforming the public sphere – either locally or nationally – in their own image. In comparative terms, the republicans erected a more coherent and pervasive oppositional culture in their local strongholds, particularly in their successful secularization of public life. In fact, the labor movement absorbed many basic republican values into its own associational culture, and never fully articulated an alternative proletarian sphere that could be clearly distinguished from a diffuse democratic culture. The result was a heterogeneous oppositional culture that was powerful enough in places like Gijón to crowd out the dominant Catholic culture, but not focused enough to provide a foundation for a new social order. At the national level, this oppositional culture was even weaker and more confused.

This cultural confusion was especially crucial during the Republic, when the new regime desperately needed symbols of unity to overcome its many weaknesses. With neither a strong program of economic and social reform nor a unifying cultural idiom, the republicans were left with little to sustain their popular leadership. However, the anarchosyndicalists could not claim hegemonic leadership either. Their political and economic muscle made them well placed to seize power in local strongholds like Gijón in the summer of 1936, but their goal of a full-fledged social revolution required more preparation – i.e., the transformation of public values and attitudes that took place largely in the public sphere. Without a strongly articulated proletarian public sphere before July 1936, the cultural framework for a revolutionary transformation of society was not in place. As a result, the wartime Republic retained a heterogeneous political culture that pursued no single hegemonic agenda. Thus, the three-way hegemonic struggle that had opened in 1898 ended inconclusively, leaving the final outcome to be decided on the battlefield.

One of the consequences of this inconclusive battle in Gijón was that no hegemonic force completely absorbed or co-opted the city's tradition of popular mobilization. Thus, as the final two chapters demonstrated, the city's rich pattern of collective action retained multiple sources and configurations. Often rooted in the networks of daily life that were constructed in neighborhoods and social activities, an informal tradition of direct action took shape alongside, and sometimes in conjunction with, the more formal protests of political parties and trade unions. The informal tradition focused on specific and practical concerns relating to the basic quality of life for the city's poorer residents, and protests often evolved through *ad hoc* alliances that coalesced around discrete issues and then dissolved until the next crisis. Participants included both men and women, but the presence of women is more notable because of their marginalization from other forms of political action.

What is the significance of this informal and gendered tradition of collective action that was never fully contained within the institutional parameters of the two major oppositional groups? First, it demonstrates the high level of mobilization in urban centers like Gijón in pre-Civil War Spain. While discontent with the status quo exists in many places, only mobilized discontent poses a serious political problem for the established order. And if extensive mobilization protrudes beyond the bounds of a few organizations, as it did in Gijón, its containment is even more problematic. Although it has often been pointed out that Spain's high level of mobilization contributed to political destabilization in the 1930s, this broader vision of political culture reveals the true scope of the challenge to the existing Catholic/ monarchist order.

And while this study focuses on only one city, it is based on the assumption that informal popular mobilization was a common feature of urban life during this period. Instead of disappearing with the advent of mass political parties and trade unions, direct community activism continued to provide an alternate form of political mobilization in the twentieth-century city. One could argue, in fact, that the

"new social movements" that appeared in the 1960s were a new version of this activist tradition, and should be understood as part of a
historical continuum.[7] During the Franco era, for example, neighborhood associations were important centers of opposition to the
regime.[8] Moreover, such opposition was a more effective weapon in an
authoritarian regime in which independent political parties and trade
unions were outlawed. Thus, instead of an anachronistic or pre-
modern form of politics, this type of sub-institutional, cross-class
mobilization has remained an important part of the repertoire of
modern mass politics.

Moreover, it enhances our understanding of modern mass politics
by bringing new and sometimes conflicting voices to the surface. In
Gijón, for example, these voices expose some of the populist limitations of the anarchosyndicalist and republican projects. Thus, the
consumer riots that demanded fixed prices and controlled exports
exposed the economic boundaries of the republicans' populism. Their
refusal to compromise principles of liberal individualism for community interest put them at odds with the strong communitarian ethic
displayed in these protests. Similarly, the protests that united different
economic groups, like owners and customers or consumers and producers, revealed the limitations of the labor movement's class-based
organization to represent the diversity of popular concerns. And
finally, the informal activism of many poor women, who repeatedly
took to the streets to defend their interests, reveals the failure of both
republicans and anarchosyndicalists to articulate a political vision that
could incorporate half the population. Instead of being apolitical or
clerical dupes, poor women were available political actors whose energies were not successfully tapped by either movement. These gaps
nicely illustrate the limitations of both counter-hegemonic projects
and their totalizing paradigms for a new Spain. In the process, they
help explain why the long struggle to define the country's political
future could not be resolved peacefully.

[7] As Christopher Johnson briefly points out, while progressives like Habermas have celebrated the potential of the "new social movements" and their "quality of life" issues,
few have acknowledged the presence of these types of movements in the past, during the
heyday of trade unionism: "Lifeworld, System and Communicative Action: The Habermasian Alternative in Social History," in *Rethinking Labor History*, ed. Lenard Berlanstein
(Urbana: University of Illinois Press, 1993), 83–84.
[8] On these associations, see Manuel Castells, "The Making of an Urban Social Movement:
the Citizen Movement in Madrid Towards the End of the Francoist Era," in *The City and
the Grassroots: A Cross-Cultural Theory of Urban Social Movements* (Berkeley: University of
California Press, 1983).

What, then, does Gijón's story tell us about the origins of the Civil War in Spain? Was the Civil War the inevitable result of long-term social and economic fissures or the product of short-term political mistakes that could have been avoided? Like most dichotomies, neither extreme provides a satisfactory explanation. On the one hand, Gijón provides ample evidence of the importance of long-term social and economic tensions. As part of the "modernizing" sector of Spanish society, Gijón illustrated the potential of economic and social change to disrupt and challenge the political order. Without growing urban centers like Gijón to furnish a fertile environment for mass mobilization, the pressure on the stagnant Restoration regime would not have been nearly as great. On the other hand, Gijón's experience demonstrates the importance of short-term political factors. Thus, the gulf between the two counter-hegemonic forces did not become unbridgeable until after 1931, when the political paths taken by republicans and anarchosyndicalists became increasingly incompatible.

What the book emphasizes, however, is the long-term evolution of Spain's political crisis after the turning point of 1898. In a period marked by hegemonic confusion and high levels of popular mobilization, no political force could successfully harness the mass political energy within a stable hegemonic framework. Furthermore, in a country that lacked significant political integration, neither force could create a national political culture that could unify the nation behind a common identity. From this perspective, Gijón's experience provides a grass-roots view of the crisis, an opportunity to peel away all the layers of hegemonic conflict and reveal its impact on the lives of ordinary men and women. The result is a social history of a polarizing society as it made the tumultuous journey from mobilization to civil war.

Appendix 1

Wage and price movement

~

Wages for typical occupations in Asturias and Gijón during the period covered by the book are listed in Tables 1.1 and 1.2. To gauge the rise in wages between 1914 and 1930, I calculated an estimate of the mean for each range. I assumed that the spread of maximum and minimum wages was a greater reflection of the spread between masters and journeymen than that between masters in different workshops. Following this assumption, I decided to set the mean at one-third above the minimum wage, since there should be fewer masters than journeymen. That is, if we could plot the curve of all painters' wages, it would probably be weighted toward the lower wage. With the mean wage for each category I set the index at the 1914 means and calculated the relative increase in wages (Table 1.3). Although this index provides a general picture of wage movement, it is still limited. It does not tell us how people at the bottom or top of each profession fared, a distinction which appeared increasingly important after 1919. That is, the trend over the 1920s seems to be towards a greater spread within professions. While top wages rose consistently, the minimum wages moved more unevenly, even dropping in 1930 in the construction industry. So, although the table can yield general information about wages, it cannot give us insight into any individual worker's fate.

Serial price movements are available on a yearly basis from 1909 in the *Anuario Estadístico de España*. However, it is more difficult to determine their applicability to Gijón. Whereas the *Anuario* included wage schedules for Oviedo, most of the price schedules are based on averages calculated from

315

Table 1.1 *Wages in Asturias, 1885–1902 (pesetas per day)*

	1885	1902
stonecutters	3.0	5.0–6.0
masons	3.0	4.5–5.0
carpenters	3.0	4.5–5.0
fitters	2.5–4.0	4.0–6.0
blacksmiths	2.5–4.0	4.0–6.0
molders	3.0–4.0	4.5–5.0
boilermakers	2.5–4.0	5.0–6.0
painters	2.5–3.0	4.0–5.0
typesetters	2.5–3.0	–
shoemakers	2.5–3.0	–
founders (metal)	3.0–3.5	4.5–5.5
tinsmiths	2.5–3.0	3.5–4.25
printers	2.5–3.0	3.5–4.25
bakers	2.25–2.5	3.5–3.75
factory boys	0.25–1.0	1.5–2.0
women in factories	0.85–1.0	1.25–2.0
loaders	1.5–2.0	5.0
dockworkers	3.5	5.0

Source: Angeles Barrio Alonso, *El anarquismo en Gijón* (Gijón: Silverio Cañada, 1982), 71 and 74.

Table 1.2 *Average wages in Oviedo, 1914–1931 (pesetas per day)*

	1914	1919	1925	1926	1931
metalworkers	4–4.5	8–10	8–12	9–12	9–13
blacksmiths	3.5–4	6–8	–	6–10	6.5–13
masons	4–4.5	8–10	8.5–10	8.5–10	6.5–13
carpenters	3–4	4–6.5	8.5–11	8.5–12	6–13
stonecutters	3–4.5	4.5–7	8.5–10	8.5–12	8–13
painters	2.5–4	5–6	6–10	6–10	6–12
shoemakers	2.75–3.1	5–8	5–8.5	5–10	5–12
tailors	2.25–4.5	5–8	5.5–10	6–12	5–12
dressmakers, seamstresses	1–1.5	2–3.5	4–6	4–6	3–9
cabinetmakers	–	–	8–12	8–12	8–13
mechanical sawyers	–	–	8–10	8–10	7–13
glassmakers	–	–	8.5–12	–	–

Source: *Anuario Estadístico de España*, 1915, 1920, 1927, 1932.

Table 1.3 *Relative index for wages, Oviedo, 1914–1930*
(1914 = 100)

	1919	1925	1930	1931
metalworkers	208	223	240	247
blacksmiths	182	198	218	236
masons	208	216	200	208
carpenters	145	278	240	250
stonecutters	152	257	257	276
painters	178	244	267	267
shoemakers	209	215	279	255
tailors	200	233	267	244
dressmakers and seamstresses	214	399	427	427

national data. Prices are divided into lists for "provincial capitals" and "everything else," with the former consistently (and understandably) reporting higher figures. I chose the capital (i.e. urban) price index, which should be a closer reflection of Gijón's reality. Nevertheless, capitals across Spain must have had vastly different food supply problems; for example, fish should be cheaper in Valencia, while olive oil should cost less in Seville. The price schedule itself gives a range for each item, which is often minimal but occasionally substantial. When the range was small, I followed the maximum prices over the years for greater consistency. For those items with a large range, I took the median price so as not to have my results affected by extremes which could have been flukes.

To supplement the national urban index, I used prices from other sources, although they are not always consistent with one another. In addition to the "capitals" index, the *Anuario* includes price schedules for the city of Oviedo for the years 1914 and 1919. For the earlier years I use figures which Tuñón de Lara has extracted from the *Boletín del IRS* for 1900 and 1908 (presumably national figures), as well as a set of local prices given at a bread rally in 1908 and the *Anuario* prices of 1909 for comparison. As is apparent from Table 1.4, the figures do not always match.

With such a variety of price schedules, I chose to use the Tuñón de Lara statistics from 1900 and 1908 to form an index (Table 1.5), since presumably the data is comparable. I also included García Arenal's data from 1885, although its comparability is probably not so reliable.

Because the Tuñón de Lara schedule is not directly comparable with the *Anuario* prices, I decided to start another and separate index in 1913, just before the war. Since the *Anuario* schedules show fairly stable prices between 1909 and 1914, I assumed that prices were probably stable in Gijón as well, even if I could not deduce the absolute value of those prices. Between 1914

317

Table 1.4 *Composite prices, 1885–1909 (quantities in kg unless noted otherwise)*

	1885	1900	1908[a]	1908[b]	1909
beef	1.28	2.00	2.60	2.10	1.60–1.79
bacon	2.00	1.75	2.20	2.40	–
sardines	0.62	0.85	1.05	–	–
cod	–	1.10	1.60	–	1.27–1.28
rice	–	0.70	0.75	0.90	0.56–0.58
garbanzos	–	1.05	1.20	1.30	0.79–0.89
green beans	–	0.70	0.75	0.70	–
potatoes	0.15	0.15	0.20	0.19	0.13–0.14
vegetables	–	0.23	0.30	–	–
oil (liter)	1.20	1.20	1.65	1.60	1.40–1.52
coke	–	0.08	0.08	–	–
eggs (12)	1.00	1.11	1.14	–	1.16–1.31
milk (liter)	0.25	0.50	0.70	–	0.42–0.44
bread	0.32	0.50	0.40	0.50	0.37–0.40
coal	–	0.20	0.19	0.18	–
hake (fish)	–	2.65	1.75	–	–
wine (*arroba*)	–	7.00	5.00	–	–
wine (liter)	–	–	–	0.25	0.30–0.33

Sources: 1885: Fernando García Arenal, *Datos para el estudio de la cuestión social* (1885; reprint, Gijón: Silverio Cañada, 1980).
1900 and 1908*a*: M. Tuñón de Lara, *El movimiento obrero en la historia de España* (Madrid: Taurus, 1972).
1908*b*: *El Noroeste*, May 21, 1909, statistics given by city councilmen Benito Conde and Ramón Alvarez García at a bread rally.
1909: *Anuario Estadístico de España*, 1915.

and 1919 I again have two sets of data to compare – the *Anuario*'s average national prices (all of Spain this time) and the same price data for the city of Oviedo in 1914 and 1919: see Table 1.6. Again, major differences do exist between the local and national data, a fact which dictates caution in using national data indiscriminately.

To gauge price rises from 1914 to 1934, I calculated one index for Oviedo only, for 1914–1919 (Table 1.7), and then another, more complete, using national urban data from the *Anuario Estadístico*, for the years 1913, 1920, 1925, 1930 and 1933/1934 (Table 1.8). Again, I assume that each index will be internally sufficiently consistent to accurately measure the general trend which prices followed.

Finally, I include the information on "market basket" estimates from two

Table 1.5 *Composite price index, 1885–1908 (1900 = 100)*

	1885	1908
beef	64	130
bacon	114	126
sardines	73	124
cod	–	145
rice	–	107
garbanzos	–	114
green beans	–	107
potatoes	100	133
vegetables	–	130
oil	96	128
coke	–	100
eggs	90	103
milk	50	140
bread	80	100
coal	–	95

Table 1.6 *Average annual prices, 1914–1919 (n = national,*
l = local, i.e. Oviedo)

	1914 (n)	1914 (l)	1919 (n)	1919 (l)
bacon	1.99–3.48	1.95–2.50	4.20–4.76	4.15–5.25
sardines	0.80–1.00	0.60–1.00	1.48–2.23	2.90–3.50
green beans	0.92–1.04	0.50–0.70	0.62–1.35	0.90–1.25
lentils	0.70–0.90	0.40–0.50	0.78–1.15	0.95–1.30
coke	0.05–0.07	0.04–0.045	0.15–0.17	0.09–0.10
coal (mineral)	0.04–0.05	0.03–0.02	0.14–0.18	0.04–0.05
coal (vegetal)	0.14–0.16	0.11–0.15	0.20–0.25	0.17–0.20
cod	–	0.75–1.00	3.75–4.50	–
bread	0.44	0.35–0.45	0.58–0.66	0.65–0.80
milk	0.52–0.62	0.10–0.15(?)	0.56–0.82	0.35–0.60
rice	0.79–1.00	0.60–0.85	0.80–1.22	0.90–1.00
garbanzos	1.02–1.32	0.75–1.25	0.90–1.84	1.25–1.50
potatoes	0.18–0.23	0.07–0.25	0.29–0.39	0.32–0.55
salt	–	0.07–0.15	–	0.20–0.30
eggs	–	0.95–1.50	–	2.25–5.50
sugar	–	0.95–1.25	–	1.50–2.10
wine	–	0.40–0.55	–	0.60–0.75
oil	–	1.00–1.25	–	1.65–2.00

Source:*Anuario Estadístico de España*, 1920.

Table 1.7 *Price index for Oviedo, 1914–1919 (1914 prices = 100)*

bacon	217
sardines	400
green beans	178
lentils	224
coke	224
coal (mineral)	170
coal (vegetal)	142
cod	460
bread	180
milk	390(?)
common fish	286
rice	132
garbanzos	137
potatoes	233
salt	245
eggs	305
sugar	164
wine	143
oil	167

Table 1.8 *Price index, 1913–1934 (provincial capitals of Spain)*
(1913 prices = 100)

	1920	1925	1930	1933/1934
bread	181	157	155	160
beef	220	220	210	220
cod	178	170	153	150
potatoes	153	158	158	150
garbanzos	163	163	151	151
rice	151	154	134	134
wine	169	138	153	102
milk	146	153	153	151
eggs	203	200	190	169
sugar	233	165	156	150
oil	159	160	132	130

sources, according to their notions of a subsistence diet: García Arenal from 1885, and Dr. Alfredo Pico from 1909 (*El Noroeste*, May 23, 1909).

García Arenal's subsistence diet (1885) (adult male input/day):

800 g bread
394 g potatoes
73 g meat
36 g fish
26 cl milk
30 g bacon
17 cl oil
one egg

Wives were supposed to consume four-fifths of the man's daily ration, while each child was slated for two-thirds. Calculated according to 1885 prices, a family of five should spend 2.4450 pts./day for basic foodstuffs, and 2.745 pts./day including fuel for cooking and condiments.

Alfredo Pico designed a more basic subsistence allowance for an adult male:

1,190 g bread
414 g meat
93 g fat

He then describes a typical meal for one adult:

breakfast: an onion omelette, bread
lunch: *garbanzos*, meat, pork fat, potatoes, bread
dinner: sardines, bread

He calculates portions and prices of each of these ingredients, and concludes that a family of three would spend 2.58 pts./day on food. If we include two more children, his family of five would spend 3.62 pts./day. Furthermore, Pico only allocates to children just over half (52%) of their father's allowance, rather than a two-thirds portion. If we re-calculate based on two-thirds for a child, the 1909 family of five would spend 4.12 pts./day on food, about a 50% rise from 1885.

Appendix 2

Occupations by status category

comandante marina (director, marine traffic)
odontólogo (teeth doctor)
naviero (ship owner, outfitter)
abogado (lawyer)
juzgado (judge)
arquitecto (architect)
ingeniero (engineer)

farmacéutico (pharmacist)
médico (doctor)
cónsul (diplomat)
profesor (professor)
catedrático (full professor)
dentista (dentist)
rentista (rentier)
teniente (lieutenant)

UPPER/LOWER MIDDLE CLASS (DIFFICULT TO DISTINGUISH)

escultor (sculptor)
artista (painter)
owner of *carbonería* (coal outlet)
industrial (factory or workshop owner)

almacenero (warehouse owner)
labrador (farmer)
comerciante (businessman)
constructor (builder)

LOWER MIDDLE CLASS

representante (agent)
oficial de marina (shipping bureaucrat)
oficial (bureaucrat)
navegante (navigator)
piloto (pilot)
notario (notary)

oficial de aduanas (customs official)
boticario (druggist)
músico (musician)
maestro (teacher)
cocinero (cook)
periodista (journalist)
barbero (barber)

contratista (contractor)
tabernero (tavern owner)
comisionista (merchant)
procurador (solicitor)
practicante (nurse)
tratante (dealer, retailer)
gestor (manager)
guardia (policeman)
carcelero (jailor)
práctico de puerto (harbor pilot)
encargado (manager)
capataz (foreman)
estanquero (tobacconist)

hostelero (innkeeper)
fondista (innkeeper)
funcionario público (bureaucrat)
ganadero (livestock breeder)
agente ejecutivo (tax assessor)
factor (salesman)
secretario judicial (legal secretary)
vinatero (wine dealer)
viajante (traveling salesman)
mayordomo (steward)
sereno (night watchman)
carabinero (rifleman)
cabo (non-commissioned officer)

WHITE COLLAR

contable (accountant)
oficinista (office worker)
cartero (postman)
dibujante (draftsman)
delineante (draftsman)

escribiente (scribe)
empleado (clerk)
conserje (concierge)
mecanógrafo (typist)
dependiente (store clerk)

SKILLED MANUAL LABORERS

sillero (chair maker)
hornero (baker)
diamantista (diamond cutter)
artes gráficas (graphic artist)
carnicero (butcher)
tablajero (butcher)
laminador (laminator – metals)
matarife (slaughterer)
bombero (fireman)
metalúrgico (metalworker)
botellero (bottlemaker)
marmolista (marble worker)
tornero (lathe operator)
gasista (gas worker)
tintorero (dyer)
afilador (knife sharpener)
litógrafo (lithographer)
tallista (wood carver)
platero (silversmith)

tapicero (carpet maker)
chalequera (jacket maker)
fundidor (smelter)
cochero (coachman)
calderero (boilerman)
zapatero (shoemaker)
pintor (painter)
ebanista (cabinet maker)
moldeador (molder)
modelista (pattern maker)
vidriero (glass maker)
joyero (jeweler)
tipógrafo (printer)
mecánico (mechanic)
cajista (typesetter)
tranviario (tram operator)
peluquero (hair stylist)
electricista (electrician)
hojalatero (tinsmith)

323

sastre (tailor)
carretero (cartwright)
cerrajero (locksmith)
panadero (baker)
aparejador (rigger)
maquinista (machinist)
albañil (mason)
chófer (chauffeur)
pescador (fisherman)
camarero (waiter)
soldador (welder)
carpintero (carpenter)
labrante (carver)
herrero (blacksmith)
forjador (forger)
impresor (printer)
mampostero (rubble mason)
maestro obrero (master artisan)
confitero (confectioner)

chocolatero (chocolate maker)
alfarero (potter)
botero (maker of *bota* bags)
cantero (stonecutter)
sombrerero (hat maker)
aserrador (sawyer)
relojero (clockmaker)
corsetero (corset maker)
esmaltador (enameler)
escalerista (stair builder)
curtidor (tanner)
latonero (brass worker)
cigarrera (cigarette maker)
tejero (tile maker)
modista (dress maker)
bordadora (embroiderer)
tornero mecánico (electric lathe operator)

SEMI-SKILLED MANUAL LABORERS

aprendiz (apprentice)
limpiabotas (shoeshiner)
asistente (assistant)
cocedor (boiler room worker)
fogonero (stoker)
marino (seaman)
picapedrero (quarry worker)
ferroviario (rail worker)
pitillera (cigarette maker)

marinero (sailor)
planchadora (ironer)
encuadernador (packer)
peinadora (hair stylist)
lavandera (clothes washer)
tejedora (weaver)
hiladora (spinner)
costurera (seamstress)

UNSKILLED MANUAL LABORERS

operario (worker)
obrero (worker)
jornalero (day worker)
barredor (street cleaner)
bracero (day laborer)

peón (assistant)
pinche (assistant)
cargador (stevedore)
corredor (runner)

The following methodological sources were used to determine categories:

Donald J. Treiman, "A Standard Occupational Prestige Scale for Use with Historical Data," *Journal of Interdisciplinary History*, 7:2 (Autumn 1976)

Erik Olin Wright, "Class and Occupation," *Theory and Society*, 9:1 (January 1980)

W. A. Armstrong, "The Use of Information About Occupation," in *Nineteenth Century Society*, ed. E.A.Wrigley (Cambridge: Cambridge University Press, 1972).

Appendix 3

Supplementary tables

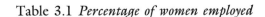

Table 3.1 *Percentage of women employed*

	Wives	Female adult children[a]	Female heads of households
Gijón			
1900	7.5%	14.6%	32.0%
1930	2.0%	17.0%	16.0%
Working-class neighborhoods			
1900	11.0%	18.3%	40.0%
1930	3.0%	15.0%	10.4%

[a]Includes only those who lived at home, and not the live-in domestic workers, who were also largely unmarried.
Source: Archivo Municipal de Gijón: *Censos de la Población.*

Table 3.2 *Residence of members of the PRLD and far right parties in Gijón*

	Falange	AP	PRLD
Center	63%	53%	57%
Center, rural *aldeas* and El Arenal	77%	76%	72%
Working-class areas	9%	10%	12%

Sizes of the lists are: 820 Acción Popular (AP) members, 301 PRLD members, 224 Falangists.
AGS, F-110 and H-1.

Select bibliography

~

Abbreviations

AGS	Archivo Histórico Nacional de la Guerra Civil, Salamanca
AHN	Archivo Histórico Nacional, Madrid
AHP	Archivo Histórico Provincial, Oviedo
BACJ	Biblioteca Asturiana del Colegio Jesuita
BCUO	Biblioteca Contemporánea de la Universidad de Oviedo
BIDEA	*Boletín del Instituto de Estudios Asturianos*
BILE	*Boletín del Instituto de Enseñanza Libre*
BJ	Biblioteca de Jovellanos, Gijón
BN	Biblioteca Nacional, Madrid
FPI	Fundación Pablo Iglesias, Madrid
HM	Hemeroteca Municipal, Madrid
HMG	Hemeroteca Municipal de Gijón
HN	Hemeroteca Nacional, Madrid

Archival sources

AGS: Sección Político-Social: Gijón

AHN: Serie, Gobernación

AHP:

    Sección Audencia Provincial de Oviedo, sumarios

    Censos Electorales de la ciudad de Gijón: 1900, 1905, 1910, 1915, 1921,
      1928, 1930, 1933

Archivo del Estado, Alcalá de Henares: Sección de Gobernación

Archivo Municipal de Gijón:

    Actas del Ayuntamiento

    Presupuestos Ordinarios, 1903, 1909, 1912, 1915, 1925, 1929, 1932

327

Censos de la Población, 1900, 1910, 1920, 1930
Delegación Regional, Oviedo, Instituto Geográfico y Estadístico:
Censos de la Población de España
Nomenclator de España: Provincia de Oviedo, 1888, 1920, 1930
Censo Electoral de la Provincia de Oviedo, 1900, 1930
Palacio de Justicia, Gijón:
Registro Civil de Matrimonios

Newspapers and periodicals

Acción, Oviedo, 1930s (HMG)
Acción Libertaria, Gijón, 1910–1911 and 1915 (BCUO)
Anales de la Universidad de Oviedo, Año II (1902–1903), IV (1906–1907)
(BN)
Anuario Estadístico de España, Madrid, 1915–1934 (BN)
Asturias, Gijón, 1937 (BJ)
Aurora Social, Oviedo, 1899–1904, 1908–1909, 1926–1932 (FPI)
Avance, Oviedo, 1931–1937 (FPI, HN)
Blanco y Negro, Madrid, 1899 (HN)
Boletín de la Biblioteca Circulante del Ateneo Obrero de Gijón, 1933–1936
(BCUO)
Boletín del Instituto de Enseñanza Libre, 1888–1900 (BN)
Boletín del Instituto de Reformas Sociales, 1904–1923 (BN)
Boletín del Norte, Gijón, 1937 (BJ)
Boletín Oficial de la Provincia de Oviedo, 1900–1930 (BN)
Boletín Oficial del Ministerio de Trabajo, Comercio e Industria, 1924–1927
(BN)
CNT, Gijón, 1937 (BJ)
El Comercio, 1900 – present (HMG)
La Defensa del Obrero, Gijón, 1901 (BCUO)
La Fraternidad, Gijón, 1898–1900 (BCUO)
El Grito del Pueblo, Gijón (BJ)
El Libertario, Gijón, 1912–1913 (BCUO)
El Metalúrgico Asturiano, Gijón, 1920 (HN)
El Noroeste, Gijón, 1897–1936 (HMG)
El Obrero Católico, Gijón, 1897 (BJ)
La Organización, Gijón, 1902 (BCUO)
El Popular, Gijón, 1904–1908 (BJ)
El Porvenir, Gijón, 1912 (BCUO)
La Prensa, Gijón, 1921–1935 (HMG)
El Principado, Gijón, 1910 (BJ)
El Productor, Gijón, 1909 (BJ)
El Publicador, Gijón, 1909 (BJ)

328

Región, Oviedo, 1934 (HMG)
Renovación, Gijón, 1916 (BACJ)
La Revista Blanca, Madrid, 1898–1905 (HM)
El Socialista, Madrid, 1900–1911 (BN, FPI)
Solidaridad, 1914, 1931–1932 (BCUO)
Solidaridad Obrera, Gijón, 1909–1910, 1921, 1923, 1925–1926 (BCUO)
Tiempos Nuevos, Gijón, 1905 (BCUO)
Unión Republicana, 1897 (BJ)
Vida Obrera, 1921 (BCUO)

Contemporary published sources

Acción Social Católica. *Reglamento de socorros mútuos de los sindicatos católicos adheridos y domiciliados en el centro de Acción Social Católica de Gijón.* Gijón, 1923.

Alas, Leopoldo. "El jornalero." In *El Señor y lo demás son cuentos.* Madrid: Talleres Calpe, 1919.

Alborñoz, Alvaro de. *El partido republicano.* Madrid: Biblioteca Nueva, 1918.

Arboleya Martínez, Maximiliano. *De la acción social: el caso de Asturias.* Barcelona: Luis Gili, 1918.

Argüelles, Ramón. *Regionalismo económico asturiano.* Gijón: La Fé, 1934.

Asociación Católica de Padres de Familia de Gijón. *Memoria.* Gijón: Imprenta Palacio, 1933.

Asociación Gijonesa de Caridad. *Memoria-Resumen de la Asociación Gijonesa de Caridad, 1905–1967.* Gijón: La Industria, 1967.

Ayuntamiento de Gijón. *Nomenclator de las calles, plazas y paseos y de las parroquias rurales con sus barrios.* Gijón: Flores, 1942.

Canals, José. *Octubre rojo en Asturias.* Gijón: Silverio Cañada, 1984 (original, 1935).

Canals, Salvador. *Asturias: información sobre su presente estado moral y material.* Madrid: M. Romero, 1900.

Canella y Secades, Fermín. *Representación asturiana: administrativa y política desde 1808–1915.* Oviedo: Imprenta de Florez, Gusano y Cañada, 1915.

Canella y Secades, Fermín, and Octavio Bellmunt y Traves. *Asturias.* Oviedo, 1895.

Castrillo Sagrado, Benito. *El aporte de los indianos a la instrucción pública, a la beneficiencia y al progreso en general de España.* Oviedo: Región, 1926.

Confederación Nacional de Trabajo. *Memoria del Congreso,* 1931; reprinted in *Revista de Trabajo.* 53 (1976): 203–420.

Díaz del Moral, Juan. *Historia de las agitaciones campesinas andaluzas: Córdoba.* Madrid: Alianza Editorial, 1973 (original, 1929).

Fernández, Rogelio. *Suplemento Revista Blanca*, May 28, 1901.

Gallego Catalán, Juan Teófilo. *La educación popular en Gijón*. Gijón, 1907. *La Escolar*. Gijón, 1907.

García Arenal, Fernando. *Datos para el estudio de la cuestión social: información hecha en el Ateneo-Casino Obrero de Gijón*. Gijón: Silverio Cañada, 1980 (original, 1885).

Gijón Veraniego. Gijón: La Industria, various years, 1913–1933.

Gimeno y Azcárate, Manuel. *La criminalidad en Asturias, 1883–1897*. Oviedo: Escuela Tipográfica del Hospicio, 1900.

González Posada. "La educación del obrero." *BILE*, 1889.

Grossi Mier, Manuel. *La insurrección de Asturias: quince días de revolución socialista*. Madrid: Crónica General de España, 1978 (original, 1935).

Guía oficial para 1930 por la Feria de Muestras Asturianas. Gijón: La Fé, 1930.

Instituto de Reformas Sociales. *Memoria del servicio de inspección en 1907*. Madrid: La Sucesora de M. Minuesa de los Ríos, 1908.

Informe acerca del conflicto obrero-patronal de Gijón. Madrid: La Sucesora de M. Minuesa de los Ríos, 1910.

Informes de los inspectores de trabajo sobre la influencia de la guerra Europea en las industrias españoles, 1917–1918. Vol. II. Madrid: La Sucesora de M. Minuesa de los Ríos, 1919.

Junta local para el fomento y mejora de casas baratas. *Memoria del ejercicio de 1916*. Gijón: La Fé, 1917.

Llano y García, Bernardo de. *Noticiero – Guía de Gijón*. Gijón, 1925.

Marsà, Graco. *La sublevación de Jaca: relato de un rebelde*. Paris: Durant, 1931.

Menéndez y Morán. *Recientes disposiciones oficiales sobre el contrato de trabajo y de las huelgas*. Oviedo, 1902.

Molins i Fabrega, N. *La insurrección proletaria de Asturias*. Gijón: Júcar, 1977 (original Catalan version, 1935).

Oliveros, Antonio L. *Asturias en el resurgimiento español*. Gijón: Silverio Cañada, 1982 (original, Madrid: Juan Bravo, 1935).

Orwell, George. *Homage to Catalonia*. (London: Secker and Warburg, 1938).

Pachín de Melás. "El Hijo del Herrero," *La Prensa*, November 18, 1934. "Convulsiones sociales en Gijón." *La Prensa*, November 25, 1934.

Patronato de San José. *Reglamento general del Patronato de San José*. Gijón: Tipógrafo Católica de L. Sangenis, 1903.

Pérez, Antonio. *Callejero de Gijón*. Gijón: La Victoria, 1924.

Pi y Margall. *Las clases jornaleras*. Barcelona: Publicaciones de la Escuela Moderna, 1915.

Portfolio Anunciador. Gijón: La Rotativa, 1916.

Portola, Felipe. *Topografía médica del concejo de Gijón*. Madrid: El Liberal, 1918.

Posada, Adolfo. *El régimen municipal de la ciudad moderna*. Madrid: Imprenta Clásica Española, 1916.

Sindicato Católico de Sirvientas. *Reglamento*. Gijón: La Reconquista, 1925.

Sociedad Económica Asturiana de Amigos del País. *Sesión pública celebrada el día 28 de enero 1901*. Oviedo: Imprenta de Eduardo Uría, 1901.

Sociedad de Socorros Mútuos de Artesanos de Gijón. *Reglamento*. Gijón: Compañía Asturiana de Artes Gráficas, 1905.

Súarez, Constantino. *Escritores y artistas asturianos*. Madrid: Sáez Hermanos, 1936.

Suárez, José. *El problema social minero en Asturias*. Oviedo: Imprenta de Pardo Gusano, 1896.

Urales, Federico. "Sobre cosas y casos en Gijón." *El Noroeste*, May 8, 1898.

Villar, Manuel. *El anarquismo en la insurrección de Asturias*. Valencia: Ediciones Tierra y Libertad, 1935.

Villar Sangenis, L. *Noticiero – Guía de Gijón*. Gijón: Imprenta Lino, 1911.

Post-Civil War published sources on Asturias and Spain

Ackelsberg, Martha. *Free Women of Spain*. Urbana: University of Illinois Press, 1991.

Aduriz, Patricio. *Pachín de Melás*. Gijón: Imprenta La Versal, 1978.

"Centenario del gijonés Ateneo-Casino Obrero." *El Comercio*, July 12, 19 and 26, 1981.

Alba, Victor. *La alianza obrera: historia y análisis de una táctica de unidad en España*. Gijón: Júcar, 1977.

Alonso Iglesias, Leontina, and Asunción García Prendes. "La Extensión Universitaria de Oviedo, 1898–1910." Tesina, University of Oviedo, 1974.

Alvarez Junco, José. *La ideología política del anarquismo español (1868–1910)*. Madrid: Siglo Veintiuno, 1976.

"El anarquismo en la España contemporánea." *Anales de Historia Contemporánea*. 5 (1986): 189–200.

El emperador del paralelo: Lerroux y la demogogía populista. Madrid: Alianza Editorial, 1990.

"Los intelectuales: anticlericalismo y republicanismo." In *Los orígenes culturales de la II República*, ed. J. L. García Delgado, 101–126. Madrid: Siglo Veintiuno, 1993.

Alvarez Palomo, Ramón. *Eleuterio Quintanilla*. Mexico: Editores Mexicanos Unidos, 1973.

"Avelino González Entrialgo." *Ruta*, 36 (1978): 7–26.

Avelino González Mallada: alcalde anarquista. Barcelona: Historia Libertaria de Asturias, 1987.

Alvargonzález Rodríguez, Ramón María. *Gijón: industrialización y crecimiento urbano*. Asturias: Ayalga Ediciones, 1977.

Industria y espacio portuario en Gijón. Vols. I and II. Gijón: Junta del Puerto de Gijón, 1985.

Arriero, María Luz. "Los motines de subsistencias en España, 1895–1905." *Estudios de Historia Social*, 30 (1984): 193–250.

Avilés Farré, Juan. *La izquierda burguesa en la II República*. Madrid: Espasa Calpe, 1985.

"Los partidos republicanos de izquierda, 1933–1936." In *La II República española: bienio rectificador y Frente Popular, 1934–1936*, ed. J. L. García Delgado, 71–82. Madrid: Siglo Veintiuno, 1988.

Azpiroz Pascual, José María, and Fernando Elboj Broto. *La sublevación de Jaca*. Zaragoza: Guara Editorial, 1984.

Balcells, Albert. "La crisis del anarcosindicalismo y el movimiento obrero en Sabadell, 1930–1936." In *Trabajo industrial y organización obrero en la Cataluña contemporánea, 1930–1936*, ed. Albert Balcells, 181–305. Barcelona: Editorial LAIA, 1974.

Balcells, Albert, ed. *El arraigo del anarquismo en Cataluña: Textos de 1928–34*. Barcelona: Júcar, 1980.

Bar, Antonio. "La CNT frente a la República." In *Estudios sobre la II República*, ed. Manuel Ramírez. Madrid: Editorial Tecnos, 1975.

La CNT en los años rojos: del sindicalismo revolucionario al anarcosindicalismo, 1910–1926. Madrid: Akal Editor, 1981.

Baragaño Castaño, María José. "La radicalización del movimiento socialista asturiano en la Segunda República, 1931–1934." Tesina, University of Oviedo, 1986.

Barragón Moriana, Antonio. *Conflictividad social y desarticulación política en la provincia de Córdoba 1918–1920*. Córdoba: Publicaciones del Ayuntamiento, 1990.

Barrio Alonso, Angeles. *El anarquismo en Gijón: industrialización y movimiento obrero, 1850–1910*. Gijón: Silverio Cañada, 1982.

Anarquismo y anarcosindicalismo en Asturias. Madrid: Siglo Veintiuno, 1988.

"Asturias en la alianza CNT – UGT, 1934–1937." In *Los nuevos historiadores ante la Guerra Civil española*. Vol. II, ed. Octavio Ruiz-Manjón Cabeza and Miguel Gómez Oliver, 9–28. Granada: Diputación Provincial de Granada, 1990.

Ben-Ami, Schlomo. *Fascism from Above: The Dictatorship of Primo de Rivera in Spain, 1923–1930*. Oxford: Oxford University Press, 1983.

Bolloten, Burnett. *The Grand Camouflage: The Communist Conspiracy in the Spanish Civil War*. London: Hollis and Carter, 1961.

Bonet, Joaquín A. *Biografía de la villa y puerto de Gijón*. Vols. I and II. Gijón: La Industria, 1968.

Pequeñas historias de Gijón. Gijón: La Industria, 1969.

Bookchin, Murray. *The Spanish Anarchists: The Heroic Years, 1868–1936*. New York: Harper and Row, 1977.

Brenan, Gerald. *The Spanish Labyrinth*. London: Cambridge University Press, 1943.

Cabezas, Juan Antonio. *Asturias: catorce meses de guerra civil*. Madrid: G. del Toro, 1975.

Capel Martínez, Rosa. *El trabajo y la educación de la mujer*. Madrid: Ministerio de Cultura, 1984.

Carcel Orti, Vicente. *La persecución religiosa en España durante la Segunda República (1931–1939)*. Madrid: Ediciones Rialp, 1990.

Caro Baroja, Julio. *El Carnaval*. Madrid: Círculo de Lectores, 1992.

Carr, Raymond. *Spain: 1808–1939*. Oxford: Oxford University Press, 1975.

Modern Spain, 1875–1980. Oxford: Oxford University Press, 1980.

Casanovas, Joan. "Pere Esteve: un anarquista català a cavall de dos mons i de dues generacions." *L'Avenç*. 162 (1992): 18–24.

Castillo, Santiago. *Historia del socialismo español*. Vol. I: *1870–1909*. Barcelona: Conjunto Editorialista, 1989.

Castro Alfín, Demetrio. "Los republicanos madrileños durante la primera fase de la Restauración." In *La sociedad madrileña durante la Restauración, 1876–1931*, ed. A.Bahamonde and L. E. Otero, 39–57. Madrid: Comunidad de Madrid, 1989.

Checa Godoy, Antonio. *Prensa y partidos políticos durante la II República*. Salamanca: Ediciones Universidad de Salamanca, 1989.

Culla i Clarà, Joan B. *El republicanisme lerrouxista a Catalunya (1901–1923)*. Barcelona: Curial, 1986.

Dardé Morales, Carlos. "Los republicanos." In *Historia General de España y América*. Vol. XVI-2. Madrid: Ediciones Rialpe, 1981.

Delgado, Manuel. *La ira sagrada: anticlericalismo, iconoclastia y antirritualismo en la España contemporánea*. Barcelona: Editorial Humanidades, 1992.

Duarte i Montserrat, Angel. *El republicanisme català a la fi del segle XIX*. Vic: Eumo Editorial, 1987.

Elorza, Antonio. "El anarcosindicalismo español bajo la Dictadura, 1923–1930." *Revista de Trabajo*. 39–40, 44–45 (1972–1974): 123–218; 315–454.

La Utopía anarquista bajo la Segunda República. Madrid: Ayuso, 1973.

Erice Sebares, Francisco. *La burguesía industrial asturiana, 1885–1920*. Madrid: Silverio Cañada, 1980.

Esenwein, George. *Anarchist Ideology and the Working Class Movement in Spain, 1868–1898*. Berkeley: University of California Press, 1989.

Espín, Eduardo. *Azaña en el poder: el partido de Acción Republicana*. Madrid: Centro de Investigaciones Sociológicas, 1980.

Fernández, Eusebio I., "Organizaciones sindicales y conflictividad social en Asturias durante la II República (1933–1934)." Ph.D. diss., University of Oviedo, 1985.

Fernández García, Aladino, *et al. Geografía de Asturias.* Vol. II: *Geografía humanal: geografía urbana: Langreo, Mieres y Gijón.* Asturias: Ayalga Ediciones, 1982.

Fox, E. Inman. *La crisis intelectual de '98.* Madrid: Edicusa, 1976.

Fusi, Juan Pablo. *Política obrera en el país vasco, 1880–1923.* Madrid: Turner, 1975.

El país vasco, pluralismo y nacionalidad. Madrid: Alianza Editorial, 1984.

Gabriel, Pere. "Clase obrera i sindicats a Catalunya, 1903–1923." Ph.D. diss., University of Barcelona, 1981.

"El marginament del republicanisme i l'obrerisme." *L'Avenc.* 85 (1985): 34–38.

"La població obrera catalana, una població industrial?" *Estudios de Historia Social.* 32–33 (enero – junio 1985): 191–260.

"Historiografía reciente sobre el anarquismo y el sindicalismo en España, 1870–1923." *Historia Social.* 1 (1988): 45–54.

"Sindicalismo y sindicatos socialistas en Cataluña. La UGT, 1888–1938." *Historia Social.* 8 (1990): 47–72.

García Venero, Maximiano. *Melquíades Alvarez: historia de un liberal.* Madrid: Ediciones Tebas, 1975.

García Peláez, Luis, and José Benito A. Buylla. "Localización geográfica de las industrias de Gijón." *BIDEA.* 45 (1962).

García-Avello Herrero, Ramón. "La música coral." *Ritmo.* 54 (1984): 18–25.

Gómez Pellón, Eloy, and Gema Coma González. *Fiestas de Asturias: aproximación al panorama festivo asturiano.* Oviedo: Caja de Ahorros de Asturias, 1985.

González Muñiz, Miguel Angel. *Los partidos políticos en Asturias.* Gijón: Centro Gráfico, 1982.

Guereña, Jean Louis. "La Projection sociale de l'Université à la fin du XIXe siècle: L'Extension Universitaire en Espagne." *Higher Education and Society. Historical Perspectives.* 1 (1985).

"Las instituciones culturales: políticas educativas." In *1900 en España,* ed. Carlos Serrano and Serge Salaün, 59–84. Madrid: Espasa Calpe, 1991.

Harding, Susan. "Women and Words in a Spanish Village." In *Toward an Anthropology of Women,* ed. Rayna Reiter, 283–309. New York: Monthly Review Press, 1975.

Harrison, Joseph. "The Inter-War Depression and the Spanish Economy." *Journal of European Economic History.* 12:2 (Fall 1983): 295–322.

Hennessey, Charles. *The Federal Republic in Spain: Pi y Margall and the Federal Republican Movement 1868–1874.* Oxford: Oxford University Press, 1962.

Hernández Andreu, Juan. *Depresión económica en España, 1925–1936.* Madrid: Instituto de Estudios Fiscales, Ministerio de Hacienda, 1980.

Heywood, Paul. *Marxism and the Failure of Organised Socialism in Spain, 1879–1936.* Cambridge: Cambridge University Press, 1990.

Hidalgo Nieto, Victoria. *La masonería en Asturias en el siglo XIX.* Oviedo: Consejería de Educación, Cultura y Deportes, 1985.

Hobsbawm, Eric. "Millenarianism II: The Andalusian Anarchists." In *Primitive Rebels: Studies in Archaic Forms of Social Movement in the 19th and 20th Centuries* (New York: Norton, 1959).

Holguin, Sandie. "The Conquest of Tradition: Culture and Politics in Spain during the Second Republic, 1931–1936." Ph.D. diss., University of California, Los Angeles, 1994.

Izard, Manuel. *Industrialización y obrerismo. Las Tres Clases de Vapor (1869–1913).* Barcelona: Ediciones Ariel, 1973.

Izquierdo Fernández, Eusebio. "Organizaciones sindicales y conflictividad social en Asturias durante la II República, 1933–1934." Tesina, University of Oviedo, 1985.

Jackson, Gabriel, P. Broué, B. Bayerlein, F. Claudin, J. L. García Delgado, G. Ojeda, J. A. Vázquez García, M. Cabrera, S. Juliá, P. Preston, A. M. Calero, J. P. Fusi Aizpurúa, J. Girón, M. Pérez Ledesma, P. I. Taibo II, A. Shubert, D. Benevides, J. M. Macarro, J. Alvarez Junco, L. Paramio. *Octubre 1934: cincuenta años para la reflexión.* Madrid: Siglo Veintiuno, 1985.

Jiménez Araya, T. "Formación de capital y fluctuación económica. Materiales para el estudio de un indicador: creación de sociedades mercantiles en España entre 1886 y 1970." *Hacienda Pública Española.* 27 (1974).

Juliá Díaz, Santos. *La izquierda del PSOE, 1935–1936.* Madrid: Siglo Veintiuno, 1977.

Orígenes del Frente Popular en España, 1934–1936. Madrid: Siglo Veintiuno, 1979.

Madrid, 1931–1934: de la fiesta popular a la lucha de clases. Madrid: Siglo Veintiuno, 1984.

Jutglar, Antoni. *Pi y Margall y el republicanismo federal.* Madrid: Taurus, 1975.

Kaplan, Temma. "Women and Spanish Anarchism." In *Becoming Visible: Women in European History,* ed. Renate Bridenthal and Claudia Koonz, 400–421. Boston: Houghton Mifflin, 1977.

The Anarchists of Andalusia, 1868–1903. Princeton: Princeton University Press, 1977.

"Female Consciousness and Collective Action: The Case of Barcelona, 1910–1918." *Signs.* 7 (1982): 545–566.

Red City, Blue Period: Social Movements in Picasso's Barcelona. Berkeley: University of California Press, 1992.

Lacomba, Juan Antonio. *La crisis española de 1917.* Madrid: Ciencia Nueva, 1970.

León-Ignacio. *Los años de pistolerismo.* Barcelona: Planeta, 1981.

Litvak, Lily. *Musa libertaria: arte, literatura y vida cultural del anarquismo español (1880–1913).* Barcelona: Antoni Bosch, 1981.

Llordén Miñambres, Moisés. *La producción de suelo urbano en Gijón, 1860–1975.* Oviedo: Gráficas Summa, 1978.

López Garrido, Diego. *La Guardia Civil y los orígenes del estado centralista.* Barcelona: Editorial Ariel, 1982.

Luis Martín, Francisco de. "Un proyecto educativo-cultural socialista: la Fundación Cesáreo del Cerro." *Historia de la Educación.* 7 (1988): 179–202.

"El Cuento en la cultura Socialista de principios del siglo XX: aproximación a la obra de J. A. Melía." *Sistema.* 93 (November 1989): 115–131.

"La cultura en la Casa del Pueblo de Barruelo de Santullán: el cuadro artístico, 1918–1936." *II Congreso de Historia de Palencia,* 1989.

Macarro Vera, José Manuel. *La utopía revolucionaria: Sevilla en la II República.* Sevilla: Monte de Piedad y Caja de Ahorros, 1985.

Magnien, Brigitte. "Cultura Urbana." In *1900 en España,* ed. Carlos Serrano and Serge Salaün, 107–130. Madrid: Espasa Calpe, 1991.

Mainer, José Carlos. *La Doma de la quimera.* Barcelona: Universidad Autónoma, Escola Universitária de traductors i intèrprets, 1988.

Malefakis, Edward. "The Civil War in Historical and Theoretical Perspective." *El País,* March 2, 1986.

Maluquer de Motes, Jordi. "De la crisis colonial a la guerra europea: veinte años de economía española." In Jordi Nadal *et. al.,* eds., *La economía española en el siglo XX.* Madrid: Ariel, 1987.

Martin, Benjamin. *The Agony of Modernization: Labor and Industrialization in Spain.* Ithaca: ILR Press, 1990.

Martínez Cuadrado, Miguel. *Elecciones y partidos políticos de España, 1868–1931.* Madrid: Taurus, 1969.

La burguesía conservadora, 1874–1931. Madrid: Alianza Editorial, 1974.

Mateo del Peral, Diego, García San Miguel, Miguel Angel González Muñiz, Bernardo Díaz Nosty and Ramón Baragaño Alvarez. *Historia de Asturias.* Vols. VIII and IX: *Edad Contemporánea I.* Vitoria: Ayalga Ediciones, 1977.

Maurice, Jacques. *El anarquismo andaluz: campesinos y sindicalistas, 1868–1936.* Barcelona: Editorial Crítica, 1990.

Meaker, Gerald. *The Revolutionary Left in Spain, 1914–1923.* Stanford: Stanford University Press, 1974.

Ministerio de Trabajo, Dirección General de Estadística. "Precios al por mayor y números índices, 1913–1941." *Boletín de Estadística.* Madrid, 1941.

Mintz, Jerome. *The Anarchists of Casa Viejas.* Chicago: University of Chicago Press, 1982.

Montañés, Enrique. *Anarcosindicalismo y cambio político: Zaragoza, 1930–1936*. Zaragoza: Institución Fernando el Católico, 1989.

Montero, José Ramón. *La CEDA: el catolicismo social y político en la II República*. Madrid: Ediciones de la Revista de Trabajo, 1977.

Nadal, Jordi. "La industria fabril española en 1900: una aproximación." In *La economía española en el siglo XX*, ed. Jordi Nadal *et al*. Madrid: Ariel, 1987.

Nadal, Jordi *et. al.*, eds. *La economía española en el siglo XX*. Madrid: Ariel, 1987.

Nash, Mary. *Mujer y movimiento obrero en España, 1931–1939*. Barcelona: Fontamara, 1981.

Nettlau, Max. *La Première Internationale en Espagne, 1868–1888*. Dordrecht: D. Reidel, 1969.

Núñez Florencio, Rafael. *El terrorismo anarquista, 1888–1909*. Madrid: Siglo Veintiuno, 1983.

Olías de Lima Gete, Blanca. *La libertad de asociación en España, 1868–1974*. Madrid: Instituto de Estudios Administrativos, 1977.

Olivé i Serret, Enric. "Els Cors de Clavé i l'obrerisme." *L'Avenç*. 104 (1987): 28–29.

Paniagua Fuentes, Xavier. *La sociedad libertaria: agrarismo e industrialización en el anarquismo español, 1930–1939*. Barcelona: Editorial Crítica, 1982.

Anarquistas y socialistas. Madrid: Historia 16, 1989.

Payne, Stanley G. *The Falange: A History of Spanish Fascism*. Stanford: Stanford University Press, 1961.

Pérez Ledesma, Manuel. *El obrero consciente: dirigentes, partidos y sindicatos en la II International*. Madrid: Alianza Editorial, 1987.

Pi y Margall, Francisco. *Pensamiento social*. Madrid: Editorial Ciencia Nueva, 1968.

Prados de la Escosura, Leandro. *De imperio a nación: crecimiento y atraso económico en España, 1780–1930*. With a preface by Gabriel Tortella. Madrid: Alianza Editorial, 1988.

Preston, Paul. *The Coming of the Spanish Civil War: Reform, Reaction and Revolution in the Second Republic*. London: Routledge, 1978.

"La Revolución de Octubre en España: la lucha de las derechas por el poder." In *Octubre 1934: cincuenta años para la reflexión*, ed. Gabriel Jackson *et.al.*, 131–158. Madrid: Siglo Veintiuno, 1985.

Quirós Corujo, Pedro G. *Alcohol y alcoholismo en Asturias*. Gijón: Arcano, 1983.

Quirós Linares, Francisco. "Patios, corrales y ciudadelas." *Ería*. 3 (1982): 3–34.

Radcliff, Pamela. "Elite Women Workers and Collective Action: The Cigarette Makers of Gijón, 1890–1930." *Journal of Social History*. 27:1 (September 1993): 85–108.

"Republican Politics and Culture in Turn of the Century Gijón." In *El Republicanismo en España*, ed. Nigel Townson, 373–394. Madrid: Alianza Editorial, 1994.

"Women's Politics: Consumer Riots in Twentieth Century Spain." In *Contested Identities: Women in Modern Spain*, ed. Victoria Enders and Pamela Radcliff. Binghampton: State University of New York Press, forthcoming.

Ramos, María Dolores. "Belén Sárraga y la pervivencia de la idea federal en Málaga, 1889–1933." *Jábega*. 53 (1986): 63–70.

Reig Armero, Ramir. *Obrers i ciutadans. Blasquisme i moviment obrer: Valencia, 1898–1910*. Valencia: Institució Alfons el Magnánim, 1982.

Blasquistas y clericales. La lucha por la ciudad de Valencia. Valencia: Institució Alfons el Magnánim, 1986.

Ringrose, David R. *Patterns, Events and Preconceptions: Revisiting the Structure of Spanish History, 1700–1900*. Cambridge: Cambridge University Press, 1996.

Robes Egea, Antonio. "La Conjunción Republicana – Socialista." Ph.D. diss., Complutense University of Madrid, 1987.

Robinson, Richard A. H. *The Origins of Franco's Spain: The Right, the Republic and Revolution, 1931–1936*. London: Newton Abbot, 1970.

Rodríguez Rojo, Martín. "Los Ateneos en Asturias durante la II República, 1931–1936." Tesina, University of Barcelona, 1985.

Romero Maura, Joaquín. "The Spanish Case." *Government and Opposition*. 5:4 (1970): 456–479.

La rosa de fuego: el obrerismo barcelonés de 1899 a 1909. Barcelona: Ediciones Grijalbo, 1975.

Rosal, Amaro del. "La taberna como centro de discusión política en Asturias, 1914–1920." *Los Cuadernos del Norte*. 14 (1982): 79–88.

Ruiz, David. *El movimiento obrero en Asturias: de la industrialización a la II República*. Oviedo: Amigos de Asturias, 1968.

Asturias contemporánea, 1808–1936. Madrid: Siglo Veintiuno, 1975.

"Clase, sindicatos y partidos en Asturias, 1931–1934." *Estudios de Historia Social*. 31 (1984): 87–100.

Insurrección defensiva y revolución obrera: el octubre español de 1934. Barcelona: Editorial Labor, 1988.

Ruiz, David, Francisco Erice, Adolfo Fernández, Carmen García, José Girón, José María Moro, and Julio Vaquero. *Asturias contemporánea, 1808–1975: síntesis histórica, textos y documentos*. Madrid: Siglo Veintiuno, 1981.

Ruiz Manjón, Octavio. *El partido Republicano Radical, 1908–1936*. Madrid: Tebas, 1976.

Samaniego Boneu, Mercedes. *La política educativa de la segunda república durante el bienio azañista*. Madrid: CSIC, 1977.

San Miguel, Luis G. *De la sociedad aristocrática a la sociedad industrial en la España del siglo XIX.* Madrid: Edicusa, 1973.

Sánchez y García Sauco, J. A. *La revolución de 1934 en Asturias.* Madrid: Editoria Nacional, 1974.

Seidman, Michael. *Workers against Work: Labor in Paris and Barcelona during the Popular Front.* Berkeley: University of California Press, 1991.

Serrano, Carlos. *Le Tour du Peuple.* Madrid: Casa de Velázquez, 1987.

Serrano, Carlos, and Serge Salaün, eds. *1900 en España.* Madrid: Espasa Calpe, 1991.

Shubert, Adrian. *The Road to Revolution in Spain: The Coal Miners of Asturias, 1860–1934.* Urbana: University of Illinois Press, 1987.

A Social History of Modern Spain. London: Unwin Hyman, 1990.

Solà, Pere. *Els ateneus obrers i la cultura popular a Catalunya, 1900–1939.* Barcelona: Ediciones la Magrana, 1978.

Las escuelas racionalistas en Cataluña, 1900–1939. Barcelona: Tusquests, 1978.

Súarez Cortina, Manuel. *El fascismo en Asturias, 1931–1937.* Madrid: Silverio Cañada, 1981.

El reformismo en España. Madrid: Siglo Veintiuno, 1986.

"La quiebra del republicanismo histórico, 1898–1931." In *El republicanismo en España, 1830–1977*, ed. Nigel Townson, 139–164. Madrid: Alianza Editorial, 1994.

Taibo, Paco Ignacio. *Asturias 1934.* Gijón: Júcar, 1984.

Tamames, Ramón. *La República y la era de Franco.* Madrid: Alianza Editorial, 1983.

Tavera, Susanna. "La ideología política del anarcosindicalismo catalán a través de su propaganda." Doctoral Thesis, University of Barcelona, 1980.

"Els anarcosindicalistes catalans i la dictadura." *L'Avenc.* 72 (1984): 62–67.

Termes Ardévol, Josep. *Anarquismo y sindicalismo en España: la Primera Internacional, 1864–1881.* Barcelona: Crítica, 1972.

Townson, Nigel. "Algunas consideraciones sobre el proyecto 'republicano' del Partido Radical." In *La II República española: bienio rectificador y Frente Popular, 1934–1936*, ed. J. L. García Delgado, 53–70. Madrid: Siglo Veintiuno, 1988.

"The Collapse of the Center: the Radical Republican Party during the Spanish Second Republic, 1931–1936." Ph.D. diss., University of London, 1991.

Townson, Nigel, ed. *El republicanismo en España, 1830–1977.* Madrid: Alianza Editorial, 1994.

Tuñón de Lara, Manuel. *El movimiento obrero en la historia de España.* Madrid: Taurus, 1972.

La quiebra del '98. Madrid: Sarpe, 1986.

Tuñón de Lara, Manuel, ed. *La Guerra Civil Española: 50 años después*. Barcelona: Editorial Labor, 1985.
Tuñón de Lara, Manuel, *et. al.*, eds. *Los orígenes culturales de la II República*. Madrid: Siglo Veintiuno, 1993.
Tusell Gómez, Javier. *Las elecciones del Frente Popular*. Madrid: Edicusa, 1971.
Las Constituyentes de 1931: unas elecciones de transición. Madrid: Centro de Investigaciones Sociológicas, 1982.
La reforma de la administración local en España, 1900–1936. Madrid: Instituto Nacional de Administración Pública, 1987.
Ullman, Joan Connelly. *The Tragic Week: a Study of Anti-Clericalism in Spain, 1875–1912*. Cambridge, MA: Harvard University Press, 1968.
Varela, Javier. *Jovellanos*. Madrid: Alianza Editorial, 1988.
Varela Ortega, José. *Los amigos políticos: partidos, elecciones y caciquismo en la Restauración, 1875–1900*. Madrid: Alianza Editorial, 1977.
Vázquez García, Juan Antonio. "El ciclo económico en Asturias, 1886–1973: un análisis comparativo." *BIDEA*. 105–106 (1982): 441–446.
La cuestión hullera en Asturias, 1918–1935. Oviedo: Instituto de Estudios Asturianos, 1985.
Vega, E. *El Trentisme a Catalunya. Divergències ideològiques en la CNT (1930–1933)*. Barcelona: Curial, 1980.
Vigil, Manuel. "Recuerdos de un octogenario." *Estudios de Historia Social*. 18–19 (1981): 311–466.
Villapadierna, Maryse. "Les 'clases populares' organisées par l'Extension universitaire d'Oviedo (début du XXe siècle)." In Jean-René Aymes *et al.*, *L'Enseignement primaire en Espagne et en Amérique Latine du XVIIIe siècle à nos jours. Politiques éducatives et réalités scolaires*. Tours: Publications de l'Université de Tours, 1986.

Other sources

Abrams, Lynn. *Workers' Culture in Imperial Germany: Leisure and Recreation in the Rhineland and Westphalia*. London: Routledge, 1992.
Accampo, Elinor. *Industrialization, Family Life and Class Relations: St. Chamond, 1815–1914*. Berkeley: University of California Press, 1989.
Aminzade, Ronald. "The Transformation of Social Solidarities in 19th Century Toulouse." In *Consciousness and Class Experience in 19th Century Europe*, ed. John Merriman, 85–106. New York: Holmes and Meier, 1979.
Class, Politics and Early Industrial Capitalism: A Study of Mid-Nineteenth Century Toulouse. Albany: State University of New York Press, 1981.
Ballots and Barricades: Class Formation and Republican Politics in France, 1830–1871. Princeton: Princeton University Press, 1993.

Armstrong, W. A. "The Use of Information About Occupation." In *Nineteenth Century Society*, ed. E. A. Wrigley, 191–310. Cambridge: Cambridge University Press, 1972.

Baron, Ava, ed. *Work Engendered: Toward a New History of American Labor.* Ithaca: Cornell University Press, 1991.

Barrows, Susanna. "After the Commune: Alcoholism, Temperance and Literature in the Early Third Republic." In *Consciousness and Class Experience in Nineteenth Century Europe*, ed. John Merriman, 205–218. New York: Holmes and Meier, 1979.

Bell, Donald. *Sesto San Giovanni: Workers, Culture and Politics in an Italian Town, 1880–1922.* New Brunswick: Rutgers University Press, 1986.

Berlanstein, Lenard R., ed. *Rethinking Labor History.* Urbana: University of Illinois Press, 1993.

Bezucha, Robert. "The Moralization of Society: the Enemies of Popular Culture in the Nineteenth Century." In *Popular Culture in France: the Wolf and the Lamb: from the Old Regime to the 20th Century*, ed. Jacques Beauroy, Marc Bertrand and Edward T. Gargan, 175–187. Saratoga: Anma Libri, 1977.

Blackbourn, David and Geoff Eley. *The Peculiarities of German History: Bourgeois Society and Politics in the Nineteenth Century.* Oxford: Oxford University Press, 1984.

Bohstedt, John. "Gender, Household and Community Politics: Women in English Riots, 1790–1810." *Past and Present.* 120 (1988): 88–122.

Bossy, John. "Godparenthood: The Fortunes of a Social Institution in Early Modern Christianity." In *Religion and Society in Early Modern Europe, 1500–1800*, ed. Kaspar von Greyerz. London: Allen and Unwin, 1984.

Boxer, Marilyn J., and Jean H. Quataert, eds. *Socialist Women: European Socialist Feminism in the 19th and Early 20th Centuries.* New York: Elsevier, 1978.

Calhoun, Craig. "Community: Toward a Variable Conceptualization for Comparative Research." *Social History.* 5:1 (1980): 105–138.

—— "The Radicalism of Tradition: Community Strength or Venerable Disguise and Borrowed Language." *American Journal of Sociology.* 88:5 (1983): 886–914.

Calhoun, Craig, ed. *Habermas and the Public Sphere.* Cambridge, MA: MIT Press, 1992.

Castells, Manuel. *The City and the Grassroots: A Cross-Cultural Theory of Urban Social Movements.* Berkeley: University of California Press, 1983.

Clarke, John, Stuart Hall, Tony Jefferson and Brian Roberts. "Subcultures, Cultures and Class." In *Resistance through Ritual: Youth Subcultures in Post-War Britain*, ed. Stuart Hall and Tony Jefferson, 5–74. London: Hutchinson, 1976.

Clarke, John, Chas Chitcher and Richard Johnson, eds. *Working Class Culture: Studies in History and Theory.* London: Hutchinson, 1979.

Clawson, Mary Ann. *Constructing Brotherhood: Class, Gender and Fraternalism*. Princeton: Princeton University Press, 1989.

Coles, Anthony James. "The Moral Economy of the Crowd: Some Twentieth Century Food Riots." *Journal of British Studies*. 18 (1978): 157–176.

Dirks, Nicholas, Geoff Eley and Sherry Ortner, eds. *Culture Power and History*. Princeton: Princeton University Press, 1994.

Eley, Geoff. "Nations, Publics and Political Culture." In *Habermas and the Public Sphere*, ed. Craig Calhoun, 322–323. Cambridge, MA: MIT Press, 1992: 322–323.

Eley, Geoff, and Keith Nield. "Why Does Social History Ignore Politics?" *Social History*. 5 (May 1980): 249–272.

Elwitt, Sanford. *The Making of the Third Republic*. Baton Rouge: Louisiana State University Press, 1975.

The Third Republic Defended: Bourgeois Reform in France. Baton Rouge: Louisiana State University Press, 1986.

Evans, Richard. "Politics and the Family: Social Democracy and the Working Class Family in Theory and Practice before 1914." In *The German Family: Essays on the Social History of the Family in 19th and 20th Century Germany*, ed. R. J. Evans and W. R. Lee, 256–287. Totowa: Barnes and Noble, 1981.

Fishman, Robert. *Bourgeois Utopias: The Rise and Fall of Suburbia*. New York: Basic Books, 1987.

Fraser, Nancy. "Rethinking the Public Sphere: A Contribution to the Critique of Actually Existing Democracy." In *Habermas and the Public Sphere*, ed. Craig Calhoun, 109–142. Cambridge, MA: MIT Press, 1992.

Friedburger, William. "War, Prosperity and Hunger: The New York Food Riots of 1917." *Labor History*. 25 (1984): 217–239.

Garrioch, David. *Neighbourhood and Community in Paris, 1740–1790*. Cambridge: Cambridge University Press, 1986.

Geertz, Clifford. *The Interpretation of Cultures: Selected Essays*. New York: Basic Books, 1973.

"Centers, Kings and Charisma: Reflections on the Symbolics of Power." In *Culture and its Creators: Essays in Honor of Edward Shils*, ed. Joseph Ben-David and Terry Nichols Clark, 150–171. Chicago: University of Chicago Press, 1977.

Goldstone, Jack, ed. *Revolutions: Theoretical, Comparative and Historical Studies*. San Diego: Harcourt, Brace, Jovanovich, 1986.

Gramsci, Antonio. *Selections from the Prison Notebooks*. New York: Lawrence and Wishart, 1971.

Gruber, Helmut. *Red Vienna: Experiments in Working-Class Culture, 1919–1934*. Oxford: Oxford University Press, 1991.

Habermas, Jurgen. *The Structural Transformation of the Public Sphere: An*

Inquiry into a Category of Bourgeois Society. Cambridge, MA: MIT Press, 1989 (original, 1962).

Hall, Stuart. "Cultural Studies and the Centre: Some Problematics and Problems." In *Culture, Media, Language: Working Papers in Cultural Studies, 1972–1979,* ed. Stuart Hall *et al.,* 15–47. London: Hutchinson, 1980.

"Notes on Deconstructing the 'Popular.'" In *People's History and Socialist Theory,* ed. Raphael Samuel, 227–241. London: Routledge and Kegan Paul, 1981.

Hall, Stuart, and Tony Jefferson, eds. *Resistance through Ritual: Youth Subculture in Post-War Britain.* London: Hutchinson, 1976.

Hanagan, Michael. *The Logic of Solidarity: Artisans and Industrial Workers in Three French Towns, 1871–1914.* Urbana: University of Illinois Press, 1980.

Hanson, Paul. "The *Vie Chère* Riots of 1911: Traditional Protests in Modern Garb." *Journal of Social History.* 21 (Spring 1988): 463–482.

Harris, David. *From Class Struggle to the Politics of Pleasure: The Effects of Gramscianism on Cultural Studies.* London: Routledge, 1992.

Hobsbawm, Eric. *Primitive Rebels: Studies in Archaic Forms of Social Movement in the 19th and 20th Centuries.* New York: Norton, 1959.

Laboring Men: Studies in the History of Labor. London: Weidenfeld and Nicolson, 1964.

"Mass-producing Traditions: Europe, 1870–1914." In *The Invention of Tradition,* ed. E. Hobsbawm and Terence Ranger, 262–307. Cambridge: Cambridge University Press, 1983.

Hobsbawm, Eric, and Terence Ranger, eds. *The Invention of Tradition.* Cambridge: Cambridge University Press, 1983.

Huard, Raymond. *Le Mouvement Républicain en Bas-Languedoc: 1848–1881.* Paris: Presses de la Fondation Nationale des Sciences Politiques, 1982.

Hunt, Lynn. *Politics, Culture and Class in the French Revolution.* Berkeley: University of California Press, 1984.

Hunt, Lynn, ed. *The New Cultural History.* Berkeley: University of California Press, 1984.

Jalla, Daniel. "Le Quartier comme territoire et comme représentation: les 'barrières' ouvrières de Turin au début du XX siècle." *Mouvement Social.* 118 (1982): 79–98.

Johnson, Christopher. "Lifeworld, System and Communicative Action: The Habermasian Alternative in Social History." In *Rethinking Labor History,* ed. Lenard Berlanstein, 55–89. Urbana: University of Illinois Press, 1993.

Johnson, Richard. "Three Problematics: Elements of a Theory of Working Class Culture." In *Working Class Culture: Studies in History and Theory,* ed. John Clarke, Chas Chitcher and Richard Johnson, 201–237. London: Hutchinson, 1979.

"Barrington Moore, Perry Anderson and English Social Development." In *Culture, Media, Language: Working Papers in Cultural Studies, 1972–1979*, ed. Stuart Hall *et. al.*, 48–70. London: Hutchinson, 1980.

Joyce, Patrick. *The Historical Meanings of Work*. Cambridge: Cambridge University Press, 1987.

Visions of the People. Industrial England and the Question of Class, c. *1848–1914*. Cambridge: Cambridge University Press, 1991.

Katznelson, Ira, and Aristide Zolberg, eds. *Working Class Formation: Nineteenth-Century Patterns in Western Europe and the United States*. Princeton: Princeton University Press, 1986.

Kerr, Clark, and Abraham Siegel. "The Interindustry Propensity to Strike – An International Comparison." In *Industrial Conflict*, ed. Arthur Kornhauser *et al.* 189–212. New York: McGraw-Hill, 1954.

Kertzer, David. *Rituals, Politics and Power*. New Haven: Yale University Press, 1988.

Kingsdale, Jon M. "The Poor Man's Club: Social Functions of the Urban Working Class Saloon." *American Quarterly*. 25 (October 1973): 472–489.

Lears, Jackson. "The Concept of Cultural Hegemony: Problems and Possibilities." *American Historical Review*. 90 (1985): 567–593.

Lidtke, Vernon. *The Alternative Culture: Socialist Labor in Imperial Germany*. New York: Oxford University Press, 1985.

Lukes, Steven. "Political Ritual and Social Integration." *Sociology*. 9:2 (May 1975): 289–308.

Magraw, Roger. *A History of the French Working Class*. Oxford: Blackwell, 1992.

Mayfield, David and Susan Thorne. "Social History and its Discontents: Gareth Stedman Jones and the Politics of Language." *Social History*. 17:2 (May 1992): 165–188.

Meacham, Standish. *A Life Apart: The English Working Class, 1890–1914*. London: Thames and Hudson, 1977.

Merriman, John. *The Red City: Limoges and the French Nineteenth Century*. Oxford: Oxford University Press, 1985.

Moch, Leslie. *Paths to the City: Regional Migration in 19th Century France*. Beverly Hills: Sage Publications, 1983.

Pateman, Carole. "Feminist Critiques of the Public/Private Dichotomy." In *The Disorder of Women: Democracy, Feminism and Political Theory*, ed. Carole Pateman, 118–140. Stanford: Stanford University Press, 1989.

Peiss, Kathy. *Cheap Amusements: Working Women and Leisure in Turn of the Century New York*. Philadelphia: Temple University Press, 1986.

Pernicone, Nunzio. *Italian Anarchism, 1864–1892*. Princeton: Princeton University Press, 1993.

Reddy, William. *Money and Liberty in Modern Europe: A Critique of Historical Understanding.* Cambridge: Cambridge University Press, 1987.

Reiter, Rayna R. "Men and Women in the South of France: Public and Private Domains." In *Toward an Anthropology of Women,* ed. Rayna Reiter, 252–282. New York: Monthly Review Press, 1975.

Ross, Ellen. "Survival Networks: Women's Neighborhood Sharing in London before World War I." *History Workshop.* 15 (Spring 1983): 4–27.

Roth, Gunther. *The Social Democrats in Imperial Germany: a Study in Working Class Isolation and National Integration.* Totowa: Barnes and Noble, 1963.

Rozenzweig, Roy. *Eight Hours for What We Will: Workers and Leisure in an Industrial City, 1870–1920.* Cambridge: Cambridge University Press, 1983.

Ryan, Mary. "The American Parade: Representations of the 19th Century Social Order." In *The New Cultural History,* ed. Lynn Hunt, 131–153. Berkeley: University of California Press, 1989.

Women in Public: Between Banners and Ballots, 1825–1880. Baltimore: Johns Hopkins University Press, 1990.

Salerno, Salvatore. *Red November, Black November.* New York: State University of New York Press, 1989.

Scott, Joan. *The Glassworkers of Carmaux.* Cambridge, MA: Harvard University Press, 1974.

Gender and the Politics of History. New York: Columbia University Press, 1988.

Sewell, William. *Structure and Mobility: The Men and Women of Marseille, 1820–1870.* Cambridge: Cambridge University Press, 1985.

Smelser, Neil J. *Theory of Collective Action.* New York: Free Press, 1963.

Smith, Judith E. "The Transformation of Family and Community Culture in Immigrant Neighborhoods, 1900–1940." In *The New England Working Class and the New Labor History,* ed. Herbert G. Gutman and Donald H. Bell, 159–183. Urbana: University of Illinois Press, 1987.

Soja, Edward W. *Postmodern Geographies: The Reassertion of Space in Critical Social Theory.* New York: Verso, 1989.

Stearns, Peter. *Revolutionary Syndicalism and French Labor.* New Brunswick: Rutgers University Press, 1974.

"Efforts at Continuity in Working Class Culture." *Journal of Modern History.* 52:4 (1980): 626–655.

Stedman Jones, Gareth. "Class Expression vs. Social Control." *History Workshop.* 4 (Autumn 1977): 163–170.

Languages of Class: Studies in English Working Class History, 1832–1982. Cambridge: Cambridge University Press, 1984.

Stovall, Tyler. *The Rise of the Paris Red Belt.* Berkeley: University of California Press, 1990.

Thompson, Edward P. *The Making of the English Working Class*. New York: Pantheon Books, 1963.

"The Moral Economy of the English Crowd in the 18th Century." *Past and Present*. 50 (1971): 76–136.

The Poverty of Theory and Other Essays (New York: 1978).

Customs in Common. London: Merlin Press, 1991.

Tilly, Charles. "The Modernization of Protest in France, 1845–1855." In *The Dimensions of Quantitative Research in History*, ed. W. O. Aydelotte et al., 192–255. Princeton: Princeton University Press, 1972.

"Charivaris, Repertoires, and Urban Politics." In *French Cities in the Nineteenth Century*, ed. John Merriman, 73–91. New York: Holmes and Meier, 1981.

"Britain Creates the Social Movement." In *Social Conflict and the Political Order in Modern Britain*, ed. James Cronin and Jonathan Schneer, 21–51. New Brunswick: Rutgers University Press, 1982.

The Contentious French. Cambridge, MA: Harvard University Press, 1986.

"European Violence and Collective Action Since 1700." *Social Research*. 53:1 (1986): 159–184.

Tilly, Charles, and Edward Shorter. *From Mobilization to Revolution*. Reading: Addison-Wesley, 1978.

Tilly, Louise. "The Food Riot as a Form of Political Conflict in France." *Journal of Interdisciplinary History*. 2 (1971): 23–57.

Politics and Class in Milan. Oxford: Oxford University Press, 1992.

Treiman, Donald J. "A Standard Occupational Prestige Scale for Use with Historical Data." *Journal of Interdisciplinary History*. 7:2 (Autumn 1976): 283–304.

White, Jerry. *The Rothschild Buildings: Life in an East End Tenement Block, 1887–1920*. London: Routledge and Kegan Paul, 1980.

Williams, Raymond. *Resources of Hope: Culture, Democracy and Socialism*. New York: Verso, 1989.

Woodcock, George. *The Anarchist Reader*. Glasgow: Fontana, 1980.

Wright, Erik Olin. "Class and Occupation." *Theory and Society*. 9:1 (January 1980): 177–214.

Index

See the glossary of terms and abbreviations, p. xvi.

Acción Popular, 150(fn29), 156–157
Agrupación al Servicio de la República,
140
Alas, Leopoldo (Clarín), 38–39
Alianza Obrera, 189, 191–193
Alianza Republicana, 145
origins of, 139
opposition to, 191(fn74), 192(fn78)
Alvarez, Melquíades, 38, 122, 125–127,
138
anarchism (*see also* CNT;
anarchosyndicalism)
and Escuela Neutra, 211
in Europe, 19th century, 44
libertarian *ateneos*, 236, 239
origins of, 11
in Gijón, 45–46
repression of, 46
strength of, in Spain, 11–12, 167–169,
189
local political context, importance of,
168–170
and terrorism, 46
anarchist leaders, 172, 183(fn48)
Martínez, José María, 172
Quintanilla, Eleuterio, 42(fn72), 134,
140(fn62), 172, 211, 235
anarchosyndicalism (*see also* CNT;
anarchism)
apoliticism, 173
in Barcelona, 168(fn4), 169(fn5)
cultural vision, alternative, 197
defined, 11
heterogeneity of, 168
ideology of, 47, 173

origins of, 46
parliamentary syndicalists, 128(fn25),
273(fn61)
and polarization, 115
and political culture in Spain,
contribution to, 311
and republicans, 115–117, 134–135,
147–148, 169–170
co-operation in Escuela Neutra, 211–
212
Socialists, conflicts with, 167–170, 172–
173, 174, 176
during Second Republic, 187–188,
285–287
co-operation with, 189–193, 263–
264, 290–291, 306(fn2)
anti-clericalism (*see also* republicanism: and
anti-clericalism; secularization),
282–283
Asturias
Civil War in, 308
economic cycles, 67–70
employment by sector, 31, 64
industrialization, patterns of, 16, 20, 64
Oviedo as capital of, 28–29
Restoration politics in, 31–32
Revolution of October 1934 in, 294–
295
ateneo
Ateneo Casino Obrero, Gijón, *see under*
cultural institutions
defined, 40(fn63)
libertarian, 236, 239

burial, 208–209, 232–233

347

Cánovas del Castillo, Antonio, 30
Catholic Church
  and education, 210
  and public culture, 137, 196, 200, 202–203
  challenge to, 203–209
  and Restoration politics, 31
  and trade unions, female, 245–246
Civil Guards, 33, 125, 275–276
Civil War, 304
  in Asturias, 307
  end of, 308
  in Gijón, 305(fn1)
  heterogeneity of regime, 306–307
  origins of, 314
class analysis, 6–7, 250
  class vs. community, 8–9
CNT (see also anarchosyndicalism; anarchism)
  abstention,
    1931 elections, 185(fn52)
    1933 elections, 151
  and Alianza Obrera, 189, 191–193, 290
  and August 1917 general strike, 271
  and Casa del Pueblo, 177, 183
  and Civil War, 306
  and consumer protests, role in, 268–269, 287–289
  Syndicate for the Defense of Public Interests, 232, 288–289
  and culture, proletarian, 227–228
  during the Dictatorship, 182–183
  and direct action, 281, 289
  formation of, 173
  and industrial unionism, 179–180
    struggle for, 277–279
  membership of, 178(fn30), 181, 184(fn49,50), 188(fn65)
    table, local CNT unions, 190
    vs. UGT (1930s), 188–189
  mutual aid, 231–232
  organization of, 173
    evolution of, 176–177, 179–180
  "political" role of, 310
  and popular community, leadership of, 252, 262, 267, 281, 283–284
  repression of
    post-First World War, 181
    recovery from, 181–182
  schism of
    background to, 1920s, 182
    FAI vs. treintismo, 186
    Gijonese federation's stance on, 186–187
  and Second Republic
    destabilization of, complex role in, 187, 289

moderation at outset of, 185, 284–285
  opposition leadership, consolidation of, 189, 191, 193–194, 280–281, 283–284
  Socialists, war on, 187–188, 285–287
  terrorism during, 186(fn58)
  transition to, role in, 184–185
  and workplace control, 229
  discipline of workers, 230–231
  employment clearinghouse, 229–230
collective action (see also consumer protests; strikes)
  building blocks of, 59–60, 77
  and a "culture of mobilization," 251, 254, 312
  defined, 249
  direct action tradition of, 312–313
  and "modernization of protest," 52, 250
  neighborhood-based, 260–262, 275–276, 291–293
  repertoires of, 35, 312–313
  waves of protest
    1909–1910, 254–266
    1914–1923, 267–279
    1931–1933, 281–289
Communist party
  and Alianza Obrera, 193
  in Civil War, 306(fn2)
  membership of, Gijón and Asturias, 188(fn66)
community (see also elite community; popular community)
  vs. class, 8–9
  defined, 8, 89(fn6)
  neighborhoods as locus of, 101, 103
  Cimadavilla as model, 109–110, 260–262
  and popular mobilization, 312
  violence in, 98
  and women, 9
Conjunción Republicana–Socialista, 122–124, 127
Conservative party
  in Asturias, 31
  and city council, 120–121
  decline of, 123
  and Dictatorship, revival under, 136–137
consumer protests, 259–260
  CNT role in, 267–268, 287–289
  Syndicate for the Defense of Public Interests, 288–289
  consumo riot, 1898, 54–56
  gender distinctions in, 256–257, 288
  in general strike, use of, 267–268
  Liga de Inquilinos and, 273–275, 288

milk tax boycott, 255–257
and republicans, 256
ambivalence towards, 257, 258, 261–
262
significance of, 56–57, 312–313
tavern closure, protest against, 258–259
transit protest, 258
typology of, 53
and women, 5, 51–53, 256–257, 269–
270, 291
cultural institutions, Gijón
Association for Culture and Hygiene,
214
branches of, 104–105, 216
mission of, 215–216
as mutual aid society, 216
and neighborhood entertainment,
106–107, 108
and neighborhood improvement,
105–106, 217
radicalization of, 218–220
and schools, 104
struggle for control of, 218
Ateneo Casino Obrero, 220
crisis of identity, 1910s, 220–221
Dictatorship, importance during, 222
founding of, 39–40
neighborhood branches of, 104
radicalization of, 222–224
and schools, 104
choral societies, 214
Anselmo Clavé, 214–215
Workers' Musical Association, 214–
215
of union movement, 235–240
artistic sections, 239–240
ateneos, libertarian, 236, 239
libraries, 237–238
culture, see cultural institutions; political
culture; workers' culture; see also
relevant headings under
anarchosyndicalism; Catholic
Church; CNT; public sphere;
republicanism; Second Republic;
trade union/labor movement

death, 208–209, 232–233
Dictatorship, of Primo de Rivera
municipal government under, 137
origins of, 136
direct action, see under CNT; collective
action; women

education
class segregation of, 90–91
neighborhood schools, 104
reform of, 36–39

secularization of, 209–211
Escuela Neutra, 211–212
resistance to, 211
trade union-sponsored, 235–236
libraries, 237
universal public, lack of, 37, 91, 209–
210
during Republic, 211
University Extension (in Asturias), 39
elections
1899, 32
1903–1909, 121–122
1922, 129
1923, 128
April 1931, 141(fn64)
October 1933, 150–151
abstention in, 151
February 1936, 159–160
rural vs. urban vote, 32 (fn37)
elite community, 8, 133–135
and Civil War, end of, 308
and Revolution of October 1934, 298,
301
employers' associations
Agremiación Patronal, 50, 134, 301
assassination of president of, 118
and Revolution of October 1934, 301
trade unions, conflicts with, 133–134,
253, 263–265, 272, 278–279, 284,
285
Unión Mercantil e Industrial, 50, 301
employment, 31, 64, 65–67, 84, 229–230

FAI, 182(fn42), 186–187
in Gijón, 187(fn62)
Falangist movement, 155
federal republicanism, Federalist party
and April 1931 coalition, 139–140
and anarchosyndicalists, 147–148, 169,
286
divisions within, 148–149, 159
and elections
June 1931, 145–146
October 1933, 150–151
Popular Front, 159
electoral program, 130, 147
leaders
Barriobero, Eduardo, 128, 135
Conde, Benito, 214
national presence during Republic, lack
of, 144
social background of, 132
and workers, 41–43
festivals
anniversary of the Republic
1935, 157
1936, 301–302
beauty pageants, 107

festivals—*cont.*
 Carnival, 106, 202
  trade union disapproval of, 234
 Jovellanos, homage to, 206
 May 1st, 240–242
  anarchist disapproval of, 241–242
  romería format, use of, 241
  trade union unity in, 1936, 302
 romerías (saints' day festivals), 106,
  202–203
 secularization of, 204–207
fishing industry, 110
 conflicts in, 112, 260–262
 Pósito de Pescadores, 111–112
 Rula (fish auction house), 112
funerals, 232–233

gender (*see also* women), 5–6, 51, 90–100,
 256–259, 288
Gijón
 commercial identity of (vs. Oviedo), 28–
  29
 declaration of Republic in, 142
 demographic evolution of, 18, 32(fn37),
  73–77
 economic growth in, 18–20
 economic insecurity in, 67, 72
 immigration into, 21(fn14), 74–75
 industries in, 65–67
 military presence in, 121
 municipal politics
  before 1900, 31–34
  1901–1909, 120–123
  1931–1935, 152–157
  1936, 163–165
  during Civil War, 307(fn3)
 significance of, 2, 12
 tourism in, 19, 21
 the "two Gijóns," 14

hegemony
 counter-hegemonic challenges, 4, 17,
  89, 115–116, 196–197, 309
 crisis of, 4, 16–17
 and lack of elite consensus, 132–133
 defined, 3–4
 monarchist/clerical hegemony, 196,
  308–309
 and the public sphere, 4–5, 195–196,
  248, 311
 and public space, 101
 republican hegemony, failure of, 224,
  313
 trade union movement hegemony,
  failure of, 228, 247–248, 306, 313
immigration, patterns of
 into Gijón, 21(fn 14), 74–75

rural/urban migration, 72–73, 75–77
industrialization, patterns of
 in Asturias, 16, 20, 64
 competitiveness, lack of, 67–68
 impact of First World War, 68
 in Gijón, 18–20, 64–67
 impact on workers, 69–72
 regional differences, 63
 in Spain, 62–63
industries, structure of (*see also* fishing
 industry)
 in Barcelona, 65
 gender segregation of, 92
 in Gijón, 65–67
 in Spain, 65(fn9)
Institución Libre de Enseñanza, 37
International, First, 41
Izquierda Republicana, 158–159, 161–162

Jovellanos, Gaspar Melchor de, 23(fn19),
 28(fn29)
 homage to, 206

labor movement, *see* trade union/labor
 movement
leisure (*see also* cultural institutions)
 neighborhood-based, 106–109
 soccer leagues, 107
 trade-union sponsored, 235–242
Lerroux, Alejandro, 126, 144
Liberal Alliance, 122–123
Liberal party, 122–123
literacy, 85, 91

mobilization (*see also* polarization), 1–9,
 12–13, 88–89, 251, 254, 312
municipal politics, *see* Dictatorship:
 municipal government under;
 Gijón: municipal politics;
 Restoration monarchy: municipal
 government under
music, 214–215
mutual aid societies (*see also* relevant
 headings under CNT; cultural
 institutions, Gijón: Association for
 Culture and Hygiene; Socialist
 party; trade union/labor
 movement; women)
Pósito de Pescadores, 112

neighborhoods (*see also* working-class
 neighborhoods)
 associational life of, 88, 95, 103–109,
  110
 city center/downtown, 23, 27–28, 80–
  81
 and political affiliation, 326

community-building, loci for, 101, 103, 109
formation of neighborhood identities, 101–109, 110–113
Humedal, 27, 84
"mixed" neighborhoods, 80(fn55), 84–85, 109
socio-economic composition of, 80–84
Tejedor, 27, 84
and women, 54

occupations (see also employment), 84, 323–324

Pachín de Melás, 95, 238–239
Partido Republicano Liberal Demócrata, see reformists
Pidal y Mon, Alejandro, 31
polarization, 1–2
after August 1917, 272, 273
and Civil War, 306, 308
and collective action, 249, 254
geographic, 78
inevitability, lack of, 60
language of, 115–116
neighborhood polarization in Cimadavilla, 291–293
in Popular Front election, 158–160
during Second Republic, 280–281
"two Gijóns," 14
"two Spains," 1
in the workplace, 50
political culture
CNT, contribution to, 310–311
defined, 3
diversity in, 254, 307(fn3)
and gender, 6
local over national, primacy of, 2, 12, 17
urban, 3
popular community, 8
agenda of, 8, 250–251, 274, 275
building blocks of, 87–88, 103, 259–260
during Civil War, 305–307
and CNT, as leaders of, 252, 262, 267, 281, 283–284
participants in, diverse, 251, 264, 266
as political actor, 89
and republicans, as leaders of, 251, 266,
decline of leadership of, 267, 270, 274–275, 280–281
and Revolution of October 1934, 298–301
as target of political groups, 89
Popular Front (in Gijón)

coalition, composition of, 158
election, 158–159
election campaign, 160
leftist critique of, 165
May 1st vs. Anniversary of Republic during, 301–303
municipal politics during, 162–165
origins of, 158
power struggle over local government, 161–163
and Revolution of October 1934, 160
rightist critique of, 165
weakness of, 162
population of Gijón, see Gijón: demographic evolution of
prices, movement of, 70–71, 315, 317–321
Primo de Rivera, Miguel, 136–137
public sphere
building blocks of, 88
defined, 4–5
emerging, 34–35
fragmentation of, 197–198
and gender, 5–6
and hegemonic struggle, 4–5, 195–196, 197–198, 248, 311
lack of, in pre-1900 Gijón, 29
oppositional culture in, 35
heterogeneity of, 228, 248, 311
proletarian, 227
weaknesses of, 227–228, 242, 243, 247–248, 311–312

Radical Socialist Party, 139–140, 145
Reformists, 119(fn1)
and April 1931 coalition, 138–139
alliance with the right, 146–147, 150, 154–157
Conjunción Republicana–Socialista, expulsion from, 127
crisis of, 1920s, 138–139
defeat of, 1936, 159–161
and Democratic Coalition, 1917, 128
as "establishment" party, 128–129, 146–147
leaders
Merediz, Mariano, 142
Morán, Dionisio, 142
leadership role in Republic, 144–145, 149–150
and Liberal Alliance, 122–123
melquiadistas, 123
origins of Reformist party, 126–127
Partido Republicano Liberal Demócrata, 146
secularization, softening of, 154–155
social background of, 132

republicanism
  and anarchosyndicalists, relations with,
    115–117, 134, 169–170
  co-operation in Escuela Neutra, 211–
    212
  and anti-clericalism (see also
    secularization), 135(fn43), 154
  as bridge to labor movement, 202
  April 1931 coalition, 138–141, 142–143
    disintegration of, 145
  citizens, creating, 36, 199
  civil and political rights, defense of,
    133–135
  and Civil War, 306
  configuration of parties under Republic,
    local vs. national, 144–146
  Conjunción Republicana–Socialista,
    122–124
  cultural agenda, alternative, 196–197,
    199
    failure of, 224, 248
    impact of, 200–201
  cultural institutions of (see also, under
    cultural institutions, Association for
    Culture and Hygiene; Ateneo
    Casino Obrero; Workers' Musical
    Association), 199–200, 213
    co-option of, 213, 218–220, 222–224
  defeat of republican political project,
    July 1936, 165–166, 306
  demonstrations, public, 33, 204
  during the Dictatorship, 137–140
  divisions among republicans, 34, 126–
    129, 140, 144, 257
  and education, 36–38, 209–211
    Escuela Neutra, 211–212
  in elections before 1900, 32
  electoral programs (and lack of), 130
  electoral union of 1903, 122(fn8)
  vs. French, 10, 198(fn8)
  "historical," 125–129
  ideology of, 9–10, 36
  and integration of masses, 115–117
  and municipal government, 118, 163–
    165
  and popular community, 251, 266, 267,
    270, 280–281
  and Popular Front, 158–163
  and private property, support of, 131
  repression of, 33–34
  social background of republicans, 132
  and social and economic reform, lack of,
    119, 129–131, 143, 152–153,
    163–165
  and trade union movement, 115–116,
    133–135, 201
  and women, 37–38, 56
  and workers, 38–41, 43, 44(fn76)

Restoration monarchy
  caciquismo in, 30
  erosion of, 121–122
  electoral apathy in, 32
  municipal government under, 29, 120–
    121, 124–125
  provincial administration during, 125
  rural districts, domination of, 31–32
  turno in, 30
  post-turno political pattern, 124
  unelected institutions, power of, 124–
    125
Revolution of October 1934
  in Asturias, three fronts of, 294–295
  casualties of, 297(fn34)
  in Cimadavilla, 295–296
  in Gijón
    community support of, 298–301
    narrative of, 295–298
    significance of, 293, 295
  national origins of, 292
  prisoners of, 300(fn46)
  ritual (see also Catholic Church;
    secularization), 201–209

Sagasta, Práxedes, 30
Sárraga, Belén, 37–38
Second Republic (see also Popular Front)
  Casas Viejas, impact of, 151
  celebration of, April 1931, 142–143
  CNT in, 183–193
  common culture, lack of, 197–198,
    224–225, 248
  and education, public, 211
  municipal government during, 152–157,
    163–165
  Popular Front, 158–165
  repression of working-class
    organizations, 156, 300–301
  second bienio, 155–157
    more anti-revolutionary than
      republican, 156–157
  similiarities to old regime, 152–155
  social reforms, lack of, 152–154
  two republican visions, 144
secularization, 200, 201–202
  of cemeteries, 208–209
  of education, 209–211
  of festival life, 204–207
  of municipal government, 203–204
  of visual symbols, 207–208
sociability
  class-segregated, 78, 87–88, 94–95, 99,
    113–114
  gendered, 51, 90–100, 258–259
  gossip, 93
  neighborhood, 88, 95, 103–114
  paseo, 94

tertulia, 40, 97
urban, 34–35
Socialist party (*see also* UGT)
vs. anarchosyndicalists, conflict with,
167–170, 172–173, 174, 176
co-operation with, 189–193, 263–
264, 290–291, 306(fn2)
and Conjunción Republicana–Socialista,
122–123(fn10), 174
and May 1st, 241–242
mutual aid, 232
origins of, in Gijón, 44
and Popular Front city government,
161, 162–163
during Second Republic, 187–9
strength of, in Asturias, 176(fn23)
weakness of, in Gijón, 169–170, 181,
188–189
strikes
Alianza Obrera, impact on, 290–291
August 1917, 178, 270–272
lessons of, 179
December 1930, 282–283
escalation of, 265, 277, 282–283, 285–
286
general strikes
1900, 253–254
December 1931, 285–287
December 1932, 284
December 1933, 290
patterns of, 254, 265
waves of
1909–1910, 262–265
1918–1920, 277–278
1931–1932, 284–287
1933–1934, 290(fn19)
1936, 304

taxes
consumo tax, 54–55, 131, 255
income tax, 153
indirect taxes, reliance on, 131
trade union/labor movement (*see also*
CNT; UGT)
and Alianza Obrera, 189–190, 193
anarchosyndicalism, strength of, 167–
169
anarchosyndicalism and socialism in
conflict between, 44, 47, 49, 167,
172–173, 174, 176, 177, 179, 181,
187–188, (over May 1st), 241–242
co-operation between, 178–179, 189,
191, 193, 263–264, 290–291,
302–303
Catholic unions, 111
culture, labor movement vs. worker, 89–
90

culture of, alternative, 226–227
hybrid nature of, 238, 240, 248
weaknesses of, 247–248
and education of workers, 235–238
and entertainment of workers, 238–240
guilds, legacy of, 45
industrial unionism, 179–180, 277
leisure activities of, 234
as antidote to worker pastimes, 234–
235
localism of, 43–44
membership in, 11(fn27)
moralizing of, 234–235
mutual aid
funerals, 232–233
at workplace, 228–229, 231
beyond workplace, 232–233
origins of, 44–45
and public sphere, proletarian, 227–228,
234, 242
and republicans, 115–116, 133–135,
201
unionization drives
1898–1901, 47–49
1909–1910, 174–175
and women, 48, 56
as "auxiliaries," 243–244
marginalization of, 247
as workers, 244–246
workers' center (Casa del Pueblo), 177
"Tragic Week," in Barcelona, 265–266
treintismo, see CNT: schism of

UGT (*see also* Socialist party)
and Alianza Obrera, 189–193
sectoral strength of, in Gijón (1930s),
188–189, 191
unemployment, 67, 69–70
Unión Republicana, 158–159
urban geography
ciudadelas, 81
ensanche, 23
evolution of, 21–28
occupations by neighborhood, 84
planning in, lack of, 28(fn25)
political affiliation by neighborhood,
326
residential segregation, 23, 27–28, 78–
84
residential stability, 76–77, 103
rural *aldeas,* 32, 75
"sexual geography," 99
transportation, 18, 102

Vigil, Manuel, 42(fn72)

wages, 70–71, 315–317

women
  anti-fascist women's groups, 246–247
  childbearing, 98
  childhood, 90–91
  comadres' banquet, 93–94, 110
  and communitybuilding, 93–94
  and consumer protests, 6, 51–53, 54–
    56, 256–257, 269–270, 291
  and direct action, 53–54, 56, 256, 261
  and mutual aid networks, 99–100
  and neighborhood communities, 54,
    100, 110, 260–261, 291–292
  and politics, 53, 56, 270
  significance of women's, 312
  and public chores, 98–99
  and the public sphere, 5–6, 51
  and republicanism, 37–38, 56
  and Revolution of October 1934, 298–
    300
  and trade union movement, 48, 243–
    247
  independent female union, 245–246
  and violence, 100
  and wage labor, 92, 326
  workplace culture, 92–94
workers
  cigarette makers, 92(fn15), 93–94, 245–
    250
  domestic servants, 92
  female, 66, 92, 326
  housing of, 81, 82–83, 99
  living conditions of, 70–71
  occupations by status, 323–324
  residential location of, 81–84
  skilled, 83
  social mobility of, 72, 91
  unemployment of, 69–70

unskilled, 83
wages of, 70–71, 315–317
white collar, 80–81, 84
workers' culture
  charivari, 110–111
  comadres' banquet, 93–94
  courtship, 94
  defined, 87
  gendered social networks, 90–100
  vs. labor movement culture, 89–90
  literacy, 85
    male vs. female, 91
  male social networks, 91, 96
    taverns, 96–97
  in neighborhoods, 103–114
  political mobilization of, 88–89, 97
  violence in, 97–98
  women's workplace networks, 92–94
working-class neighborhoods (*see also*
    neighborhoods), 81–82, 101, 109
  Cimadavilla, 21–22, 82–83, 109–114
    and fishing industry, 110–111
    as model for working-class
      neighborhoods, 109–110, 113
    neighborhood-based protest in, 260–
      262, 291–293
    Revolution of October 1934 in, 296–
      297
  condition of, 27–28, 82–83, 102
  El Llano, 27, 82–83
    Revolution of October 1934 in, 297
  La Calzada, 27, 82–83
    Revolution of October 1934 in, 297
  Natahoyo, 26–27
  residential stability of, 103
  "traditional" vs. "modern," 22–23, 27,
    109, 111, 113